Introduction to Multidimensional Scaling

THEORY, METHODS, AND APPLICATIONS

Introduction to Multidimensional Scaling

THEORY, METHODS, AND APPLICATIONS

Susan S. Schiffman

Departments of Psychiatry and Psychology
Duke University
Durham, North Carolina

M. Lance Reynolds

Research and Development Department
Brown and Williamson Tobacco Corporation
Louisville, Kentucky

Forrest W. Young

L. L. Thurstone Psychometric Laboratory
University of North Carolina
Chapel Hill, North Carolina

WITH CONTRIBUTIONS BY

J. Douglas Carroll   James O. Ramsay
James C. Lingoes   Edward E. Roskam

With a Foreword by Joseph B. Kruskal

ACADEMIC PRESS, INC.

(Harcourt Brace Jovanovich, Publishers)

Orlando   San Diego   San Francisco   New York   London
Toronto   Montreal   Sydney   Tokyo   Sao Paulo

ACADEMIC PRESS, INC.
Orlando, Florida 32887

United Kingdom Edition published by
ACADEMIC PRESS, INC. (LONDON) LTD.
24/28 Oval Road, London NW1 7DX

Library of Congress Cataloging in Publication Data

Schiffman, Susan.
    Introduction to multidimensional scaling.

    Includes bibliographies and index.
    1. Multidimensional scaling. 2. Multidimensional
scaling--Computer programs. 3. Psychometrics.
4. Social sciences--Methodology. I. Reynolds, M. Lance.
II. Young, Forrest W. III. Title.
BF39.S33   001.4'2   81-10842
ISBN 0-12-624350-6   AACR2

Contents

I
Basic Concepts and Data Bank

6
How to Use POLYCON   103

7
How to Use KYST-2   127

8
How to Use INDSCAL and SINDSCAL   143

9
How to Use ALSCAL   169

10
How to Use MULTISCALE   211

11
Comparison of Programs

12
Interpreting Stimulus Spaces   253

13
Interpreting Subject Spaces   299

14
Treating Rectangular Matrices by Multidimensional Scaling   321

List of Contributors

Numbers in parentheses indicate the pages on which the authors' contributions begin.

J. Douglas Carroll (371), Bell Telephone Laboratories, Inc., Murray Hill, New Jersey 07974

James C. Lingoes (362), Department of Psychology, The University of Michigan, Ann Arbor, Michigan 48109

James O. Ramsay (389), Department of Psychology, McGill University, Montreal, Quebec, Canada

Edward E. Roskam (362), Psychologisch Laboratorium, University of Nijmegen, Nijmegen, The Netherlands

Foreword

At the age of twenty-odd, multidimensional scaling should be in the full vigor of youth—and I am happy to report that it is just graduating from college and doing very well. A word about its family history may be helpful. Some hint of things to come appeared in the methods long used by surveyors to reconcile slightly discrepant measurements, and also in a 1928 comparison of serum and antiserum from five different animal species. Conception took place in 1936, and after a delayed gestation, multidimensional scaling was baptized in the 1950s by Warren Torgerson. Like any child, it owed its progress to the help of many people. In the early 1960s these included first and foremost Roger Shepard, and also Louis Guttman, James Lingoes, Edward Roskam, Victor McGee, and myself. Later on, there were Douglas Carroll together with Jih-jie Chang and Sandra Pruzansky, and Forrest Young and Jan de Leeuw and James Ramsay and Phipps Arabie and Yoshio Takane and Richard Harshman and . . ., but even commencement addresses must come to a stop.

Indications are that MDS, to use its nickname, should continue to do well. Consider, for example, computer programs for MDS, a central theme of this book. Look in the table of contents at the wide variety of programs, and you will see abundant evidence of vitality. Indeed, it is just this variety and diversity that make a book like this one necessary. New methods, even more forcefully than the new programs that embody them, display the continuing vigor of the field. The programs covered in this book contain a succession of significant methods that are in wide current use at present writing.

New applications and uses are the lifeblood of any statistical technique. Though a discussion of the full range of applications is not central to this book, it does draw on an interesting and significant new area: applications to olfaction and taste. For years I had been hoping to see what contribution MDS could make to our knowledge of olfactory perception—but MDS was younger then, and I could not persuade the reluctant teenager to turn its attention to smell. I am happy that a few more years of maturity have changed reluctance to enthusiasm and much progress is now being made in this area, as Susan Schiffman and her colleagues demonstrate in this volume.

It is only because the concept of statistics has expanded in the last few decades that MDS can be admitted without contradiction to the family of statistical methods. Indeed, one of the programs discussed in this book is part of a major computer-based statistical analysis system. Even so, to gain greater respect in the family it needs to develop further the self-critical tools of assessment and diagnosis. How *well* do we know what we know? How do we spot warning signals—and bring them effectively to the attention of first-time users? Fortunately, this book helps to answer these questions: MDS is starting to face up to these adult problems.

This important new method for analyzing data continues to grow. When MDS is joined with suitable techniques for collecting data and assessing its own results, it grows from a merely statistical method into a useful *scientific* method. I am glad that Schiffman, Reynolds, and Young have put together this introductory volume about models and computer programs for MDS, as well as techniques for collecting data and assessing MDS results. I am sure that many people will find it a very useful volume.

JOSEPH B. KRUSKAL
Bell Laboratories
Murray Hill, New Jersey

Preface

Multidimensional scaling (MDS) is a powerful mathematical procedure which can systematize data by representing the similarities of objects spatially as in a map. This book covers the design, execution, and analysis of multidimensional scaling experiments and includes detailed descriptions and examples of six major MDS computer programs: MINISSA, POLYCON, KYST, INDSCAL/SINDSCAL, ALSCAL, and MULTISCALE. Discussed are various program options that allow the user, for example, to select the model—classical, replicated, or weighted—most appropriate to a particular data set, and to examine the effect of different measurement level assumptions. Later chapters show how to fit properties and preferences to derived stimulus spaces, how to interpret vector spaces of subject weights, and how to analyze rectangular data matrices.

The book is organized into three sections. Part I, "Basic Concepts and Data Bank," describes MDS in nonmathematical terms, covers experimental designs and procedures, includes test data, and gives an overview of MDS models and programs. Part II, "Methods and Applications," gives examples for each of the MDS programs and compares the results. Methods for interpreting stimulus and subject spaces are described and evaluated. Part II concludes with a chapter on the use of MDS in product development. Part III, which includes contributions by Edward E. Roskam and James C. Lingoes, J. Douglas Carroll, and James O. Ramsay, gives detailed descriptions of the MDS models and how the programs work.

The book may be used by the newcomer to MDS, yet it contains information and examples that the specialist may find difficult to obtain elsewhere. Its genesis arose from the need for documentation of the range of MDS procedures available to the potential user who had many questions that no current text could answer in full.

Since the pioneering work of Warren Torgerson, Roger Shepard, Louis Guttman, and Joseph B. Kruskal, multidimensional scaling has rapidly evolved to include an ever-increasing range of analytic procedures. Those chosen for this book are by no means exhaustive. However, we have selected these six because they are currently the most frequently used approaches, and because they are sufficiently fundamental that continuing developments in the field will build on the principles presented here. By including worked examples from a variety of data sets (including two chapters on how to interpret the results), by describing the advantages and limitations of each program, and by including a chapter on the theoretical basis of each program, the authors have attempted to provide both a handbook and a scientific text.

The authors greatly appreciate the helpful comments of Robert P. Erickson, Joel Huber, and Gregory Lockhead of Duke University, as well as the incisive technical reviews of J. Douglas Carroll, Joseph B. Kruskal, James C. Lingoes, Cynthia H. Null, Sandra Pruzansky and James Ramsay on various aspects of Chapters 1–15. Any residual errors are clearly the responsibility of the authors.

Part I

Basic Concepts and Data Bank

1

Introduction

1.1. Why Multidimensional Scaling (MDS)?

A problem encountered by researchers in many disciplines—ranging from the physical, biological, and behavioral sciences to product development, marketing, and advertising—is how to measure and understand the relationships between objects when the underlying dimensions are not known. The rate of increase of human understanding has depended on organizing concepts that allow us to systematize and compress large amounts of data. Systematic classification generally precedes understanding.

The purpose of this book is to demonstrate how multidimensional scaling can help systematize data in areas where organizing concepts and underlying dimensions are not well developed. Multidimensional scaling (MDS) is simply a useful mathematical tool that enables us to represent the similarities of objects spatially as in a map. All that we need to apply computer-based MDS procedures is a set of numbers that expresses all (or most) combinations of pairs of similarities within a group of objects. MDS procedures represent objects judged experimentally similar to one another as points close to each other in a resultant spatial map. Objects judged to be dissimilar are represented as points distant from one another.

Multidimensional scaling procedures, which use direct similarity (or dissimilarity) measures as input, have the advantage of being low in experimenter contamination. They do not require a priori knowledge of the attributes of the stimuli to be scaled. Rather, they provide a space that reveals dimensions relevant to the subjects. Experiments designed to collect similarity data for MDS analysis generate a large amount of information and generally yield stable spaces with only a few subjects. The major disadvantage of MDS is that such experiments can be time consuming and expensive.

This book gives step-by-step instructions in how to:

1. Gather experimental measures of similarity among objects
2. Apply multidimensional scaling procedures to the experimental similarity data to represent the underlying structure spatially or geometrically as in a map
3. Understand individual differences in judgments of similarity that yield differing geometrical maps
4. Interpret the geometrical maps to gain an understanding of the configurations of points

The examples used in this book are based on data from taste and smell experiments. They have been chosen, however, so that researchers in most disciplines can find illustrations useful for their own work. Understanding the dimensions of taste and smell, like many other fields, is still in its infancy. This is so for the chemist concerned with molecular architecture; for the neurophysiologist concerned with the mechanisms of reception, transmission, and coding; for the psychophysicist studying perception; for the technologist developing consumer products; and for the market researcher evaluating consumer products. An underlying cause of the problem is that people have difficulty in articulating the nature of taste and smell sensations, and that different people experience similar things in different ways. In addition, the relationships between chemical structure and sensation are not well understood.

Thus, for taste and smell (as well as most areas of research) we need a measurement system in which language is kept to a minimum. We need a method for analyzing the measurements that allows for individual differences in experience and yet can relate the measurements to objective properties of the items. Similarity judgments and their subsequent analysis by MDS meet these requirements.

1.2. What MDS Can Do

An example from color vision illustrates what MDS can do. Ekman (1954) obtained measures of similarity among pairs of 14 colors varying in hue. Subjects made ratings of qualitative similarity for each pair of combinations of colors ranging in wavelength from 434 nm to 674 nm. The mean ratings were transformed to range from 0 (no similarity at all) to 1 (identity).

Shepard (1962) applied an MDS procedure to the mean transformed similarity ratings and extracted the underlying structure represented by the two-dimensional spatial configuration shown in Figure 1.1. His computational strategy was to find a spatial arrangement of low dimensionality where the *rank order* of the distances in the space corresponded with the *rank order* of the similarity measures with minimal error. The underlying structure recovered from Ekman's similarity data was very simply the conventional color circle with the colors arranged along the smooth contour in order of increasing wavelength. Thus, MDS yielded a parsimonious solution with a high degree of interpretability and minimal error in only two dimensions.

The solution in Figure 1.1 is much preferable to one achieved by Ekman using factor analysis. He treated the 14 by 14 matrix of mean transformed similarity ratings as a correlation matrix and found that five factors were needed to account for the data. He identified the factors as violet, blue, green, yellow, and red. Section 1.5 explains the differences between factor analysis and MDS. It simply suffices here to conclude that MDS gives a more meaningful and interpretable solution than factor analysis for these data.

This brings us to several important points about MDS. First, for a single subject, n stimuli can always be fitted into $n - 1$ dimensions so that the distances in the derived space correspond exactly with the experimental similarity measures in a linear fashion. However, although a higher-dimensional solution generally gives a better fit to the data, this does not mean that the high-dimensional solution is necessarily correct. Data will always contain noise. Second, with a little "smoothing," 15 stimulus points may be forced from a 14-dimensional solution to one as low as 4, 3, or

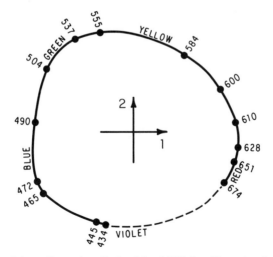

Figure 1.1. Spatial configuration derived by MDS for Ekman's similarity judgments among 14 colors. (Adapted from Shepard, 1962.)

even 2 dimensions with minimal error. This is, of course, what actually occurs when spaces are computed to dimensionalities specified by the user. Third, if the computation criterion is to relate the *rank order* of distances to the *rank order* of experimental similarity measures (rather than directly relate the distance and similarity measures in a linear fashion), the stimuli can be perfectly represented in $n - 2$ dimensions and generally in fewer dimensions than when using the measures themselves.

This last point represents the essential difference between *metric* and *nonmetric* scaling. In general, *nonmetric* scaling, where only *rank order* relationships are maintained, provides spaces with better fit in low dimensionality than metric solutions. This book includes discussion of both metric and nonmetric procedures.

1.3. How MDS Works

Presenting one with a map of the United States and asking one to measure with a ruler the distances among 10 diversely located American cities is a straightforward project. Multidimensional scaling does the opposite of this; it takes a set of distances (such as those often found in a table at the bottom of maps) and recreates the map. This is a more difficult project, but it can be solved in two dimensions with a ruler and compass. For real sets of data it is necessary to use a computer. This book describes six computer programs (MINISSA, POLYCON, KYST, INDSCAL, ALSCAL, and MULTISCALE) which have been developed to tackle such data sets containing "noise," or error. We will present first, conceptually, how one of these programs, ALSCAL, recovers a map showing locations of U.S. cities from the distances between them.

The two-dimensional map in Figure 1.2, which was constructed from the distances using ALSCAL, shows the cities in proper relative positions to one another. This solution was found in two iterations by ALSCAL with very little error (SSTRESS = .003). The meaning of an iteration and SSTRESS will become clear shortly. First it is necessary to point out that the space in Figure 1.2 was determined with the assumption that the data obey the ratio level of measurement. The four levels of measurement— nominal, ordinal, interval, and ratio—are defined in the glossary at the end of this chapter. (Each of the programs discussed in this book varies in the data measurement level it can treat; see Chapter 4.) It is sufficient to state that the ALSCAL procedure as used here attempts to fit the data such that the distances in the derived space are in the same ratio as the flying distances used as data.

A space can also be derived such that the distances are merely in the same rank order as the flying distances. This is called an *ordinal analysis*.

Figure 1.2. ALSCAL ratio scale analysis of intercity flying distances: iteration 2.
SSTRESS = .003.

However, MDS procedures do not immediately achieve solutions which
fit the data at any level of measurement. They require numerous trials or
iterations. First, a starting configuration is assumed such as the straight line
shown in Figure 1.3. (Computation of starting configurations varies from
procedure to procedure and ALSCAL will ordinarily use a better one than
this. We are making it a very poor one for the sake of illustration.) ALSCAL
attempts to move the points to match the flying distances used as data. On
the first iteration, the rank order of distances along the line is compared
with the rank order of the flying distances and a large measure of error
(SSTRESS = .727) is found. On the second iteration, the points are moved
by the ALSCAL procedure to the positions indicated by the arrows to
reduce the differences and thus the error (SSTRESS = .454) between the
rank order of the distances in the space and the data which consist of flying
distances. Further iterations are shown in Figures 1.4 and 1.5.

By the eighth iteration, the value of SSTRESS has decreased to .052 and
the positioning of the cities begins to resemble a map of the U.S. (rotated
45°). The rotation illustrates an important point about MDS. Multidimensional scaling simply recovers underlying structure among stimuli which
is "hidden" in the data. Meaningful directions through the space such as

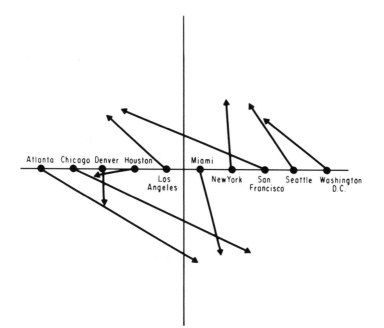

Figure 1.3. Ordinal analysis of flying distances: iterations 1 and 2. SSTRESS = .727, .454.

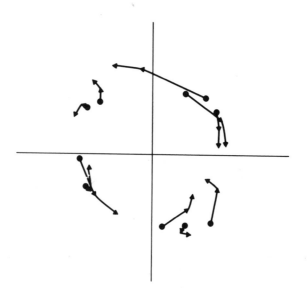

Figure 1.4. Iterations 3, 4, and 5 in ordinal analysis of flying distances. SSTRESS = .267, .137, .100.

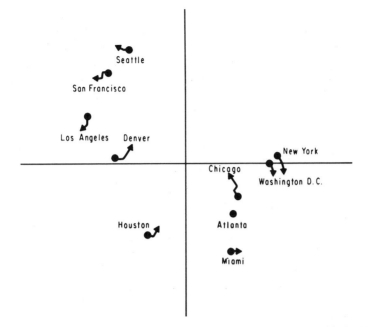

Figure 1.5. Iterations 6, 7, and 8 in ordinal analysis of flying distances. SSTRESS = .080, .065, .052.

north–south or east–west may have to be determined by the experimenter. Also, interpretation of the dimensions is only part science and is a skill that develops with experience and a thorough knowledge of the properties of the stimuli.

Having shown conceptually how MDS recovers structure from a collection of distances, we now show a little more formally the mathematical problem which the various MDS computer programs have been written to solve. The data we will obtain are normally the amount of perceived difference between each pair of a set of stimuli. These data sets are often called *dissimilarities* or *proximities*, or even just *data*. What we want to find out are positions in space or coordinates for each of the stimuli such that the distances between them will correspond as closely as possible to these proximities or transformations of them. Our success will be reflected by how well the distances, *d*, in this space match the proximities, δ, or their transformations.

The position of a stimulus in a space is specified by its coordinates on each dimension. For simplicity we will use just two dimensions. The coordinates to be found for stimulus 1 are then x_{11} and x_{12}, for stimulus 2, x_{21} and x_{22}, and so on. Using this notation, the distance between stimulus 1 and stimulus 2 is, from the Pythagorean theorem:

$$d_{12} = [(x_{11} - x_{21})^2 + (x_{12} - x_{22})^2]^{1/2}.$$

In essence, what an MDS program does is to assume or calculate some set of coordinates for the stimuli called the starting configuration. Distances are calculated from these coordinates and compared with the data. Depending on how large the differences are, the program then moves the coordinates around a bit and recomputes the distances. This process is repeated until the distances fit the data as well as practical. Each of the programs contains specific criteria for determining when this state is achieved.

While Chapter 16 describes in detail the computation strategies used in each of the programs, there are two more important concepts to present— *nonmetric scaling* and *individual differences scaling*.

The first, nonmetric scaling, has already been referred to earlier. Nonmetric scaling only tries to fit the rank order of the proximities to the distances in the stimulus space, whereas classical metric scaling attempts to fit the proximities to the distances. To perform nonmetric scaling it is necessary to apply some transformation to the data to allow the performance of arithmetic operations on it. This process is called a *monotone transformation* and the transformed data are called *disparities*. The goodness of fit is then determined between the disparities and the distances in the stimulus space.

Individual differences scaling allows for differences in individual perceptions. This is described in greater detail in Chapter 4, but basically the solutions contain, in addition to stimulus coordinates, a measure of how important each dimension is to the perceptions of each subject.

So far we have considered the basic principles for a two-dimensional solution. In actuality, some of the programs described in this book allow the user to specify a solution with as many as 10 dimensions. The computer programs do not determine the true dimensionality of the space but do provide a number of guides for determining the appropriate dimensionality. Thus, it is fairly normal procedure in the analysis to develop solutions of several dimensionalities and then from an examination of the output determine which one to investigate for structure. This is the topic of the next section, but we would like to point out here that for none of the examples described in this book did we find more than three dimensions.

1.4. How Many Dimensions and What Do They Mean?

When we refer to dimensions at this point we are considering the number of coordinate axes in the stimulus space. Should there be two, three, four, or just one? The first step is to examine the change in goodness of fit with change in dimensionality. All the algorithms provide some measure of goodness of fit: coefficient of alienation in MINISSA, stress in POLYCON and KYST, correlations and/or variance accounted for in INDSCAL, stress and squared correlations in ALSCAL, and standard error in MULTISCALE. In general, stress will decrease and correlations will increase with increasing numbers of dimensions. If these values are plotted against the number of dimensions, there will frequently be an elbow in the curve (Figure 1.6). The number of dimensions at this elbow are the maximum number that are generally considered.

Another guideline uses so-called Monte Carlo methods to set upper limits to the number of dimensions. MDS programs will supply *stimulus spaces* from a set of random numbers. Several investigators have determined the stress values obtained for different numbers of *stimuli* using *data sets* derived from random number tables. From these investigations they have developed guidelines as to the maximum number of dimensions it is appropriate to consider for a given number of stimuli. Unfortunately, it is not always possible to have enough stimuli to follow these guidelines.

There are several ways to overcome this problem. The most reliable, but not necessarily the most expedient, is to repeat the whole experiment and see if the new data set provides the same solution as the old. A more likely course of action is to split the data set (assuming that it has been collected from a number of subjects) and determine if equivalent solutions are obtained from each set. A third method is to include a few replicated stimuli in the original stimulus set and analyze these as if they were different stimuli. The closeness of these replicated stimuli to each other in the stimulus spaces provides not only a measure of the *noisiness* of the data but also an indication of dimensionality. In higher, meaningless dimensions they will move apart. With MULTISCALE it is possible to examine chi-square values as a guide to dimensionality.

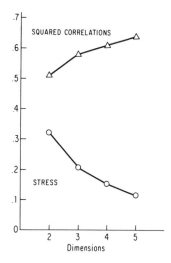

Figure 1.6. Changes in stress and squared correlations with dimensionality; from nonmetric individual differences analysis of colas by ALSCAL, Chapter 9.3.

The final criterion for number of dimensions is interpretability. While considerable effort and intuition may be necessary to interpret a dimension, dimensions that cannot be interpreted probably do not exist. We come, therefore, to the meaning or interpretation of the dimensions. The first point is that the coordinate axes in the stimulus spaces may not lie in the same directions as the perceptual dimensions. While the MDS programs can provide a map of city locations from intercity distances, they cannot align the map in a north–south direction. A rotation of the coordinate system may be necessary to properly orient the axes. However, the programs we describe in this book frequently provide coordinate axes which can be interpreted as perceptual dimensions. This is particularly true for the individual differences analyses provided by INDSCAL, ALSCAL, and MULTISCALE. Thus, the coordinate axes are a first place to look. Proximities of cola beverages are analyzed later in this book by each program using a variety of options. In all cases the first coordinate axis, dimension 1, separates diet from nondiet drinks.

This illustrates an important point in interpretation of dimensions. The first step is to look at the properties of stimuli at each end of the dimension to determine if there is some attribute that changes in an obvious fashion. One property of the strawberry-flavored beverages analyzed later in this book is sugar content. A rapid inspection will show if the beverages are arranged along a dimension in order of sugar content. If they are, sweetness is that dimension, or at least a component of it.

A perceptual space representing the qualities of a set of stimuli will, however, generally contain two kinds of attributes—qualitative and quantitative. The ordering of quantitative attributes along a dimension (e.g., more sweet–less sweet) is straightforward. The arrangement of qualitative attributes is not. In dichotomous cases (diet taste–regular taste of soft drinks, chocolate flavor–coffee flavor of liqueurs, or simple red color–green color) one dimension of the space will reflect the two attributes. But how about the more general case when the stimuli contain a number of qualitative attributes? Can any useful descriptions be given to the dimensions? Are they unique? If so, do they reflect hedonic or intensity differences?

Hedonic dimensions can be found if a separate experimental ranking of preference or rating of good–bad is available. A number of property fitting algorithms are available (see, for example, PREFMAP, Chapter 12) which show if a rank order of the stimuli can be projected through the stimulus space.

In taste and smell experiments, intensities are usually equalized by appropriate dilution to avoid intensity dimensions. For consumer products, however, intensity may very well be a dimension, although *strength* is a particularly vague and elusive attribute for alcoholic beverages and cigarettes.

Another approach is to determine if physicochemical parameters can be projected through the stimulus space. An example of this is provided in

Chapter 12, where molecular weight and departure from pH 7 are projected into a space derived from the taste of chemicals.

Finally, no dimensions as such may be found. Nevertheless, the stimuli are arranged in a sensible manner. Probably the most striking example of this is the color circle described in Section 1.2. Our example of food flavors analyzed later in the book shows no interpretable dimensions as such, but the flavors are grouped in an intuitively reasonable way.

Geometrical representations are not always the best way to portray similarities, such as with some linguistic data. A hierarchical clustering procedure (e.g., Johnson, 1967) may indeed be more appropriate. However, derivation of the color circle just mentioned shows that MDS can usefully be applied to visual cues. Although MDS is not universally applicable, the fact that a dimension cannot always be labeled does not mean that a geometric representation is not necessarily useful. There are examples in this book where dimensions can be labeled and examples where they cannot. In the latter case, useful groupings of stimuli can still occur and be, for example, related to chemical composition. An MDS perceptual space is useful in revealing and (perhaps) understanding order. It provides an alternative taxonomy to those derived from traditional psychophysical methods. Mostly we have found perceptual spaces derived from MDS of similarity judgments to be useful. However, there have been in the past, and there no doubt will be in the future, occasions when they are not.

1.5. How MDS Differs from Factor Analysis

Just as MDS refers to a collection of data analysis procedures (not a single procedure), factor analysis (FA) refers to a family of procedures used to analyze multivariate data sets such as various attribute ratings for a number of stimuli. The MDS model is based on distances between points whereas the FA model is based on the angles between vectors. Both models generally use Euclidean space, but MDS has the advantage in that it is easier to interpret distances between points than angles between vectors. Also, FA often results in a relatively large number of dimensions mainly because most procedures are based on the assumption of linear relationships between the variables. This is a severe assumption with regard to perceptual data. The MDS approach does not contain this assumption, and the result is that it normally provides more readily interpretable solutions of lower dimensionality.

Apart from these reasons for our preference for MDS over FA, there is a fundamental reason for preference concerned with the type of data normally collected for analysis by each procedure. As discussed earlier, data for MDS, when collected by direct judgment of dissimilarities, are least subject to experimenter contamination and most likely to contain relevant structure. Data for FA generally contain scores for each stimulus on a shopping list of attributes which may or may not be relevant.

Our preference, therefore, from experimental, mathematical, and interpretative viewpoints for the data described in this book is for MDS over FA. Even if the experimental procedure has not provided direct proximities, it is still possible to convert the type of data normally analyzed by FA to *derived proximities* for subsequent analysis by MDS. Some examples of how to do this are discussed in Chapter 14.

1.6. Glossary of MDS Terminology

Most disciplines develop their own terminology. MDS is no exception. Specialized terminology is useful when it speeds communication. Its other uses need no elaboration. We have minimized as much specialized terminology as possible, but find some essential. Following are definitions of terms which will be used in the book, arranged under the following headings:

- Definition of terms concerning data
- Definition of terms concerning perceptual spaces
- Definition of terms concerning MDS computer programs

Terms Concerning Data

Object.   A thing or event, for example, an apple.

Stimulus.   A perceived object, for example, a tasted apple.

Attribute.   A perceived characteristic of a stimulus, for example, sweet.

Proximity.   A number that shows the amount of similarity or difference between a pair of stimuli. Input data values are often referred to as proximities. The usual symbol is δ.

Data Matrix.   Arrangement of the data into a table where the first column shows the proximities between stimulus 1 and each of the succeeding stimuli, the second column shows the proximities between stimulus 2 and succeeding stimuli, and so on. The proximities between all pairs of stimuli can be shown in the *lower-half matrix* lined in below:

$$
\begin{array}{cccc}
\delta_{11} & \delta_{12} & \delta_{13} & \delta_{14} \\
\delta_{21} & \delta_{22} & \delta_{23} & \delta_{24} \\
\delta_{31} & \delta_{32} & \delta_{33} & \delta_{34} \\
\delta_{41} & \delta_{42} & \delta_{43} & \delta_{44}
\end{array}
$$

The total matrix shown above is said to be *square*. It is also *symmetric* if the proximities in the upper-half matrix are equal to the proximities in the lower-half matrix, for example, $\delta_{42} = \delta_{24}$. MDS procedures often assume this is so.

Measurement Level (of Data).

Nominal.   Objects are sorted into groups only, such as males and females. This is the *weakest* or *lowest* measurement level. It is also referred to as *categorical*.

Ordinal.   Objects are arranged in rank order of magnitude. For example, bus–van–car is the ranking of these vehicles in terms of size. At the ordinal level of measurement, there is no indication of whether the size difference between bus and van is more or less than the size of the difference between van and car.

Interval.   Objects are placed on a scale such that the magnitude of the differences between objects is shown by the scale. However, interval scales do not have true zeros. The Fahrenheit temperature scale is an interval scale. The difference between 20°F and 50°F is the same as the difference between 50°F and 80°F. However, it is not true to say that 80°F is four times as hot as 20°F.

Ratio.   Objects are placed on a scale such that the position along the scale represents the absolute magnitude of the attribute. This is the most stringent level of measurement. Mass and velocity are examples of ratio scales. A car traveling at 60 m.p.h. is traveling twice as fast as a car traveling at 30 m.p.h.

Terms Concerning Perceptual Spaces

Point.   A position in a space that is an abstract representation of a stimulus.

Dimension.   A characteristic that serves to define a point in a space; an axis through the space.

Space.   The set of all potential points defined by a set of dimensions.

Configuration.   A particular organization of a set of points, that is, a map.

Direction.   A vector through a space that relates to an attribute. A vector is a quantity which possesses both magnitude and direction.

Orthogonal.   This means perpendicular to. Most MDS spaces are developed with orthogonal axes.

Subject Weights.   Numbers showing the relative importance a subject attaches to each of the stimulus dimensions when making his or her similarity judgments. Sometimes they are also referred to as dimensional saliences.

Subject Space. A map showing the vectors of subject weights. The length of the weight vector in INDSCAL and ALSCAL indicates how much of the subject's data (or some transformation of that data) is explained by the model. The subject space has as many dimensions as the stimulus space.

Euclidean Distance. This is the distance that corresponds to everyday experience. The distance between two stimuli can be calculated from their coordinates according to the Pythagorean formula. In a three-dimensional map, for example, the distance between stimulus A (coordinates X_A, Y_A, Z_A) and stimulus B (coordinates X_B, Y_B, Z_B) is

$$[(X_A - X_B)^2 + (Y_A - Y_B)^2 + (Z_A - Z_B)^2]^{1/2}.$$

Minkowski Distance. This is a generalization of Euclidean distance. The interstimulus distances, instead of being given by the *square root* of the sum of the *squares* of the coordinate differences, are given by the *rth root* of the sum of the *rth powers* of the absolute coordinate differences. In the example above, for a Minkowski *r* of 3, the distance between A and B is:

$$(|X_A - X_B|^3 + |Y_A - Y_B|^3 + |Z_A - Z_B|^3)^{1/3}$$

City-Block Distance. This is a Minkowski distance with $r = 1$. The distance between two stimuli roughly corresponds to "walking" halfway round a city block contained in a regular grid of streets. Interstimulus distances for the city block *metric* (see following), Euclidean space, and a space with Minkowski metric with *r* of 3 are shown in Figure 1.7.

The meaning of Minkowski *r* greater than 2 is complicated. A large Minkowski *r* emphasizes the dimension on which two stimuli are most different. Gregson's (1965) suggestion that it is a measure of the importance a subject places on stimulus dimensions is more straightforwardly handled by subject weights (INDSCAL, ALSCAL). While the city-block metric ($r = 1$) is conceptually attractive for stimuli judged with more than one sense (taste and texture, for example), Euclidean solutions have been found to be adequate in practice.

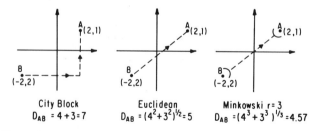

Figure 1.7. Illustration of city-block, Euclidean, and Minkowski distances. The representation of a Minkowski distance for $r = 3$ is symbolic.

Terms Concerning MDS Computer Programs

MDS. Multidimensional scaling.

Algorithm. The mathematical procedure used to solve the problem. The word becomes tied to the computer program based on the procedure: "The INDSCAL algorithm allows for individual perceptual differences." Or it is dropped entirely: "INDSCAL allows for individual perceptual differences." While perhaps formally incorrect, we use the word program rather than algorithm in this book.

Metric. The type of measuring system. The word is used very widely in different contexts which can be confusing. It is common in MDS to refer to metric and nonmetric solutions for the stimulus space. The distances in metric solutions preserve (as far as possible) the original similarity data in a linear fashion. The distances in *nonmetric* solutions preserve only the rank order of the original similarity data. The actual computation of the coordinates of the stimulus space is, of course, a metric (numerical) operation. Monotone transformations (see the following) of the original similarity data provide the bridge between rank order and distances in the stimulus space.

Transformations. Nonmetric MDS programs apply *monotone* transformations to the original data to allow performance of arithmetic operations on the rank orders of proximities. A monotone transformation need only maintain the rank order of the proximities. The logarithm function is an example of a monotone transformation.

Disparities. Monotonic transformations of the data which are as much like the distances (usually in a least-squares sense) as possible.

Stress. A particular measure that shows how far the data depart from the model. There are several stress formulas available in the various algorithms.

Shepard Diagram. Also scattergram or scatter diagram. A plot comparing the distances derived by MDS and the transformed data (disparities) with the original data values or proximities.

References

Ekman, G. Dimensions of color vision. *Journal of Psychology,* 1954, *38,* 467–474.
Gregson, R. A. M. Representation of taste mixture cross-modal matching in a Minkowski *r*- metric. *Australian Journal of Psychology,* 1965, *17,* 195–204.
Johnson, S. C. Hierarchical clustering schemes. *Psychometrika,* 1967, *32,* 241–254.
Shepard, R. N. The analysis of proximities: Multidimensional scaling with an unknown distance function. II. *Psychometrika,* 1962, *27,* 219–246.

2

Gathering Data for
Multidimensional Scaling Experiments

2.1. General Comments

Multidimensional scaling of similarity judgments has many applications. These can range from analysis of neurophysiological data to an examination of people's perceptions of politicians. There is no way that this total spectrum can be covered here. By concentrating on a specific area of perceptual psychology—the measurement of taste and smell—the major principles and procedures can be illustrated with stimuli to which we can all relate. Further, gathering data for sensory experiments generally involves more variables and is more time consuming than most other MDS applications. Thus, while the safeguards and procedures described are not always necessary for all experiments, conceptual, for example, we hope that they will alert the potential user to consider carefully variables in his or her own work. Though the psychological process involved in making the judgments will vary with the stimulus set, the need to collect reliable data remains invariant.

An ideal multidimensional scaling experiment involves gathering four types of data: (*a*) similarity judgments among all pairs of stimuli, (*b*) ratings of stimuli on descriptors such as adjectives, (*c*) objective measures (such as physicochemical parameters) relating to the sensory properties of the stimuli, and (*d*) information about the subjects. The *similarity judgments* are the *primary* means for recovering the underlying structure of relationships among a group of stimuli. It should be emphasized that the spatial arrangement derived by MDS from similarity judgments is the heart of the analysis. The use of similarity judgments allows us to find a mathematical solution based on experimental quantitative data without having to rely on a highly subjective and often conceptually incomplete list of verbal descriptors. It is highly unlikely that all the relevant dimensions which account for differences among stimuli can be achieved using adjective descriptors. We simply do not have a complete enough vocabulary in any language to describe most sensory processes, especially taste and smell. It will also be shown that adjective data is extremely noisy and contains less structure when compared with similarity spaces. The adjective descriptors are best used to help understand a multidimensional space derived from the similarity judgments, not to derive one.

A general procedure used for MDS experiments is as follows:

Day 1. Exposure to range of stimuli; explanation of similarity judgments; practice similarity judgments.

Days 2 to N. Similarity judgments.

Last Day(s). Adjective ratings and preferences.

2.2. Time Required to Do an Experiment

The total time taken for an experiment depends on the number and nature of the stimuli. For example, the time required to gather conceptual data will be shorter than for taste data for equal numbers of stimuli. In taste and smell experiments, the more intense and/or lingering the taste or smell, the longer the time needed between stimulus pairs and the fewer pairs that can be judged in a session. With the musks (Section 3.5), for example, only one pair could be judged per session. Both fatigue and cross-adaptation effects that stimuli exert on one another are ever-present dangers. The minimum time between stimulus pairs is never less than 1 min. Average times range from 3 to 15 min. It is rarely feasible, from the viewpoints of sensory fatigue, interest, and personal schedules, to retain subjects for more than $1\frac{1}{2}$ hours per session. A shorter session is preferable. We recommend that no more than 55 verbal or visual judgments be attempted in one session. These can be accomplished in 1 hour or less. From the outset we wish to emphasize the importance of gathering data in a very sound experimental fashion. Hastily gathered data under uncontrolled conditions seldom yield results which can be replicated.

The number of sessions necessary to complete experiments with differing numbers of stimuli and different intervals between stimulus pairs is shown in Table 2.1.

TABLE 2.1
Sessions Needed to Perform all Pairwise Comparisons[a]

Number of stimuli	7	10	15	20
Number of pairs	21	45	105	190
Approximate minutes at 5-min intervals	100	220	520	945
Approximate number of 90-min sessions	2	3	6	11
Approximate minutes at 15-min intervals	300	660	1560	2835
Approximate number of 90-min sessions	4	8	18	32

[a] In order to compute the number of pairs for a given number of stimuli (e.g., seven stimuli), C_2^7 (the combination of seven stimuli two at a time) is found.

$$C_2^7 = \frac{7!}{2!\,5!} = \frac{7\times6\times5\times4\times3\times2\times1}{(2\times1)\times(5\times4\times3\times2\times1)} = 21.$$

A simpler calculation is $N(N-1)/2$.

Some general guidelines from our own experience for a variety of stimuli are:

Stimulus type	Between pairs interval
Weak tastes	2–5 min
Moderate tastes	5–10 min
Weak and moderate odors	3–5 min
Strong and lingering odors and tastes	15+ min

2.3. Presentation of Taste and Smell Stimuli

With taste stimuli, subjects generally take about 10 cc into their mouths from cups. With strong stimuli, for example, liqueurs, the volume is less. They rinse with water within and between pairs. Neither stimuli nor rinse water are swallowed, although subjects may drink water if thirsty. Subjects are instructed to let the stimulus solutions come in contact with all parts of the mouth, including the back of the tongue. This is to activate as many receptors as possible and to keep the tasting procedure standard. If taste sensations only are the objective of the experiment, the subjects wear nose plugs to reduce olfactory input.

For both taste and smell experiments, subjects are required not to eat, drink (except water), or smoke for at least 1 hour before a session. Where practical it is desirable to extend this period of abstinence to 2 hours.

Immediately before the start of the experiment subjects brush their teeth using water only to remove food particles. Subjects are requested not to wear lipstick or perfumes. For certain stimuli, where visual cues are unavoidable, subjects wear blindfolds.

With odor stimuli there are two general methods of stimulus presentation: from an olfactometer or from wide-mouthed bottles. The latter is of course much simpler, and suitable for most experiments. All odors in the stimulus set must then be adjusted to approximately equal intensity if the desired space is to be strictly qualitative. This is usually achieved by dilution with odorless grades of either dipropylene glycol or diethyl phthalate.

Subjects normally sniff one odor, wait about 10 sec, then sniff the other. They keep their eyes closed while sniffing to avoid stimulation of the eye by the odorants. Repeat sniffs are not encouraged as confusion and fatigue increase. With moderately intense odors 3 to 5 min between stimulus pairs is a sufficient rest period. With stronger or lingering odors more time may be needed. It is best, in the absence of specific information, to run some pilot trials to determine an appropriate interval. With cigarettes, which provide taste, smell, trigeminal sensations, and nicotine absorption, 15-min intervals are needed between pairs even with only three puffs from each cigarette.

2.4. Recording Similarity Judgments

For all the examples given in this book similarity judgments were recorded by making a mark on a 5-in. line. In our experience, subjects seem to be comfortable with a 5-in. line—with a 4-in. line their judgments are compressed and with a 6-in. line they do not use the right-hand end of the scale often. Three different anchors were used:

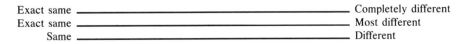

Exact same ———————————————————————— Completely different
Exact same ———————————————————————— Most different
Same ———————————————————————— Different

When the stimulus range is wide, as in the taste of chemicals (Section 3.4) or odor of chemicals (Section 3.7), the first seems most appropriate. When the stimulus range is narrow, as in cigarettes (Section 3.6), the second or third represent a better choice. We do not know of an experiment which has been performed to examine the effect of different anchors which may in any case be minor provided subjects understand the task. We do believe it important, however, to provide an undifferentiated line scale rather than a series of boxes or numbers. This is for several reasons. First, people attach different meanings to verbal descriptions such as *fairly* and *some-*

what. Second, subjects tend to lose sight of the similarity task while debating the relative merits of *fairly* and *somewhat*. Third, many subjects feel uncomfortable with segmenting the line with words and especially with numbers. If boxes or numbers are used, and the only reason we can see for this is to simplify data work-up, they should definitely *not* be labeled *fairly similar, somewhat different*, and so forth.

A separate sheet of paper is provided for each judgment so that subjects do not refer back to previous judgments. The judgments as measured from the left-hand end of the scales above are dissimilarities. Larger numbers mean that a pair is more dissimilar. Judgments may be recorded either in millimeters (scale becomes 0 to 127) or 1/20 in. (scale becomes 0 to 100).

Two other methods of recording judgments should be mentioned. While not generally applicable to taste and smell experiments, they are valuable for large visual and verbal stimulus sets and can be performed easily in the field and with children. The first of these is a sorting method. The subject is presented with the total stimulus set and asked to sort them into groups of like stimuli. Normally the subject determines the number of groups, but the experimenter can specify a number, say 5, if desired. The stimuli can be the actual articles, say packages of cereals, but it is obviously more convenient to use photographs or cards with the stimulus names. When the sort is completed the experimenter records the allotment of the stimuli to the groups then sets up a square matrix for each subject. The entries in the matrix are binary coded using 0 if a stimulus pair is allocated to the same group and 1 if to a different group. The matrices are then summed over subjects (or subsets of the subjects) to give the dissimilarity judgments.

The second method is conditional rank order. Here each stimulus in turn is used as a standard and the subject is asked to rank the remaining stimuli in order of their similarity to this standard. Again this is a relatively easy task to perform, particularly with visual stimuli. The task can be further simplified, particularly when a large number of stimuli are involved, by requiring the subjects to rank only a smaller number against each standard. With 15 stimuli, for example, they might be asked to order the 5 most like each standard and the 5 least like each standard. The data would then be coded 1, 2, 3, 4, 5 for the 5 most similar, 6 for the 4 unranked samples, and 7, 8, 9, 10, 11 for the least similar. Another variation is to exclude each standard after it has been used from the stimulus set. That is to say, although all stimuli will be ranked with respect to stimulus A, A will be excluded from the comparisons with B, A and B will be excluded from the comparisons with C, and so on. This procedure effectively halves the time required to gather data. On the other hand, if time and subject interest allow collection of the full data matrix, then it is possible to determine how consistent the subject is in making his or her judgments.

Conditional rank order data are most easily analyzed by using the row conditional options available in KYST, POLYCON, or ALSCAL. Each row of the data matrix is set up showing similarity or dissimilarity with respect to the standard.

2.5. Order of Stimulus Presentation

Ideally the order of stimulus presentation is random across subjects as well as across stimulus pairs. Also half the subjects for a pair AB will experience A first while the other half will experience B first. (It is assumed in almost all similarity experiments and MDS scaling procedures that $d_{AB} = d_{BA}$. There is no proof that this is so, however, and a balanced design compensates for any such effects.) With a large number of subjects and stimuli, randomization across subjects poses practical problems. We do not see this precaution as essential. There is one exception to the otherwise mandatory randomization across stimulus pairs. If the experimental design includes a number of same–same comparisons (cigarettes in Section 3.6 are an example) it is not desirable to have such comparisons occurring sequentially in a session. Subjects will begin to question their perceptions. Therefore, after randomization, the pair sequence is checked to determine if any adjustments to avoid such effects need to be made.

2.6. Selection of a Stimulus Set

It is desirable to include as many stimuli as practically possible in an experiment. This is because the number of dimensions which can be explored increases with the number of stimuli. Use of a small data set can lead to loss of the more subtle nuances which can only be observed at higher dimensionalities. Ideally one should have about 12 stimuli for two-dimensional solutions and 18 stimuli for three-dimensional solutions. Kruskal and Wish (1978) recommend 9 stimuli for 2 dimensions, 13 for 3, and 17 for 4; Young (1970) and Spence and Domoney (1974) recommend 6 for 1 dimension, 11 for 2, and 17 for 3. There are several places in this book where we violate these recommendations because of time constraints, unavailability of sufficient stimuli, or to illustrate a specific point. But note that the recommendations just given are for a single matrix of data, and all of our data sets have several matrices. While no studies have been done, it seems reasonable to assume that the recommendations can be weakened somewhat when there are more than, say, 10 matrices being analyzed. We do not know, though, just how much these recommendations can be weakened, or what effect there would be on the quality of the results. It is, of course, desirable to have as many stimuli as possible and to reduce all sources of error in the data. With very few stimuli and many matrices it is important to split the data into two or more subsamples, and then to perform parallel analyses on each subsample. This allows one to check on the reliability of the analyses.

One way around the time–number of judgment problems, if sufficient stimuli are available, is to use incomplete data designs. Suppose we wish to compare 20 stimuli. This requires 190 similarity judgments. We can use twice as many subjects as intended and have them each make 95 judgments. The judgment pairs can be assigned randomly for each subject or, alternately, after numbering the matrix, half the subjects can perform even-numbered judgments and the other half odd-numbered judgments.

We do not give examples in this book of incomplete data designs although all of the programs except INDSCAL will accept matrices with missing data. The subject is discussed briefly in Section 4.4 and more fully in the references contained there. This area needs more experimental work.

Since we are concerned in this section, with discovering the underlying properties that cause similarities and differences among a group of objects, if one or two objects are very different from the remainder, these large differences will obscure more subtle differences. Suppose the stimulus set is white wine. If the stimuli all represent extreme examples of the suspected attributes the solution will be an unsurprising collection of clusters. Inclusion of a champagne may collapse the structure to the single dimension of bubbly–not bubbly. If it is taste or odor *qualities* that are sought, it is important to equalize *intensities* as much as possible. If this is not done, intensity may become the dominant dimension.

On the other hand, if all stimuli are very similar, it is important to build in checks for reproducibility. One way to do this is to include replicate stimuli as in the cigarette example (Section 3.6). If time and money allow, the entire experiment can be repeated. What is needed is some way of determining if each subject's judgments do represent real perceptual differences. Or are they just guesses? Many of the programs provide some measure of fit for each subject which is of course a guide to the reliability of their judgments. This brings us to the area of subject selection and explanation of the task.

2.7. Selection of Subjects

Whether the experiment is academic or industrial (e.g., concerned with consumer products), many of the same general principles apply to screening and retaining subjects. For an MDS experiment with consumer products one needs subjects who are users of the product class and of at least one of the brands of interest. While nonusers could provide difference judgments, the intent of the experiment is to uncover those differences which are relevant to the users. In this respect, therefore, normal consumer research methods identify the appropriate population. However, further screening is necessary, and this screening applies also to an academic experiment in which college students are the probable subjects.

An MDS experiment concerns separation of stimuli. The subjects need to be both physiologically sensitive to differences in the stimulus set, and psychologically capable of performing the experiment. Beer and cigarettes are two product categories notorious for their difficulty. Many users seem unable to tell the difference between competing brands. Obviously one wishes to use for subjects only those people who can discriminate. While anosmia and taste blindness are interesting topics in their own right, partial anosmics or nontasters may not be suitable for certain smell or taste experiments. The simplest way to screen out insensitive subjects is to apply two or three triangle tests on the stimuli of interest during a screening interview. While this does not guarantee that all those who pass the test are "good" (the probability of three out of three guessed responses being correct is .036), it does weed out those who are insensitive. Two other simple criteria are to disqualify denture wearers and people over 55, unless of course they are the population of interest.

We use psychological capability in a very broad sense. One needs subjects who understand the task, remain motivated, are punctual for panel or group sessions, abide by panel instructions, and are willing to make judgments. On this last point we invariably find about 5% of the subjects who never use more than 20% of the difference scale.

Understanding and motivation are to a large extent the responsibility of the panel leaders. With experience they can determine during screening interviews those people who will not respond well during panel sessions. We have explored numerous psychological scales as instruments for subject selection. While some of these work satisfactorily for college students, it has not in our experience been useful on the general population. Unless the obese are the subjects of actual interest they are probably best avoided. While their pattern recognition is good, they tend to exaggerate the hedonic aspect of stimuli in making judgments.

It is usually possible to rationalize after the fact why a subject performs poorly: A had one trouble after another during the 3 weeks of the experiment—car trouble, a sick wife, sick children, little sleep. His thoughts were on his troubles, not the stimuli. His scores were random. At the end of the first week we realized B was taking an excessive amount of medications.

2.8. How to Get Subjects to Understand What to Do

We assume that you will have elected to use the undifferentiated line scale with the anchor words: exact same–most different. Your task is to relate to the subjects how to judge the stimuli, *without* influencing the way in which they make their judgments. This is by no means trivial. One way is to have them practice using images as the stimulus set. One could, for example, use four cuts of steak: sirloin, porterhouse, T-bone, and filet. An alternative set could be citrus fruits: oranges, lemons, tangerines, and grapefruit. The instructions to the subjects could be as follows:

During this experiment you will be judging how similar or different a number of stimuli are. You will be comparing them two at a time. For us to know how similar or different you find each pair to be we will have you mark a form for us. (Pass forms around.)

You can see that on the form there is a line with the words *exact same* at one end, and *most different* at the other. If you find no difference between the two stimuli[1] make a mark at the end of the line by *exact same*. If you find there is a difference make a mark somewhere along the line showing how much difference you find. *Most different* is in the setting of the group of stimuli you will be comparing for us.[2] In order for you to get an idea of how much difference there is in this group of stimuli we will have you try them first one at a time over the next few days.

One thing we would like you to remember is that different people judge things in different ways. This means that there are no right or wrong answers. Two stimuli that are very similar to one person may be quite different to another. Both results are important to us. We are interested in finding out how you as an individual compare these stimuli.

Let's now practice marking these forms, and then see if you have any questions. Imagine you are comparing four fruits: oranges, lemons, tangerines, and grapefruits. We are going to ask you to compare them two at a time. There will be six pairs in all. You should have six forms in front of you stapled together. Use one form for each pair. Remember all you have to do is to make a mark on the line showing how similar or different you feel each pair to be. Allow about 15 seconds between each pair.

The first pair is .... oranges–grapefruit
The second pair is .... oranges–tangerines
The third pair is .... lemons–grapefruit
The fourth pair is .... oranges–lemons
The fifth pair is .... lemons–tangerines
The sixth and last pair is .... grapefruit–oranges

Now write your name on the top form and we will collect them. Any questions?

[1] Obviously you will name the item class, beer, cigarettes, sausages, etc., and not use the word stimuli.

[2] It is sometimes helpful to describe the bounds of the product category: bourbon whiskey, not scotch; only menthol cigarettes; only fruity flavors.

There are a number of important points in this explanation. First, there are no right or wrong answers. Well motivated subjects tend to worry if they are "doing all right." The scientific panel atmosphere, which is necessary for a serious approach, tends to work against the intuitive responses which are sought. Subjects need reassurance. . . . "We are interested in you as an individual." And indeed one is. There are generally a number of people who really cannot tell the difference, even if they think they can, or pretend they can. This in itself is a useful statistic. Second, practice on a fairly easy stimulus set is the best way to generate familiarity with the scale. This avoids questions of "How far along should I mark if they seem fairly different?" Explanations here quickly degenerate into providing a form of category scale, which you do not want to do. Third, it provides an idea of the bounds of the stimulus set, and encourages full use of the scale.

If exposure to the stimulus set will take several days, a number of practice runs of this nature can be performed. It is best to use stimulus sets that evoke sensory images rather than cognitive or abstract responses. Of course with images as the stimulus set it is difficult to avoid altogether cognitive responses. The fruits above could be ordered by color or size, as well as sweetness.

2.9. Summary

This chapter has described the procedures needed to collect similarity judgments for subsequent multidimensional scaling. We cover the time needed to perform an experiment, how to present stimuli, how to record judgments, and how to select stimuli and subjects. Since these experiments are relatively time-consuming compared with other ways of collecting perceptual data, performing a pilot experiment before the main data collection commences can be helpful. This permits determination of the number of judgments subjects can make per session and the appropriateness of the stimulus set. You will find, as you study the examples in this book, that good data are vital. While the underlying models for the programs we discuss do vary, none can achieve a meaningful solution from noise. We cannot overemphasize the need to carefully select the stimulus set and ensure that the judgments asked of the subjects lie within their capabilities.

References

Kruskal, J. B., & Wish, M. *Multidimensional scaling*. Beverley Hills: Sage Press, 1978.

Spence, I., & Domoney, D. W. Single subject incomplete designs for nonmetric multidimensional scaling. *Psychometrika*, 1974, *39*, 469–470.

Young, F. W. Nonmetric multidimensional scaling: Recovery of metric information. *Psychometrika*, 1970, *35*, 455–474.

3

Data Bank Used
throughout This Book

The eight classes of stimuli described in this chapter cover a range of taste and smell experiences. These examples were chosen because the form and structure of the data represent situations likely to be encountered in a wide variety of MDS applications—sensory and conceptual. The data provide, therefore, an opportunity to compare the strengths and weaknesses of the various programs. The experimental procedures, which are typically more involved than for visual or verbal experiments, for example, will hopefully stimulate the potential user into a careful examination of key variables for any study. Table 3.1 shows where our experiments are used in the book to illustrate the various programs. Each section in this chapter describes the purpose behind the experiment, the stimulus class, the subjects partaking in the experiment, and the experimental procedure. In the cola example, Section 3.1, we provide the raw data set for those who wish to check their own systems or make comparisons with other algorithms.

3.1. Colas

This exploratory experiment (Schiffman, 1977) was to determine if there was enough difference between cola drinks to map their taste qualities by MDS.

Table 3.1
Chapter Sections Which Illustrate Treatment of a Specific Stimulus Set with a Specific Program

Stimuli	Program					
	MINISSA	POLYCON	KYST	INDSCAL[a]	ALSCAL	MULTISCALE
Colas	5.3	6.3	7.3	8.3	9.3	10.3
Food flavors	5.4	6.4	7.4	8.4	9.4	10.4
Strawberry-flavored beverages	5.5	6.5	7.5	8.5	9.5	10.5
Taste of chemicals	5.6					
Musk odors	5.7			8.6	9.7	
Cigarettes				8.7		
Odor of chemicals					9.6	

[a] Section 8.10 describes application of SINDSCAL to colas.

Stimuli

Ten colas (see Table 3.2) were bought (in glass containers) from retail outlets. Fresh bottles were used each day. Two hours before use, the colas were opened to remove carbonation (thus minimizing this variable). The drinks were served at room temperature in 5-ounce plastic cups.

Subjects

The 10 subjects, aged 18–21 years, were all university students—5 were male, 5 were female. They were paid $17.50 for their participation in the

Table 3.2
Colas Used as Stimuli in Section 3.1

Stimulus number	Cola
01	Diet Pepsi
02	RC Cola
03	Yukon
04	Dr. Pepper
05	Shasta
06	Coca-Cola
07	Diet Dr. Pepper
08	Tab
09	Pepsi-Cola
10	Diet Rite

7-day experiment. None were smokers. The subjects were blindfolded throughout the experiment to eliminate visual cues.

Procedure

The experiment was performed in a partitioned classroom with three or four subjects present at any one time. In the first session, subjects tasted the 10 colas and were told that these beverages represented the full range of tastes they would be comparing. They did not swallow the drinks and rinsed their mouths with distilled water between tastes. They were also instructed in the use of the scoring sheet, a 5-in. line anchored as shown below:

Same ————————————————————————————————— Different

During the course of the experiment they were told that they could expect to be making marks along the full length of the line. Practice similarity judgments were made during the first session.

The 45 pairwise similarity judgments were made over a 5-day period. Each day nine judgments were made with 5-min intervals between pairs. Order of stimulus presentation was randomized to balance cross-adaptation effects. Upon instructions from the experimenter, the blindfolded subjects first tasted a cola beverage which was placed in front of them, letting it swirl around their mouths for about 5 sec. Then they spit the substance into a spittoon; this was followed by rinsing the mouth with distilled water. Next they tasted another beverage placed in front of them, again ejecting it into the spittoon. After the cups were taken away by the experimenter, the subjects removed their blindfolds and made a rating of similarity by marking an X along the 5-in. line above. Five minutes of rest was allowed between pairs.

On the seventh day subjects rated each cola on the series of adjective scales shown in Table 3.3. The adjectives were anchored at the ends of a 5-in. line.

Similarity judgments and adjective ratings were transcribed on a scale from 0 to 100, 0 representing *same* or the left-hand adjective and 100 representing *different* or the right-hand adjective.

The complete data set is given in Tables 3.4 and 3.5.

3.2. Food Flavors

This experiment (Schiffman & Pasternak, 1978) was to determine if aged subjects discriminate food odors differently than a young control group.

Table 3.3
Adjective Scales on Which Colas in Section 3.1 Were Rated

Adjective number	Adjective scale
01	Good; Bad
02	Strong; Weak
03	Sweet; Not sweet
04	Bitter; Not bitter
05	Sour; Not sour
06	Fruity; Not fruity
07	Spicy; Not spicy
08	Coats mouth; Does not coat mouth
09	Sharp; Not sharp
10	Puckers mouth; Does not pucker mouth
11	Fresh; Stale
12	Chemical; Not chemical
13	Complex; Simple

Stimuli

The stimuli were 14 commercial food flavors (see Table 3.6) supplied by Firmenich, New York. Apart from butter and chocolate, the stimuli represented three basic groups: fruits, vegetables, and meats. The flavors were diluted with an odorless grade of dipropylene glycol until they were judged of approximately equal intensity by 14 young college students. The odorants were sniffed from opaque wide mouth bottles.

Subjects

The 32 subjects comprised two groups:

1. Sixteen aged—all female, aged 72–78 years, healthy residents of a retirement home, nonsmokers.
2. Sixteen young—11 female and 5 male, aged 19–25 years, healthy university students, nonsmokers.

The subjects were paid $27.50 for their participation in the 11-day experiment. Subjects kept their eyes closed during sniffing to eliminate stimulation of the surface of the eyes by the odorants.

Procedure

The experiment was performed in two locations: (a) an assembly room in a retirement home and (b) a university classroom. Both locations were

Table 3.4
Similarity Data among All Pairs of Ten Colas for Ten Subjects in Section 3.1, in Format (2X, 9F2.0)[a]

```
0116
018147
01563271
0187684471
016035219834
018494985799 99
0150877973199245
019925539852179984
0116929083794424 1898
0209
029070
0287 6506
0287778383
023379258939
0286869922904 0
028130578869 3 997
027420947805819288
022326729402768 12005
0349
039696
03979294
0368129093
037744889026
03979394259349
0354769294202493
034748929435 189423
032147909268 67875515
0423
049951
04992378
0490 16 2249
047455509913
04 148877755070
0425954 899997999
046036692421539999
040089728177717 45171
0562
057716
05981455
0576224047
058416168107
05178036936090
0576938680943619
0574201638051 80671
05107278929286160299
```

(cont'd.)

Table 3.4 (cont'd.)

```
0685
068215
06972856
0651313643
067927078207
0613843887682
0682997368804020
0669243027161221880
0615807890726170595
0710
075375
07999999
0787276599
076066729999
079699901090175
0798999198883499
0773159099009569575
0754628499955385149
0814
086147
08799677
0872211273
086612288113
086664754171812
0851673293496686
080720677115567669
0819510688258150088?
0911
099069
09722690
0993176924
093934369880
0926827785539?
0980747599938713
09730891351717917991
0924629076856477472465
1069
106358
10768579
1052145181
106139358336
10809093067885
102887839464444490
1080209298512238033
10782840993671826213
```

---

[a] Columns 1–2 give subject code, for example, 01 refers to subject 1 and 16 is the dissimilarity measure between RC Cola and Diet Pepsi (Table 3.2).

Table 3.5

Ratings of Ten Colas on Thirteen Adjective Scales for Ten Subjects in Section 3.1, in Format (4X, 13F2.0)[a]

```
0101989891049999998482710470803
0102039102999999196969099069393
0103027407997627509990220684 75
0104473107789962319949994 83838
0105900543088198069902900993941
0106990096011790997980003990101
0107103303878940786099314 74247
0108393934991817999979313 59091
010937180080101032959981494 134
0110763399158599990607709 80709
0201358911929179837885828782 82
0202848282838577717370481871734
020397189605053616161003471421
020413700390840233888991308375
020594288716034711290603640040
020622731380842026637683438478
020729771687851746838089779284
020888378515158907121519602138
020940333464681748697072697451
021084268221148246131416503742
030140834487959393759483264946
030289457687989492788921951950
030399757849479594944905970450
030425191395951097509593089450
030547351996949494492950701221
030669425096959593493795493938
030770222392761196493097284137
030867453772819705537386792540
030946411596969696559596716557
031084637292949396499384923049
040178358914519999511872792250
040273642180998099799989687677
040374467320522680245125517425
040408510099992058879988159926
040585299900149999072400821982
040628793978999073268988238876
040770507025523580801617657629
040899009009199999821700612248
040932535382842186859999509190
041093539918188799513110772136
050188798318745844112117950809
050251283164744967577184264557
050380167819279221251219181712
050409751391922453918387259183
050592128612198553141225821329
050615391694904889667794208772
050799119408099871100805980714
050885169805159899100706990137
050923531070009899627883267985
051010099602301086080504990025
```

(cont'd.)

Table 3.5 (cont'd.)

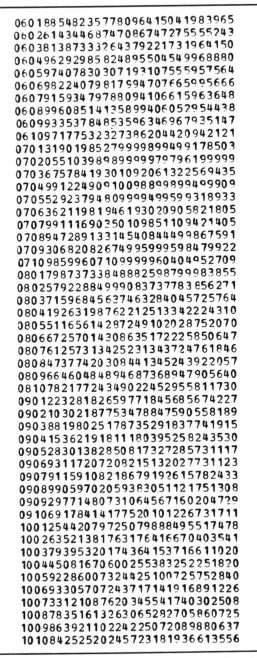

```
060 188 548 235 778 096 4 150 4 198 3 965
060 261 434 468 74 7086 747 275 55 55 243
060 381 387 333 264 379 221 731 964 150
060 496 292 985 824 89 55045 49 968 880
060 597 407 830 307 193 107 555 957 564
060 698 224 079 817 994 707 665 995 666
060 791 593 4 797 880 94 106 6 159 63 648
060 899 608 514 1358 994 060 52 954 438
060 993 353 784 853 596 346 967 935 147
061 097 177 532 327 386 204 420 942 121
070 131 901 985 279 999 89 94 9 9 178 503
070 205 510 398 989 999 97 9 796 199 999
070 367 578 4 19 301 092 061 322 569 435
070 499 122 490 9 100 98 899 899 49 990 9
070 552 923 794 809 99 49 995 99 318 933
070 636 211 981 946 193 020 905 821 805
070 799 111 690 350 109 851 109 421 405
070 894 728 9 133 14 540 844 499 867 591
070 930 682 082 674 995 999 598 479 922
071 098 599 607 109 999 960 404 952 709
080 179 873 733 848 882 598 799 983 855
080 257 922 884 999 083 737 783 856 271
080 371 596 845 637 463 284 045 725 764
080 419 263 198 762 212 513 342 224 310
080 551 165 614 287 249 102 028 752 070
080 667 257 014 308 635 172 225 850 647
080 761 257 3 134 252 313 437 247 618 46
080 847 377 420 308 44 134 524 392 2057
080 966 460 48 489 468 736 89 47 905 640
081 078 217 724 349 022 452 955 811 730
090 122 328 182 659 77 184 568 567 4227
090 210 302 187 753 478 847 590 558 189
090 388 198 025 178 735 291 837 741 915
090 415 362 191 811 180 395 258 243 530
090 528 301 382 850 817 327 285 731 117
090 693 117 207 208 215 132 027 731 123
090 791 159 108 218 679 1926 157 824 33
090 899 059 702 059 383 051 121 751 308
090 929 771 480 731 064 567 160 204 729
091 069 178 414 177 520 101 226 731 711
100 125 442 079 725 079 888 495 517 478
100 263 521 381 763 176 416 670 403 541
100 379 395 320 174 364 153 7 166 11 020
100 445 081 670 600 255 383 252 251 820
100 592 286 007 324 425 100 725 752 840
100 693 305 707 243 717 141 916 891 226
100 733 121 087 620 345 541 740 302 508
100 878 351 613 263 065 282 705 860 725
100 986 392 110 224 225 072 089 880 637
101 084 252 520 245 723 181 936 613 556
```

[a] Columns 1–2 give subject code, Columns 3–4 give stimulus code (Table 3.2), adjectives are in order shown in Table 3.3.

well ventilated with exhaust fans. In the first session, subjects were exposed to the 14 stimuli and told that these represented the full range of odors they would be comparing. They were also instructed in the use of the scoring sheet, a 5-in. line anchored as shown below:

Same ———————————————————————————— Different

They were told that during the course of the experiment, they could expect to be making marks along the full length of the line. Practice similarity judgments were made during the first session.

The 91 pairwise similarity judgments were made over a 9-day period. Each day, 10 judgments (11 in the last similarity session) were made, allowing 3-min intervals between pairs. The subjects were presented with pairs of stimuli at the level of the nostrils by the experimenter. The time interval between presentation of two stimuli of a pair was approximately 10 sec. A rating of similarity was made after each pair by marking an X along the 5-in. line. Order of stimulus presentation was randomized across stimuli to balance cross-adaptation effects.

Finally, on the eleventh day the subjects rated each flavor on a hedonic scale:

Good ———————————————————————————— Bad

Similarity judgments and hedonic ratings were transcribed on a scale from 0 to 99, 0 representing *same* or *good* and 99 representing *different* or *bad*.

Table 3.6
Food Flavors Used as Stimuli in Section 3.2

Fruit flavors	Vegetable flavors	Meat flavors	Other flavors
Apple	Corn	Bacon	Butter
Cherry	Green bean	Beef	Chocolate
Grape	Potato	Chicken	
Lime	Tomato		
Strawberry			

3.3 Strawberry-Flavored Beverages

The purpose of this experiment (Skinner & Schiffman, 1979) was to determine the perception of 11 different formulations of strawberry-flavored beverages which varied in color and sweetness.

Stimuli

The stimuli were 11 noncarbonated strawberry-flavored beverages (see Figure 3.1) varying only in sweetness (sugar content) and color (redness). They were served in 5-ounce clear plastic cups at 50°F.

Subjects

The 46 subjects, aged 22–44, were Caucasian mothers recruited by a market research company. They were paid $100 for their participation in 10 sessions lasting 1¼ hours each.

Procedure

The experiment took place in a panel room fitted with individual booths twice a day for 1 week. In the first session, subjects tasted five strawberry drinks representing the full range of sweetness and color. They did not swallow the drinks and rinsed their mouths with tap water between tastes. They were also instructed in the use of the scoring sheet, a 5-in. line

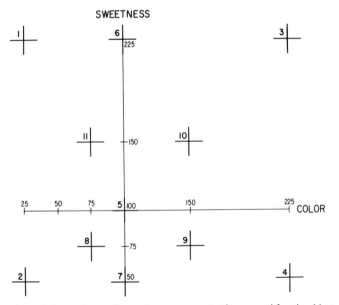

Figure 3.1. The relative color and sweetness concentrations used for the 11 strawberry-flavored drinks in Section 3.3.

anchored as shown below:

Same _____ Different

During the course of the experiment, they were told that they could expect
to be making marks along the full length of the line. Practice similarity
judgments were made during the first session.

The 55 pairwise similarity judgments, along with seven same–same pairs
(a stimulus was compared with itself), were made in seven sessions. When
instructed by the experimenter, the subjects first tasted the right-hand beverage of a pair placed in each booth. They let it swirl around their mouths
for about 5 sec and spit it into a spittoon. After rinsing their mouths, they
tasted the left-hand beverage. The subjects then made a rating of similarity
along the 5-in. line. The order of the presentation balanced cross-adaptation
effects.

Finally, in the last sessions, the subjects rated each of the 11 stimuli on
the adjective scales shown in Table 3.7.

Table 3.7
Adjective Scales on Which Each of the Strawberry-Flavored Beverages Was Rated in
Section 3.3

Good	Bad
Strong	Weak
Refreshing	Not refreshing
Sweet	Not sweet
Sour	Not sour
Watery	Thick
Full-bodied	Not full-bodied
Complex	Simple
Fragrant	Not fragrant
Like	Dislike
Fruity	Not fruity
Bitey	Not bitey
Tingling	Not tingling
Sharp	Not sharp
Coats mouth	Doesn't coat mouth
Bitter	Not bitter
Salty	Not salty
Fresh	Stale
Chemical	Not chemical
Red	Not red
Orange	Not orange
Pink	Not pink
Strong color	Weak color
Strong taste	Weak taste
Like color	Dislike color
Like taste	Dislike taste
Pleasant	Unpleasant

Both similarity and adjective ratings were transcribed on a scale from 0 to 99, with 0 representing *same* or the left-hand adjective and 99 representing *different* or the right-hand adjective.

3.4. Taste of Chemicals

The purpose of this experiment was to determine whether the taste realm is limited to four basic tastes (Schiffman & Erickson, 1971). Traditionally the range of gustatory quality has been assumed to be limited to four primary tastes: sweet, sour, salty, and bitter. A geometric model in the form of a hollow tetrahedron was proposed by Henning (1916) to represent the range of gustatory quality. Henning's model arranges the four primary tastes at the four corners of an equilateral tetrahedron. Sensations which are mixtures of two primaries are located on the edges of the tetrahedron. Sensations, which are mixtures of three primaries, are located on the faces of the tetrahedron. Henning's model is hollow because he believed there were no sensations produced by mixtures of four primaries.

Henning's model, though helpful for guiding research, is troublesome as a complete gustatory model. First, it does not allow for ordering of stimuli which cannot be described in terms of the traditional primary qualities; thus it is *closed-ended*. Second, it is quantitatively imprecise because it is not based on quantitative experimental measures.

The problems encountered in ordering stimuli with Henning's model can be eliminated using multidimensional scaling procedures. Multidimensional scaling procedures are open-ended so that all stimuli can be ordered even if they cannot be described in terms of sweet, sour, salty, and bitter. Also the distances achieved in a multidimensional scaling arrangement are based on quantitative experimental measures.

Stimuli

The stimuli, shown in Table 3.8, were 19 reagent grade chemicals chosen for their ranges of gustatory quality and chemical structure. All stimuli are traditionally assumed to be describable in terms of the four primary tastes. They were tested at room temperature (72°F).

Subjects

The subjects were four nonsmoking males, aged 16–34 years. They were paid $100 for their participation in the total experiment, which required 35–40 1-hour sessions.

Table 3.8
Concentrations of Chemicals Used as Stimuli in Section 3.4[a]

Stimulus	Subjects			
	1	2	3	4
NaCl—Sodium chloride	.2	.2	.2	.2
LiCl—Lithium chloride	.2	.2	.2	.2
NH₄Cl—Ammonium chloride	.1	.1	.1	.1
KCl—Potassium chloride	.3	.3	.3	.3
MgCl₂—Magnesium chloride	.1	.1	.1	.1
CaCl₂—Calcium chloride	.025	.025	.05	.05
K₂SO₄—Potassium sulphate	.3	.3	.3	.3
NaAc—Sodium acetate	.7	.7	1.0	1.0
PbAc—Lead acetate	.05	.005	.05	.05
Glucose	1.2	1.2	1.2	1.2
Sucrose	.8	.8	1.0	1.0
Saccharin	.0025	.0025	.0025	.0025
HCl—Hydrochloric acid	.01	.01	.01	.01
HNO₃—Nitric acid	.01	.01	.01	.01
HAc—Acetic acid	.05	.01	.1	.1
NaOH—Sodium hydroxide	.05	.006	.05	.05
Na₂CO₃—Sodium carbonate	.1	.05	.1	.1
QHCl—Quinine hydrochloride	.002	.0004	.002	.002
Q₂SO₄—Quinine sulphate	.001	.00025	.001	.001

[a] The molarity of solutions used for each subject was judged to be equal in intensity.

Procedure

The experiment took place in a psychology laboratory. In the first few sessions, the subjects compared each stimulus to .2M NaCl, a stimulus of moderate intensity. The concentrations shown in Table 3.8 for the stimuli were found to be approximately equal in perceived intensity to .2M NaCl. In the next sessions, each stimulus was compared with every other on the basis of taste, 171 pairs in all. Subjects made judgments of similarity by marking an X along a 5-in. line shown below:

Exact same ——————————————————— Completely different

The two stimuli to be compared were placed in front of the subject by the experimenter. The subject sipped the first substance, letting it swirl around his mouth, and then rinsed his mouth with distilled water. Then he tasted the second stimulus of the pair in the same manner. The time between two stimuli in a pair ranged from 20 sec to 1 min allowing the subject to get a good impression of the taste. One stimulus was used throughout any given session as the standard for comparison with the other stimuli. (Note: The order of the presentation of the stimuli can be randomized as well, and the choice of randomization versus use of a standard frequently depends on the particular experiment. In the experience of the authors, the order of presentation of pairs has not affected the subsequent arrangement achieved by MDS.) A minimum of 40 for one subject and a maximum of 171 additional similarity judgments for another subject were made to determine reliability of the ratings.

Finally, in the last sessions the subjects rated each stimulus on the 45-adjective scales shown in Table 3.9. The adjectives were anchored at the ends of a 5-in. line much like that for similarity judgments.

Both similarity and adjective ratings were transcribed on a scale from 0 to 100, with 0 representing *exact same* or the left-hand adjective and 100 representing *completely different* or the right-hand adjective.

Table 3.9
Adjective Scales on Which Chemicals Were Rated in Section 3.4[a]

1	2
Good; Bad	Salty; Unsalty
Foodlike; Not foodlike	Bitter; Not bitter
Obnoxious; Not obnoxious	Sweet; Unsweet
Repulsive; Not repulsive	Sour; Not sour
Pleasant; Unpleasant	Acid; Alkaline
Flavorous; Not flavorous	Bitey; Not bitey
Nauseous; Not nauseous	Tingling; Not tingling
Urinous; Not urinous	Hot; Cold
Poisonous; Not poisonous	Sharp; Not sharp
Strangling; Not strangling	Burning; Not burning
Soft; Hard	Warming; Chilling

3	4
Refreshing; Not refreshing	Soapy; Not soapy
Smooth; Rough	Spicy; Not spicy
Metallic; Not metallic	Fatty; Not fatty
Taste changes; Taste constant	Meaty; Not meaty
Weak; Strong	Fruity; Not fruity
Dry; Wet	Odorous; Not odorous
Minerally; Not minerally	Pungent; Not pungent
Complex; Simple	Smokey; Not smokey
Flat; Not flat	Sensual; Not sensual
Clear; Unclear	Watery; Thick
Taste develops slowly;	Fresh; Stale
Taste develops rapidly	Dilute; Concentrated

[a] The adjectives in Column 1, as will be shown in Chapter 12, tend to be associated with a hedonic dimension. The adjectives in Column 2 refer to the four so-called basic primaries as well as to tactile, temperature, and pain qualities of the stimulus. Columns 3–4 contain additional adjectives which have been used in reference to taste stimuli. Those adjectives in Column 4, however, were found to be either irrelevant or to reveal inconsistent information about the particular stimuli used in this experiment.

3.5. Musk Odors

Musks have complex and lingering odors which are all fairly similar. The purpose of this experiment is to demonstrate that a multidimensional scaling of similarity judgments provides an ordering of odor qualities not attainable by adjective ratings (Schiffman & Dackis, 1976).

Stimuli

The stimuli were the 14 musks shown in Figure 3.2. Purities were better than 95%. They were presented to the subjects as 10% (w/w) solutions in perfumer grade diethyl phthalate. The powerful and lingering nature of musk odors prevented assurance of equal intensity across stimulants. The 10% (w/w) concentration was chosen because it was discernible to all subjects for all stimuli.

Subjects

The subjects were 20 college students, aged 20–25, split evenly by gender. Five subjects out of an initial 25 were eliminated from the experiment because they failed to discriminate at least 4 of the first 10 test pairs. Subjects were paid $100 for the entire experiment.

Procedure

The experiment took place in well-ventilated classrooms with exhaust fans. The first sessions were used to familiarize the subjects with the range of the 14 stimuli and for practice similarity judgments.

Because the stimuli are all fairly similar, a special two-step procedure was devised for obtaining similarity judgments. The purpose of this was to reduce the amount of guessing on the subject's part when marking the amount of difference on the 5-in. line:

Exact same ——————————————————————————— Completely different

The first step consisted of a triangle test. If the subject correctly identified which of three stimuli present was different, then he or she made an actual similarity judgment. In addition to the similarity judgment, subjects also indicated whether the odd stimulus was more or less intense.

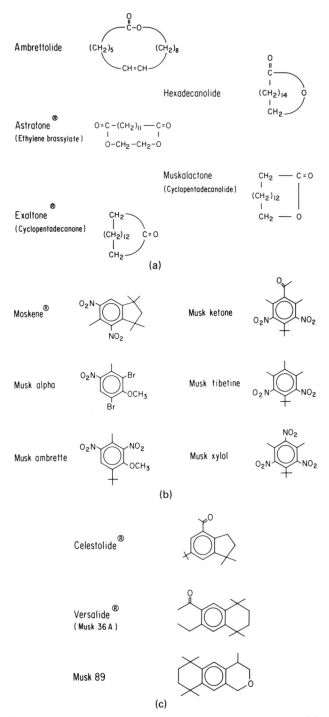

Figure 3.2. The chemical structure of the 14 musks used in this study: (a) macrocyclic musks; (b) nitro musks; (c) bicyclic and tricyclic musks. (From Schiffman & Dackis, 1976).

To balance cross-adaptation effects, random selection of the six stimulus presentation orders was used. That is, any subject could receive at any time one of the six orders AAB, ABA, BAA, BAB, ABB, and BBA. Neither rooms nor subjects were used for more than one trial in any 2-hour period. Development of all 91 comparisons took 4 months.

Table 3.10 is a confusability matrix for the 14 musks. The number in each cell refers to the number of subjects who failed to select the odd stimulus in that triangle test. The larger the number, the more similar that pair of musks.

Another matrix was developed which incorporated similarity judgments. Here, the total of all judgments for a pair was divided by 20 (the number of subjects). A similarity value of 0 was assigned to a given pair if the subject was unsuccessful in the triadic comparison; if successful, his or her rating on the 5-in line (transcribed from 0 to 99) was used as a similarity measure. Here, smaller numbers mean greater similarity.

After all similarity judgments were completed, subjects were asked to provide descriptive adjectives. Their responses provided the basis for four semantic differential scales:

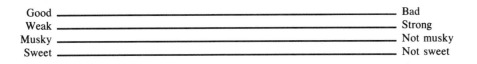

Good ———————————————————————————— Bad
Weak ———————————————————————————— Strong
Musky ——————————————————————————— Not musky
Sweet ——————————————————————————— Not sweet

Subjects then rated each of the 14 musks, on the four scales by making a mark on a 5-in. line anchored by the descriptors.

Both similarity and adjective ratings were transcribed on a scale from 0 to 99, with 0 representing *exact same* or the left-hand adjective and 99 representing *completely different* or the right-hand adjective.

3.6. Cigarettes

This experiment (Brotzge & Crain, 1977) is included to provide a paradigm for people in industry who are unsure if MDS of similarity judgments is applicable to their products. The design answers two basic questions. First, how well can consumers judge differences in a laboratory sip test? This is particularly relevant for products such as beer, soft drinks, and cigarettes. Second, how robust is the stimulus space? With a fairly large amount of noise expected (and usually found), can criteria be developed to ensure that the stimulus space makes sense? This was a pilot experiment and was not designed to uncover all the true dimensions of the stimulus space.

Table 3.10
Confusability Matrix[a]

	Ambretto-lide	Astra-tone®	Exaltone®	Hexadec-anolide	Muska-lactone	Moskene®	Musk alpha	Musk ambrette	Musk ketone	Musk tibetine	Musk xylol	Celest-olide®	Versa-lide®	Musk 89
Ambrettolide	—													
Astratone®	6	—												
Exaltone®	12	5	—											
Hexadecanolide	6	8	6	—										
Muskalactone	11	6	10	6	—									
Moskene®	10	11	12	10	9	—								
Musk alpha	7	5	11	7	8	9	—							
Musk ambrette	7	8	6	8	8	8	8	—						
Musk ketone	8	9	8	5	7	12	7	8	—					
Musk tibetine	8	8	8	8	9	14	6	7	11	—				
Musk xylol	6	7	10	3	9	13	6	7	13	12	—			
Celestolide®	12	9	12	9	12	13	7	9	5	13	10	—		
Versalide®	4	12	10	6	6	11	5	7	9	12	8	11	—	
Musk 89	6	9	7	8	10	5	7	10	9	9	7	12	8	—

[a] This table shows the number of subjects out of 20 who were unable to discriminate between two musks in triadic comparison tests in Section 3.5.

Stimuli

The stimuli were three commercially available king-size "cork" tipped filter cigarettes, Marlboro, Winston, and Viceroy. Brand names were covered with a half inch strip of masking tape. Each cigarette was replicated in the design matrix (in *Procedure*) so that there were six *apparent* stimuli. It should be noted here that in most instances we would discourage the use of only six stimuli for an MDS experiment (see Section 2.6).

Subjects

Ninety-nine smokers of king-size filter cigarettes were recruited from the general public, 39 male and 60 female, aged 21–55.

Procedure

Subjects attended a panel room for 1 hour a day for 3 weeks. They were paid $75 for their participation. The first 2 days were devoted to familiarization with the cigarettes and making practice similarity judgments. Similarity judgments were expressed as a mark on a 5-in. line:

Exact same ———————————————————————————— Completely different

The three pairs of replicated cigarettes were considered as six stimuli. Six stimuli require comparison of 15 pairs. Three additional same–same comparisons above those provided by replication of the stimuli were included to better define individual performance. The 18 pairs smoked are shown, the replicated stimuli being Marlboro (Marlboro), etc.

	Marlboro	(Marlboro)	Viceroy	(Viceroy)	Winston
Marlboro	X				
(Marlboro)	X				
Viceroy	X	X	X		
(Viceroy)	X	X	X		
Winston	X	X	X	X	X
(Winston)	X	X	X	X	X

The raw data were expressed as millimeters from the exact same end of the 5-in. line.

As a first step in analysis the data were statistically treated at the aggregate level to determine if average scores for different pairs were different from average scores for same pairs. Table 3.11 shows average scores,

Table 3.11
The Mean Similarity Score ± Standard Deviation for Each Comparison of Cigarettes[a]

	Marlboro versus Viceroy	Marlboro versus Winston	Viceroy versus Winston
Mean–standard deviation	53 ± 42	47 ± 30	48 ± 41
Marlboro versus Marlboro 42 ± 30	$p < .001$	$p < .002$	$p < .002$
Viceroy versus Viceroy 43 ± 31	$p < .001$	$p < .002$	$p < .002$
Winston versus Winston 40 ± 31	$p < .001$	$p < .001$	$p < .002$

[a] Thus, the mean similarity score for comparing Marlboro versus Viceroy is 53 with a standard deviation of 42. The difference between the mean for the Marlboro versus Viceroy when compared with the mean for Marlboro versus Marlboro is significant at the .001 level. The scores were in millimeters from the Same anchor on a 5-in. Same–Different scale.

standard deviations, and the significance of the differences between the pairs of means.

The subjects were then divided into three groups depending on the ratio of their average *different* scores to average *same* scores. Tentatively, subjects with ratios greater than 1.5 were classified as good discriminators. Those with ratios of different to same scores less than 1 were considered bad discriminators. The group with ratios lying between 1 and 1.5 were considered to have intermediate discriminating ability.

3.7. Odor of Chemicals

The purpose of this experiment was to provide an ordering of odor qualities to correlate with physicochemical properties of the stimuli (Schiffman, Robinson, & Erickson, 1977).

Stimuli

The stimuli were the 19 reagent grade chemicals shown in Table 3.12. Subjects received stimuli via the sniffing port of an olfactometer. This device allowed mixing of an air stream with odorants to provide a constant

Table 3.12
Chemicals Used as Stimuli in Section 3.7

Acetic acid
Acetone
Anisole
1-Butanethiol
1-Butanol
Ter-butanol
1,2-Dichloroethane
2-Ethoxyethylacetate
Ethyl acetate
Formic acid
3-Heptanone
Methyl acetate
1-Nitropropane
Pentanoic acid
2-Pentanone
Propyl acetate
Propyl sulfide
Salicylaldehyde
1,3,5Trimethylbenzene

concentration. Air streams to each of the 19 stimuli were adjusted to provide moderate sensations of approximately equal intensity.

Subjects

The subjects were 12 nonsmoking university students, aged 18–21 years; 6 were male and 6 were female. They were paid $27.50 for their participation in the experiment.

Procedure

This experiment took place in a room with cross-currents and exhaust fans. The first sessions were devoted to familiarization with the olfactometer, the odor quality of the stimuli, and practice similarity judgments. Then 171 similarity judgments were then made during 5–8 1-hour sessions. Stimulus pairs were presented in random order. The time interval between a pair of stimuli was 10 sec with a recovery period of at least 90 sec before the next pair. Similarity judgments were made by marking an X along a 5-in. line:

Exact same ——————————————————————————— Completely different

When all similarity judgments were completed subjects rated each of the 19 stimuli on 22 semantic differential scales, Table 3.13. Ratings were made by marking a 5-in. line anchored by the descriptors.

Both similarity and adjective ratings were transcribed on a scale from 0 to 99 with 0 representing *exact same* or the left-hand adjective and 99 representing *completely different* or the right-hand adjective.

3.8. Blended Foods

The purpose of this study was to determine whether the taste and smell of foods are perceived differently by obese and normal weight subjects (Schiffman, Musante, & Conger, 1978).

Stimuli

The stimuli were fresh, unseasoned blended fruits, vegetables, meat, fish, nuts, dairy products, and grains. Four standards: sucrose (sweet), NaCl

Table 3.13
Adjective Scales on Which Chemicals Were Rated in Section 3.7

Odorous	Not odorous
Good	Bad
Smell develops slowly	Smell develops quickly
Fruity	Not fruity
Meaty	Not meaty
Vegetable-like	Not vegetable-like
Milk product	Not milk product
Fishy	Not fishy
Burnt	Not burnt
Foul	Not foul
Fragrant	Not fragrant
Smokey	Not smokey
Pungent	Not pungent
Putrid	Not putrid
Urinous	Not urinous
Ethereal	Not ethereal
Flowery	Not flowery
Fresh	Rotten
Sharp	Dull
Burning	Not burning
Musky	Not musky
Resinous	Not resinous

(salty), lemon (sour), and coffee (bitter) in a thin cornstarch base were included as well. The fruits, vegetables, and grains were lightly steamed to yield a soft texture after blending. The meats and fish were roasted without fat and bones in aluminum foil. The eggs were fried in a Teflon pan without butter. Slight amounts of water were added to some of the blended foods to minimize any differences in the consistencies. The foods were tested at 160°F.

Subjects

The normal weight subjects were 27 Duke University students ranging in age from 18–22 years. The obese subjects, aged 19–31, were 16 patients at a weight reduction clinic at Duke Medical Center. According to the Metropolitan Life Insurance tables, none of the students was overweight; the obese patients were at least 45% overweight (mean = 56.3%). All subjects were Caucasian, unmarried, and nonsmokers and were approximately equal with regard to intelligence and socioeconomic status. Eighteen of the students were female; nine were male. All the obese patients were female.

Procedure

The experiment was performed in well ventilated rooms with fans. The subjects were blindfolded and given a container of blended food to smell at the level of the nostrils. Next, they were given a spoonful to taste and instructed to swirl it around all parts of the mouth. After tasting, the food was ejected into a paper napkin and placed into a paper bag to ensure that the subjects did not see the color of the food substance.

After the blindfolds were removed, the subjects rated the blended food stimulus on 51 semantic differential scales. Forty five of the scales are shown in Table 3.9. In addition, ratings were made on six more scales: flowery–not flowery; smell develops slowly–smell develops fast; foul–not foul; fragrant–not fragrant; sulphurous–not sulphurous; and resinous–not resinous.

The adjective ratings were transcribed on a scale from 0 to 100, such that a rating at good, for example, was transcribed as 0 and a rating at bad was transcribed as 100.

References

Brotzge, R. F., & Crain, W. O. Multidimensional scaling of dissimilarity judgments of smoking quality. Thirty-first Tobacco Chemists' Research Conference, Greensboro, N.C., 1977.

Henning, H. The quality continuum of taste. *Zeitschrift für Psychologie*, 1916, *74*, 203–219.

Schiffman, S. S. Unpublished experiments at Duke University, 1977.

Schiffman, S., & Dackis, C. Multidimensional scaling of musks. *Physiology and Behavior*, 1976, *17*, 823–829.

Schiffman, S. S., & Erickson, R. P. A psychophysical model for gustatory quality. *Physiology and Behavior*, 1971, *7*, 617–633.

Schiffman, S., Musante, G., & Conger, J. Application of multidimensional scaling to ratings of foods for obese and normal weight individuals. *Physiology and Behavior*, 1978, *21*, 417–422.

Schiffman, S. S., & Pasternak, M. Decreased discrimination of food odors in the elderly. *Journal of Gerontology*, 1978, *34*, 73–79.

Schiffman, S., Robinson, D. E., & Erickson, R. P. Multidimensional scaling of odorants: Examination of psychological and physicochemical dimensions. *Chemical Senses and Flavor*, 1977, *2*, 375–390.

Skinner, E., & Schiffman, S. S. Multidimensional scaling of model beverages. Described in Schiffman, S. Preference: A multidimensional concept. In J. H. A. Kroeze (Ed.), *Preference behaviour and chemoreception*. London: Information Retrieval Ltd., 1979. Pp. 63–69.

Additional References on Multidimensional Scaling in Chemoreception

Erickson, R. P., & Schiffman, S. S. The chemical senses: A systematic approach. In M. S. Gazzaniga & C. Blakemore (Eds.), *Handbook of psychobiology*. New York: Academic Press, 1975. Pp. 393–426.

Schiffman, S. S. Contributions to the physicochemical dimensions of odor: A psychophysical approach. *Annals of the New York Academy of Sciences,* 1974, *237,* 164–183.

Schiffman, S. S. Physicochemical correlates of olfactory quality. *Science,* 1974, *185,* 112–117.

Schiffman, S. S. Multidimensional scaling: A useful tool to measure flavor. *Cereal Foods World,* February, 1976, 64–68.

Schiffman, S. S. Food recognition by the elderly. *Journal of Gerontology,* 1977, *32,* 586–592.

Schiffman, S. S. Changes in taste and smell with age: Psychophysical aspects. In J. M. Ordy & K. R. Brizzee (Eds.), *Sensory systems and communication in the elderly* (Vol. 6). New York: Raven Press, 1979. Pp. 227–246.

Schiffman, S. S. Contribution of the anion to the taste quality of sodium salts. In M. R. Kare, M. J. Fregley, & R. A. Bernard (Eds.), *Biological and behavioral aspects of NaCl intake.* Nutrition Foundation Monograph Series. New York: Academic Press, 1980. Pp. 99–111.

Schiffman, S. S., & Dackis, C. Taste of nutrients: Amino acids, vitamins, and fatty acids. *Perception and Psychophysics,* 1975, *17,* 140–146.

Schiffman, S. S., & Engelhard, H. H. Taste of dipeptides. *Physiology and Behavior,* 1976, *17,* 523–535.

Schiffman, S. S., & Leffingwell, J. C. Perception of odors of simple pyrazines by young and elderly subjects: A multidimensional analysis. *Pharmacology, Biochemistry, and Behavior,* 1981, *14,* 787–798.

Schiffman, S. S., McElroy, A. E., & Erickson, R. P. The range of taste quality of sodium salts. *Physiology and Behavior,* 1980, *24,* 217–224.

Schiffman, S. S., Moroch, K., & Dunbar, J. Taste of acetylated amino acids. *Chemical Senses and Flavor,* 1975, *1,* 387–401.

Schiffman, S. S., Nash, M. L., & Dackis, C. Reduced olfactory discrimination in patients on chronic hemodialysis. *Physiology and Behavior,* 1978, *21,* 239–242.

Schiffman, S. S., Reilly, D. A., & Clark, T. B. Qualitative differences among sweeteners. *Physiology and Behavior,* 1979, *23,* 1–9.

4

Overview of the Multidimensional Scaling Programs Used in This Book

This chapter provides a nonmathematical overview of the six MDS programs used in this book. Our selection is not exhaustive for MDS programs. It is, however, based on four criteria:

1. Ready availability and wide current use of the chosen programs
2. Coverage of the spectrum from simple nonmetric scaling of one data matrix to metric and nonmetric individual differences scaling of several data matrices
3. Use of different computation strategies for fitting the stimulus configuration to the data
4. Our own familiarity and experience with these algorithms

The six MDS programs along with their authors are listed in Table 4.1. These programs are capable of performing a wide variety of analyses, all of which are generically known as MDS. However, the analyses and the kinds of data suited for analysis by the six programs are not all the same. In this chapter we discuss the various types of data that these programs can analyze and the various kinds of analyses that can be performed. We organize the discussion according to the concepts of the data theory developed by Young (in preparation), although the presentation here is simpler and less complete.

Table 4.1
MDS Programs Discussed in This Book and Their Authors

Program	Author
MINISSA, Chapter 5	Guttman (1968); Lingoes (1973); Roskam (1968)
POLYCON, Chapter 6	Young (1972, 1973)
KYST, Chapter 7	Kruskal (1964a,b); Kruskal, Young, and Seery (1973)
INDSCAL and SINDSCAL, Chapter 8	Carroll and Chang (1970); Pruzansky (1975)
ALSCAL, Chapter 9	Takane, Young, and de Leeuw (1977); Young and Lewyckyj (1979)
MULTISCALE, Chapter 10	Ramsay (1977, 1978a,b)

4.1. Basic Data Concepts

A schematic of our data theory is presented in Table 4.2. The schematic has three organizing principles that are discussed in this section and the next two. There are six cells, one for each of the six types of analyses. Each cell is labeled with an abbreviation which is the name of the type of

Table 4.2
Types of Multidimensional Scaling Performed by the Six Programs

	Shape		
	Square	Rectangular	
No matrix weights	CMDS	CMDU	One matrix
	MINISSA POLYCON KYST ALSCAL MULTISCALE	POLYCON KYST ALSCAL	
	RMDS	RMDU	More than one matrix
	POLYCON KYST ALSCAL MULTISCALE	POLYCON KYST ALSCAL	
Matrix weights	WMDS	WMDU	
	INDSCAL ALSCAL MULTISCALE	ALSCAL	

MDS. We will explain these abbreviations momentarily. In each cell is a list of the programs which can perform the specific type of MDS. Together, the six programs can perform all six MDS types. However, most of the programs can only perform some of the six types of analyses. (The schematic does not show that many of the programs can perform other types of analyses not covered by the data theory presented here. However, in this book we limit ourselves to those types of analyses which we judge are relevant to the largest number of researchers. More detail is given by Young [in preparation], Carroll and Arabie [1980], and by the program guides for each computer program.)

Our data theory has three major organizing concepts, the *shape* of the data, the *number of ways* of the data, and the nature of the MDS model. Note that two of the data theory concepts refer to the data, and one to the MDS model. This may sound a bit strange. Should not data theory have to do only with data? Actually, the answer is no; data theory has to do with both the nature of the data and the nature of the model being used to understand the data. This is explained further in Young (in preparation). For our purposes here we simply note that the two data concepts are discussed in this section, and the model concept in the next two.

Shape

One of the organizing concepts of our data theory is the *shape* of the data. This refers to whether the data matrix is *square* or *rectangular*. Thus, as we see in Table 4.2, the columns of each portion of the schematic are labeled *square* and *rectangular*. A square data matrix has the same number of rows as it has columns. A rectangular data matrix does not have the same number of rows and columns. Regardless of its shape, we denote the data matrix by the symbol **O**.

In a rectangular data matrix, the set of things represented by the rows *necessarily* differs from the set of things represented by the columns. An example of rectangular data is ratings, obtained from a single subject, of a set of foods on a variety of rating scales. The rows are rating scales and the columns foods (or the other way around). Another example is ratings, obtained from several subjects, of the degree of liking each subject has for each food. Here the rows are subjects and the columns foods (or the other way around).

In a square data matrix, it is *usually* (but not necessarily) the case that the set of things represented by the rows are the same as the set of things represented by the columns. An example of a square data matrix is judgments from a single subject of the similarity of all pairs of foods to each other. Here the rows would be foods and the columns would also be foods.

Another example is the proportion of subjects, from a large group of subjects, who said, for each pair of foods, that the two foods in the pair tasted the same. Again, the rows are foods and the columns foods.

A particular type of square data matrix is a *triangular* data matrix. For triangular data it is not only the case that the row and column stimuli are the same, but it is also the case that the data are symmetric. If, in the preceding example, the data are symmetric, then it would be the case that the similarity of (say) tuna and lettuce would be the same as the similarity of lettuce and tuna. Thus, data are symmetric when the order of presentation of the two stimuli in a pair is irrelevant. By implication, not all square data matrices are symmetric: Some are asymmetric.

Note that a square matrix does not necessarily have to have rows that represent the same set of things as the columns. For example, we might ask a subject to rate 23 foods on 23 rating scales. While such data actually do form a square matrix, we would call them rectangular. This points up the fact that the important feature distinguishing square data from rectangular data as defined here is whether the rows represent the same set of things as the columns. If the rows are the same as the columns, we call the data square. If the rows represent a different thing from the columns we call the data matrix rectangular.

Thus the *shape* of the data is an important organizing principle of our data theory. A more accurate (but also more unfamiliar) set of terminology can be used to refer to this same organizing principle. This terminology focuses on the *number of modes* in the data. Square data, which involve only one set of things, are called *one-mode* data. Rectangular data, which involve two sets of things, are called *two-mode* data. This terminology emphasizes that the important data theory concept is the number of distinct sets of things (number of modes) represented in the data matrix.

Number of Ways

The second concept central to our data theory is the *number of ways* in the data. A single matrix of data *always* has exactly *two ways:* the rows and the columns. Note that it does not matter whether the two ways are the same or not; we still refer to them as two ways (but there is one mode if the two ways are the same, two if not). Even though a single matrix of data is always two-way, it is often the case that the data are contained in several matrices. In such a case the data are *multi-way* data, having at least three ways. For example, if *several* subjects are asked to judge the similarity of all pairs of foods to each other, then the data are three-way. One way is subjects, and the other two are foods. (These data are also two-mode, the modes being subjects and foods.) If this same experiment were conducted before and after an advertising campaign, the data would be four-way, one of the ways being occasions, another being subjects, and the other two foods. (These data would also be three-mode: foods, subjects, and occasions.) As a final example, say that an experimenter has asked several subjects to rate several foods on several rating scales. These would be three-way, three-mode data.

4.2. Unweighted MDS

What is an MDS model? An MDS model is an algebraic equation used to summarize some of the information in the data. What all MDS models share is that the algebraic equation has a geometric counterpart that allows us to make a picture of the information in the data. Thus, an MDS model is also a geometric picture that summarizes some of the information in the data. The practical value of MDS is based on the fact that it is often easier and more informative to look at a picture of the data, than to look at the data themselves, particularly when the set of data is large. Stated simply, a picture is worth a thousand numbers!

Most MDS programs share the ability to present the user with a *Euclidean* picture of the data, that is, the picture corresponds to a Euclidean model of the data. Such a model always represents information in the data which concerns the *stimuli* being used in the experiment. In the example we presented earlier where a single subject judged the similarity of a set of foods, the foods are the stimuli, and they are represented as *points* in a space. The space is called the *stimulus space;* it is usually (but not always) a Euclidean space, and it often has only two or three dimensions.

Classical MDS (CMDS)

Let us look at an example of the simplest type of MDS, the type called Classical MDS (CMDS) in Table 4.2. At the top of Figure 4.1 we present a list of four food stimuli. (In a real experiment there should be many more than four stimuli.) Say that we asked a subject to order the pairs of foods according to their apparent similarity. The subject's judgments are shown in the data matrix, the 1 meaning that the subject picked that pair of stimuli (lettuce and spinach) as most similar, the 2 meaning that pair was picked second, etc. Note that the data are triangular. Note also that the shaded cells on the diagonal mean that the subject was not asked to judge the similarity of a stimulus to itself.

What CMDS does is to represent these four food stimuli as four points in a stimulus space. How is the information in the data used to form the stimulus space? In our example the data indicate that the subject judged

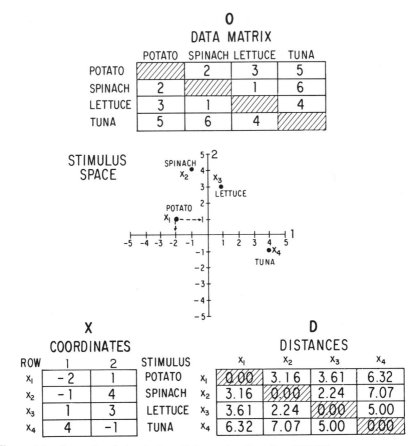

Figure 4.1. Example of classical multidimensional scaling (CMDS).

lettuce and spinach as most similar, and tuna and spinach as least similar. CMDS tries to locate points for the four stimuli so that lettuce and spinach will be located closest together, and tuna and spinach farthest apart. In the stimulus space presented in the middle of Figure 4.1 we see that lettuce and spinach are closest together, and spinach and tuna are farthest apart. (With real data, we might not have been so fortunate.)

At the bottom of Figure 4.1 we present two additional matrices. One of these is the matrix of stimulus coordinates, denoted by the symbol $\mathbf{X}$. This matrix is the algebraic equivalent of the stimulus space just discussed. Specifically, the algebraic row $\mathbf{x}_1$ is equivalent to the geometric point $\mathbf{x}_1$, row $\mathbf{x}_2$ to point $\mathbf{x}_2$, etc. Thus, row $\mathbf{x}_1$ has entries -2 and 1, which correspond to the projection of point $\mathbf{x}_1$ onto the two dimensions of the stimulus space (the projections are indicated by the dashed lines).

The other matrix at the bottom of Figure 4.1 consists of Euclidean distances between the points in the stimulus space. We denote this matrix by the symbol **D**. Each element of the matrix gives the Euclidean distance between a pair of points. Note that the smallest distance (2.24) is between points x_2 and x_3 and that these points correspond to the two stimuli which were judged as being most similar (lettuce and spinach). Further, the order of the distances is the same as that of the judgments. That is, d_{12}, the distance between x_1 and x_2, is less than d_{43}, the distance between x_4 and x_3. Correspondingly, o_{12}, the dissimilarity between potato and spinach, is less than o_{43}, the dissimilarity between tuna and lettuce.

At this point we need to make explicit the type of notation we are using. We have been denoting matrices by boldface capital letters (a data matrix is denoted **O**), and rows of such matrices by boldface lowercase letters with a subscript (a row of the stimulus matrix **X** is x_i). We are now ready to define the distance between two points, and to do this we must refer to elements of the matrix of stimulus coordinates. We use italicized lowercase letters with subscripts for this task (an element of row x_i of matrix **X** is x_{ia}).

Each distance is calculated according to the Euclidean distance formula for two dimensions:

$$d_{ij} = [(x_{i1} - x_{j1})^2 + (x_{i2} - x_{j2})^2]^{1/2} , \qquad (4.1)$$

or, in summation notation:

$$d_{ij} = \left[\sum_{a=1}^{2} (x_{ia} - x_{ja})^2 \right]^{1/2} , \qquad (4.2)$$

where d_{ij} is the Euclidean distance between points i and j, and where x_{i1} is the coordinate of point i on dimension 1, x_{i2} is the coordinate on dimension 2, and x_{ia} is the coordinate on some unspecified dimension a. As a concrete example, the distance between points x_1 and x_3, in Figure 4.1 is equal to:

$$d_{13} = [(-2 - 1)^2 + (1 - 3)^2]^{1/2} . \qquad (4.3)$$

The programs which perform CMDS are listed in the CMDS cell of Table 4.2.

The algebra of the Euclidean distance formula corresponds to the geometry of the Pythagorean theorem. The formula, in two dimensions, takes the square root of the sum of two differences which have been squared. The geometry, in two dimensions, is shown in Figure 4.2. The heavy solid line connecting points x_1 and x_2 represents the Euclidean distance we wish to calculate. The two dashed lines from each point represent the projection of each point onto each dimension. The dashed lines and the solid line together form a right triangle. The solid line is the hypotenuse of this right triangle. The lengths of the triangle's dashed sides are indicated by the large brackets. The length of the hypotenuse is the unknown distance we wish to determine. According to the Pythagorean theorem, the length of the hypotenuse of a right triangle equals the square root of the sum of the

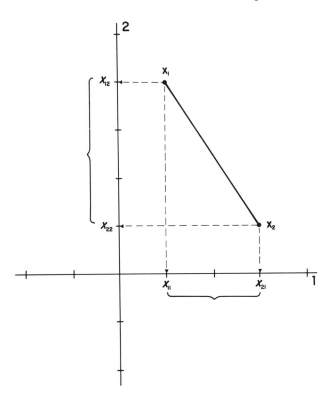

Figure 4.2.   Illustration of geometry for utilizing the Euclidean distance formula.

squared lengths of the remaining two sides. The Euclidean distance formula given above makes the same statement, except it does it for any number of dimensions, not just two.

Classical Multidimensional Unfolding (CMDU)

So far we have only discussed the representation of square data. When the data form a single rectangular matrix (are two way, two mode), MDS always represents *both* sets of things as points in a single low-dimensional space (which is usually Euclidean). This space is called a *joint* Euclidean space because the two modes are jointly represented in a single space. The information in the data that is used to form the space is the degree of relation between the rows and columns. We call this type of MDS classical multidimensional unfolding (CMDU), following the terminology of Coombs (1964).

CMDU can be used, for example, when several subjects rate their liking for each of several foods. What CMDU does is to represent both foods and subjects as points in a joint space. Each subject point is located close to points for foods the subject likes, and far from points for foods the subject does not like. Conversely, each food point is located close to points for subjects who like the food, and far from points for subjects who dislike the food. In the example involving ratings of foods on adjectives, the adjective points are located near to points for foods rated high on those adjectives, and far from points for foods rated low on those adjectives.

When used with this type of data (i.e., data in which one of the ways is subjects), CMDU is an individual differences analysis which portrays differences in perception or cognition. For the example presented in the previous paragraph, CMDU displays individual variation in liking of the several foods. This is done by placing individuals in different parts of the space. Those individuals who are near each other in the space have the same food preferences. Those who are far from each other have different preferences.

CMDU can also be used with other types of rectangular data. One of the modes does *not* have to be subjects. We could apply CMDU to a matrix of ratings of foods on several scales, where the ratings have all been obtained from a single subject. For example, we could ask the subject to rate each food on scales of color, texture, taste, etc. In this case, CMDU does not provide an individual differences analysis. More will be said on the important topic of individual differences in Section 4.5.

A concrete example of CMDU is presented in Figure 4.3. At the top of the figure is a list of the same four foods that were used in the example in Figure 4.1. In the present example, three hypothetical subjects have rank ordered the four foods in terms of how much they like each food. The data matrix O, then, has the numbers 1 through 4 in each row, each 1 indicating the food most liked by each subject, each 4 the food least liked by each subject. These data are represented by the joint Euclidean space presented in the middle of Figure 4.3. The stimulus points and the person points are jointly arranged in this figure so that each person is close to liked foods, and far from disliked ones. For example, Subject 1, who is represented by the y_1 point in the space and by the y_1 row in the data matrix, is close to the x_1 point, which is for potato, the food he or she liked best.

At the bottom of Figure 4.3 there are three matrices, two labeled coordinates and one labeled distances. The two coordinate matrices are for stimuli and subjects, matrix X is for stimuli (as in Figure 4.1) and matrix Y for subjects. There is still just one distance matrix, matrix D, but it is now rectangular instead of square. Just as before, the elements in the distance matrix give the Euclidean distance between points in the joint space, but now the distances are between the points in two different sets (subjects and foods), and not between the points within either set. Note that the order of the distances in each row is the same as the order of the observations in the corresponding row of the data matrix O. Each distance

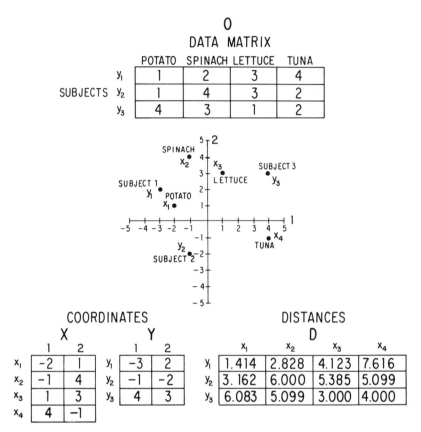

Figure 4.3. Example of classical multidimensional unfolding (CMDU).

is calculated according to the joint Euclidean distance formula in two dimensions, which is, in summation notation:

$$d_{ij} = \left[\sum_{a=1}^{2} (y_{ia} - x_{ja})^2 \right]^{1/2}, \tag{4.4}$$

where y_{ia} is the coordinate of subject i on dimension a, and where the other symbols are defined as before. Thus, the distance between subject y_1 and food x_1 in Figure 4.3 is equal to:

$$d_{11} = [(-3 + 2)^2 + (2 - 1)^2]^{1/2}. \tag{4.5}$$

The programs that perform CMDU are listed in Table 4.2. Due to notorious difficulties with local minima and degenerate solutions, we only discuss CMDU very briefly (in Chapters 12 and 14). While all MDS programs are susceptible to these difficulties, with care the experienced user may find the model useful. Alternative analyses are suggested in Chapter 14.

Replicated MDS and MDU

So far we have discussed two types of unweighted MDS. But, as can be seen from Table 4.2, there are four types of unweighted MDS. The two that we have not mentioned are replicated multidimensional scaling (RMDS), and replicated multidimensional unfolding (RMDU). These analyses are identical to their CMDS and CMDU counterparts, except that the data are three-way, not two-way. That is, they use more than one matrix of data instead of just one. The programs that incorporate each of these analyses are listed in cells RMDS and RMDU of Table 4.2.

The difference between classical and replicated analysis lies not only in the nature of the data. There also is a very important philosophical difference. Depending on the *conditionality* of the data (see Section 4.4), it is possible to allow for individual differences in response style (response bias) with a replicated analysis. This is not possible with a classical analysis since it involves data from only one individual. But, with a replicated analysis individual response bias can be accommodated since there is more than one matrix. This is done by simply permitting different response transformations for each subject (matrix).

Fortunately, it appears that RMDS has none of the computational difficulties associated with CMDU. Indeed, RMDS is probably the most robust and reliable type of MDS discussed in this book. Thus, RMDS is the first practical method for looking at individual variation that we have discussed. We will go into this more in Section 4.5.

Unfortunately, the problems with CMDU seem to extend to RMDU. Also, these problems seem to be present for all of the programs. Thus, we do not discuss RMDU further in this book. However, the experienced user may wish to perform RMDU analyses, and to carefully evaluate the adequacy of the results.

4.3. Weighted MDS

All types of unweighted MDS (CMDS, CMDU, RMDS, RMDU) represent the stimuli as points in space. This is also true for the two types of weighted MDS introduced in this section. For all six types of MDS the space is usually Euclidean, and frequently has only a few dimensions. Also, stimuli are represented as points when the data are square as well as when they are rectangular. In addition, when the data are rectangular, all six types of MDS (and all of the programs that can accept rectangular data) represent the second set of things (people, rating scales, whatever) as points in the space that already contains the stimulus points. For both types of data the points are arranged so that the distances between them reflect the information in the data. When the data are square the distances reflect the similarity of pairs of stimuli. When the data are rectangular the distances reflect the degree of relation between the stimuli and the other set of things.

The new notion here is weights. The types of weighted MDS discussed in this book are simple *matrix-weighted* MDS. These types of MDS involve a component which represents information about variation between the matrices. In the previous section, none of the types of MDS for three-way data contained a component to represent differences between the matrices. Those types of MDS contained one or two components to represent the rows and columns of each matrix, but none to represent the variation from one matrix to the next. The matrix-weighted types of MDS contain such a component.

While the replicated types of MDS permit individual differences in response bias, this is done via different data transformations. There is nothing in the Euclidean model, equation (4.2), which explicitly relates to individual differences. With the weighted types of MDS, on the other hand, there are weights which specifically portray differences between matrices. If each matrix of data corresponds to an individual, then the weights model portrays differences in the way individuals think or perceive. Specifically, each individual (matrix) has a weight for each dimension of the stimulus space. The weight represents the salience of the dimension to the individual. If the weight is relatively large, the dimension is very important. If small, very unimportant. Therefore, the subject's weight on a dimension is a measure of the importance of the dimension to the subject.

An extreme example should help explain the nature of the weighted Euclidean model. Suppose the stimulus set consists of a number of fruit juices varying in odor, sweetness, and color. We would expect the stimulus space to contain at least three dimensions. Normal subjects will show weights indicating the importance of each dimension to them in making their judgments. A subject for whom sweetness is important will have a relatively large weight on the sweetness dimension(s). The largest weight(s) for the subject who finds color to be most important will be on the color dimension(s). If any of the subjects are color blind, however, color will not be represented in their stimulus space. These subjects should have zero weights on the color dimension(s). They will have positive weights on the other dimensions, however. Likewise, if any of the subjects are anosmic, odor will not be a dimension of their space. For these subjects, the odor dimension(s) should have zero weights.

One of the nice aspects of the weighted types of MDS is that they clearly separate the group information which is in common to all of the subjects from the information which is unique to each subject. The stimulus space represents the group information, although not all dimensions of the space are necessarily common to all subjects. The weight space gives the pattern of individual differences.

Another nice characteristic of the weighted types of MDS is the fact that the stimulus space, while Euclidean, is *not rotatable*. While the reasons for this are too technical to go into here, it is a characteristic which has a very important consequence. The dimensions of the stimulus space are frequently claimed to be directly interpretable. We should not have to wonder whether there are some other directions in the space which should be interpreted. Thus, in the example just given, the dimensions ought to directly correspond to odor, sweetness, and color.

It is our opinion, though, that this aspect of weighted MDS has been oversold. When looked into carefully, it is seen that the stimulus space is rigidly oriented only when there is no error in the data. When there is error, the space can be rotated at least a small portion of a degree, with the freedom to rotate increasing as the amount of error increases. In the extreme, when the data are totally error, the space can be rotated at will. Furthermore, for a given amount of error, the tightness of the orientation depends on the pattern of weights. If all the weights fall along a straight line then the orientation is not defined, and as the weights depart from being on a straight line the orientation is more tightly fixed.

In the remainder of this section we discuss two types of matrix-weighted MDS. We call them weighted MDS (WMDS) and weighted MDU (WMDU). These two types of MDS involve the same basic Euclidean stimulus space of the four types of MDS discussed in Section 4.2. WMDU involves the joint space notion discussed for CMDU and RMDU. Just as with the un-weighted analyses, there is a scaling analysis (WMDS) for square data and an unfolding analysis (WMDU) for rectangular data.

There are a number of types of weighted MDS which we do not discuss in this book. Some of these use more complex matrix-weighted models, and some use row-weighted models. These models are beyond the scope of our presentation, but those who are interested should see Carroll and Arabie (1980) or Young (in preparation).

Weighted MDS (WMDS)

Other writers generally refer to WMDS as individual differences scaling (INDSCAL) as it was originally called by the authors who developed the first successful computer program (Carroll & Chang, 1970). However, to avoid confusion with their INDSCAL *program,* we will refer to the analysis as WMDS, and the program as INDSCAL. Our nomenclature also emphasizes the fact that WMDS is not reserved for individual differences, since the third way of the data may be occasions or experimental conditions, instead of individuals. Thus, WMDS can be used to account for differences between occasions, or between experimental conditions, as well as between individuals.

A concrete example of weighted MDS (WMDS) is presented in Figure 4.4. At the top of the figure is the familiar list of four foods. Directly below this list are two matrices of data, O_2 and O_5. The two data matrices in the figure contain data from two of five hypothetical subjects, Subjects 2 and 5. The data from Subjects 1, 3, and 4 are not presented. (Note the new notation. When there are several matrices we refer to a specific one of them by a boldface capital letter with a subscript. Thus, one of the many data matrices O is the specific one O_i.)

GROUP STIMULUS SPACE

The middle left-hand portion of Figure 4.4 presents a hypothetical configuration of four points in Euclidean space. This has the same character-

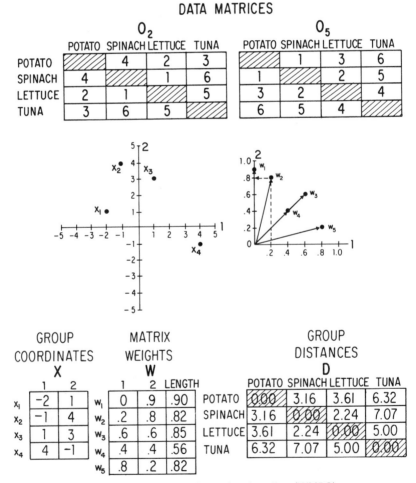

Figure 4.4. Example of weighted multidimensional scaling (WMDS).

istics as the stimulus space used with the CMDS example in Figure 4.1 except for one *very important* difference: The stimulus space for the WMDS model is *not rotatable,* as we have already discussed. As previously, we represent the numerical version of the stimulus space by the matrix **X**. This matrix is given at the bottom of Figure 4.4.

As with RMDS, the WMDS stimulus space contains a configuration of stimuli which is appropriate to the entire group of subjects (matrices). Thus, we call this space the *group* stimulus space. The algebraic formula for the distances d_{ij} in the group stimulus space is:

$$d_{ij} = \left[\sum_{a=1}^{r} (x_{ia} - x_{ja})^2 \right]^{1/2} . \tag{4.6}$$

The matrix **D** in Figure 4.4 is calculated by this formula. This is the same as the formula for Euclidean distance given earlier (4.2).

Unlike RMDS, however, the group stimulus space of the WMDS model is not appropriate to any particular subject. This is because each subject differs from the other subjects in the way the dimensions are weighted. In fact, each subject's weights modify the group space to yield a space which is more nearly appropriate to his or her own data. Thus, with WMDS each subject has his or her own personal stimulus space.

WEIGHT SPACE

To understand the difference between the group and personal stimulus spaces, we must look at the new component of the WMDS model, the weights. The right-hand middle portion of Figure 4.4 presents a space of matrix (subject) weights that represents the variation between the five hypothetical matrices (subjects). This space displays the new weight component of the matrix-weighted model. Matrix **W**, at the bottom of Figure 4.4, is the numerical equivalent of the weight space. How do we interpret the weight space? First of all, each data matrix O_i is represented by a *weight vector* $\mathbf{w}_i$, not by a weight point. Thus, the second data matrix, denoted O_2, is represented by weight vector $\mathbf{w}_2$ drawn from the origin of the space, not by a point $\mathbf{w}_2$. What does this vector tell us? Specifically, the weight vector tells us the relevance of each dimension of the stimulus space to each matrix of data. When the matrices correspond to subjects each weight vector tells us the relative salience of each dimension of the stimulus space to each subject.

The degree of relevance of each dimension to a matrix is determined by projecting the matrix's weight vector onto each dimension of the weight space. This projection gives us the elements w_{ia} of the weight matrix **W**. For example, the projections for data matrix O_2's weights are shown by the dashed lines drawn from $\mathbf{w}_2$ to the two dimensions of the weight space. These two projections correspond to the two weights in row $\mathbf{w}_2$ of the weight matrix **W**. If a projection is relatively far from the origin of the space, then the weight for that dimension is relatively large, and the dimension has a relatively large contribution to the information in the data matrix. Thus, dimension 2 contributes a relatively large amount to data matrix O_2 since the weight of the second data matrix on dimension 2 is .8. If the projection is close to the origin the weight is relatively small, and the dimension does not contribute very much to the data matrix. Thus, dimension 2 does not contribute very much to data matrix O_5 since the matrix's weight on that dimension is only .2. Furthermore, if a weight vector points along a dimension of the weight space (as is the case for w_1), then that dimension is an important contributor to the information in that data matrix, and the dimension it is pointing away from is not important. If a weight vector is pointing at a 45° angle from the two dimensions (as is the case for w_3 and w_4), then both of the dimensions are equally important in determining the data in the matrix.

Numerically, a projection which is relatively far from the origin corresponds to a relatively large weight w_{ia}. A projection which is close to the origin corresponds to a small weight. Furthermore, a projection which falls onto the origin of the space corresponds to a weight of zero. Negative weights, which are difficult to interpret, are generally not obtained.

In INDSCAL and ALSCAL (but not in MULTISCALE) the length of a subject's weight vector reflects the amount of variation in the subject's data which is accounted for by the multidimensional scaling: the longer the vector, the more variation accounted for. The length of the vector is determined by squaring all of the subject's weights, summing them, and then taking the square root. For the example in Figure 4.4, the lengths of each weight vector are given next to matrix **W**.

The square of the length of the weight vector tells us something very useful. Specifically, for a given subject the sum of that subject's *squared* weights indicates the *proportion of variance* in a transformation of that subject's data which is accounted for by the distances in that subject's personal space. Note that the data transformation is *not the same* in INDSCAL and ALSCAL, thus the specific interpretation is a bit different in the two programs. In INDSCAL it is the scalar product transformation, whereas in ALSCAL it is the optimal scaling transformation. However, for these two programs (but not for MULTISCALE) the length of the weight vector can be loosely taken to reflect the variance accounted for by the analysis.

PERSONAL SPACES

We can now return to the personal stimulus space notion we alluded to earlier. Algebraically, each subject k has his or her own personal space X_k. The personal distances for subject k are defined by the equation for the weighted Euclidean model:

$$d_{ijk} = \left[\sum_{a=1}^{r} (x_{kia} - x_{kja})^2 \right]^{1/2} , \qquad (4.7)$$

where x_{kia} is an element of matrix $\mathbf{X}_k$, and is the coordinate of point i on dimension a of subject k's personal stimulus space. Personal space $\mathbf{X}_k$ is related to group space $\mathbf{X}$ and to subject k's weights $\mathbf{w}_k$ by the equation

$$x_{kia} = w_{ka}^{1/2} x_{ia} , \qquad (4.8)$$

where $w_{ka}^{1/2}$ is the square root of an element of matrix $\mathbf{W}$, and x_{ia} is the coordinate of stimulus i on dimension a of the group stimulus space. By substitution, we see that subject k's personal distances can also be expressed as:

$$d_{ijk} = \left[\sum_{a=1}^{r} w_{ka} (x_{ia} - x_{ja})^2 \right]^{1/2} . \qquad (4.9)$$

This is the fundamental equation for the WMDS model.

Geometrically, the weights stretch and shrink the dimensions of the group stimulus space to yield each subject's personal space. The stretching and shrinking is done separately for each subject according to that subject's own idiosyncratic weighting scheme. If the subject has a heavy weight on a dimension, then that dimension is stretched. If a dimension has a low weight, the dimension is shrunk. Thus, the subject's personal stimulus space is just like the group stimulus space, except that the dimensions of the personal space have been stretched or shrunk according to the subject's pattern of weights. Note that each personal space is a Euclidean space. The programs that perform WMDS are listed in the WMDS cell of Table 4.2.

In Figure 4.5 we present three personal spaces—one each for Subjects 2, 4, and 5. For each subject k the matrices of personal coordinates $\mathbf{X}_k$ and of distances $\mathbf{D}_k$ are presented along with the geometric version of the personal space. Each matrix $\mathbf{X}_k$ contains the coordinates x_{kia} of stimulus i on dimension a for subject k. These coordinates are derived by applying the formula for x_{kia} (given earlier) to the relevant information in Figure 4.4. Thus, the first column of $\mathbf{X}_2$ is obtained by multiplying the square root of the second subject's weight on dimension 1—that is, $(.2)^{1/2}$—times the first column of the group coordinate matrix.

Each distance is calculated according to the weighted Euclidean distance formula for two dimensions:

$$d_{ijk} = [w_{k1}(x_{i1} - x_{j1})^2 + w_{k2}(x_{i2} - x_{j2})^2]^{1/2} , \qquad (4.10)$$

which, in summation notation, is the fundamental formula for the weighted Euclidean model given above. Thus, the distance between point $\mathbf{x}_1$ (whose

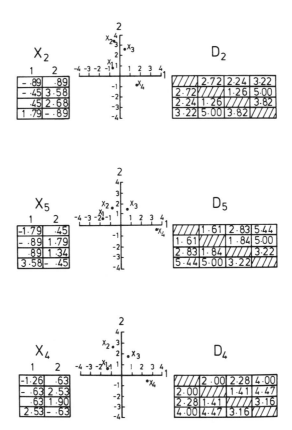

Figure 4.5. Personal spaces for weighted multidimensional scaling (WMDS).

coordinates are given in Figure 4.4 as -2 and 1) and point x_3 (with co-ordinates 1 and 3) as viewed by Subject 2 (with weights w_2 of .2 and .8) is calculated as:

$$d_{132} = [.2(-2-1)^2 + .8(1-3)^2]^{1/2}. \quad (4.11)$$

This formula should be compared with formula (4.5) in the discussion of the classical Euclidean model. By carrying through the multiplication of the square root of the weights times the coordinates, we obtain Subject 2's own personal coordinates:

$$d_{132} = [(-.89-.45)^2 + (.89-2.68)^2]^{1/2} \quad (4.12)$$

These coordinates correspond to the coordinates given in matrix X_2 in Figure 4.5. (Note that there are minus signs in the formula that arise due to the fact that the second coordinate is always subtracted from the first.)

By comparing each individual's personal space with the group space presented in Figure 4.4, we can see that each dimension of the group space has been shrunk to become a dimension of a personal space. Some of the personal dimensions have been shrunk more than others. These are the dimensions resulting from applying small subject weights. Such a dimension is relatively unimportant to the subject. Thus, Subject 2's personal space is predominantly composed of dimension 2 which is much more important to her than dimension 1. Furthermore, the reverse is true for Subject 5. On the other hand, Subject 4 has equal weights on each dimension, and his space is the same as the group space except for being smaller.

Weighted MDU (WMDU)

We do not need to dwell very long on the Weighted MDU (WMDU) situation. The analysis is relatively new (Young & Lewyckyj, 1979), and has not yet been fully evaluated (see also Carroll & Arabie, 1980). Furthermore, WMDU is a simple combination of notions already discussed for other analysis situations. In particular, WMDU combines the joint space notion of CMDU with the weight notion of WMDS, and thereby extends unfolding to three-way, three-mode data. An example of data appropriate to WMDU is ratings of several stimuli, on several rating scales, the ratings being made by several subjects. For this example, the stimuli and rating scales are represented as points in a joint Euclidean space, with the subjects being represented by a weight space. The joint Euclidean space has the same characteristics as with CMDU except for the very important difference that it is *unrotatable*. The weight space is the same as with WMDS. It is not known whether the computational difficulties associated with CMDU and RMDU are also present here, although they probably are.

4.4. Additional Data Concepts

In the previous sections of this chapter we compared the six programs in terms of what types of data they can analyze and how they can analyze it. We noted, in Table 4.2, that one of the programs (MINISSA) is limited to analyzing a single square matrix of data; two of the programs (INDSCAL and MULTISCALE) can analyze any number of square data matrices, and three (KYST, POLYCON, and ALSCAL) can analyze any number of rectangular or square data matrices. We also noted, in Table 4.2, that those programs which can analyze a given type of data do not necessarily analyze it in the same way.

In this section we discuss some additional ways in which the programs differ with regard to the types of data which can be analyzed. The discussion, which is summarized in Table 4.3, is in terms of the assumptions made about the data's measurement characteristics, whether the data must be symmetric and/or must be dissimilarities, and whether the data may have missing values.

MEASUREMENT LEVEL

One of the distinguishing features of the six programs discussed in this book is whether they perform *metric* MDS or *nonmetric* MDS. While the terminology is a bit unfortunate (due to other meanings for these words), the distinction is very important. Metric MDS assumes that the data are quantitative, whereas nonmetric MDS assumes that they are qualitative. Stated differently, the distinction refers to assumptions about the *measurement level* of the data. Nonmetric MDS assumes that the data are either *nominal* or *ordinal,* whereas metric MDS assumes that the data are either *interval* or *ratio.*

The entries in the row labeled *level* in Table 4.3 are the first letter of the measurement levels available in the program (*N*ominal, *O*rdinal, *I*nterval, or *R*atio). Thus, one of the programs (MINISSA) is exclusively nonmetric, two of the programs (INDSCAL and MULTISCALE) are exclusively metric, and three of the programs (KYST, POLYCON, and ALSCAL) are either metric or nonmetric. Of the various levels, we feel that the ordinal and interval levels are most useful, with the nominal level being rarely if ever of any use, and the ratio level being occasionally useful. Our experience suggests that the metric–nonmetric distinction rarely makes a crucial difference in the outcome of the analysis. It is desirable to have a program which provides a choice, though, since then the user can compare the results of the two types of analyses.

MEASUREMENT PROCESS

The notion of *measurement process* refers to whether the process which generated the data should be thought of as *discrete* or *continuous.* The assumption has implications about the treatment of ties in the data. If the process is viewed as discrete, then ties remain tied throughout the analysis. If it is viewed as continuous, then the ties become untied during the analysis.

If the data are judgments obtained from a subject, then the distinction refers to the nature of what one thinks is going on inside the subject. If the subject really has a continuous *internal* scale, but is required to give discrete numbers, then the data are continuous. If the internal scale is *really* discrete, then the data are properly thought of as being discrete.

The discrete–continuous distinction is relevant for all levels of measurement. However, the six programs only implement the distinction for the ordinal level of measurement. For other levels of measurement, the process is implicitly discrete. Thus, the metric programs (INDSCAL and MUL-TISCALE) are implicitly discrete, whereas the nonmetric programs (MIN-

Table 4.3
Characteristics of Six MDS Programs[a]

	MINISSA	KYST	POLYCON	INDSCAL	ALSCAL	MULTISCALE
Level	O	OIR	NOIR	IR	NOIR	IR
Process	DC	DC	DC	D	DC	D
Conditionality	M	UMR	UMRA	M	UMR	UM
Symmetry	S	AS	AS	S	AS	AS
Dis/similarity	DS	DS	DS	DS	DS	DS
Missing data	Yes	Yes	Yes	No	Yes	Yes
Rectangular data	No	Yes	Yes	No	Yes	No
Three-way data	No	Yes	Yes	Yes	Yes	Yes

[a] Code: Level, N = nominal, O = ordinal, I = interval, R = ratio; Process, D = discrete, C = continuous; Conditionality, U = unconditional, M = matrix conditional, R = row conditional, A = arbitrary; Symmetry, A = asymmetric, S = symmetric; Dis/similarity, D = dissimilarity, S = similarity.

ISSA, KYST, POLYCON, and ALSCAL) provide a choice when the measurement level is ordinal, but are implicitly discrete for all other levels (see Table 4.3). (The terminology used here corresponds to the ALSCAL terminology. In KYST, POLYCON, and MINISSA the terminology is *primary* [continuous] and *secondary* [discrete].)

The chosen measurement process is not very crucial unless there are a very large number of ties in the data. In this situation the results of the two types of analyses may be very different. This situation arises, for example, when subjects have been asked to rate the similarity of pairs of stimuli on a scale of 1 to 5. If there are, say 20 stimuli, then there are 190 pairs, and the 190 similarity judgments fall into only five categories. There are a lot of ties, and the assumed measurement process may make a big difference in the results of the analysis.

MEASUREMENT CONDITIONALITY

The notion of measurement conditionality was first discussed by Coombs (1964). It refers to the fact that in some empirical situations some of the numbers in the observations cannot be meaningfully compared to other numbers in the observations. For example, when we ask several subjects to judge, on a scale which is transcribed from 1 to 9, the similarity of pairs of odors, it is reasonable to assume that one subject's response of two is smaller than his response of four, but it is not reasonable to assume that his response of two is smaller than *another* subject's response of four. It is not meaningful to compare between subjects because there is nothing in the experimental paradigm that convinces us that the different subjects are using the response scale in exactly the same fashion. Indeed, there is a great deal of evidence that just the opposite is true. Thus, the *meaning* of the numbers is *conditional* upon which subject is responding.

The entries in the *conditionality* row in Table 4.3 are the first letter of each type of conditionality available for each program. The six programs permit four types of conditionality. All of the programs permit the data to be *matrix conditional*, the type of conditionality described in the example just given. For two of the programs (MINISSA and INDSCAL) this is the only type of conditionality permitted. All of the rest of the programs also permit the data to be *unconditional*, the situation where all of the observations can be meaningfully compared with each other. Three programs (KYST, POLYCON, and ALSCAL) also permit the data to be *row conditional*, an option appropriate to asymmetric and rectangular, but not symmetric data. This type of conditionality means that only numbers within one row of one matrix can be meaningfully compared with each other.

In addition to these types of conditionality, POLYCON permits the user to have data whose conditionality is completely arbitrary. This is useful for experimental designs in which there may be order effects or in which some observations are gathered on one day and some on another day. In odor research there can be pronounced order effects (the perception of a stimulus pair is effected by which pairs were previously presented). For this reason, it is common that an experiment is run over many days, with only a few pairs being presented on a given day, the pairs separated by many minutes. With POLYCON it would be possible to analyze the data as if all of the judgments which were first on a day were comparable to each other but not to any other judgments, those which occured second were in another comparability group, etc. If five judgments were made on one day, then there would be five partitions, to use POLYCON terminology.

Each of the programs obtains a separate transformation of the raw data for each partition, whether the partitions are for rows, for matrices, or are arbitrary. The transformation meets the requirements placed on it by the measurement level and process of the data. If the data are ordinal then the order of the raw observations *within* each partition is preserved, but not between partitions. There is a separate monotonic transformation for each partition. If the data are interval, there is a separate linear transformation for each partition. If the data are discrete, then ties within partitions are maintained.

SYMMETRY

As shown by the S in each cell of the symmetry row of Table 4.3, all of the programs permit the data to be symmetric. That is, they can all analyze data when it is the case that $o_{ijk} = o_{jik}$ for all pairs of stimuli i and j. Thus, whenever we observe (or can assume that) subject k always judges the similarity of stimuli i and j (in that order) to be the same as stimuli j and i (in that order), the data are symmetric and can be analyzed by any of the programs. However, when it is the case that $o_{ijk} \neq o_{jik}$ for at least one pair of stimuli, the data are *asymmetric*. That is, if we observe that subject k does not always judge the similarity of stimuli i and j (in that order) to be the same as j and i (in that order), then the data are asymmetric. As shown by the A in four of the cells of the symmetry row of Table 4.3, all of the programs except MINISSA and INDSCAL permit proximities data to be asymmetric.

DIS/SIMILARITIES

Throughout this chapter we have been using the words *similarity* and *dissimilarity* interchangeably. However, the two words do not mean exactly the same thing. They differ as to the meaning of large versus small numbers. For *similarity* data, large numbers mean "a lot of similarity." For *dissimilarity* data, large numbers mean "a lot of dissimilarity." Correspondingly, for similarity data small numbers mean "not much similarity," and for dissimilarity data small numbers mean "not much dissimilarity." As shown in the dissimilarity row of Table 4.3, all of the programs can analyze both types of data. For various technical reasons, however, we generally recommend that dissimilarity data be gathered, and that the user convert similarity data into dissimilarity data in whatever way seems reasonable.

MISSING DATA

There are some experimental designs which have been suggested (Spence, 1975; Young, Null, & Sarle, 1978) that specifically incorporate missing data to increase the number of stimuli being judged by the subject. Missing data may also be obtained inadvertently. As shown in the missing data row of Table 4.3, all of the programs except INDSCAL can analyze data with missing elements. In all of these programs, there are virtually no restrictions on the amount or pattern of missing data. We do recommend, however, that those interested in missing data designs read the references just given.

4.5. Individual Differences

As has been mentioned in several places in this chapter, there are a number of different ways in which individual differences can be allowed for in MDS. In this section we compare these different ways. The various approaches to individual differences are obtained by applying a specific MDS model to data having a specific *shape* and *conditionality*. We have discussed two types of MDS models: unweighted and weighted models. We have mentioned two fundamental data shapes: square and rectangular. And, we have discussed three types of data conditionality: unconditional, matrix conditional, and row conditional. When a specific MDS model is combined with a specific data shape, we obtain a specific way of thinking about individual differences in perception or cognition. On the other hand, a specific data conditionality implies something specific about individual differences in response style. Thus, we have four types of individual differences situations. One permits no individual differences, one only permits differences in perception–cognition, one only permits differences in response style, and one permits both types of differences. The programs which incorporate each of these four basic approaches to individual differences are listed in Table 4.4.

Unfortunately, the situation is complicated by the basic nature of the data. If none of the ways of the data corresponds to individuals, then it is certainly the case that there can be no provision for individual differences. Thus, if we have a single subject judging the similarity of pairs of stimuli, there can be no way of looking at individual differences since there is only one individual. This would be true even if we had the individual perform the experiment on several different occasions. Similarly, if we had one individual rate several stimuli on several scales under several different experimental conditions, there is no way of getting at individual differences. Thus, just because we have, for example, three-way, two-mode data, we cannot necessarily provide for individual differences, although individual differences models can be used to analyze the data. The third way (and

Table 4.4
Four Types of Individual Difference Situations Permitted by Various Programs

	No response differences	Response differences
No perceptual differences	MINISSA KYST POLYCON ALSCAL MULTISCALE	KYST POLYCON ALSCAL MULTISCALE
Perceptual differences	ALSCAL INDSCAL MULTISCALE	ALSCAL MULTISCALE

second mode) of the data may correspond to a *data source* other than individuals.

It is also important *which* way of the data corresponds to individuals. In particular, if the first and/or second way of the data is for individuals, then they are portrayed as points in a Euclidean space. However, if individuals correspond to the third way of the data, then they are portrayed as vectors in a weight space.

Let us look at the case where the first (or second) way of the data is individuals, that is, where there are one or more matrices of data, with the rows (and/or columns) of each data matrix corresponding to individuals. Table 4.5 summarizes the relationship between the types of individual differences, the conditionality of the data, and the presence or absence of weights.

From the table we see that the presence or absence of weights is irrelevant to individual differences for this type of data. This is because weights are always associated with the third way of the data and individuals are associated with the first or second way. Further, since individuals are always

Table 4.5
Individual Differences When Rows Correspond to Individuals

| | Conditionality | | |
	Unconditional	Matrix conditional	Row conditional
Unweighted	Individual differences in perception–cognition permitted	Individual differences in perception–cognition permitted	Both types[a] of individual differences permitted
Weighted	Individual differences in perception–cognition permitted	Individual differences in perception–cognition permitted	Both types[a] of individual differences permitted

[a] Response style and perception–cognition.

associated with the first or second way of the data they are always represented as points in a Euclidean space. Since analysis of these data *always* represents the individuals as points, the analysis *always* implies that there are individual differences in perception or cognition. For these data we do not have the choice of treating individuals as replicates.

The table also shows that these data provide us with the option of permitting individual variation in response style. When we state that the data are row conditional we imply that the individuals vary in response processes since rows correspond to individuals. When we opt for some other type of conditionality we imply that the individuals do not vary in response style.

These data may consist of matrices all of which are either square or rectangular. When the data are square we have the CMDS, RMDS, or WMDS situations, but with individuals taking the role played by stimuli in our previous discussions. When the data are rectangular we have the CMDU, RMDU, or WMDU situations in which the rows are individuals. It is important to note that it is not possible to have row conditional symmetric (square) data.

Hoadley (1974) (see also Young, in preparation), who used similarity data concerning United States Senators, provides us with an example of square data where the "stimuli" are individuals. He defined the similarity of the Senators on the basis of the frequency that each pair of Senators voted the same way on all of the issues that came before the Senate over a 2-year period. His data, then, formed a single square data matrix whose mode is Senators. Hoadley's CMDS displayed each Senator as a point in a Euclidean space. His interpretation of the two-dimensional space revealed systematic variation related to the political affiliation of the Senator, and to the liberal or conservative views of the Senator. Specifically, as one moved from the right to the left side of the space the Senators became more liberal. Also, all of the Republicans were on the top of the space, and all Democrats on the bottom. Hoadley's individual differences model postulates that the Senators vary along two attributes, and that each Senator has a specific amount of each attribute. His analysis displays systematic individual variation related to the political (cognitive) characteristics of the Senators.

We have already presented examples of individual differences when the data are rectangular and the first way is individuals. The classic example is an experiment in which individuals are asked to rate their preference for stimuli. Here the rows correspond to individuals and the columns to stimuli. Analysis of these data portrays the individuals and the stimuli as points in one Euclidean space. The individual differences model postulates that individual preferences vary over individuals on several attributes, and that each individual has a specific amount of each preference attribute.

We now turn to the case where the *third* way of the data is individuals, that is, where there is more than one matrix of data, each matrix being obtained from a different individual. Table 4.6 summarizes the relationship between the types of individual difference situations, the conditionality of the data, and the presence or absence of weights.

From the table we see that the presence or absence of weights is an important determiner of the implied nature of individual variation. This is the case, of course, since weights are always associated with the third way of the data, and since we are now dealing with data whose third way is individuals. Here the individuals *may* be represented as vectors in a weight space (or they may not be represented at all). If the model is a weighted model then individual variation is represented in the weight space, for unweighted models individual variation is not represented. The type of individual variation represented by the weights is perceptual–cognitive variation. Thus Table 4.6 shows that the unweighted models provide no representation of this type of individual variation, and shows that the weighted models do make such a provision. For the unweighted models the individuals are treated as replications.

The table also shows that these data provide us with the option of permitting individual variation in response style. Data assumed to be matrix or row conditional imply that individuals vary in their response processes. Unconditional data imply that they do not.

These data may either be all square matrices or all rectangular matrices. The types of analyses correspond straightforwardly to the discussion in previous parts of this chapter. While it is not possible to have row conditional symmetric (square) data matrices, this does not imply that symmetric data rule out provisions for response bias since symmetric data can be matrix conditional.

We do not really need to go into examples in any detail since we have already presented several in previous sections of this chapter. Briefly, any data whose third way is individuals falls into the classification presented in Table 4.6. We could have several individuals judge the similarity of all pairs of several odors. RMDS or WMDS analysis of these data pictures

Table 4.6
Individual Differences When Matrices Correspond to Individuals

	Conditionality		
	Unconditional	Matrix conditional	Row conditional
Unweighted	No individual differences allowed	Individual differences in response style permitted	Individual differences in response style permitted
Weighted	Individual differences in perception–cognition permitted	Both types[a] of individual differences permitted	Both types[a] of individual differences permitted

[a] Response style and perception–cognition.

the stimuli as points in a Euclidean space. WMDS analysis also portrays the individuals as vectors in the weight space. Three-way rectangular data are exemplified by an experimental paradigm in which several stimuli are rated on several scales by several individuals. RMDU or WMDU analysis of these data displays both the stimuli and rating scales as points in a joint Euclidean space. WMDU also shows the individuals as vectors in a weight space.

4.6. Program Characteristics

The final comparison of the six programs is presented in Table 4.7. This comparison involves some of the basic limitations and characteristics of the programs. The first three columns give the three major limitations placed on the size of the biggest set of data which can be analyzed by each program. The limitations are on the maximum number of stimuli, subjects (or matrices), and data points. Column four of the table presents the maximum dimensionality of an analysis. (These limitations are for the specific version of each program which we are using in this book. There may be other versions of each program which have different limitations.)

Note that MINISSA can analyze an unlimited number of matrices, however, each matrix is submitted to a completely separate CMDS. Thus, the limitation is one matrix per CMDS analysis, although an unlimited number of matrices may be analyzed in totally independent CMDS analyses. The limitations for ALSCAL are functions of the characteristics of the computer on which the program is running, since ALSCAL is a dynamic core allocation program. That is, ALSCAL will attempt to analyze any size data, the only limitation being the total amount of core available to the user at the computer center. The limitation on total amount of data for MULTISCALE is 5000 when WMDS analyses are performed, and 15,000 otherwise. In addition, for MULTISCALE the product of the number of subjects and dimensions must not exceed 500.

Column 5 of Table 4.7 indicates whether the program optimizes a least-squares index (LS) or a maximum likelihood index (ML). All of these six programs except MULTISCALE are in some sense least squares. The maximum likelihood aspect of MULTISCALE is its most important feature, since it provides the user with certain potentially useful statistical tests unavailable in the other programs. This is explained further in Chapter 10 on MULTISCALE.

All of the least-squares programs can be said to optimize either sums of squares or variance accounted for in a transformation of the data. MINISSA optimizes the variance accounted for in an order-preserving transformation

Table 4.7
Characteristics of Six MDS Programs Described in This Book[a]

Program	Stimuli	Matrices	Data	Dimensions	Optimize	Converge	Start	Iteration
MINISSA	100	1–no limit	4950	10	LS	No	IU	I
POLYCON	60	No limit	4000	9	LS	No	IU	IC
KYST	100	No limit	1800	6	LS	No	IUR	ICA
INDSCAL/SINDSCAL	100–No limit	99–no limit	18000–dynamic	10	LS	Yes	IU	IC
ALSCAL	No limit	No limit	Dynamic	6	LS	Yes	IU	IC
MULTISCALE	50	100	5000–15000	10	ML	No	IU	ICA

[a] Code: Optimize, LS = least-squares index, ML = maximum likelihood; Start, I = internal computation, U = user defined, R = random; Iteration, I = maximum number of iterations specified, C = critical improvement-optimization criterion, A = additional control of iteration process.

of the data or a least-squares transformation of the data. INDSCAL optimizes the variance accounted for in scalar products computed from the data. POLYCON, KYST, and ALSCAL optimize either the sums of squares or the variance accounted for in a least-squares transformation of the data, although these three do not optimize precisely the same index.

We have the unfortunate situation that the six programs optimize six different indices. This makes comparing results somewhat difficult, since one cannot compare one program's index of fit to another program's. However, many of the programs print out Kruskal's original STRESS index, and these values can be compared between programs. Strictly speaking, this is not entirely adequate because only KYST and MINISSA (one option) optimize Kruskal's STRESS, thus, the comparison is somewhat overly favorable to these two programs.

Column 6 of Table 4.7 refers to a basic characteristic of the computational nature of each program. Each program is iterative, that is, they all try over and over again to improve their index of fit. Two of the programs are said to be "convergent," that is, every time they try to improve the fit, they do. The remaining four programs are not convergent. That is, sometimes they make the fit worse when trying to make it better. It has been conjectured that a program which is not convergent may produce spurious results (called "local optimum solutions") somewhat more frequently than a convergent program. While there is no empirical evidence one way or the other, Takane, Young, and de Leeuw have argued that this might be the case. All of the programs do produce local minimum solutions on occasion, although they are often very difficult to detect.

Column 7 of Table 4.7 refers to the ways in which the program computes its initial starting values (its initial configuration). Since all of the programs are iterative, they must all have some way to get started. All of the programs have an internal computational procedure for doing this. This is denoted by I in the seventh column. The internal strategy is generally related to Torgerson's (1952) classic procedure. All of the programs also let the user read in a set of starting values. This user-defined start is denoted by the letter U in the table. KYST also permits random (R) starts.

The last column of Table 4.7 refers to the ways in which the user has control over the details of the iterative procedure. All of the programs let the user specify a maximum number of iterations (denoted by the letter I). All of the programs except MINISSA let the user specify the minimum amount of improvement in the optimization criterion which is a critical improvement from one iteration to the next (C). Two of the programs (KYST and MULTISCALE) provide the user with several additional ways of controling the iterative process (A).

If the user is worried that the solution may be spurious, then two things can be done. First, the user can read in a set of starting values. Second, the user can modify the details of the iterative process. The first option may help improve the fit of the derived solution since arrival at a spurious solution may be caused by the initial starting procedure. However, it may not change anything since the spurious solution can also be caused by certain details of the iterative procedure, particularly for nonconvergent algorithms. Thus, the user may also modify some of these details, as shown in the table.

References

Carroll, J. D., & Arabie, P. Multidimensional scaling. In M. R. Rosenzwieg & L. W. Porter (Eds.), *Annual review of psychology*. Palo Alto, Calif.: Annual Reviews, Inc., 1980.

Carroll, J. D., & Chang, J. J. Analysis of individual differences in multidimensional scaling via an *n*-way generalization of "Eckhart–Young" decomposition. *Psychometrika*, 1970, *35*, 283–319.

Coombs, C. H. *A theory of data.* New York: Wiley, 1964. (Reprinted by Mathesis Press, Ann Arbor, Mich., 1976.)

Guttman, L. A. A general nonmetric technique for finding the smallest coordinate space for a configuration of points. *Psychometrika*, 1968, *33*, 469–506.

Hoadley, J. *Spatial analysis of Senate voting patterns*. Master's thesis, University of North Carolina, 1974.

Kruskal, J. B. Multidimensional scaling by optimizing goodness of fit to a nonmetric hypothesis. *Psychometrika*, 1964, *29*, 1–27. (a)

Kruskal, J. B. Nonmetric multidimensional scaling: A numerical method. *Psychometrika*, 1964, *29*, 115–129. (b)

Kruskal, J. B., Young, F. W., & Seery, J. B. *How to use KYST, a very flexible program to do multidimensional scaling and unfolding*. Murray Hill, N.J.: Bell Laboratories, 1973.

Lingoes, J. C. *The Guttman-Lingoes nonmetric program series*. Ann Arbor, Mich.: Mathesis Press, 1973.

Pruzansky, S. *How to use SINDSCAL. A computer program for individual differences in multidimensional scaling*. Murray Hill, N.J.: Bell Laboratories, 1975.

Ramsay, J. O. Maximum likelihood estimation in multidimensional scaling. *Psychometrika*, 1977, *42*, 241–266.

Ramsay, J. O. Confidence regions for multidimensional scaling analysis. *Psychometrika*, 1978, *43*, 241–266. (a)

Ramsay, J. O. *MULTISCALE: Four programs for multidimensional scaling by the method of maximum likelihood*. Chicago: National Educational Resources, Inc., 1978. (b)

Roskam, E. E. C. I. *Metric analysis of ordinal data in psychology*. Voorschoten, Amsterdam, 1968.

Spence, I. Complete and incomplete pairwise designs for multidimensional scaling. Unpublished paper, 1975.

Takane, Y., Young, F. W., & de Leeuw, J. Nonmetric individual differences multidimensional scaling: An alternating least squares method with optimum scaling features. *Psychometrika*, 1977, *42*, 7–67.

Torgerson, W. S. Multidimensional scaling: I. Theory and method. *Psychometrika*, 1952, *17*, 401–419.

Young, F. W. A model for polynomial conjoint analysis algorithms. In R. W. Shepard, A. K. Romney, & S. B. Nerlove (Eds.), *Multidimensional scaling*. New York: Seminar Press, 1972.

Young, F. W. *Conjoint scaling*. Chapel Hill, N.C.: University of North Carolina, 1973 (April, No. 118). (Revised March 1977.)

Young, F. W. *Theory and methods of multidimensional scaling*. Hillsdale, N.J.: Erlbaum, in preparation.

Young, F. W., & Lewyckyj, R. *ALSCAL-4. User's guide*. Chapel Hill, N.C.: University of North Carolina, 1979.

Young, F. W., Null, C. H., & Sarle, W. Interactive similarity ordering. *Behavioral Research Methods and Instrumentation*, 1978, *10*, 273–280.

Part II
Methods and Applications

5

How to Use MINISSA

5.1. Setting Up a MINISSA MDS Job

This chapter describes MINISSA applications to a single matrix of dissimilarity judgments (CMDS, see Section 4.1). MINISSA is an easy program to use since only three parameter cards are required. The scaling is nonmetric, but a city-block metric can be used if desired. Up to 100 variables (stimuli) can be analyzed in as many as 10 dimensions. The main options concern treatment of missing data and the addition of further points to a fixed configuration. The version described here is MINISSA-I(M)/SSA-I revised 1/1/73 (see Appendix and Chapter 16).

Figure 5.1 shows the deck setup for analysis of 10 colas (Chapter 3.1).

```
              5        10        15        20        25
I M E A N S   C O L A S - 1 0   S U B J E C T S
        1 0         1       5           O
( 9 F 2 . 0 )
3 4
7 9 5 4
8 6 5 6 7 0
7 6 3 0 5 1 6 6
6 3 4 0 3 7 9 0 3 5
5 7 8 6 7 7 5 0 7 6 7 7
6 2 8 0 7 1 8 8 6 7 5 4 6 6
6 5 2 3 6 9 6 6 2 2 3 5 7 6 7 1
2 6 6 0 7 0 8 9 6 3 6 7 5 9 3 3 5 9
```

Figure 5.1. Deck setup for analysis of 10 colas by MINISSA.

Card 1. This is the title card. A 1 is punched in column 1 followed by a title of choice in columns 2 to 72.

Card 2. This is the parameter card. There are 15 four-column fields. Only the first four are necessary for simple analysis of dissimilarity data.

Identifier	Columns	
NR	1–4	The number of variables (stimuli) which must be less than or equal to 100 and greater than or equal to 4.
MIND	5–8	The minimum number of dimensions. If you set MIND = 0, the program will determine MIND.
MAXD	9–12	The maximum number of dimensions must be 10 or NR-2, whichever is smaller.
ISIM	13–16	Blank or zero for dissimilarity data. For similarity data, enter 1 in column 16.

The remaining 11 fields on this card may be left blank unless the options shown are required.

Identifier	Columns	
IFD	17–20	A 1 in column 20 will cause distance matrices to be printed for two or more dimensions.
IFC	21–24	A 1 in column 24 will cause coordinates to be punched for two or more dimensions.
IFGLK	25–28	A 1 in column 28 will cause Kruskal's stress to be minimized.
IFCONF	29–32	Put 1 in column 32 if a configuration is to be input.
IFFIX	33–36	Put 1 in column 36 if input configuration is to remain fixed and additional points are to be fitted to this space.
IFSR	37–40	Blank or zero unless data are to be generated by a subroutine.
MISS	41–44	Enter 1 in column 44 if at least one cell is considered missing or to be ignored.
IFE	45–48	Blank or zero for Euclidean metric. Put 1 in column 48 for city block. MIND must then be 1 or greater.
IFG	49–52	Blank or zero for global monotonicity. Put 1 in column 52 for local monotonicity (errors in small distances weighted more than errors in large distances). This option only available when IFE + IFFIX + MISS = 0.
CODE	53–56	Use a value with decimal point to ignore cells in the data punched with the same code.
CUT	57–60	Value at or above/below which all input coefficients considered tied. Its use is not normally recommended.

Card 3. Format for input in FORTRAN F-notation, in this case (9F2.0).

Input Configuration Cards (Not shown). This is the point at which an input configuration is entered. It must be in (10F8.3) format with NR sets of cards each having MAXD coordinates.

Data Cards. These are the data entered as a lower-half dissimilarity matrix without diagonals. There should be NR-1 cards. Other forms of input are possible by using a number of subroutines (see IFSR).

Next Cards (Not shown). This is the point at which data to be modified by a subroutine (IFSR. NE. 0) are entered. Also, this is the point at which variables to be added to a fixed configuration (IFFIX = 1) are added.

5.2. Understanding MINISSA Output

The first page simply reproduces the input data. Solutions are then given starting at MIND (unless MIND is set to zero in which case solutions are produced downward from MAXD), the minimum number of dimensions, and proceed to MAXD, the maximum number of dimensions. At each dimensionality MINISSA provides a table of coordinates and configuration plots. Figure 5.2 shows the table for the two-dimensional cola solution. SEMI-STRONG MONOTONICITY refers to the way in which tied data are treated. Ties, when they occur, are broken on an optimal basis.

The CENTRALITY INDEX is the distance of each stimulus from the true origin of the stimulus space. Unlike the other MDS programs, MINISSA does not normalize the coordinates to zero mean. Stimulus coordinates are given in the next two columns.

```
MEANS COLAS-10 SUBJECTS

GUTTMAN-LINGOES' SMALLEST SPACE COORDINATES FOR M =  2 (SEMI-STRONG MONOTONICITY).

DIMENSION                      1        2
-----------------------------------------------------------------------------------
           CENTRALITY
VARIABLE     INDEX
   1          74.438      -78.062     0.573
   2          48.193       42.609    15.941
   3         109.029       79.735    85.355
   4         135.898       62.817  -100.000
   5          56.107       47.162    36.634
   6          82.955        2.563   100.000
   7         118.661      -60.031   -87.977
   8         109.363     -100.000    72.593
   9          36.343       30.760    18.719
  10          79.066      -83.162    32.593

GUTTMAN-LINGOES' COEFFICIENT OF ALIENATION = 0.19053 IN  16 ITERATIONS.
KRUSKAL'S STRESS = 0.14885
```

Figure 5.2. MINISSA output for two-dimensional solution of mean cola data.

The Guttman–Lingoes COEFFICIENT OF ALIENATION of .19053 means that approximately 96% of the variance in the mean cola data is accounted for in the two-dimensional solution achieved after 16 iterations. Kruskal's STRESS is a measure of fit defined as the sum of the squares of the differences between distances and disparities divided by the sum of the squares of the distances.

5.3. Colas

Solutions for the mean cola data (Section 3.1) were found by MINISSA in one, two, three, four, and five dimensions. MINISSA, like most MDS programs, will find a five-dimensional solution (50 coordinates for 10 stimuli) for the colas, although the result is not meaningful because the mean similarity matrix contains only 45 data elements. The values of error (coefficient of alienation) are shown in Figure 5.3. The two-dimensional solution is shown in Figure 5.4. The diet drinks fall to the left-hand portion of the space and nondiet drinks fall to the right. Thus, dimension 1 appears to be a diet–nondiet dimension. Drinks made by the same company tend to

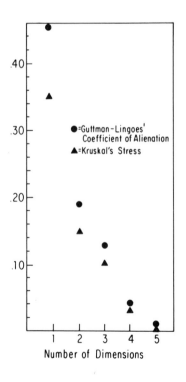

Figure 5.3. The change in the coefficient of alienation and stress for one- to five-dimensional solutions for the mean cola data.

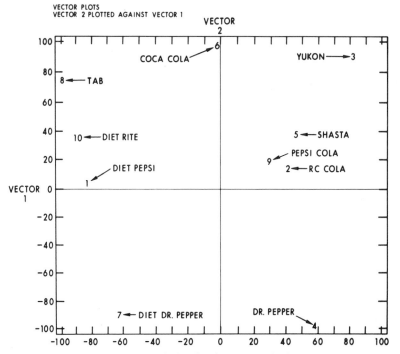

Figure 5.4. The two-dimensional solution for the mean cola data achieved by MINISSA.

be related to each other at similar projections along dimension 2, which appears to be a cola–cherry cola dimension.

Little new information is gained in going from a two- to a three-dimensional solution even though there is a continued reduction in error. Stimuli are not nearly as differentiated on dimension 3 compared to dimensions 1 and 2. A three-dimensional model made from the three-dimensional solution also confirmed little gain in information from two to three dimensions. This will be shown not to be the case for the INDSCAL space where the solution can accommodate all the individual differences. When a solution is found using mean values over the group of 10 subjects, frequently information, and thus one or even several dimensions, can be lost in averaging the data. The INDSCAL solution will be found to be more readily interpretable, giving information about individual differences and not forcing the solution into two dimensions.

Although another algorithm (INDSCAL) will be shown to yield more information for this data set, it can be seen that an arrangement of colas achieved by MINISSA using mean measures of similarity reveals diet–nondiet as well as proprietary flavor information.

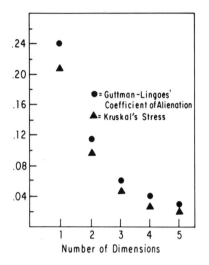

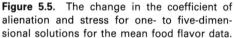

Figure 5.5. The change in the coefficient of alienation and stress for one- to five-dimensional solutions for the mean food flavor data.

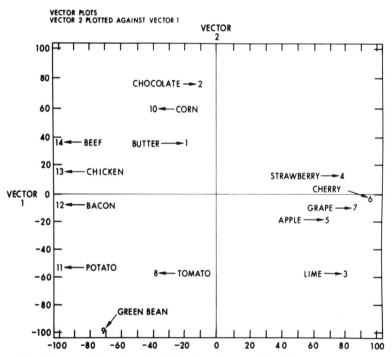

Figure 5.6. The two-dimensional solution for the mean food flavor data achieved by MINISSA.

5.4. Food Flavors

Mean similarity measures for food flavors (Section 3.2) were found over all 32 subjects (16 young and 16 elderly) and MINISSA was applied to the mean matrix. There was a great deal of noise in the data for individual elderly subjects as will be shown when INDSCAL is applied to these data. However, averaging the data smoothed out the noise, resulting in a meaningful solution in two dimensions. A plot of the decrease of error for the food flavors is shown in Figure 5.5. The MINISSA solution for the mean food flavors is shown in Figure 5.6. The fruits are clustered together on the right. The meats are far to the left. Potato, tomato, and green beans are in the lower left-hand quadrant. In the center upper part of the space are chocolate, corn, and butter. Individual solutions for aged subjects indicate that some of the subjects could not tell one substance from another. For example, the application of MINISSA to data for one elderly subject revealed the space shown in Figure 5.7. It is obvious that this subject cannot discriminate odors from one another. All the young subjects had meaningful individual spaces. Smoothing of the data by finding means for

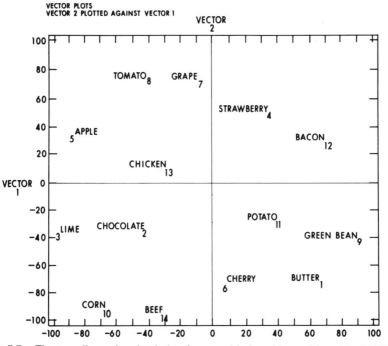

Figure 5.7. The two-dimensional solution for one elderly subject achieved by MINISSA. Obviously the solution is meaningless because this subject had a severely diminished sense of smell.

young and elderly subjects allowed MINISSA to find a meaningful arrangement.

5.5. Strawberry-Flavored Beverages

The mean similarity measures over all 46 subjects (Section 3.3) were found and used as input to MINISSA. Four- and five-dimensional solutions were not found because an examination of the first three dimensions revealed that the solution was at most two dimensional. A plot of the error is shown in Figure 5.8. For the three-dimensional solution, the stimuli clustered together on the third dimension showing no differentiation among the stimuli. The two-dimensional solution is shown in Figure 5.9. The results indicate that the first dimension, which is very important since a one-dimensional solution accounts for 87% of the variance, is related to sweetness. The 225% sweet stimuli fall to the far left, and the 50% sweet to the far right. The second dimension appears to be related to what subjects see as a departure from the marketed product. Subjects perceive 75% color, 75% sweet, and 100% color, 100% sweet as most like the marketed product. It is shown in Chapter 12 that most subjects prefer beverages sweeter than the marketed product (i.e., 100% color, 100% sweet). For this reason, they probably see the 75% color, 75% sweet as most like the marketed product.

It is shown that when INDSCAL and ALSCAL are applied to these data that the second dimension is meaningful for approximately one-fourth of the subjects. The remainder are predominantly one-dimensional, attuned mainly to sweetness.

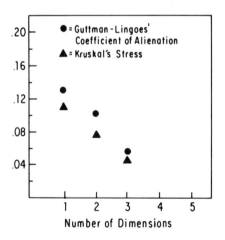

Figure 5.8. The change in the coefficient of alienation and stress for one- to three-dimensional solutions for the mean data on strawberry-flavored drinks.

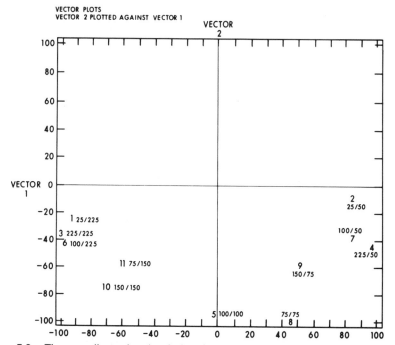

Figure 5.9. The two-dimensional solution for the mean data on strawberry-flavored drinks achieved by MINISSA (percentage color/percentage sweetness).

5.6. Taste of Chemicals

Application of MINISSA to measures of taste dissimilarity among 19 chemicals resulted in the three-dimensional space shown in Figure 5.10. A three-dimensional solution was deemed appropriate because the coefficient of alienation indicated that the variance was largely accounted for in three dimensions (see Figure 5.11), and no further structure was revealed by the fourth or fifth dimensions. Henning's prism, which is supposed to span the totality of the taste realm, accounts for part of the space. There are groupings of sweet (glucose, sucrose, saccharin, and PbAc), sour (HCl, HAc, and HNO_3), salty (NaCl, NaAc, and LiCl), and bitter (Q_2SO_4 and QHCl) which represent the corners of Henning's prism. KCl, NH_4Cl, $CaCl_2$, K_2SO_4, and $MgCl_2$ are found between the salty tastes and bitter quinines. NaOH and Na_2CO_3 form a fifth group which falls outside the tetrahedral structure. Henning had originally placed NaOH on the salty–sweet edge of the tetrahedron and Na_2CO_3 on the salty–sour edge. Yoshida (1963) has also found two substances, potassium alum and monosodium glutamate,

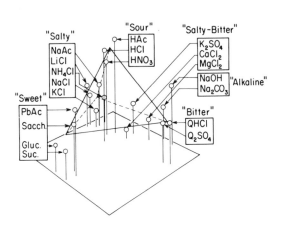

Figure 5.10. Three-dimensional composite Euclidean solution for similarity judgments achieved by the Guttman–Lingoes–Roskam method. The sweet-tasting substances (glucose, sucrose, saccharin, and PbAc) are grouped together, as are the sour acids (HCl, HAc, and HNO_3), the alkaline stimuli (NaOH and Na_2CO_3), the bitter stimuli (Q_2SO_4 and QHCl), and the salty stimuli (NaCl, NaAc, and LiCl). The remaining salts— KCl, NH_4Cl, $CaCl_2$, K_2SO_4, and $MgCl_2$—are found in between the strong salty tastes and the bitter quinines.

which violate a tetrahedral structure. Thus, it appears that tastes are not limited to the sweet, sour, salty, bitter domain.

It can be seen that MINISSA ordered the stimuli by a procedure that did not constrain the arrangement with our limited taste vocabulary. The only requirement to develop the space in Figure 5.10 was experimental similarity measures. In Chapter 12 it is shown how an underlying set of rules or dimensions can be found so that a taste model can be developed from the space in Figure 5.10.

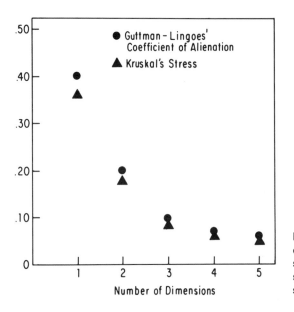

Figure 5.11. The change in the coefficient of alienation and stress for one- to five-dimensional solutions for the mean similarity data on 19 chemicals.

5.7. Musk Odors

MINISSA was applied to two different matrices which utilized different aspects of the data (see Section 3.5). MINISSA was first applied to the lower-half confusability matrix shown in Table 3.10, which indicates the number of subjects out of 20 who could not discriminate between two musks using a triadic comparison. MINISSA was also applied to the mean measures of similarity for each pair of stimuli over the 20 subjects. Similarity measures of zero (when subjects could not differentiate stimuli in a triadic comparison) were averaged with actual ratings which subjects made when they were successful with a triadic comparison. The resultant space from the latter application of MINISSA is shown in Figure 5.12. A similar arrangement was found from the confusability matrix. The macrocyclic musks (M) were arranged in the upper and right-hand portions of the space, while the nitro musks (N) were arranged toward the left. Musk alpha, the only nitro musk with bromine groups, fell apart from the other musks.

Individual spaces for each of the 20 subjects were also derived using MINISSA. They were quite similar to one another as well as similar to the space in Figure 5.12. There was much less variation among individual subject similarity spaces than was found for the subject's distribution of ratings on adjective scales shown in Figure 5.13. Thus, application of multidimensional scaling to similarity measures and confusability data proved to be a more stable means of characterizing differences among the 14 musks tested than ratings on adjective scales.

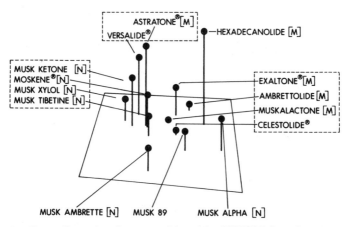

Figure 5.12.   Three-dimensional space achieved by MINISSA based on mean confusability and similarity data for musks. The macrocyclic musks (M) are ordered in the upper and right-hand portions of the space. The nitro musks (N) tend to be located toward the left.

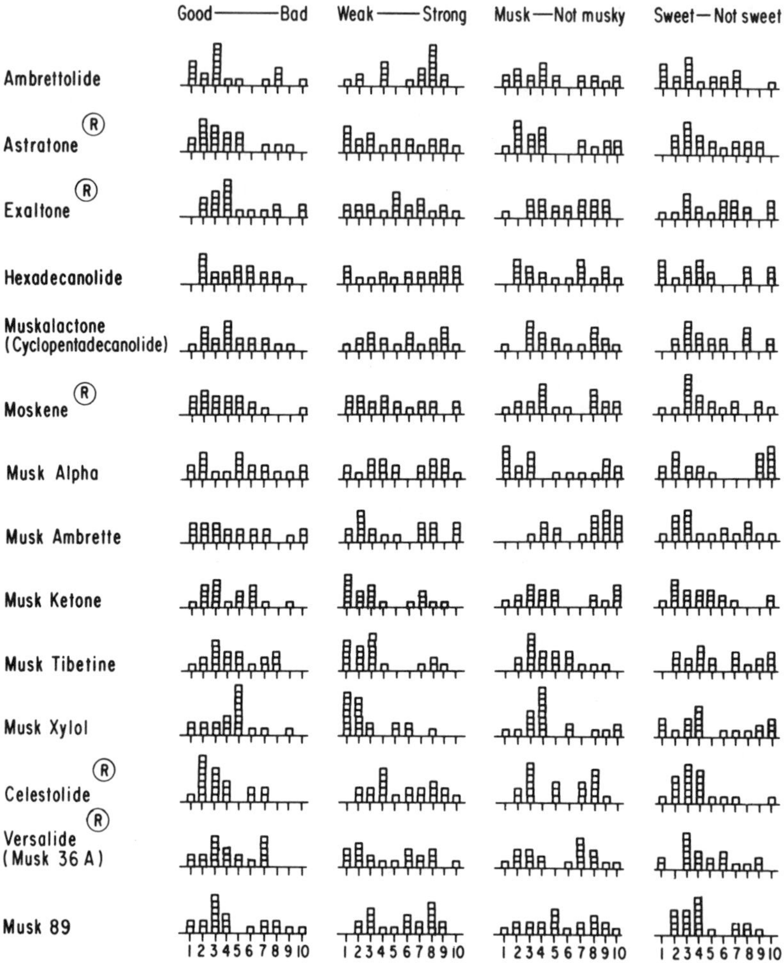

Figure 5.13. Histograms indicating the distribution of adjective ratings for the 20 subjects. Each box represents an individual subject rating.

5.8. General Comments

MINISSA is a very useful program for finding a multidimensional space from a single matrix based on individual or mean similarity ratings. In the examples given in this chapter, it was most effectively applied to the 19 chemical stimuli (Section 5.6) and musk odors (Section 5.7). It is shown later (Chapters 8 and 9) that application of individual differences models (INDSCAL and ALSCAL) to the cola, food flavor, and strawberry-beverage data yield more information than application of MINISSA.

MINISSA has two helpful options for the user of MDS. The first is a simple method of treating missing data, and the second is a method to input a fixed space to which additional points are added.

Two forms of MINISSA are presently available: the Michigan version, MINISSA (M), described in this chapter (see also Appendix) and the Nijmegen (Holland) version, MINISSA (N). There are slight differences between the two versions that relate to the minimization of stress and calculation of stepsize (see Section 16.4). However, the differences between the two versions are negligible for practical purposes.

Reference

Yoshida, M. Similarity among different kinds of tastes near the threshold concentration. *Japanese Journal of Psychology,* 1963, *34,* 25–35.

6

How to Use POLYCON

6.1. Setting Up a POLYCON MDS Job

This chapter describes POLYCON applications to a single matrix of dissimilarity judgments (CMDS, see Section 4.1) and to several matrices of dissimilarity judgments (RMDS). POLYCON is a very flexible program which permits many types of analyses to be performed on many types of data. However, for nonmetric analysis of dissimilarity data in two dimensions, only the following four control cards are mandatory:

START
INPUT (which describes the data)
COMPUTE
STOP

In practice a few more control cards are generally used to title and label the output as well as expand the analysis. The first 10 columns of PO-LYCON control cards are reserved for the *commands*. Columns 11–72 specify the *parameters*, which are the details of the command. The last 8 columns can be used to sequence the cards. The control cards can be placed in any order between START and COMPUTE.

The version described here is POLYCON 2.06 (see Appendix) which can handle a maximum of 4000 data points. For example, data consisting of

```
        5      10      15      20      25      30      35      40      45      50      55      60      65
START
LABEL                 1D PEPSI,2RC,3YUKON,4DR PEPP,5SHASTA,6COKE,7D DR PE,8TAB
                      ,9PEPSI,0D RITE C.
TITLE                 COLAS-TEN INDIVIDUAL MATRICES
INPUT                 DATA,TRIANGULAR((10),FORMAT(2X,9F2.0)),REPLICATIONS((10)).
0116
018147
0156327 1
0187684471
01603521 9834
018494985799 99
0150877973199245
0199255398521799 84
0116929083794424189 8
(9 MORE DATA MATRICES FOLLOW)
ANALYSIS              DIMENSIONS((5,4,3,2,1)).
PLOT                  DERIVED CONFIGURATION, TRANSFORMATION, GOODNESS OF FIT,
                      STRESS.
COMPUTE
ANALYSIS              POLYNOMIAL((1)).
COMPUTE
STOP
```

Figure 6.1. Input deck of POLYCON control cards for cola study described in Section 3.1.

lower-half similarity matrices from 38 subjects on 15 stimuli (38 × (15 × 7) = 3990 data points)[1] can just be accommodated.

Figure 6.1 shows the input deck of control cards for the analysis of dissimilarities for 10 cola drinks by 10 subjects (Section 3.1).

Card 1. START card: START is punched in columns 1–5.

Card 2. LABEL card: LABEL is punched in columns 1–5. Columns 11 through 72 contain each label separated by a comma as: 1D PEPSI,2RC,3YUKON, etc. Continuation cards may be used, as in this example, with the first entry in column 11 being a comma. The final character is a period. Labels may contain up to eight characters including blanks and excepting commas and periods. Any configuration plotted uses the first character of a point's label to identify the point. There may be no more than 60 labels. If the LABEL card is omitted, points will be designated by letters.

Card 3. TITLE card: TITLE is punched in columns 1–5. Any information may appear in columns 11–72 and will appear in columns 1 through 62 on each page of the output. A second TITLE card may be included to provide information on columns 63 through 124 of the output. A title card may not be continued.

---

[1] 15 × 7 is $N \times (N - 1)/2$, where N is 15. This is the total number of combinations of 15 stimuli taken two at a time.

Card 4. INPUT card: INPUT is punched in columns 1–5. Columns 11–72 on this card and any subsequent continuation cards contain parameter names separated by commas. Three parameter categories are mandatory:

1. Type of matrix—for example, DATA. The POLYCON users guide specifies the parameter name DATA MATRIX. However POLYCON only uses the first four characters of a parameter for identification; hence DATA is sufficient.
2. Shape and size of matrix—for example, TRIANGULAR(10). The matrix in the cola example is triangular and has 10 stimuli.
3. Format parameter—for example, FORMAT(2X,9F2.0). The format statement should utilize standard Fortran F-type conventions, but there must not be more than 150 characters between the parentheses.

Following these three mandatory parameters are a number of optional parameters. For our applications, the most important one is REPLICA-TIONS(i). This indicates that there are i matrices to be read in which are all of the same type, shape, size, and format as previously described. In this example, there are 10 replications because there are 10 subjects. The final character on the INPUT card is a period.

Data cards must immediately follow the INPUT card *unless* the optional input parameter TAPE(i) is used. The i in this case indicates the number of the logical unit containing the data which must be in card images. If there are replications, all the data for the first replication are entered first and so on.

There are other optional INPUT type and shape parameters which will only be mentioned briefly here. In addition to triangular matrices, the data may be arranged in square matrices that are either symmetric or asymmetric and either have or do not have diagonals. The appropriate parameter options are called: SQUARE(i), DIAGONAL, NO DIAGONAL, SYMMETRIC, and ASYMMETRIC. There are also options which permit partitioning of the data matrix into subsets so that POLYCON performs a separate trans-formation for each subset. This is useful when the elements of one subset of data are not measured on the same scale as those in another subset (e.g., subsets were gathered on different days). It is also possible to input an initial configuration or a target configuration, the latter to be used as a target for rotating the derived configuration. In addition, it is also possible to input a weight matrix which permits differential weighting of individual data values.

Card 5. ANALYSIS card: ANALYSIS is punched in columns 1–8. Analysis parameters appear in columns 11–72 on this and as many suc-cessive cards as needed. This card in the cola example is used to describe the solution dimensionalities sought, for example, DIMENSIONS(5,4,3,2,1).

The last character on the card is a period. The maximum number of dimensions is nine. The most efficient analysis is obtained if one specifies the dimensions in descending order. This is because the five-dimensional arrangement can be utilized in the initialization process for the four-dimensional analysis. For nonmetric analysis of dissimilarities data, the DIMENSIONS option is generally the only parameter required on the ANALYSIS card.

The ANALYSIS card is optional. If it is omitted, POLYCON will make certain default assumptions about the wide range of nonmetric analyses which can be selected with an ANALYSIS card. The wide range of options fall into three basic categories: (*a*) measurement model parameters, (*b*) regression parameters, (*c*) minimization parameters.

MEASUREMENT MODEL PARAMETERS. The default measurement model options are:

COLUMN   COLUMN
1   11
ANALYSIS   EUCLIDEAN,DIMENSIONS(2).

Another measurement model parameter which can replace EUCLIDEAN is MINKOWSKI(*a*). This parameter utilizes the Minkowski metric for the measurement model. Of course, MINKOWSKI(1.0) and MINKOWSKI(2.0) are equivalent to city-block and EUCLIDEAN models, respectively.

REGRESSION PARAMETERS. The default options for the regression parameters which control the ordinal rescaling (or monotonic transformation) of the data are the following:

COLUMN   COLUMN
1   11
ANALYSIS   ASCENDING REGRESSION,LEAST SQUARES
                TRANSFORMATION,SECONDARY,MATRIX
                COMPARISON,NO WEIGHTS.

ASCENDING REGRESSION indicates that the monotonic transformation is performed so that larger data values correspond with larger distances in the derived configuration. Large data values in the input matrices mean greater dissimilarities. ASCENDING REGRESSION is equivalent to saying, on the INPUT card, that the data are DISSIMILARITIES DATA.

LEAST SQUARES TRANSFORMATION refers to the fact that the monotonic transformation used is that developed by Kruskal (1964).

SECONDARY indicates that ties in the data will be left tied. This corresponds to the DISCRETE option in ALSCAL.

MATRIX COMPARISON refers to the fact that separate transformations are performed for each data matrix. It is assumed that all elements within a data matrix can be compared but that elements between replications (if any) cannot be compared. This corresponds to MATRIX CONDITIONAL in ALSCAL.

NO WEIGHTS indicates that all data points are weighted equally.

Other POLYCON ANALYSIS options available which can be substituted for the corresponding default options given are:

DESCENDING REGRESSION indicates that the monotonic transformation is performed so that larger data values correspond with smaller distances. This is equivalent to saying, on the INPUT card, that the data are SIMILARITIES DATA.

RANK IMAGE transformation refers to the fact that the monotonic transformation used is that developed by Guttman (1968).

PRIMARY indicates that the ties in the data will be untied.

CUBE COMPARISON refers to the fact that all matrices undergo the same transformation, implying that elements between replications can be compared.

ROW COMPARISON can be used with asymmetric row conditional data; there are separate transformations for each row.

There are numerous other regression parameters, two of which are frequently helpful to add to the ANALYSIS command. The first is FIX POINTS($i,j,. . .,k$). This permits the initial coordinates of points, i,j, etc., to remain fixed throughout the nonmetric phases of the analysis. This is helpful when comparing newly scaled points with a subset of points that are fixed relative to one another as determined in a previous experiment.

The second is CUTOFF(a,b) which specifies the range of the data elements to be included in the analysis. Data elements smaller than (or equal to) the value a or larger than (or equal to) the value b will be excluded from the analyses. The default values for a and b are 0 and 10^{40}, respectively. This points out an important aspect of POLYCON, that is, zeros are treated as missing data. Therefore, if there are zeros in your data, either the CUTOFF parameter should be used (e.g., CUTOFF(-1)), or any data values which are zero should be entered as .01 or some other number which is appropriately small for the numerical range of the data.

MINIMIZATION PARAMETERS. The minimization parameters and their defaults are:

COLUMN 1	COLUMN 11
ANALYSIS	ITERATIONS(5,25),STRESS FORMULA(2), ESTIMATION METHOD(1).

ITERATIONS(5,25) indicates that, in the first phase of the analysis, five iterations are permitted to compute a Young–Torgerson quasi-nonmetric (intermediate between metric and nonmetric) initial configuration (Young, 1968). In the second phase, a maximum of 25 iterations are permitted for

the Young–Torgerson gradient method (Young, 1968). STRESS FOR-
MULA(2) selects Kruskal's stress formula two to be minimized. There are
three possible stress formulas which can be minimized. All three formulas,
which are measures of badness of fit, have the same numerator, that is,
the sum of weighted squared differences between the disparities and distances (see Young, 1972). STRESS FORMULA(1) selects Kruskal's stress
formula one to minimize; the denominator is the sum of the weighted
squared distances. The denominator for Kruskal's STRESS FORMULA(2)
is the variance of the weighted distances.[2] STRESS FORMULA(3) utilizes
Young's least-squares criterion. The denominator for this measure of fit is
the variance of the weighted disparities. ESTIMATION METHOD(1) eliminates all missing data elements from the analysis.

Note in Figure 6.1 that other new ANALYSIS cards may be inserted to
perform different analyses on the same data set. These are each succeeded
by a COMPUTE card.

Card 6. PLOT card: PLOT is punched in columns 1–4, and columns
11–72 contain the PLOT parameter names which are separated by commas
and terminate with a period. The PLOT card must precede the COMPUTE
card if plots are required. While the card is optional, no plots are provided
without it. PLOT with no parameter names and a period in column 11
terminates all previous plot requests and provides no plotted output. The
plot parameter names are:

DERIVED CONFIGURATION
TRANSFORMATION (disparities versus data)
GOODNESS OF FIT (disparities versus distances and data versus
                distances)
STRESS (stress of each solution versus dimensionality of the solution)
ROTATED CONFIGURATION
INITIAL CONFIGURATION
TARGET CONFIGURATION

Care should be taken, in use of configuration parameter names with high-
dimensional solutions, not to generate excessive output. Solutions in one
through nine dimensions with all configurations plotted result in 484 pages
of plotted output.

Card 7. COMPUTE card: COMPUTE is punched in columns 1–7. This
card is mandatory. Computations are performed according to the parameters
specified on the ANALYSIS card or provided by the default options.

---

[2] The definitions for both STRESS FORMULA(1) and STRESS FORMULA(2) in the RMDS
case do not correspond precisely to Kruskal's definitions. The difference in definition leads
to larger stress values for POLYCON than for KYST. The differences in values do not indicate
differences in the adequacy of the solution, however, but only differences in function.

Card 8. New ANALYSIS card: ANALYSIS is punched in columns 1–8. The new analysis required is a metric analysis of the same data set. POLYNOMIAL(1) is punched in columns 11–23. The last character on the card is a period. In order to switch the analysis back to nonmetric, LEAST SQUARES TRANSFORMATION or RANK IMAGE TRANSFORMATION must appear on the next ANALYSIS card.

Card 9. COMPUTE card.

Card 10. STOP card: STOP is punched in columns 1–4. This must be the last card and is mandatory.

Other output options.　Other output commands not used in this example include the PUNCH and PRINT output options. Punched output in (8F10.5) format may be obtained by including a card with PUNCH in columns 1–5 before COMPUTE. PUNCH parameters include:

DISPARITIES MATRIX
DISTANCES MATRIX
RESIDUALS MATRIX
DERIVED CONFIGURATION
ROTATED CONFIGURATION

Matrices are punched row by row, configurations point by point, with new cards for new rows or new points.

The PRINT card is inserted before COMPUTE if additional information is required. The default option basically provides the values of STRESS and the derived configuration. By punching PRINT in columns 1–5, many additional parameters, such as those in the PUNCH option, may be printed by designating the desired parameters in columns 11–72.

6.2. Understanding POLYCON Output

POLYCON output contains four main parts:

1. A listing of the POLYCON control cards used
2. A brief history of the analysis which shows results for the best iteration
3. Plots of the configurations
4. Plots of transformations and fits

Figure 6.2(a) and (b) shows the first two pages of a POLYCON output. Page 1 repeats the LABEL and TITLE information and the INPUT, ANALYSIS, and PLOT parameters. Page 2 contains three main sections: (*a*) computational results after BEST ITERATION of Phase 2, (*b*) DERIVED CONFIGURATION, (*c*) PARTIAL DERIVATIVES. It also indicates that a minimum for STRESS(2) was found in the first two phases of the analysis

FORREST W. YOUNG
PSYCHOMETRIC LABORATORY
UNIVERSITY OF NORTH CAROLINA

POLYCOM
VERSION   2.06
NOVEMBER 1974

POLYNOMIAL CONJOINT ANALYSIS

SEQUENCE
FIELD

COMMAND   PARAMETER
FIELD   FIELD

START
LABEL   1D PEPSI,2RC,3YUKON,4DR PEPP,5SHASTA,6COKE,7D DR PE,8TAB
               ,9PEPSI,0D RITE C.

TITLE   COLAS-TEN INDIVIDUAL MATRICES

INPUM   DATA,TRIANGULAR(10),FORMAT(2X,9F2.0),REPLICATIONS(10).

ANALYSIS   DIMENSIONS(5,4,3,2,1).

PLOT   DERIVED CONFIGURATION, TRANSFORMATION, GOODNESS OF FIT,
               STRESS.

COMPUTE

(a)

COLAS-TEM INDIVIDUAL MATRICES

SOLUTION IN 3 DIMENSIONS FOR 30 COORDINATES FROM 1 PASSIVE AND 449 ACTIVE DATA ELEMENTS PARTITIONED INTO 10 SUBSETS.

PHASE 1

MINIMUM STRESS FOUND

PHASE 2

MINIMUM STRESS FOUND

BEST ITERATION

ITER	P	NP	DIST M	DISP M	DIST V	DISP V	DIST SQ	DIFF SQ	STRESS 1	STRESS 2	STRESS 3	PART SQ	PART MAX	STRESS
3	0	1	0.6886	0.6886	0.0	0.0	0.4741	0.0	0.2090	0.7222	1.0443			
3	1	45	1.2358	1.2358	6.2788	3.0034	74.9998	3.2752	0.2251	0.7781	1.2386			
3	2	45	1.2358	1.2358	6.2788	2.4778	74.9998	3.8010	0.2353	0.8131	1.3968			
3	3	45	1.2358	1.2358	6.2788	2.1277	74.9998	4.1511	0.1924	0.6797	0.9267			
3	4	44	1.2482	1.2482	5.9726	3.2131	74.5257	3.5157	0.2165	0.7483	1.1280			
3	5	45	1.2358	1.2358	6.2788	2.7630	74.9998	3.0632	0.2021	0.6985	0.9760			
3	6	45	1.2358	1.2358	6.2788	3.2156	74.9998	3.9208	0.2286	0.7902	1.2895			
3	7	45	1.2358	1.2358	6.2788	2.3580	74.9998	2.4193	0.1796	0.6207	0.7917			
3	8	45	1.2358	1.2358	6.2788	3.8595	74.9998	2.9942	0.1998	0.6906	0.9548			
3	9	45	1.2358	1.2358	6.2788	3.2845	74.9998	3.9604	0.2298	0.7942	1.3070			
3	10	450	1.2358	1.2358	6.2788	2.3184	74.9998	33.8605	0.2125	0.7362	1.0877			
					62.4818	28.6210	749.9976	33.8605				0.1604	0.2158	0.7362

STRESS(2) = 0.736

DERIVED CONFIGURATION

	1	2	3	4	5	6	7	8	9	10
	1D PEPSI	2RC	3IUKCN	4DP PEPP	5SHASTA	6COKE	7D DR PE	8TAB	9PEPSI	OD RITE
DIMENSION 1	-0.565	0.458	0.314	0.121	0.637	0.467	-0.605	-0.679	0.577	-0.724
DIMENSION 2	-0.233	-0.092	0.002	1.124	-0.035	-0.460	0.742	-0.403	-0.216	-0.430
DIMENSION 3	-0.704	-0.611	0.704	-0.050	0.125	0.312	0.083	0.520	-0.408	-0.063

PARTIAL DERIVATIVES

	1	2	3	4	5	6	7	8	9	10
	1D PEPSI	2RC	3IUKCN	4DP PEPP	5SHASTA	6COKE	7D DR PE	8TAB	9PEPSI	OD RITE
DIMENSION 1	-0.097	0.141	0.066	-0.009	0.011	0.073	-0.046	-0.074	0.034	-0.100
DIMENSION 2	-0.057	-0.087	-0.059	0.216	-0.106	0.074	0.010	-0.051	0.025	-0.060
DIMENSION 3	-0.063	0.036	-0.011	0.010	0.016	-0.002	0.010	0.018	-0.030	0.018

(b)

Figure 6.2. (a) First page of POLYCON output for the nonmetric cola analysis which lists the control cards used. (b) Second page of POLYCON cola output which, in this case, gives computational information for the three-dimensional nonmetric cola solution.

which utilize the Young–Torgerson quasi-nonmetric initialization procedure and the Young–Torgerson gradient method. The columns under BEST ITERATION (in Phase 2) provide certain computational results for each subject (partition P). The zero value of P is for missing data elements, in this case one from Subject 4 who shows only 44 elements in column NP. Actually, this element was not missing but was a zero which was interpreted by POLYCON as missing data. The last row in the table with a blank value of P is for all data elements combined, that is, 450. This information is also indicated under the heading where it is stated that there are 449 active elements and 1 passive element in this replicated three-dimensional analysis of 10 colas for 10 subjects.

The meaning of other column headings is:

NP	Number of elements in a partition. Here each subject's complete cola matrix consists of 45 elements.
ITER	Number of iterations required to minimize stress in Phase 2 or the maximum number of iterations specified in the control cards if no minimum was found.
DIST M	Mean of the distances in partition P. For the standard analyses these will all be the same.
DISP M	Mean of the disparities in partition P. These likewise will be the same.
DISP V	Weighted variance of the distances in partition P. Their sum over all partitions is the denominator for stress formula 2.
DISP V	Weighted variance of the disparities in partition P. Their sum is the denominator for stress formula 3.
DIST SQ	Sum of weighted squared distances in partition P. Their sum is the denominator for stress formula 1.
DIFF SQ	Sum of weighted squared differences between the disparities and distances. The numerator for all stress formulas.
STRESS 1	Value of stress formula 1 for partition P on iteration ITER.
STRESS 2	Value of stress formula 2 for partition P on iteration ITER.
STRESS 3	Value of stress formula 3 for partition P on iteration ITER.
PART SQ	Sum of squared partial derivatives. Larger values indicate greater imprecision in the solution.
PART MAX	Maximum absolute value of partial derivative.
STRESS	Value of selected stress formula (here STRESS(2)) over all data partitions on iteration ITER.

Values for three stress formulas are given, but unless specified otherwise in the ANALYSIS statement STRESS(2) is minimized. When a number of data sets are analyzed simultaneously, stress values are provided for each matrix. This allows a comparison of how each individual fits the model and is loosely related to the distance of subject weights from the origin in

INDSCAL (Chapter 8) or ALSCAL (Chapter 9). When solutions are obtained in a number of dimensionalities (as will normally be the case), the change in stress with dimensionality provides an initial guide to the dimensionality of the solution.

The matrix labeled PARTIAL DERIVATIVES may be ignored by the average user. The size of the partial derivative indicates the uncertainty in each coordinate's value. The larger the partial derivative, the greater the uncertainty. As the fit improves, the partial derivatives tend to zero. The largest absolute value is for dimension 2 for Dr. Pepper and this is shown in the last row of the BEST ITERATION table in the PART MAX column. The size of the partial derivative is loosely related to the size of Ramsay's ellipsoids (Chapter 10).

The next pages of the printout after the computational results for the best iteration show the derived cola configurations which will be discussed shortly and are illustrated in Figure 6.4. Examples of the final three pages in the printout shown in Figure 6.3(a), (b), and (c) are:

1. MONOTONIC TRANSFORMATION
2. MONOTONIC FIT
3. LINEAR FIT

MONOTONIC TRANSFORMATION shows the transformed data (disparities) plotted against the original data. The disparities are normalized so that the mean squared datum is unity. An X refers to an individual coordinate. Numbers indicate the number of overlapping points with the letter M representing 10 or more overlapping points.

MONOTONIC FIT represents the distances as a function of the raw data and, in this example shows considerable scatter.

LINEAR FIT is an ordinary scattergram whose width represents departure from perfect fit. In this plot, the residual differences between the transformed data and the distances which POLYCON is attempting to minimize are presented directly. Residual differences are measured relative to a perfect fit, which would be represented by a straight line extending from the lower left corner of the plot to the upper right corner. A point close to the hypothetical perfect line indicates the datum is being fit better than a point falling further away. The stress which is optimized, in this case STRESS(2), is related to a measure of the residuals from a perfect fit.

Subsequent pages of the printout show solutions of lower dimensionality. The final page is a plot of stress versus dimensionality.

6.3. Colas

This data set (Section 3.1) is from 10 subjects for 10 decarbonated commercial colas. The analyses described here make two comparisons:

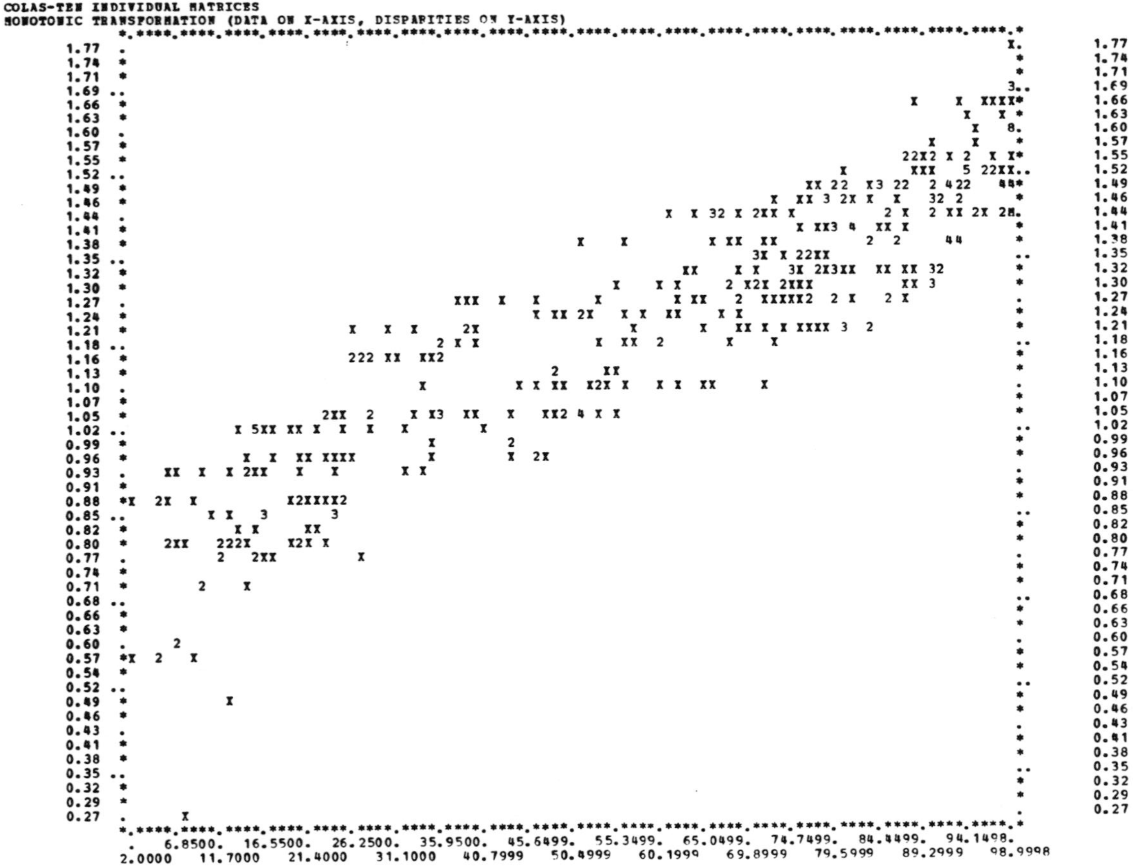
COLAS-TEN INDIVIDUAL MATRICES
MONOTONIC TRANSFORMATION (DATA ON X-AXIS, DISPARITIES ON Y-AXIS)
1.77
0.27
2.0000
98.9998

Figure 6.3(a). MONOTONIC TRANSFORMATION of 10 subjects' data for 10 colas.

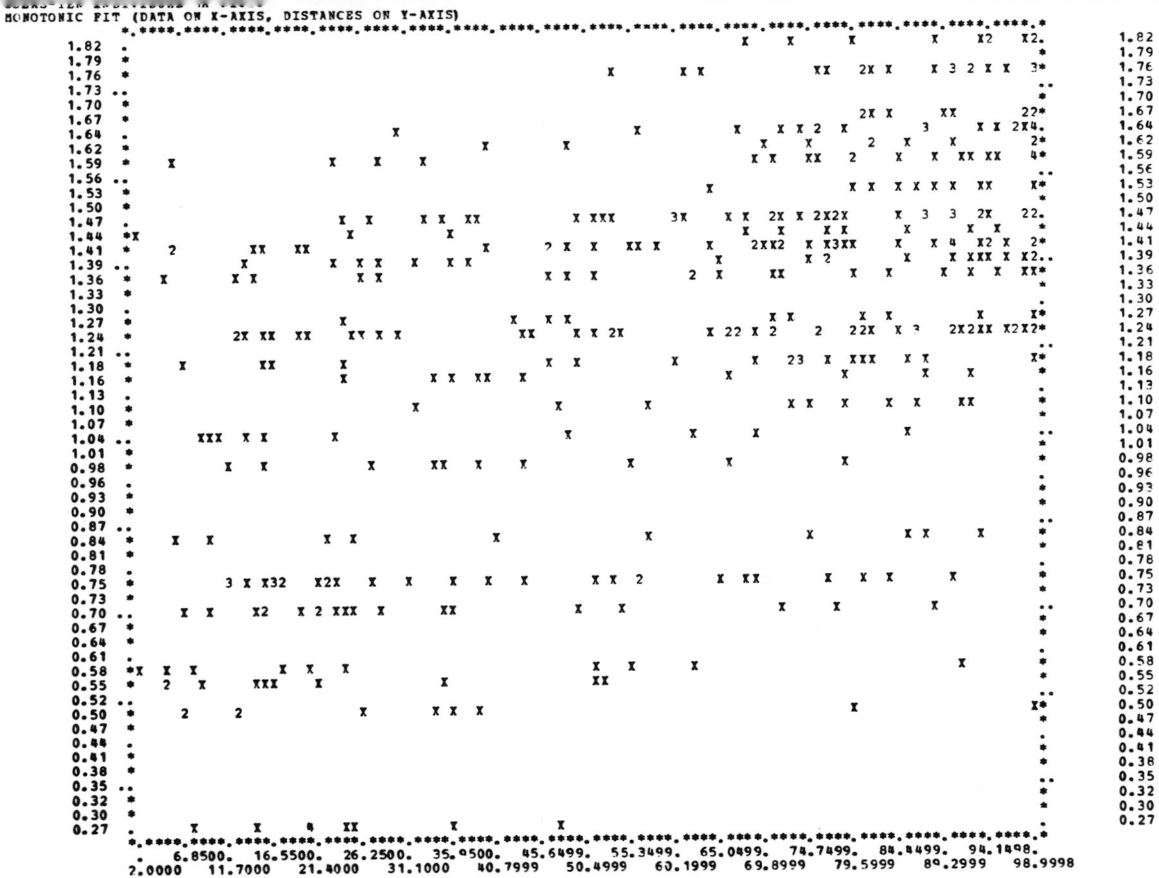

Figure 6.3(b). MONOTONIC FIT presents the distances found by POLYCON as a function of the raw cola data for the three-dimensional nonmetric solution.

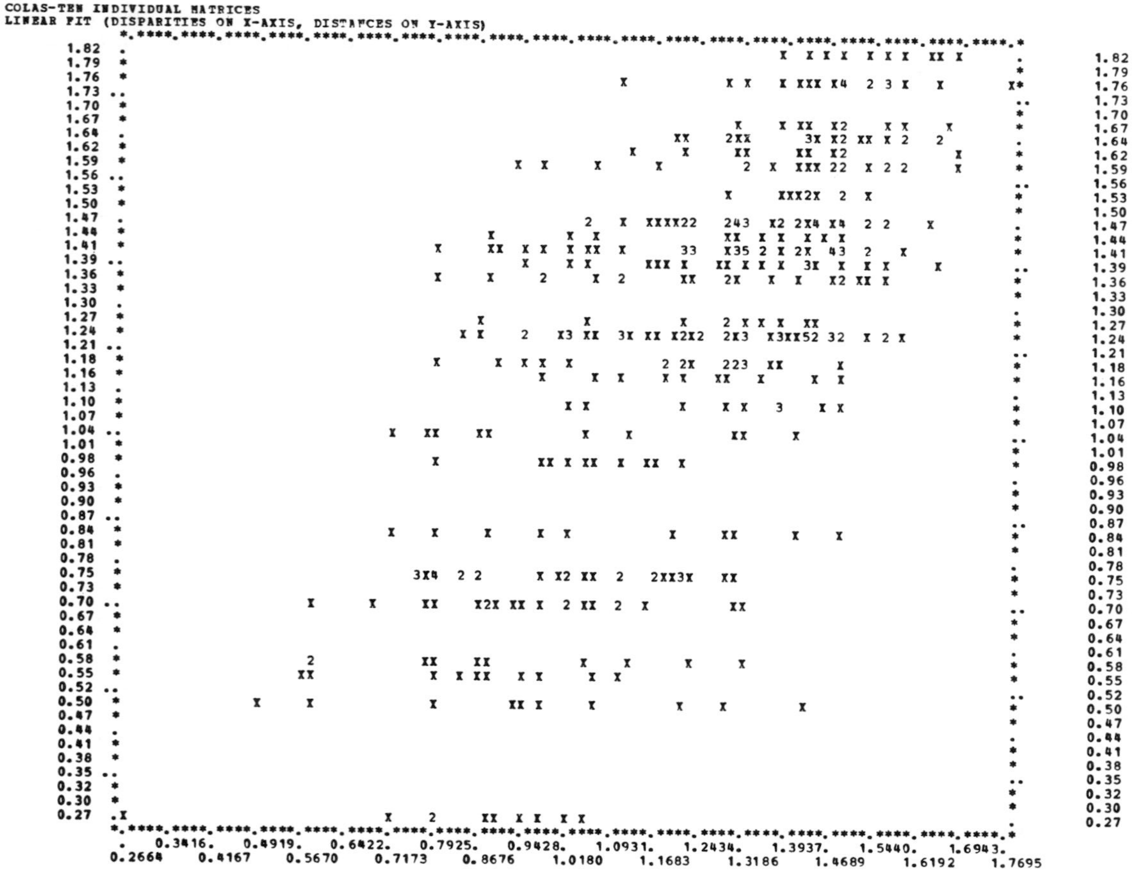

Figure 6.3(c). LINEAR FIT presents the distances found by POLYCON as a function of the transformed cola data (disparities).

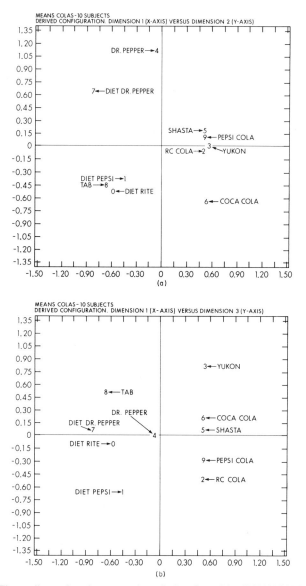

Figure 6.4. Three-dimensional nonmetric solution found by POLYCON for mean data on 10 colas. Points are specified by numbers as indicated on the LABEL card. (a) Dimension 1 versus dimension 2. (b) Dimension 1 versus dimension 3.

1. Metric versus nonmetric scaling
2. Analysis of mean (externally averaged) data versus simultaneous analysis of internally averaged data, that is, classical multidimensional scaling (CMDS) versus replicated multidimensional scaling (RMDS).

The mean analyses commenced at four dimensions and proceeded through to one dimension while the replicated analyses commenced at five dimensions. A five-dimensional solution has 50 coordinates for 10 stimuli. The mean similarity matrix contains only 45 data elements so it is meaningless to search for a five-dimensional solution in the analysis of the mean data.

Metric versus Nonmetric for Mean Data

The decrease in STRESS(2) with increasing dimensionality for metric (use ANALYSIS parameter POLYNOMIAL(1)), and nonmetric solutions is shown below:

	Dimensionality			
	1	2	3	4
Stress (metric)	.776	.508	.319	.231
Stress (nonmetric)	.638	.357	.204	.117

The nonmetric solution reveals, as expected, lower stress at each dimensionality. The decrease in STRESS(2) is fairly smooth over the four dimensions with no sharp elbow in the curve to suggest appropriate dimensionality.

The stimulus spaces from metric and nonmetric solutions are very similar and require no rotation for interpretation. In the three-dimensional solution, Dimension 1 separates the diet and nondiet colas. Dimension 2 separates the two Dr. Pepper colas (cherry flavor) from the remaining eight (cola flavor). Dimension 3 to some extent appears to represent a manufacturer flavor type. Pepsi Cola and Diet Pepsi, RC and Diet Rite, Dr. Pepper and Diet Dr. Pepper, and Coca-Cola and Tab are paired somewhat on this dimension. When a fourth dimension is added, the stimulus order on Dimension 4 is similar in the metric and nonmetric solution (RC, Shasta, and Tab clearly separated from Yukon and Diet Pepsi); however, there is no obvious interpretation. For this reason, a three-dimensional solution was considered reasonable. Figure 6.4(a) and (b) shows the three dimensional nonmetric solution.

Metric versus Nonmetric (Ten Replications)

The decrease in stress with increasing dimensionality for metric and nonmetric solutions is shown as follows:

	Dimensionality				
	1	2	3	4	5
Stress (metric)	.893	.853	.816	.811	.790
Stress (nonmetric)	.840	.761	.736	.729	.708

The stress values are very large when the 10 matrices are analyzed simultaneously. Even the five-dimensional solution has a larger stress value than the one-dimensional solution for the externally averaged data shown. However, this does *not* mean that the externally averaged data provide a better representation of the stimuli because replicated and nonreplicated stress values cannot be compared with POLYCON. Stress values will inevitably increase as the number of matrices entered increases. Here, as with the mean data, the decrease in STRESS(2) with increasing dimensionality is relatively smooth. Also, the nonmetric solutions result in lower stress values.

The three dimensional metric and nonmetric spaces are virtually identical and require no rotation for interpretation. Dimension 1 separates the diet and nondiet colas. Dimension 2 separates the two Dr. Pepper colas from the remaining eight. Dimension 3 is related to manufacturer type. The stimulus space derived from simultaneous analysis of the individual matrices shown in Figure 6.5(a) and (b) is basically the same as that derived from externally averaged data in Figure 6.4(a) and (b). The three dimensions have the same interpretation. The only difference of note is the ordering of the five nondiet regular flavor colas on dimensions 1 and 2. The externally averaged data provides no separation of these colas from each other on dimension 1, and separates only Coca-Cola on dimension 2. The replicated analysis provides some separation of the five colas on both dimensions. External averaging probably compresses and obscures small differences which are perceived better by some individuals than others.

In this example the main features of the stimulus space are revealed whether the analysis is (*a*) metric or nonmetric, or (*b*) based on external averaging or simultaneous analyses of individual matrices. This indicates that the data are reasonably good for derivation of the stimulus space. However, as mentioned earlier, external averaging will have the tendency to obscure differences between more similar stimuli.

Table 6.1 shows the change in stress with dimensionality for each subject and gives some support to the selection of a three-dimensional stimulus space. For Subjects 5 and 6, minimum stress is achieved in one dimension. For Subject 4, minimum stress is achieved in two dimensions. Subject 1 has a dip at dimension 2. For Subject 8, the minimum stress is found in three dimensions. The other five subjects (2, 3, 7, 9, and 10) who continue

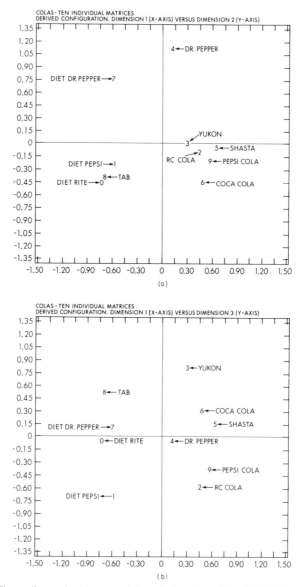

Figure 6.5. Three-dimensional nonmetric solution found by POLYCON for replicated data on 10 colas. (a) Dimension 1 versus dimension 2. (b) Dimension 1 versus dimension 3.

to show reduced stress with increasing dimensionality, however, have elbows in their stress curves after dimension 3 or a dip at dimension 3.

While POLYCON does not provide an individual differences analysis as such, examination of individual stress can provide some clues as to indi-

Table 6.1

Individual Stress(2) Values—Nonmetric Analysis[a]

Subject	Dimension				
	1	2	3	4	5
1	.719	.693	.722	.667	.689
2	.969	.886	.778	.749	.727
3	.980	.897	.813	.773	.784
4	.755	.661	.680	.744	.685
5	.599	.663	.748	.695	.664
6	.573	.650	.699	.658	.661
7	.979	.846	.790	.775	.760
8	.927	.685	.621	.709	.652
9	.777	.758	.691	.700	.656
10	.978	.813	.794	.803	.783

[a] The dimensionality of minimum stress for each subject is underlined with a solid line. The dimensionality which has an elbow in the stress versus dimensionality curve or a local minimum for stress is underlined with a broken line.

vidual differences. For Subjects 5 and 6 the diet–nondiet dimension seems all important. Other subjects show larger stress reductions than others (e.g., compare Subjects 7 and 8) with the introduction of dimension 2. The distinction cherry cola–regular cola, therefore, holds relatively different importance for these subjects.

6.4. Food Flavors

This data set (Section 3.2) comprises similarity judgments for the odor of 14 food flavors. The 32 subjects include two groups, 16 students and 16 elderly people. These will be referred to as YOUNG and AGED, respectively.

Three nonmetric solutions are discussed: (a) mean data for the YOUNG alone, (b) mean data for the YOUNG and AGED together, and (c) individual data for the YOUNG and AGED analyzed together.

Mean Data for YOUNG (Nonmetric)

The decrease in stress with dimensionality is:

	Dimensions				
	1	2	3	4	5
Stress	.396	.255	.149	.105	.083

A two- or three-dimensional solution appears appropriate. The first dimension of the three-dimensional stimulus space separates the five fruit flavors from the other flavors. Meat (bacon, chicken, and beef) and vegetables (potato and green bean) are at the other extreme. Butter, chocolate, corn, and tomato flavors are in between. The second dimension separates the vegetables from the meats. While the third dimension separates butter from chocolate and chicken, no obvious flavor typology is apparent. The order of the stimuli on the third dimension is:

Stimuli	Coordinates on dimension 3
Chicken	0.51
Beef, chocolate, cherry	0.33, 0.30, 0.26
Potato, green bean, lime, grape	0.12, 0.12, 0.08, 0.03
Apple, strawberry	−0.04, −0.11
Corn	−0.19
Bacon	−0.36
Tomato	−0.47
Butter	−0.57

Since the third dimension reveals no new interpretable arrangement of the stimuli, a two-dimensional solution is appropriate. The two-dimensional solution is almost identical to that reported below in Figure 6.6.

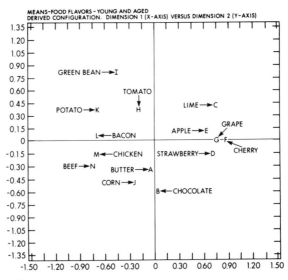

Figure 6.6. Two-dimensional nonmetric solution found by POLYCON for mean data of young and aged subjects on 14 food flavors.

Mean data for YOUNG and AGED (Nonmetric)

The change in stress with dimensionality for the mean similarity judgments of the YOUNG and AGED data combined is given below:

	Dimensions				
	1	2	3	4	5
Stress	.387	.239	.150	.108	.083

Incorporation of the AGED data into the mean dissimilarities has not markedly altered the stress for the solutions. Likewise, the stimulus spaces are very similar to those for the YOUNG alone. Apparently the increased noise contributed by the AGED data is averaged out in the mean data. The two-dimensional solution is shown in Figure 6.6.

Replicated data for YOUNG and AGED (Nonmetric)

In this analysis a two-dimensional solution is clearly the most that is appropriate:

	Dimensions		
	1	2	3
Stress	.869	.833	.831

The stimulus space is very similar to that developed from the mean data and is not reproduced here.

Comparison of the individual STRESS(2) values in the two-dimensional replicated solution is, however, of interest. Whereas those for the YOUNG range from .62 to .90, those for the AGED range from .75 to .99. The mean stress for the YOUNG is .73, for the AGED it is .93. Data for the AGED therefore fit the model less well than for the YOUNG. In the one-dimensional solution the stress range for the YOUNG is .68 to .93; for the AGED, .87 to .99. Mean stresses are .79 for the YOUNG and .95 for the AGED. The YOUNG, therefore, gain somewhat more from the addition of a second dimension than do the AGED.

6.5. Strawberry-Flavored Beverages

This data set (Section 3.3) is for 11 strawberry-flavored beverages varying only in sweetness and depth of color. The 46 subjects were mothers of young children. With these stimuli in which only two attributes were varied, the opportunity exists of examining false higher dimensionality solutions.

Stress values for mean matrices found by metric and nonmetric analyses and for the replicated (nonmetric) analyses are:

	Dimensions				
	1	2	3	4	5
Stress (mean, metric)	.259	.223	.216	.176	.135
Stress (mean, nonmetric)	.205	.171	.139	.077	.070
Stress (replicated, nonmetric)	.562	.576	.579	.574	.537

Analysis of the replicated matrices clearly suggests that a one-dimensional solution is appropriate. Stress *increases* with a second dimension. The mean metric analysis suggests a possible second dimension. One might be tempted with the mean nonmetric analysis to seek a fourth dimension!

The one-dimensional solutions for the three analyses are identical. The drinks are ranked in order of sweetness. Further, the discrimination between the five sweetness levels is excellent. This can be determined since three stimuli (of different color depth) were included at 50% and 225% of normal sweetness and two stimuli at 75% and 150% of normal sweetness. The maximum distance between drinks of identical sweetness in the replicated analysis is .17 scale units. The minimum distance between drinks of different sweetness is .28 scale units. The coordinates for the five sweetness levels are:

Sweetness	Coordinates on dimension 1
225%	.94, .87, .83
150%	.55, .49
100%	−.01
75%	−.43, −.48
50%	−.83, −.92, −1.00

The second dimension in the replicated solution shows no obvious order. Color depth is not a dimension. Since the stress value *increased* with the addition of a second dimension, a search for meaning is, in any case, unlikely to be successful. The two-dimensional solutions provided for the mean data by both metric and nonmetric analyses, however, are somewhat similar to each other and totally different from the replicated analysis. The metric solution is shown in Figure 6.7. The second dimension appears to represent (roughly) increasing distance from the standard color. The 25% and 225% colors are furthest from the 100% standard. The 75% colors are closest to the standard. The effect seems confounded, however, by sweetness level since the 100% colors at extreme high or low sweetness are further removed than the 150% colors at intermediate sweetness. Overall, the dimension can perhaps be called "similarity to the standard (commercial) product." None of the higher-dimensional analyses reveal any further order in the data.

It is perhaps surprising that the second dimension, if real, emerged from the externally averaged data and not from analysis of the individual matrices. As will be seen later, the INDSCAL and ALSCAL analyses provide support for existence of the second dimension in this data set.

Finally the stress values for the replicated two-dimensional solution indicate fairly wide differences in ability to rank sweetness. Although the overall stress is .58, the range is from .45 to .87.

6.6. General Comments

POLYCON is a very flexible program with options which can be helpful to both the novice and the sophisticated user. Although it tends to use

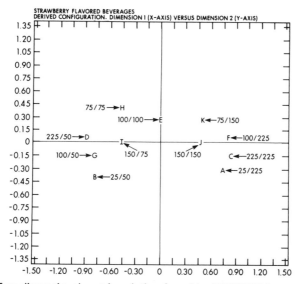

Figure 6.7. Two-dimensional metric solution found by POLYCON for mean data on 11 strawberry-flavored drinks (percentage color/percentage sweetness).

more computer time than some of the other programs, many of POLY-CON's alternatives, such as the partitioning option, are not available in most of the other programs.

References

Kruskal, J. B. Multidimensional scaling by optimizing goodness-of-fit to a nonmetric hypothesis. *Psychometrika*, 1964, *29*, 1–27. (a)

Kruskal, J. B. Nonmetric multidimensional scaling: A numerical method. *Psychometrika*, 1964, *29*, 115–129. (b)

Guttman, L. A general nonmetric technique for finding the smallest coordinate space for a configuration of points. *Psychometrika*, 1968, *33*, 469–506.

Young, F. W. TORSCA-9: A FORTRAN IV program for nonmetric multidimensional scaling. *Behavioral Science*, 1968, *13*, 343–344.

Young, F. W. A model for polynomial conjoint analysis algorithms. In R. N. Shepard, A. K. Romney, & S. Nerlove (Eds.), *Multidimensional scaling: Theory and applications in the behavioral sciences*. New York: Academic Press, 1972.

7

How to Use KYST-2

7.1. Setting Up a KYST MDS Job

KYST, like POLYCON, is a very versatile program which can analyze either a single matrix of similarity judgments (CMDS, see Section 4.1) or a number of matrices which are assumed to differ only in error of measurement (RMDS). The job control language is similar to POLYCON but some of the control phrases and formats are different. It is not necessary, for example, to label control cards with INPUT and ANALYSIS in KYST as required by POLYCON. In general, a control phrase may appear anywhere on a control card and is not restricted to being placed in particular columns on the card.

As with the description of POLYCON, this discussion will concentrate on the scaling of dissimilarity judgments. For other uses of KYST, see the users manual available from Bell Laboratories referenced in the Appendix. The version described here is KYST-2, February 1976.

Figure 7.1 shows the input deck for the nonmetric and metric analysis of dissimilarities of 10 cola drinks by 10 subjects (Section 3.1), and is an example of replicated scaling (RMDS). The input deck contains three types of cards.

1. Analysis control cards, cards 1 and 2 in the example
2. Output control cards, cards 3 and 4 in the example
3. Data cards, card 5 and subsequent cards

```
        5        10        15        20        25        30        35        40
DIMMAX = 5, DIMMIN = 1
REGRESSION = ASCENDING, SECONDARY
PRINT = DATA, PRINT = DISTANCES
PLOT = SCATTER = SOME, PLOT = CONFIGURATION = ALL
DATA, LOWERHALFMATRIX, DIAGON = ABSENT
COLAS - TEN INDIVIDUAL MATRICES
10    1    10
(2X, 9F2.0))
0116
018147
01563271
0187684471
016035219834
01849498579999
0150877973199245
019925539852179984
01169290837944241898
(9 MORE DATA MATRICES FOLLOW)
COMPUTE
REGRESSION = POLYNOMIAL = 1
PRINT = NODATA
COMPUTE
STOP
```

Figure 7.1. Input deck of KYST control cards for cola study described in Section 3.1.

As with POLYCON, the final two cards are COMPUTE and STOP. Different analyses may be performed on the same or different data during a run by placing new analysis control cards and, optionally, new data cards between COMPUTE cards, see Figure 7.1.

KYST is limited to 1800 data points (which is rather small compared to other programs) and six dimensions. This amount of data points means a limit, for example, of one lower half similarity matrix of 60 stimuli (1770 points), or 20 replications on 13 stimuli (1560 points). Twenty replications on 14 stimuli give 1820 points, which exceeds the limit. Up to 100 stimuli can be used with an incomplete data matrix having no more than 1800 data values.

Analysis Control Cards

Card 1. DIMENSION card: This shows the maximum and minimum number of dimensions required in the analysis, in this case five and one. Unless specified by DIMDIF = integer, each succeeding analysis will be performed in one less dimension. The equal signs and commas are optional. They improve visual clarity but are interpreted as blanks. Blanks may be freely inserted at the natural places for visual appearance. Thus the two following cards are equivalent:

DIMMAX = 5, DIMMIN = 1, DIMDIF = 1
DIMMAX   5   DIMMIN   1

With DIMDIF = 2, solutions would be provided in five, three, and one dimensions.

If the dimensions card is omitted, the default option provides only a two-dimensional solution.

Card 2. ANALYSIS type: The example shows that the regression is ASCENDING, that is, that data values are treated as dissimilarities and thus large values correspond to large distances in the derived space. This is the default option and may be omitted. The converse (large data values correspond to small distances) is specified by REGRESSION = DESCENDING.

SECONDARY indicates that ties in the data will be left tied. In contrast to POLYCON, this is not the default option. The default option in KYST is PRIMARY, that is, ties are broken.

Like POLYCON, KYST offers a variety of regression types. Unless specified, the regression is monotone which corresponds to nonmetric scaling. If metric scaling is required, this is most often called by the control phrase REGRESSION = POLYNOMIAL = 1. Figure 7.1 shows how to call for a metric analysis after a nonmetric analysis by placing this card after the first COMPUTE card and before a second one.

Output Control Cards

With no output control cards KYST will provide a list of analysis and data control cards, a history of the analysis, the coordinates for the final configuration, scatter plots, and configuration plots. Since this is all that is normally required, print and plot cards may be omitted; however, we show here how they can be used.

Card 3. PRINT card: The data will not be printed unless PRINT = DATA is entered. If data listings are not required for subsequent analyses of the same data deck, enter PRINT = NODATA before the next COMPUTE card.

PRINT = DISTANCES provides a list of data values in order of size, the stimulus pair they pertain to, the distances between these stimuli in the configuration, and the regression value (DHAT or disparity) for that distance. Again this will not be provided unless called for.

On the other hand, a history of the computation through each iteration is provided unless PRINT = NOHISTORY is entered.

Note that for each print option the word PRINT must be repeated as in the example.

Card 4. PLOT card: The phrases PLOT = SCATTER = SOME, PLOT = CONFIGURATION = ALL shown in Figure 7.1 are adequate for most analyses. The scatter plots show distances and disparities versus data.

Additionally, if solutions are determined in more than one dimension, a plot of stress versus dimensions is provided automatically.

Either scatter or configuration plots may be totally suppressed by PLOT = SCATTER = NONE   or   PLOT = CONFIGURATION = NONE. Configuration plotting may be limited by PLOT = CONFIGURATION = SOME. With this option, each dimension is plotted against only one other dimension unless there is an odd number of dimensions in which case dimension 1 is plotted with both dimensions 2 and 3. In a five-dimensional solution, for example, this option reduces the number of configuration plots from 10 to 3.

Data Cards

Card 5.   DATA shape: This is a mandatory card which must precede the rest of the data deck and must contain the word DATA. The shape of the data and presence or absence of a diagonal can be put on this same card or a separate preceding card. Depending on how the similarities data are key punched, the three alternative cards for full as well as half matrices are:

DATA,MATRIX
DATA,LOWERHALFMATRIX,DIAGON = ABSENT
DATA,UPPERHALFMATRIX,DIAGON = PRESENT

Card 6.   TITLE card: This provides the title which will be printed before the history and with each configuration plot.

Card 7.   Parameter card indicating size of data: This is in I3 format and must contain three integers. The first integer which must end in column 3 shows the number of rows in the matrix. Note that this is the number of rows in a dissimilarity (or similarity) matrix with the diagonal present. Even though data are entered with DIAGON = ABSENT the integer punched must correspond to the full matrix size. Similarity data on 10 stimuli provides nine rows of data but the integer to be punched is 10.

The second integer which must end in column 6 shows the number of replications for each subject. With one data set for each subject as is normally the case 1 is punched in column 6.

The third integer which must end in column 9 shows the number of subjects, in this example, 10.

Card 8.   FORMAT card: Use a floating-point FORTRAN format, for example, (9F2.0), which corresponds to the longest row of data.

Data Cards.   These are entered subject by subject.

Card 9. COMPUTE card: COMPUTE starts the computation. Every-thing relevant to the analysis must come before this card.

Card 10. New ANALYSIS card: The example shows a request for a new analysis on the same data set. REGRESSION = POLYNOMIAL = 1 calls for a metric analysis.

Card 11. New PRINT card: PRINT = NODATA suppresses relisting of the data.

Card 12. A COMPUTE card for the new job.

Card 13. STOP card: STOP on the card signals the end of the computer run and is mandatory.

As in the example, other KYST jobs may be run by inserting new control cards before the STOP card. If no new data are entered, the new job is run on the initial data deck. Each new job requires a COMPUTE card to start the computation.

Other Analysis Options

As with POLYCON, city block and general Minkowski metrics are avail-able. The appropriate control phrase entered on an analysis card is:

R = number with decimal point,
for example, $R = 1.0$ for city block.

Computation is slower for Minkowski metrics other than $R = 2.0$, (the de-fault Euclidean option), and $R = 1.0$ (city-block distance).

In addition to the default option for stress, SFORM1, an alternative formula SFORM2 may be specified. Selection of SFORM1 or SFORM2 indicates which of Kruskal's two stress formulas are to be minimized.

Like POLYCON, the default option for developing an initial configuration uses the classical Torgerson scaling technique followed by one iteration of the quasi-nonmetric Young method to improve it. A second option is to use RANDOM = integer, small values, any under 100 are suggested. This is useful if solutions with local minima are suspected. Use of a different integer for each run will produce different initial starting configurations.

A third option is to enter a starting configuration using the control phrase CONFIGURATION, followed by a title card, followed by a parameter card in 2I3 format, followed by the configuration itself. The first parameter shows the number of points in the configuration; the second, the number of di-mensions. The next card is a FORTRAN format statement showing the format for the coordinates of one point. The subsequent cards give the configuration itself with a new card for each point.

If desired, the first several points may be fixed (prevented from changing) during the scaling by use of the control phrase FIX = integer. The number of points indicated by the integer value remain fixed. The points one wishes to fix must be entered first in the configuration deck. Even with this option, these coordinates may not appear in the final configuration as entered, since they will be subjected to standardization and rotation unless the phrase COORDINATES = AS-IS is also entered.

The default option which provides the final form of the configuration sets the centroid to the origin, the mean square distance of the points from the centroid to 1, and rotates the configuration so that its principal components lie along the coordinate axes. Standardization and rotation may be suppressed by the AS-IS phrase above. Rotation alone may be suppressed by COORDINATES = STANDARDIZE.

There is an option in KYST, as there is in POLYCON, that permits partitioning the data into subsets or sublists with a separate regression performed on each sublist. This option is useful when elements of separate sublists are not measured under the same conditions (e.g., sublists were gathered on different days).

Punch Option

The only punched output available is the coordinates of the final configuration. These may be obtained by use of the control phrase CARDS.

Missing Data

KYST treats all numbers more negative than a very large negative threshold (-1.23×10^{20}) as missing data. Thus, by default all numbers, including zero, are analyzed. If the user wishes to change this threshold this is indicated by:

CUTOFF = number with decimal point

If zeros in the data should not be analyzed, a positive value of CUTOFF should be used.

7.2. Understanding KYST Output

The standard KYST output contains three main parts—a full history of the analysis, plots of the configuration, and scatter plots. In the history

KYST provides more information about progress toward convergence than POLYCON but no information (which POLYCON does) about how well each subject's data fit the solution. A final plot of stress versus dimensions is an initial guide to the appropriate dimensionality.

Figure 7.2(a) and (b) shows the first two pages of a KYST output. The first page shows the analysis, output, and data control cards. The second page shows the history of the computation, reason for termination (e.g., minimum was achieved), and final configuration coordinates. The latter are standardized with the centroid at the origin and the mean square distance set equal to 1.

The history of computation shows eight values for each iteration. The meaning of these, which most users may skip, is:

STRESS	Stress calculated by stress formula 1
SRAT	Stress ratio. Shows how fast stress is decreasing
SRATAV	Another indicator of how fast stress is decreasing
CAGRGL	Cosine of the angle between a gradient and the previous gradient
COSAV	Weighted average of CAGRGL values
ACOSAV	Weighted average of absolute value of CAGRGL values
SFGR	Scale factor, essentially length of the gradient. This is zero at a minimum configuration
STEP	Shows the stepsize for the iteration

When data are partitioned into groups (as when a separate regression is performed on each subject's matrix in the replicated case), the groups are referred to by SERIAL numbers 1,2, . . . , etc. In this case, the default option does not partition the data so all 10 subject matrices with 45 values each are treated as one group. (Thus, COUNT refers to the 450 data points.) If the partitioning option SPLIT = BYGROUPS had been used to cause a separate regression on each subject's data, there would have been 10 values under SERIAL (1 . . . 10), under COUNT(each value would be 45), and under STRESS (values of stress for each of the 10 subjects). REGRESSION ASCENDING indicates that large data values correspond to large distances in the derived space. COEFFICIENTS refers to coefficients of the polynomial transformation and can be ignored by the average user.

The next page, unless the PRINT = DISTANCE option is used, is the scatter plot, Figure 7.3. Two values are plotted on the page versus the original data. The first, using the symbol D, shows the distances and corresponds to POLYCON's MONOTONIC FIT plot. The second, using the symbol − , shows the transformed distances and corresponds to POLYCON's MONOTONIC TRANSFORMATION. Subsequent pages give configuration plots, see Figure 7.4, and finally a plot of stress versus dimensions.

7.3. Colas

This data set is from 10 subjects for 10 decarbonated commercial colas (see Section 3.1). Two nonmetric scalings are discussed here: (a) CMDS (see Section 4.1) of mean data (externally averaged by the experimenter prior to analysis), and (b) RMDS or simultaneous analysis of replicated data decks for 10 subjects. Both analyses used the control phrases:

DIMMAX = 5, DIMMIN = 1
REGRESSION = ASCENDING,SECONDARY

The first control phrase indicates that solutions were obtained in five through one dimension. The second control phrase treated the data as dissimilarities (large observations correspond to large distances) and kept ties tied.

Changes in stress (formula 1) with dimensionality for the two solutions are:

	Dimensions				
	1	2	3	4	5
Stress (CMDS, mean data)	.352	.140	.061	.029	.010
Stress (RMDS, 10 data matrices)	.497	.303	.199	.151	.120

Stress values are obviously greater when 450 data points are analyzed (10 replications) than 45 (mean data). Note that KYST will inappropriately yield a solution for the mean data from 10 colas in five dimensions, providing

```
DIMMAX=5,DIMMIN=1

REGRESSION=ASCENDING,SECONDARY

PRINT=DATA,PRINT=DISTANCES

PLOT=SCATTER=SOME,PLOT=CONFIGURATION=ALL

DATA,LOWERHALFMATRIX,DIAGON=ABSENT

COLAS-TEN INDIVIDUAL MATRICES
 10   1 10

(2X,9F2.0)

COMPUTE
```
                                          (a)

Figure 7.2. (a) First page of KYST printout which shows the analysis, output, and data control cards. (b) (facing page) Second page of KYST output which describes the history of the computation, reason for termination (e.g., minimum was achieved), and coordinates of the final configuration.

HISTORY OF COMPUTATION. N= 10.   THERE ARE 450   DATA VALUES, SPLIT INTO 1   LISTS.   DIMENSION = 3

ITERATION	STRESS	SRAT	SRATAV	CAGRGL	COSAV	ACSAV	SVGR	STEP
0	0.235	0.800	0.800	-0.000	-0.000	0.000	0.0046	0.0272
1	0.230	0.978	0.855	0.987	0.652	0.652	0.0042	0.0729
2	0.219	0.950	0.886	0.888	0.808	0.808	0.0031	0.2252
3	0.208	0.950	0.907	0.563	-0.097	0.646	0.0028	0.1229
4	0.203	0.975	0.929	-0.636	-0.452	0.639	0.0015	0.0516
5	0.201	0.990	0.949	0.051	-0.120	0.251	0.0006	0.0348
6	0.200	0.997	0.965	0.263	-0.132	0.259	0.0005	0.0323
7	0.200	0.999	0.976	-0.350	-0.186	0.319	0.0006	0.0187
8	0.200	0.999	0.983	-0.219	-0.208	0.253	0.0003	0.0112
9	0.199	1.000	0.989	0.202	-0.063	0.219	0.0002	0.0087
10	0.199	1.000	0.992	0.091	0.081	0.135	0.0002	0.0075
11	0.199	1.000	0.995	-0.116	-0.049	0.122	0.0001	0.0053
12	0.199	1.000	0.997	-0.154	-0.118	0.143	0.0001	0.0035
13	0.199	1.000	0.998	0.129	0.045	0.134	0.0001	0.0028
14	0.199	1.000	0.998	0.286	0.204	0.234	0.0001	0.0029
15	0.199	1.000	0.999	-0.001	0.069	0.080	0.0001	0.0025
16	0.199	1.000	0.999	-0.408	-0.246	0.296	0.0001	0.0014

MINIMUM WAS ACHIEVED

THE FINAL CONFIGURATION HAS BEEN ROTATED TO PRINCIPAL COMPONENTS.

THE FINAL CONFIGURATION OF 10 POINTS IN 3 DIMENSIONS HAS STRESS 0.199 FORMULA 1

LABEL FOR CONFIGURATION PLOTS

		FINAL CONFIGURATION	
		1	2	3

		1	2	3
A	1	-0.628	-0.136	-0.766
B	2	0.390	-0.392	-0.738
C	3	0.291	-0.191	0.967
D	4	0.011	-1.104	0.126
E	5	0.911	-0.199	0.073
F	6	0.527	0.729	-0.359
G	7	-0.868	-0.481	0.338
H	8	-0.578	0.632	0.591
I	9	-0.575	0.497	-0.577
J	10	-0.630	0.645	-0.373

DATA GROUP(S)

SERIAL COUNT STRESS REGRESSION COEFFICIENTS (FROM DEGREE 0 TO MAX OF 4)
1   450   0.199   ASCENDING

(b)

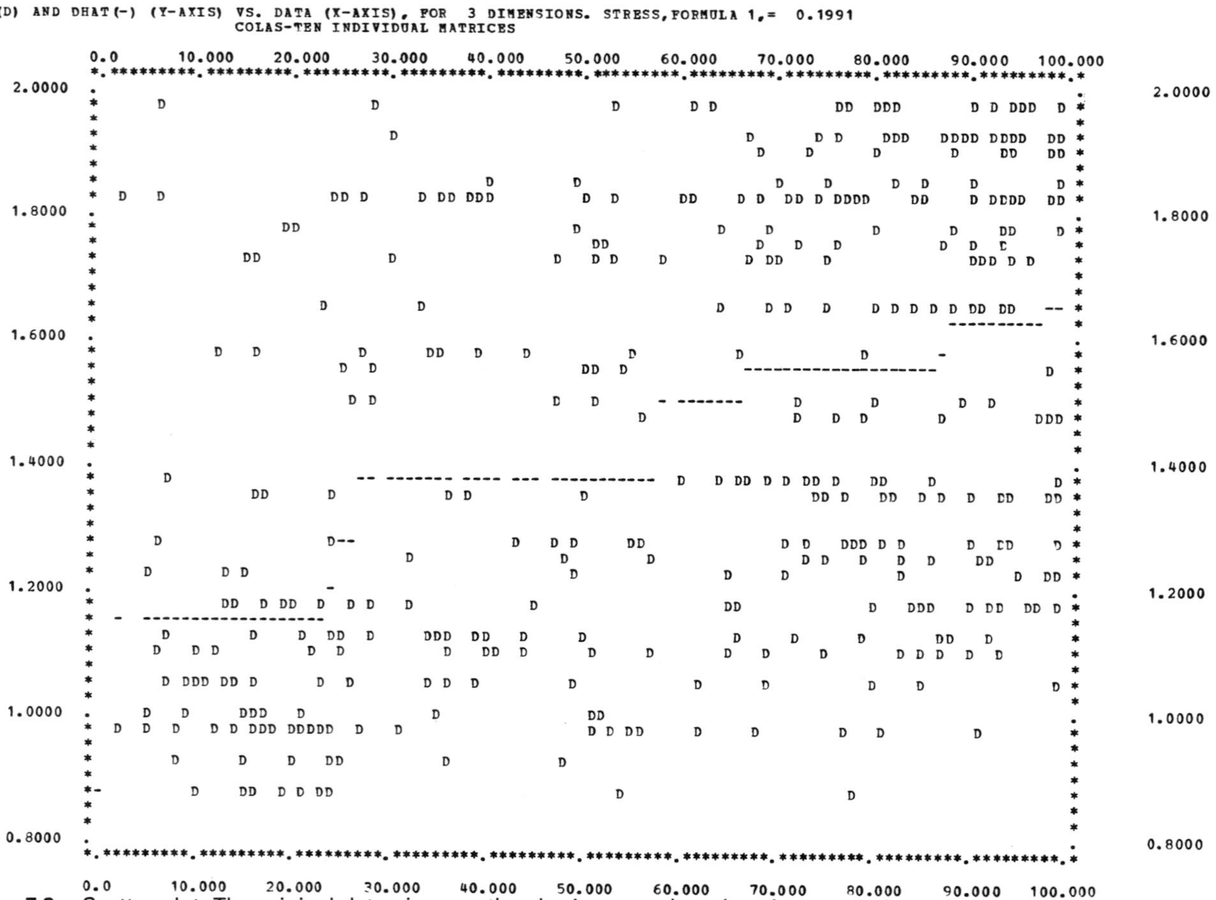

Figure 7.3. Scatter plot. The original data given on the abscissa are plotted against two values given on the ordinate. The symbol D refers to distances and the symbol - corresponds to transformed distances, that is, disparities.

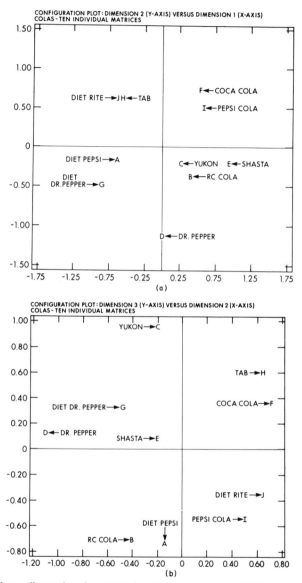

Figure 7.4. Three-dimensional nonmetric solution found by KYST for replicated data on the 10 colas. (a) Dimension 2 versus dimension 1. (b) Dimension 3 versus dimension 2.

50 coordinates, which is more than the original 45 data points. POLYCON has a built-in error message for the unwary experimenter. Three-dimensional solutions seem appropriate even though there were relatively few, 45, data values used in the CMDS analysis.

Figure 7.4(a) and (b) show plots of dimensions 1 versus 2 and 2 versus 3, respectively, for the three-dimensional solution for the replicated data. Dimension 1 separates the diet colas, on the left, from the nondiet colas on the right.

Dimension 2 appears to be a cherry–regular flavor dimension: Dr. Pepper, a cherry-flavored cola is at the bottom extreme in Figure 7.4(a); Tab, Diet Rite, Coca-Cola, and Pepsi Cola are at the top. Diet Dr. Pepper is next closest to Dr. Pepper on dimension 2.

Dimension 3 in Figure 7.4(b) appears to be associated with manufacturer's flavor. Products produced by a specific manufacturer, such as Pepsi and Diet Pepsi, RC and Diet Rite, Dr. Pepper and Diet Dr. Pepper, Coca Cola and Tab, have fairly close coordinates on dimension 3. This interpretation is fairly weak here, but appears with greater clarity in the INDSCAL analysis in Chapter 8.

Solutions for the mean data (CMDS) are basically similar to those produced for the replicated data (RMDS) and not reproduced here. The major difference is that fairly similar stimuli, for example, Pepsi, Shasta, RC, and Yukon, are less well separated from each other in the mean data analysis than with the replicated data analysis. External averaging probably compresses and obscures small differences that can be maintained with replicated analysis.

7.4. Food Flavors

This data set (Section 3.2) comprises similarity judgments for the odor of 14 food flavors from 32 subjects, 16 young college students and 16 elderly people. We discuss here only the nonmetric solution for the mean data (CMDS) for the entire group.

The analysis control phrases were:

DIMMAX = 5, DIMMIN = 1
REGRESSION = ASCENDING,SECONDARY

Solutions were derived therefore in five through one dimensions. The data were dissimilarities (large observations corresponding to large distances), and ties were left tied.

The change in stress (formula 1) with dimensionality is:

	Dimensions				
	1	2	3	4	5
Stress	.214	.101	.054	.032	.023

Since no elbow occurred in the curve which plots dimensions versus stress, each of the five solutions was examined to determine the appropriate dimensionality.

The two-dimensional KYST solution is shown in Figure 7.5. It is identical, except for reflection, to the POLYCON solution, and has the same value, .101, for stress (formula 1). The first dimension of the three-dimensional solution separates fruits, on the left, from meats and vegetables, on the right. Butter and chocolate are in the center. The second dimension separates the tarter flavors from the sweeter, lime from strawberry, green beans from corn, and also vegetables such as potato and green beans from the meats.

The third dimension separates butter from chocolate but does not provide any obvious flavor groupings. The order of the stimuli on dimension 3 is:

Stimuli	Coordinates on dimension 3
Butter	.73
Tomato	.62
Corn	.26
Bacon	.17
Strawberry, lime	.14, .10
Apple, green bean	− .07, − .09
Grape, potato	− .15, − .17
Chocolate, cherry, beef	− .35, − .36, − .38
Chicken	− .44

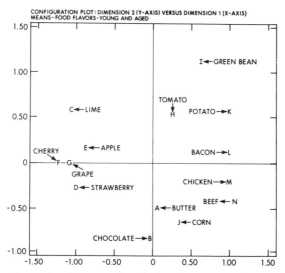

CONFIGURATION PLOT: DIMENSION 2 (Y-AXIS) VERSUS DIMENSION 1 (X-AXIS)
MEANS-FOOD FLAVORS-YOUNG AND AGED

Figure 7.5. Two-dimensional nonmetric solution found by KYST for young and aged subjects on 14 food flavors.

While this dimension does not appear interpretable, it is interesting to note that the order of the stimuli follows closely that provided by the three-dimensional POLYCON analysis (Section 6.4). This coincidence is most likely due to the similarity of KYST and POLYCON rather than meaning-fulness of the third dimension. The fourth and fifth dimensions were not interpretable.

It is not possible to compare KYST and POLYCON replicated solutions for the 32 subjects since the number of observations, 2912, exceeds the KYST maximum of 1800.

7.5. Strawberry-Flavored Beverages

This data set (Section 3.3) is for 11 strawberry-flavored drinks varying only in sweetness and depth of color. The 46 subjects were mothers of young children.

With these stimuli, in which two attributes are controlled and there are no other variables, the opportunity exists for examining solutions with dimensionality higher than two which are unlikely to be appropriate.

We discuss here only the nonmetric solution for the mean data for the entire group.

The analysis control phrases were:

DIMMAX = 5, DIMMIN = 1
REGRESSION = ASCENDING,SECONDARY

Solutions were derived therefore in five through one dimensions. The data were dissimilarities (large observations corresponding to large distances), and ties were left tied.

The change in stress (formula 1) with dimensionality is:

	Dimensions				
	1	2	3	4	5
Stress	.113	.078	.047	.025	.017

Stress values here are all so small that it is difficult to see an elbow in the stress versus dimensions plot. The one-dimensional solution orders the beverages in terms of sweetness:

Sweetness	Coordinates for one-dimensional solution
225%	−1.11, −1.16, −1.30
150%	−.74, −.80
100%	.06
75%	.55, .74
50%	1.13, 1.29, 1.33

This order also appears in the first dimension of the five-dimensional solution. Thus, although a five-dimensional solution is inappropriate, the first dimension nevertheless is correct and not distorted by the search for higher dimensionality.

Application of KYST to similarity judgments provides a consistent relative ranking of the beverages on a sweetness scale without requiring direct ratings of sweetness. The maximum distance between beverages of identical sweetness in the one-dimensional solution is .20 scale units. The minimum distance between beverages of different sweetness is .31 scale units which occurs between the two highest sweetness levels.

The two-dimensional solution is shown in Figure 7.6. Dimension 2 does not order the beverages in terms of color depth as shown:

Coordinate on dimension 2	Color	Sweetness
.69	25%	50%
.42	225%	225%
.37	25%	225%
.31	75%	150%
.21	225%	50%
.14	100%	225%
−.16	75%	150%
−.20	150%	75%
−.32	150%	150%
−.65	75%	75%
−.82	100%	100%

The salient feature on dimension 2 is that the normal color–sweetness level, that commercially sold, is at one extreme while abnormally high or low values of sweetness or color are at the other. One could perhaps label this dimension, therefore, as a "familiarity" dimension or that "most like a normal strawberry-flavored soft drink." The familiarity dimension appears to be real because it appears in the POLYCON, INDSCAL, and ALSCAL analyses.

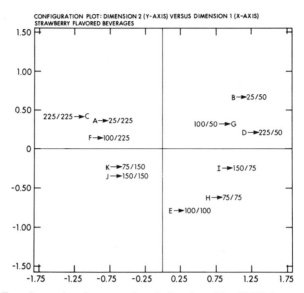

Figure 7.6. Two-dimensional nonmetric solution found by KYST for mean data on 11 strawberry-flavored drinks (percentage color/percentage sweetness).

While a search for color depth order was made in the higher dimensionality solutions, none was found. Therefore, the two-dimensional solution seems best even though it did not reveal an attribute order that was anticipated.

7.6. General Comments

Provided that the user does not require individual differences scaling and the number of observations does not exceed 1800, KYST (see Appendix) is an excellent MDS program. KYST provides a very clear Shepard diagram showing both distances and disparities against data (Figure 7.3). One feature of KYST that differs from POLYCON is that individual matrices in the replicated cases are assumed to be matrix unconditional (see Section 4.2) by default.

8

How to Use INDSCAL and SINDSCAL

8.1. Setting Up an INDSCAL Job

This chapter describes applications of INDSCAL and a specialized version (SINDSCAL) to two or more matrices of dissimilarity judgments. Individual differences models require at least two data matrices to provide dimension weights as well as stimulus coordinates. INDSCAL contains no simple provision for analysis of a single data matrix. INDSCAL is a very popular program and numerous modified versions exist. We strongly recommend acquisition of an official Bell Laboratories version (see Appendix). The one we have used is the IBM version from Bell Laboratories which is limited to 99 data matrices, a maximum of 10 dimensions, and a maximum of 45 stimuli, with the constraint that the product of the number of subjects and the square of the number of stimuli must be less than or equal to 18,000. For example, with 20 stimuli, analysis would be limited to 18,000/400 = 45 subjects' data.

Unlike POLYCON and KYST, INDSCAL does not use a free format job control language. Instead, data and analysis parameters are specified in a fixed format on a series of cards which must be in a fixed order. The only alphanumeric information, apart from the data format, found in an INDSCAL input deck is the job title. Figure 8.1 shows the input deck for the cola analysis.

Card 1. PARAMETER card: For most jobs you will need only to alter the maximum number of dimensions. The other 12 parameters are rarely changed for the majority of applications. The format is 10I4, I6, 2I4. The parameters are as follows:

Identifier	Columns	
N	1–4	Gives the number of ways (see Section 4.1) of the input matrices, here three, that is, people by stimuli by stimuli.
MAXDIM	5–8	The maximum dimensionality sought must be less than or equal to 10.
MINDIM	9–12	The minimum dimensionality sought must be greater than or equal to 1, and less than or equal to MAXDIM.
IRDATA	13–16	Describes data type 1 Lower half similarity matrices 2 Lower half dissimilarity matrices 3 Euclidean distances 4 Lower half correlation matrices 5 Lower half covariance matrices with diagonals 6 Full symmetric similarity matrix 7 Full symmetric dissimilarity matrix Enter appropriate number, in this case, 2.
MAXIT (also called ITMAX)	17–20	The maximum number of iterations must be less than or equal to 50. In many cases, iterations cease well before this (see CRIT, Card 4). We recommend 50.
INORM (also called ISET)	21–24	1 Equate matrix 2 to matrix 3 after the first set of computations and iterate again keeping these matrices constant. This is the normal mode for three-way symmetric data. 0 Do not set matrix 2 equal to matrix 3.
IOY	25–28	0 Compute all dimensions simultaneously. This is the normal mode. 1 Do separate one-dimensional solutions. This option can be used if analyzing a single matrix, but we do not recommend it.
IDR	29–32	1 Compute correlations between data and solutions. Use this option. 0 Do not compute correlations.
ISTI (also called ISAM)	33–36	1 Keep matrices 2 and 3 unchanged and solve for remaining matrices. Use this when it is desired to fit subject weights to an already obtained stimulus space. 0 Solve for all matrices. This is the normal mode for MDS.
IPUNSP	37–40	−1 An option to punch scalar product matrices on cards. 0 Do not punch. Use this option.
IRN	41–46	Random number for generating the random initial matrices. Enter a five-digit odd integer. Make sure there is an odd digit in column 46. If a target configuration will be read in, enter 0 in column 46.

(cont'd.)

Identifier	Columns	
IVEC (option in some versions)	47–50	0 To read in a matrix. 1 To read in Tricon type output (see Green and Rao, 1972).
IT (option in some versions)	51–54	This is the symbol for the read device at your installation. Enter appropriate number in column 54.

Card 2. The title card is restricted to one card and 72 columns.

Card 3. This gives the number of subjects NWT(1) and the number of stimuli NWT(2) and NWT(3). The format is 7I4, but for three-way symmetric data, only three integers are needed.

Card 4. This gives the criterion for ending the iterations, CRIT. Mathematically, if $[y - \hat{y}(I - 1)]^2 - [y - \hat{y}(I)]^2 \leqslant$ CRIT, iteration stops where: y = original data, $\hat{y}$ = estimated data, I = an iteration number.

A value of .001 is the smallest value the program will allow and is recommended.

Card 5. The format card for reading in the data in a FORTRAN F format.

Card 6. The data set entered subject by subject.

Card 7. Present only if IRN = 0. These will be the format and coordinates for an a priori stimulus configuration. Coordinates are read in by dimension. After the format card the next card gives all stimulus coordinates

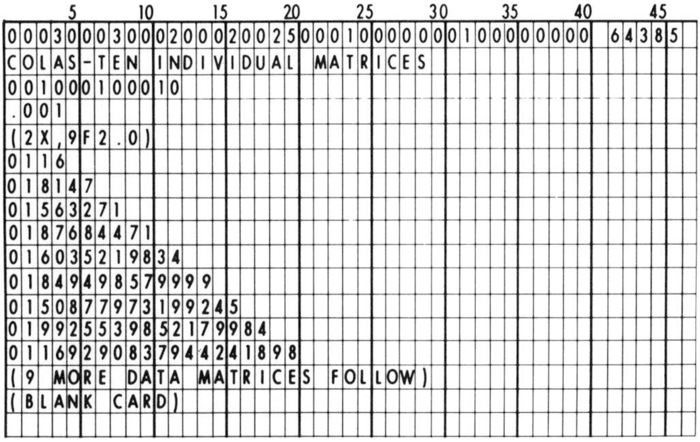

Figure 8.1. Input deck for cola analysis by INDSCAL.

on dimension 1, the following card all stimulus coordinates on dimension 2, and so on.

Card 8.   Blank or repeat of cards 1 through 7. A blank card must be the last data card to signal the end of all computation.

8.2. Understanding INDSCAL Output

INDSCAL output contains seven parts:

1. A listing of the job title, parameters used, and matrix sizes
2. Several pages showing the values of each matrix through the iteration procedure
3. A history of the computation
4. Subject weight and stimulus coordinate matrices
5. Sums of products for the preceding two matrices
6. Plots of subject weights and stimulus configurations
7. Correlations between computed scores and original data

The printout begins with: INDIVIDUAL DIFFERENCES ANALYSIS USING CANONICAL DECOMPOSITION OF 3 WAY TABLE IN N DIMENSIONS. If solutions in several dimensions were called for, the first N is MAXDIM, and later sections of the printouts move through lower dimensions to MINDIM. For example, a four-dimensional solution will be printed before a three-dimensional solution. JOB TITLE is then given followed by a listing of the PARAMETERS and MATRIX SIZES (number of subjects and stimuli).

The next three to six pages of printout show the values of each matrix through the iteration procedure. While these are of perhaps theoretical interest to the programmer, they can be ignored or deleted for the average practitioner (ourselves included). Finally, the HISTORY OF COMPUTATION appears showing the overall correlation between original and computed distances, (Y(DATA) and YHAT), the square of the correlation, and the residual variance (1-R**2). At this point JOB TITLE is repeated (perhaps with the knowledge that the previous pages will be discarded). The practical output of the analysis follows (Figure 8.2).

NORMALIZED A MATRICES

MATRIX 1 gives the subject weights W for each dimension. There should be few if any negative weights. Negative weights have no conceptual meaning and should be considered as zero. Many large negative weights indicate that the dimensionality is too high, that the INDSCAL model is inappro-

COLAS-TEN INDIVIDUAL MATRICES

NORMALIZED A MATRICES

MATRIX   1

1	0.63600	0.34404	0.25248
2	0.19073	0.58033	0.38598
3	0.19595	0.73744	0.29552
4	0.66531	0.25070	0.42670
5	0.80621	0.07248	0.23908
6	0.79873	0.08349	0.26433
7	0.21039	0.65035	0.32371
8	0.42846	0.55952	0.40662
9	0.62916	0.20309	0.38978
10	0.20465	0.68979	0.22290

MATRIX   2

1	-0.33533	0.18274	0.37953
2	0.29926	0.24273	0.30893
3	0.18808	-0.10158	-0.55596
4	0.22448	-0.63063	0.28790
5	0.30484	0.15496	-0.06768
6	0.20093	0.11129	-0.37596
7	-0.32062	-0.57294	0.12459
8	-0.40174	0.13734	-0.38731
9	0.30862	0.27559	0.23300
10	-0.46850	0.20059	0.05296

MATRIX   3

1	-0.33533	0.18274	0.37953
2	0.29926	0.24273	0.30893
3	0.18808	-0.10158	-0.55596
4	0.22448	-0.63063	0.28790
5	0.30484	0.15496	-0.06768
6	0.20093	0.11129	-0.37596
7	-0.320 62	-0.57294	0.12459
8	-0.40174	0.13734	-0.38731
9	0.30862	0.27559	0.23300
10	-0.46850	0.20050	0.05296

MATRIX   1

SUMS OF PRODUCTS

1	2.87541	1.41141	1.51304
2	1.41141	2.32710	1.34611
3	1.51304	1.34611	1.08090

SUM OF SQUARES=   6.28341

MATRIX   2

SUMS OF PRODUCTS

1	1.00000	0.03992	-0.00818
2	0.03992	1.00000	-0.08281
3	-0.00818	-0.08281	1.00000

SUM OF SQUARES=   2.99999

MATRIX   3

SUMS OF PRODUCTS

1	1.00000	0.03992	-0.00818
2	0.03992	1.00000	-0.08281
3	-0.00818	-0.08281	1.00000

SUM OF SQUARES=   2.99999

Figure 8.2.   Printed output for cola analysis.

priate for this set of data, or that there is an error in the deck setup. For any given subject the sum of the squares of the weights across the dimensions gives an estimate of how well the weighted stimulus space fits an individual subject's data. A more direct measure of fit is given by correlations to be discussed later. Weights on an individual dimension of .2 or less are only adding 4% to the variance. Whether these are noise or small but meaningful contributions will depend on the stability of the data.

MATRIX 2 gives the stimulus coordinates. These are normalized on each dimension t such that:

$$\sum_i X_{it} = 0, \quad \sum_i X_{it}^2 = 1.$$

MATRIX 3 is a repeat of MATRIX 2.

Before looking closely at MATRIX 1 or MATRIX 2, it is worthwhile to look at the next two items, SUMS OF PRODUCTS for each of these matrices. The *main diagonal* of MATRIX 1, SUMS OF PRODUCTS, shows the sums of squares of subject weights for each dimension. These values when divided by NWT(1) (the number of subjects) show the relative importance of each dimension. These usually decrease moving from the upper left to the lower right. The off-diagonal elements can be ignored by most users. Underneath the SUMS OF PRODUCTS MATRIX is given SUM OF SQUARES of this main diagonal. This value divided by NWT(1) should be close to the final R^2 value found in HISTORY OF COMPUTATION (not shown).

The *off diagonal* elements of MATRIX 2, SUMS OF PRODUCTS, are important. These show the degree of correlation between the dimensions. If the dimensions are orthogonal, these values are zero. Large values indicate either strong coupling between dimensions or that the program may not have converged. If large values are found, particularly in solutions of high dimensionality, rerun the data starting at a lower dimensionality. The main diagonals are unity since the stimulus coordinates of matrix 2 are normalized to give $\Sigma_i X_{it}^2 = 1$. The SUM OF SQUARES that follows is the number of dimensions in that solution. The calculation is repeated for MATRIX 3. Following this are PLOTS of the subject weights for all pairs of dimensions and stimulus spaces for all pairs of dimensions.

The last page of the printout is labeled CORRELATIONS BETWEEN COMPUTED SCORES AND ORIGINAL DATA FOR SUBJECTS. The correlations are actually between the computed scores and scalar products derived from individual subject's original data. The average subject correlation coefficient is the simple arithmetic mean of the individual correlation coefficient. The mean square correlation coefficient is the square of the correlation between the derived scalar products and the estimated data.

Some Warnings about INDSCAL

1. There are several versions of INDSCAL, some official, some modified. We strongly recommend that a tape of the program is obtained from Bell Laboratories.

2. INDSCAL cannot easily provide a similarity space from the data for one individual.
3. Two-dimensional stimulus spaces derived when the program starts at two dimensions are not necessarily the same as those when the program is started at three dimensions. The main reason for this is that a local minimum has been reached in a higher dimensional solution, and then the lower-order dimensional solutions are not the optimal ones. Alternatively the lower-order solution itself may be at a local minimum.

8.3. Colas

This data set (Section 3.1) is from 10 subjects (5 male, 5 female) for 10 decarbonated commercial colas. The data illustrate differences in individual perceptions for the *relevance* of different attributes in judging degrees of similarity. It will be shown that for some individuals the distinction cherry cola–regular cola is more important than diet–nondiet. For others, the reverse is true.

The Stimulus Space

A three-dimensional solution is appropriate in terms of *explained variance* and interpretability. The three dimensions are orthogonal as shown by SUMS OF PRODUCTS, MATRIX 2:

```
1    1.00
2     .04    1.00
3    -.01    -.08    1.00
```

The off-diagonals are close to 0. The group stimulus space is shown in Figure 8.3(a) and (b).

Interpretation of dimensions 1 and 2 is straightforward. They are, respectively, diet–nondiet and cherry cola–regular cola. Diet drinks are on the left side of the space in Figure 8.3(a), nondiet drinks on the right. The two Dr. Pepper cherry colas are located in the lower half of the space. Dimension 3 is less obvious but appears to be another component of flavor quality associated with specific manufacturer's practices. Note the proximities of Coca-Cola–Tab, Pepsi Cola–Diet Pepsi, and Dr. Pepper–Diet Dr. Pepper in Figure 8.3(b).

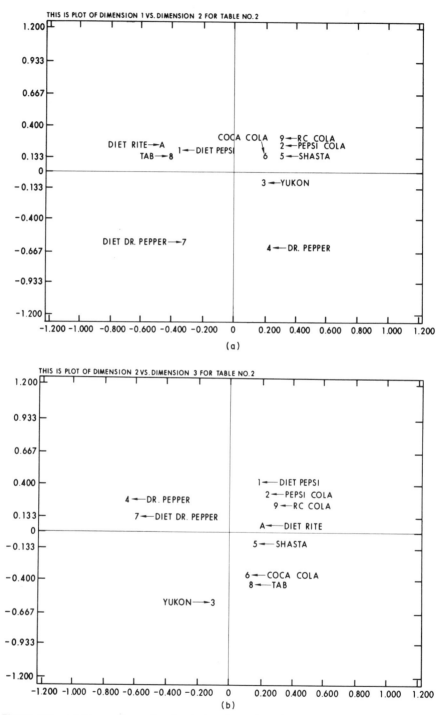

Figure 8.3. (a) Three-dimensional solution for colas: 1 versus 2 plane. (b) Three-dimensional solution for colas: 2 versus 3 plane.

The relative importance of the three dimensions for the group of 10 subjects as a whole (the diagonal of SUMS OF PRODUCTS, MATRIX 1) is:

Dimension	Sum of products
1	2.88
2	2.33
3	1.08

Dimensions 1 and 2 are therefore of similar importance to the hypothetical average subject. Dimension 3 is, however, of lesser importance. The perceptual space of the average subject would in fact be squashed on dimension 3 compared with the representations in Figure 8.3(b).

Individual Differences

The subject weights for the three dimensions of the cola space are shown in Figure 8.2 (MATRIX 1). Figure 8.4(a) and (b) shows the subject weights graphically.

One can calculate the perceptual spaces for individuals by multiplying the stimulus coordinates on each dimension by the square root of the subject weights for that dimension

$$y_{ijt} = \mathbf{W}_{it}^{1/2} \, x_{jt}$$

where y_{ijt} is the stimulus j coordinate for individual i on dimension t and x_{jt} is the jth stimulus coordinate on dimension t in the group stimulus space.

Figure 8.5(a) and (b) compares the perceptions for Subjects 2 and 9 for six of the colas on dimensions 1 and 2. Subject 2 emphasizes dimension 2, cherry versus regular more than dimension 1, whereas for subject 9 the reverse is true. Diet versus nondiet is more important. The stimulus coordinates for Subjects 2 and 9 are given in Table 8.1.

Interestingly, those subjects, Figure 8.4(a), who weight dimension 1 heavily (1, 4, 5, 6, and 9) are PTC tasters. PTC is a compound which tastes bitter to some and is tasteless to others. The remaining subjects, who give little weight to this diet–nondiet dimension, are nontasters of PTC.

8.4. Food Flavors

This data set (Section 3.2) is from 32 subjects (16 elderly, 16 young) for 14 food flavors. This example shows the effects of lack of ability to dis-

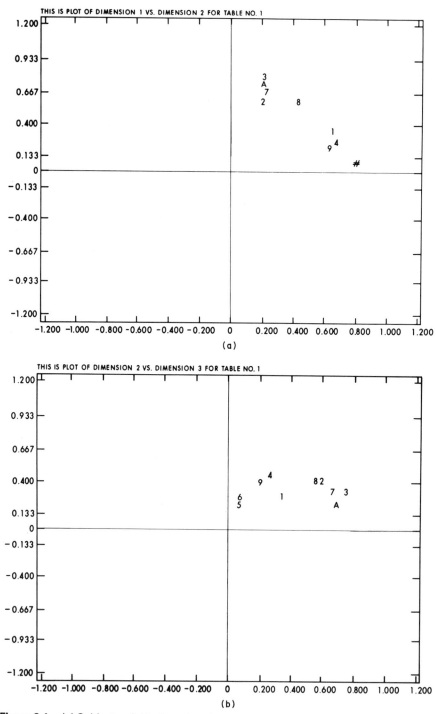

Figure 8.4. (a) Subject weights for colas: 1 versus 2 plane. # indicates a duplicate point for 5 and 6; (b) Subject weights for colas: 2 versus 3 plane.

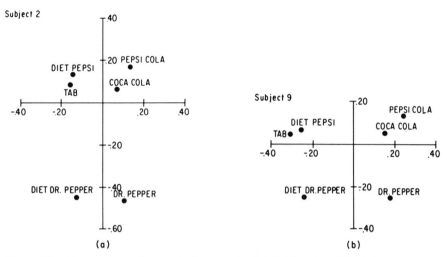

Figure 8.5. Comparison of perceptual spaces for (a) Subject 2 and (b) Subject 9 for six colas.

criminate by the elderly rather than differences in the relevance of the dimensions. The data were analyzed for both the 16 young subjects alone as well as for all 32 subjects.

The Stimulus Space

The common stimulus spaces from both groups were very similar. Two-dimensional solutions were selected because the addition of a third dimension added little to the explained variance.

	Explained variance (as a percentage)		
Group	Two dimensions	Three dimensions	Increase
Young	44	49	5
Young and elderly	35	40	5

The dimensions are not totally orthogonal; the off-diagonal element in SUMS OF PRODUCTS, MATRIX 2, is .30 ($\cos^{-1}$ 72.5°).

The stimulus space for the normal–elderly group is shown in Figure 8.6. Fruits fall in the upper-right quadrant, meats in the lower left. Chocolate and butter flavors come close together in the lower right. The corn flavor is more similar to butter and chocolate than it is to the other three vegetable flavors found in the upper left. The interest in this example, however, is more in how the different subject groups react to the stimuli than to the

Table 8.1
Stimulus Coordinates for Subjects 2 and 9

		Subject 2		Subject 9	
		$W_1 = .19$ $W_1^{1/2} = .44$ X_1	$W_2 = .58$ $W_2^{1/2} = .76$ X_2	$W_1 = .63$ $W_1^{1/2} = .79$ X_1	$W_2 = .20$ $W_2^{1/2} = .45$ X_2
Stimulus					
Diet Pepsi	1	-.15	.14	-.27	.08
Pepsi Cola	2	.13	.18	.24	.11
Yukon	3	.08	-.08	.15	-.05
Dr. Pepper	4	.10	-.48	.17	-.28
Shasta	5	.13	.12	.24	.07
Coca-Cola	6	.09	.08	.16	.05
Diet Dr. Pepper	7	-.14	-.44	-.25	-.25
Tab	8	-.17	.10	-.32	.06
RC	9	.14	.21	.25	.12
Diet Rite	10	-.20	.15	-.37	.09

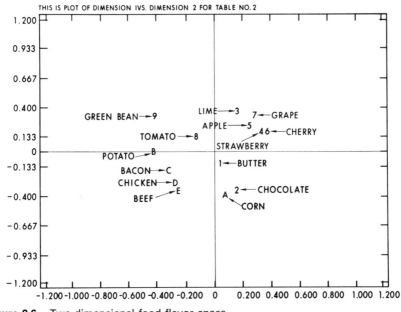

Figure 8.6. Two-dimensional food flavor space.

stimulus locations. With such a wide range of odors included in the stimulus set, only the grosser differences emerge.

Individual Differences

As shown earlier, the group stimulus space containing elderly subjects explains less of the variance in the original data than the space for the young alone. This suggests that either the elderly subjects used different dimensions than young, or that their data contain a great deal more noise. Higher-dimensionality solutions did not provide better correlations. Therefore, it is probable that as a group they were much less sensitive in differentiating the stimuli.

Whereas individual correlations for the young ranged from .45 to .81, those for the elderly ranged from .22 to .64. Some of the elderly subjects had higher correlations than two or three of the young subjects. This is to be expected. However, considering the groups as a whole, data from the young subjects are better represented by the space.

Figure 8.7 shows individual subject weights for the young–elderly space. Elderly subjects are circled and, as a group, are obviously less discriminating than the young. Elderly Subject H, for example, has such low weights

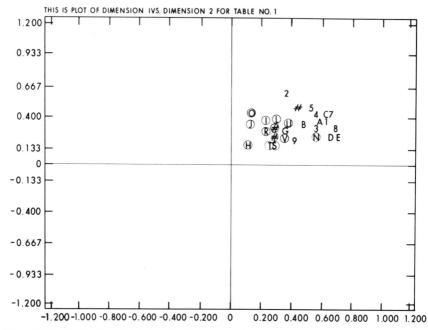

Figure 8.7. Subject weights for food flavors. Circles represent elderly; # overlapping points.

on both dimensions that she exhibits no real discrimination. On the other hand, elderly Subject N performs as well as the young.

8.5. Strawberry-Flavored Beverages

This data set (3.3) is for 11 strawberry-flavored drinks varying only in sweetness and depth of color. The 46 subjects were mothers of young children. Since the stimuli are known to vary in only two physicochemical dimensions, the stimulus space should be readily interpretable. As will be seen, this is not entirely so.

The two-dimensional solution accounts for about 68% of the variance. The MATRIX 1, SUMS OF PRODUCTS, is:

$$
\begin{array}{ccc}
1 & 3.09 & - \\
2 & - & 27.18 \\
\end{array}
$$

The fact that the subject weights for dimension 2 are larger than dimension 1 is of no concern. Some versions of the INDSCAL program do not necessarily rearrange the solution to show dimension 1 as that with the largest explained variance. The two dimensions are also not orthogonal. The MATRIX 2, SUMS OF PRODUCTS, off-diagonal element is $-.268$ ($\cos^{-1}$ 106°).

The order of the stimuli on dimension 2, which is almost nine times more important than dimension 1 is:

Sweetness	Number of stimuli	Dimension 2 coordinates		
225%	3	.354,	.320,	.309
150%	2	.284,	.257	
100%	1	.033		
75%	2	$-.159$,	$-.239$	
50%	3	$-.373$,	$-.392$,	$-.392$

Dimension 2 clearly reflects sweetness. Figure 8.8 shows the plot for the two-dimensional solution.

Dimension 1 does not indicate intensity of color. Both very pale (25%) and very intense (225%) beverages lie adjacent to each other. The beverages

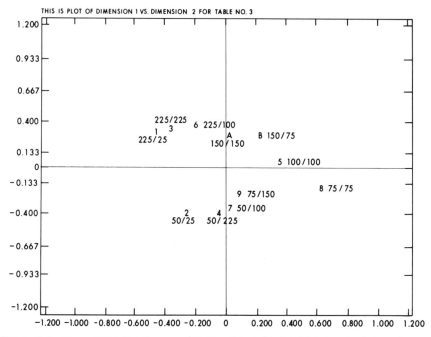

Figure 8.8. Two-dimensional space for strawberry-flavored beverages (percentage of sweetness/percentage of color).

lying closest to the standard beverage (100/100) are those which are closest in overall sweetness–color formulation. These are 75/75 on the extreme right and 150/75 and 75/150. As with the POLYCON solution, this dimension may perhaps be considered as "similarity to the standard (commercial) beverage."

Individual subject weights show that only Subject 1, who moreover has a low correlation, has a greater weight on dimension 1 than on dimension 2. For most subjects, the dimension 2 weights are about three times greater than the dimension 1 weights. Use of other random numbers (IRN) in an attempt to get the sweetness dimension to appear as dimension 1 were unsuccessful. The spaces were essentially the same except for very minor differences in subject weights and degree of orthogonality.

8.6. Musk Odors

This data set (Section 3.5) is from 20 subjects for 14 musks. This example is included to show a data set with which INDSCAL is unable to cope. The perceptual differences among the stimuli are difficult to judge, and an individual's data matrix typically contains a large number of no differences or zeros. The data for an individual are therefore only weakly, if at all, at the interval level of measurement. A nonmetric scaling algorithm is clearly more appropriate.

The problem is immediately apparent on reviewing the INDSCAL solution for the 20 subjects. The SUMS OF PRODUCTS, MATRIX 1 (subject weights), reads:

$$
\begin{array}{lll}
1 & 1.06 & \\
2 & & 1.46 \\
3 & & \quad 1.47 \\
\end{array}
$$
SUMS OF SQUARES = 3.99

So little of the variance is accounted for in total $(3.99/20 = 20\%)$ that the solution is unlikely to be of any value. The stimulus space, as expected, bears little if any relation to the MINISSA or ALSCAL spaces and no relationship to the physicochemical properties of the musks.

The teaching from this failure of INDSCAL is not that there is an inherent weakness in the algorithm, but rather that certain data sets are inappropriate for analysis by it. INDSCAL provides a metric analysis. As such it works well with interval data and much ordinal data. However, when the data tend to be categorical, as in the present case, INDSCAL is probably inappropriate.

8.7. Cigarettes

This data set (Section 3.6) is from 99 subjects for just three stimuli. Although we generally discourage the use of small numbers of stimuli (see Section 2.6), the importance of this pilot experiment lies in the design. Each stimulus was duplicated. The similarity judgments were developed and analyzed as if there were six different stimuli. Additionally, subjects performed extra same–same comparisons to allow calculation of a "signal-to-noise" ratio, (average different score)/(average same score). On the basis of this signal-to-noise ratio, subjects were divided into three groups

Classification		Signal-to-noise
Good discriminators	(38)	> 1.5
Intermediate discriminators	(26)	1.0–1.4
Poor discriminators	(35)	< 1.0

INDSCAL analysis of the data for the three groups supported this initial separation. The three two-dimensional group stimulus spaces are shown in Figure 8.9(a), (b), and (c). Each cigarette pair is close together and separated from the other two in the "good" discriminator space. The intermediate discriminators separate Marlboro and Viceroy from Winston on the horizontal dimension but lose order on the vertical dimension. The bad discriminators' space is clearly nonsense.

INDSCAL provides correlations between a transformation of the original data and the distances in the stimulus space. These are not sufficient to establish the validity of the spaces as the values in Figure 8.9 show. While none of the correlations is high, the difference in correlation coefficients between the three groups is not large. On the other hand, even though the good discriminator space accounts for only 44% of the variance, it provides a reliable separation of the three different stimuli. We have seen cases where this much of the variance is accounted for, yet the stimulus space is not meaningful. With random numbers for six stimuli and 20 subjects INDSCAL shows about 35% of the variance accounted for in two dimensions. The bad discriminator space in this example accounts for 34% of the variance.

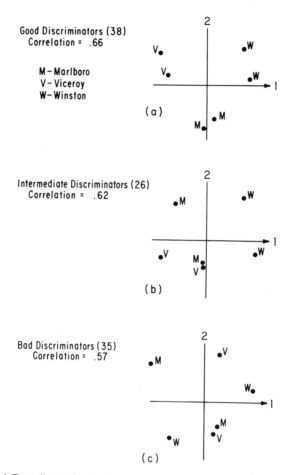

Figure 8.9. (a) Two-dimensional cigarette space for 38 good discriminators. (b) Two-dimensional cigarette space for 26 intermediate discriminators. (c) Two-dimensional cigarette space for 35 bad discriminators.

8.8. Setting Up a SINDSCAL Job

SINDSCAL uses the same general arrangement as INDSCAL. The main difference in deck setup is that SINDSCAL's 9 parameters are entered on two cards whereas INDSCAL's 13 are entered on one. Figure 8.10 shows the input deck. SINDSCAL's first four parameters, Card 1, are those most likely to change between analyses. The maximum values for these are interdependent and depend also on the core size of the computer used.

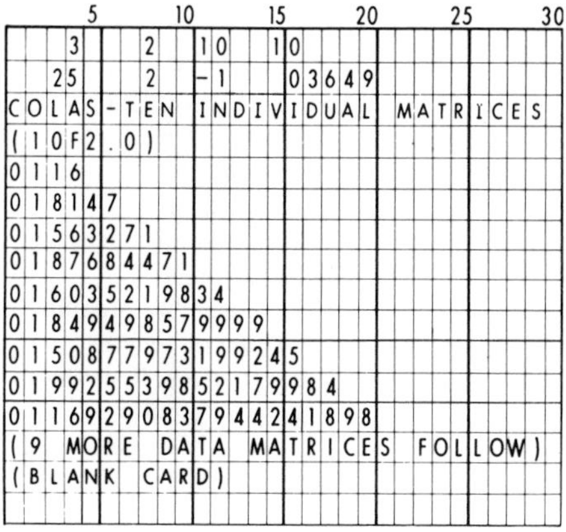

```
              5      10      15     20      25      30
      3       2     1 0    1 0
    2 5       2     - 1    0 3 6 4 9
C O L A S - T E N   I N D I V I D U A L   M A T R I C E S
( 1 0 F 2 . 0 )
0 1 1 6
0 1 8 1 4 7
0 1 5 6 3 2 7 1
0 1 8 7 6 8 4 4 7 1
0 1 6 0 3 5 2 1 9 8 3 4
0 1 8 4 9 4 9 8 5 7 9 9 9 9
0 1 5 0 8 7 7 9 7 3 1 9 9 2 4 5
0 1 9 9 2 5 5 3 9 8 5 2 1 7 9 9 8 4
0 1 1 6 9 2 9 0 8 3 7 9 4 4 2 4 1 8 9 8
( 9   M O R E   D A T A   M A T R I C E S   F O L L O W )
( B L A N K   C A R D )
```

Figure 8.10. Input deck for cola analysis by SINDSCAL.

Card 1. This shows the main problem parameters.

Identifier	Columns	
MAXDIM	1–4	The maximum dimensionality sought must be less than or equal to 10.
MINDIM	5–8	The minimum dimensionality must be greater than or equal to one, and less than or equal to MAXDIM.
NMAT	9–12	The number of input matrices. This is usually the number of subjects. For the default core size, this can be 200 with NSTIM = 12 and MAXDIM = 5.
NSTIM	13–16	The number of stimuli.

These parameters are entered in I4 format.

Card 2. This contains the remaining five parameters which will usually be changed infrequently.

Identifier	Columns	
ITMAX	1–4	The maximum number of iterations. There is no maximum to the number of iterations allowed; a large number, such as 200, may be necessary to achieve the proper orientation in some circumstances. (ITMAX = 0 if you are only solving for subject weights and are supplying an input stimulus configuration.)

(cont'd.)

Identifier	Columns	
IRDATA	5–8	Form of input data. For all options except 5, 6 and 7, the matrices are lower half without diagonals.
		1 similarities
		2 dissimilarities
		3 Euclidean distances
		4 correlations
		−4 same as 4 but program normalizes each matrix so sum of squares = 1
		5 covariances, lower half with diagonals
		−5 same as 5 but program normalizes each matrix so sum of squares = 1
		6 full symmetric matrix of similarities
		7 full symmetric matrix of dissimilarities
PUNCH	9–12	Punch options. All options except −1 include normalized solution.
		−1 no output
		0 normalized solution only
		1 scalar products matrices
		2 three unnormalized matrices
		3 all of the above
IPLOT	13–16	Plotting options
		−1 no plots
		0 plot all pairs of planes
IRN	17–20	Starting configuration
		0 user supplied
		4 digit integer. Primes generation of random starting configuration.

Card 3. The title card is restricted to one card with only 72 columns allowed.

Card 4. This shows the data format which must be F or E enclosed in parentheses. The user can supply a subroutine to read in data matrices. In this case, MYREAD is entered in columns 1–6 of card 4.

Card 5. The data set in the format specified on card 4. Each row of a matrix is on one card or cards. The matrices are stacked subject by subject. That is, all the data for Subject 1 come before Subject 2 and so on. If IRN = 0, configuration cards follow. The first card supplies in F or E format the format for the coordinates. The second configuration card gives the coordinates on dimension 1 for all stimuli. The next card gives the coordinates on dimension 2 and so on.

Last Card. This must be blank in columns 1 to 20.

8.9. Understanding SINDSCAL Output

SINDSCAL printouts are basically similar to INDSCAL but contain less detailed descriptions of the computation. Unless there are a large number of subjects, the information will be contained on two pages (Figure 8.11).

After the title and analysis parameters, coordinates for the initial stimulus matrix are given. This is generated randomly or has been supplied by the user (when IRN = 0). The HISTORY OF COMPUTATION shows the improvement in CORRELATIONS, the variance accounted for (VAF), the residual (LOSS), and the reason for termination. In this case the maximum iterations specified, 25, were reached. The criterion for convergence is built into the program and is .000001.

In the example shown, convergence was not achieved. In the extreme right-hand column, LOSS, Figure 8.11(a), the difference between the values for iterations 24 and 25 is .000017. This is larger than the built-in criterion of .000001. In practical terms this means that the solution may not have attained the proper orientation of the axes although the interstimulus distances are likely to be correct. The SUBJECTS WEIGHT MATRIX and STIMULUS MATRIX follow. These are analogous to INDSCAL's MATRIX 1 and MATRIX 2.

SINDSCAL next provides SUM OF PRODUCTS matrices for SUBJECTS and STIMULI. While the latter is equivalent to INDSCAL's SUM OF PRODUCTS (MATRIX 2), the former is normalized to unity on the main diagonal by SINDSCAL.

While INDSCAL does not provide a measure of APPROXIMATE PROPORTION OF TOTAL VARIANCE accounted for by each dimension (one must divide the main diagonal of SUM OF PRODUCTS (MATRIX 2) by the number of subjects to obtain this), SINDSCAL performs the calculations. Finally, SINDSCAL, like INDSCAL, provides CORRELATION BETWEEN COMPUTED SCORES AND SCALAR PRODUCTS.

8.10. Colas by SINDSCAL

This data set (Section 3.1) is from 10 subjects (5 male, 5 female) for 10 decarbonated commercial colas. We compare here the SINDSCAL analysis with the INDSCAL analysis discussed in Section 8.3. Both are in three dimensions.

Comparison of Stimulus Spaces

The SINDSCAL stimulus spaces are shown in Figure 8.12(a) and (b). Dimension 1, as with INDSCAL, separates diet and nondiet drinks. Likewise, dimension 2 separates cherry and regular colas. Dimension 2, like INDSCAL dimension 3, appears to represent manufacturer flavor type.

The axes of the SINDSCAL space are also reasonably orthogonal as shown by the small values of the off-diagonal elements in the SUM OF PRODUCTS (STIMULI) matrix, Figure 8.11(b). As with INDSCAL, these numbers are the cosines of the angles between the axes which are:

Dimension pair	SINDSCAL	INDSCAL
1 and 2	87.5	87.7
1 and 3	89.0	90.5
2 and 3	94.3	94.7

```
                       SYMMETRIC INDSCAL

 COLAS-TEN INDIVIDUAL MATRICES

 ****************************************************
 PARAMETERS
  DIM  IRDATA  ITMAX IPUNCH  IPLOT    IRN
   3     2      25     -1      0     3649
 NO. OF MATRICES =  10   NO. OF STIM. =  10


 ****************************************************

 INITIAL STIMULUS MATRIX
  1 -0.229  0.190 -0.295  0.214  0.398  0.090  0.160 -0.120 -0.194  0.147

  2 -0.353 -0.047  0.495 -0.140 -0.336 -0.069 -0.034 -0.271 -0.287  0.316

  3 -0.282  0.255  0.293 -0.393  0.251 -0.064 -0.096  0.304  0.066  0.274
```

```
                          HISTORY OF COMPUTATION
  ITERATION         CORRELATIONS BETWEEN      VAF              LOSS
                      Y(DATA) AND YHAT        (R**2)         (Y-YHAT)**2
      0                  0.137572           0.018926          0.981074
      1                  0.613671           0.376592          0.623408
      2                  0.749687           0.562030          0.437970
      3                  0.777591           0.604648          0.395352
      4                  0.784859           0.616004          0.383996
      5                  0.787935           0.620842          0.379158
      6                  0.789650           0.623547          0.376453
      7                  0.790764           0.625307          0.374693
      8                  0.791561           0.626569          0.373431
      9                  0.792162           0.627521          0.372479
     10                  0.792631           0.628264          0.371735
     11                  0.793000           0.628848          0.371152
     12                  0.793291           0.629311          0.370689
     13                  0.793519           0.629672          0.370328
     14                  0.793699           0.629957          0.370043
     15                  0.793837           0.630177          0.369823
     16                  0.793946           0.630350          0.369650
     17                  0.794030           0.630484          0.369516
     18                  0.794095           0.630587          0.369413
     19                  0.794144           0.630664          0.369336
     20                  0.794182           0.630725          0.369275
     21                  0.794210           0.630770          0.369230
     22                  0.794233           0.630806          0.369194
     23                  0.794249           0.630832          0.369168
     24                  0.794261           0.630851          0.369149
     25                  0.794272           0.630868          0.369132
 REACHED MAXIMUM ITERATIONS
     FINAL               0.794275           0.630872          0.369128
```

(a)

Figure 8.11. Printed SINDSCAL output for cola analysis. (Continued on facing page.)

```
                    NORMALIZED SOLUTION

SUBJECTS WEIGHT MATRIX
 1     0.641  0.192  0.201  0.663  0.807  0.798  0.206  0.429  0.624  0.206

 2     0.346  0.579  0.737  0.252  0.073  0.085  0.651  0.562  0.203  0.692

 3     0.235  0.388  0.286  0.429  0.235  0.265  0.333  0.404  0.400  0.219


STIMULUS MATRIX
 1    -0.348  0.290  0.205  0.214  0.306  0.214 -0.323 -0.390  0.302 -0.470

 2     0.179  0.239 -0.096 -0.633  0.156  0.115 -0.574  0.141  0.273  0.199

 3     0.357  0.322 -0.553  0.286 -0.036 -0.364  0.104 -0.410  0.260  0.033


NORMALIZED SUM OF PRODUCTS (SUBJECTS)
 1     1.000
 2     0.548  1.000
 3     0.854  0.845  1.000

SUM OF PRODUCTS (STIMULI)
 1     1.000
 2     0.044  1.000
 3     0.018 -0.075  1.000

APPROXIMATE PROPORTION OF TOTAL VARIANCE ACCCUNTED FOR BY EACH DIMENSION
        1       2       3
       0.288   0.234   0.108

CORRELATION BETWEEN COMPUTED SCORES AND SCALAR PROD. FOR SUBJECTS


 1     0.766598
 2     0.724976
 3     0.817676
 4     0.830240
 5     0.844252
 6     0.845299
 7     0.761165
 8     0.816045
 9     0.760824
10     0.756282                              (b)
```

Figure 8.11 (Cont'd.)

The approximate proportions of total variance accounted for by each dimension are:

Dimension	SINDSCAL	INDSCAL
1	.288	.288
2	.234	.233
3	.108	.108
Total	.630	.629

The stimulus space provided by SINDSCAL is thus almost identical to that provided by INDSCAL.

Comparison of Subject Weights

Complete subject weights are shown for the SINDSCAL analysis in Figure 8.11(a) and in Figure 8.2 for the INDSCAL analysis. They are closely

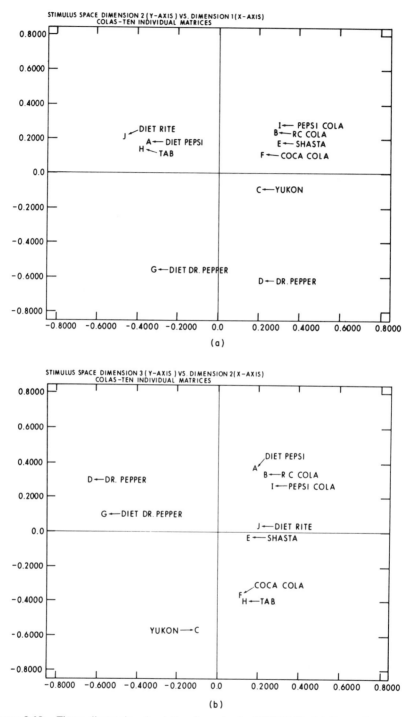

Figure 8.12. Three-dimensional solution for colas by SINDSCAL: (a) dimension 2 versus dimension 1; (b) dimension 3 versus dimension 2.

comparable. If INDSCAL indicates a high weighting on dimension 1 and a low weighting on dimension 2 for a subject, then so will SINDSCAL. Three examples are shown here, (S) indicating SINDSCAL weights and (I) INDSCAL weights:

Subject	\multicolumn{6}{c}{Dimension weights}

Subject	1(S)	1(I)	2(S)	2(I)	3(S)	3(I)
1	.64	.64	.35	.34	.24	.25
7	.21	.21	.65	.65	.33	.32
9	.62	.63	.20	.20	.40	.39

In summary, SINDSCAL provides a virtually equivalent solution to that provided by INDSCAL.

8.11. General Comments

INDSCAL has probably received greater attention than other MDS programs. It is easy to use, and the output is relatively simple to understand. With "good" data analyzed at the appropriate dimensionality, INDSCAL solutions are reliable; however, it is not designed to cope with data that are highly nonmetric.

It is helpful, in interpreting INDSCAL spaces, to have independent checks of subjects' ability to discriminate as well as replicate stimuli. In the absence of an independent measure of subject performance, it is sometimes possible to "refine" an INDSCAL analysis as follows. First develop a two-dimensional space for all subjects. Then separate the subjects into two groups, those whose correlations are .7 or greater, and those whose correlations are less. (A correlation of .7 corresponds to about 50% explained variance.) Repeat the INDSCAL analysis for each group, including higher-dimensional solutions as considered appropriate. The stimulus spaces for the first group will most likely represent better fits with the data, and be interpretable. While the stimulus spaces for the second group may show a different set of perceptions which were initially obscured, they are more likely to continue to be noise.

A further feature of INDSCAL, particularly when compared with ALSCAL, is that noise is absorbed to a large part by subject weights. The poor perception of food flavors by the elderly described in Section 8.4 is an example of this. This effect, in extreme cases, is for the stimuli to become bunched around the origin in the stimulus space while subject weights show considerable diversity.

J. D. Carroll and S. Pruzansky of Bell Laboratories recommend use of SINDSCAL over INDSCAL for analyzing the type of similarity data described in this book. There is a considerable reduction in memory requirements and simplification of the main computation subroutine. It should run as much as 30% faster than INDSCAL. Input is simpler and more flexible, and the output more compact. SINDSCAL also has dynamic core allocation, thus allowing analysis of data from larger numbers of subjects (if your computer core is sufficient) than INDSCAL.

Reference

Green, P. E., & Rao, V. R. *Applied multidimensional scaling: A comparison of approaches and algorithms.* New York: Holt, Rinehart & Winston, 1972.

9

How to Use ALSCAL

9.1. Setting Up an ALSCAL Job

This chapter describes ALSCAL applications to a single matrix of dissimilarity judgments (CMDS, see Section 4.1) and to several matrices of dissimilarity judgments (both RMDS and WMDS). ALSCAL is an extremely flexible program which can provide metric and nonmetric scaling with or without individual differences models. We concentrate here on the use of ALSCAL for scaling of dissimilarity judgments. For other uses of ALSCAL, see the users' manual available from the University of North Carolina, referenced in the Appendix.

There are two versions of ALSCAL, called ALSCAL and PROC ALSCAL. The input for ALSCAL is very different from that for PROC ALSCAL. The output of both is the same.

PROC ALSCAL is a Statistical Analysis System (SAS) procedure. SAS (see Helwig & Council, 1979) is a general statistical system which is available from the SAS Institute as referenced in the Appendix. The input to PROC ALSCAL for an individual differences analysis (WMDS) is shown in Figure 9.1(a) for 10 cola drinks for 10 subjects (Section 3.1). As you can see, PROC ALSCAL uses a plain language for its control cards which is similar to KYST and POLYCON.

We do not explain input to PROC ALSCAL in this chapter. It is fully explained in Reinhardt (1980). We do wish to say, however, that PROC ALSCAL, as part of a unified statistical system, can be very easily used

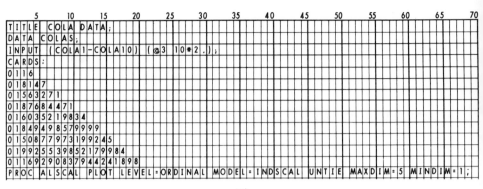

(a)

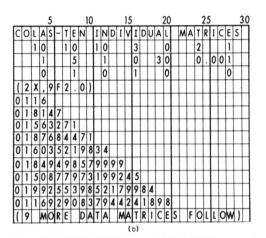

(b)

Figure 9.1. Input deck of (a) PROC ALSCAL and (b) ALSCAL control cards for the cola study described in Section 3.1.

in conjunction with other SAS procedures. In one job it is possible to do a scaling, followed by other analyses such as multiple regression and cluster analysis.

The ALSCAL (not PROC ALSCAL) input deck for the same WMDS cola analysis is shown in Figure 9.1(b). ALSCAL does not use the plain language job control features found in PROC ALSCAL and in KYST and POLYCON. Instead, data and analysis parameters are coded in a fixed format using a specific card order as in INDSCAL. The deck setup described below is for ALSCAL-4 and *not* for the earlier versions 1, 2, 3, and not for SAS PROC ALSCAL.

The first five cards are mandatory and contain all the specifications and options for normal scaling of dissimilarity judgments. Card 6 is the data deck unless data is read from a tape or disk. Cards 7 through 14 are optional and allow input of configurations or weights.

The number of stimuli, subjects, and observations is limited only by the size of the core at your computer installation.

Card 1. Gives an alphanumeric title information in 20A4 format.

Card 2. Data description card. This card is in (9I4) format. Integers are entered as follows:

Identifier	Columns	
NROW	1–4	Number of row stimuli, 10 in this example.
NCOL	5–8	Number of column stimuli, 10 in this example. Note these two numbers must be the same unless the data to be analyzed are rectangular.
NS	9–12	Number of matrices (subjects), also 10 here.
NDTYP	13–16	Measurement level of the data 1 = ratio 2 = interval 3 = ordinal, this example (this is also the default option) 4 = nominal Most direct dissimilarity judgments, particularly those made by marking a line anchored "exact same–completely different," are probably ordinal.

Binary data, same–different or right–wrong answers in a triangle test, are of course nominal. Analysis at the ratio level is not recommended. While most similarity data are probably ordinal, analysis at the interval level provides solutions most similar to INDSCAL. If ALSCAL solutions at the ordinal and interval levels are the same, the data can be considered to be interval.

Identifier	Columns	
NSIM	17–20	Shows the type of data 0 = symmetric—dissimilarity (default) 1 = symmetric—similarity 2 = asymmetric—dissimilarity 3 = asymmetric—similarity 4 = rectangular—dissimilarity 5 = rectangular—similarity For the nominal measurement, column 13–16, the similarity—dissimilarity distinction is irrelevant and either option associated with symmetric or asymmetric is permissible.
NPS	21–24	Determines whether for ordinal data ties will be maintained (discrete) or broken (continuous) 1 = discrete (default) 2 = continuous (this example)

(cont'd.)

Identifier	Columns	
NWC	25–28	Determines whether there will be separate transformations for each matrix (subject), or each row, or whether the same transformation is applied to all data. 1 = matrix conditional (default, this example) 2 = row conditional 3 = unconditional
	29–32	Only for ratio or interval data, provides the degree of the polynomial for scaling the data which can range from 1 to 4. The default value is 1.
	33–36	Maximum number of memory locations reserved for ties in ordinal data. The default is equal to the total number of observations or 1000, whichever is less.

Card 3. Problem card in (5I4,F8.0) format.

Identifier	Columns	
NWE	1–4	Describes the model type 0 = simple Euclidean model (default), CMDS, or RMDS 1 = individual differences model, WMDS (this example) 2 = asymmetric model (see Chapter 4) 3 = asymmetric individual differences model For individual differences models there must be at least two subjects.
NDIM	5–8	Maximum number of dimensions. The maximum is 6 with a default of 2. One-dimensional solutions may only be called for the simple Euclidean model.
NDMN	9–12	Minimum number of dimensions. Solutions are provided for all dimensionalities between the maximum and minimum. In the example we call for 1 but ALSCAL refuses to accept this and substituted 2 for an individual differences model.
NNC	13–16	0 = no negative weights (default) 1 = negative weights allowed
MAXIT	17–20	Maximum number of iterations (default = 30).
EPSI	21–28	Convergence criterion for improvements in SSTRESS (default is .001). SSTRESS is computed by the Takane–Young–de Leeuw formula in terms of normalized disparities and distances (Young, 1979).

Card 4. This card in (8I4) format provides a number of input–output options.

Identifier	Columns	
NDI	1–4	0 = do not print data, distances, or disparities
		1 = print data, distances, and disparities
NPI	5–8	0 = do not plot derived configuration, transformations, and goodness of fit
		1 = plot derived configuration, transformations, and goodness of fit
NPH	9–12	0 = do not punch derived configuration
		1 = punch derived configuration
		2 = punch initial and derived configuration
DATA	13–16	0 = read data from cards
		n = read data from FORTRAN logical unit n
INITX	17–20	0 = compute initial stimulus configuration
		1 = compute and print initial stimulus configuration
		2 = read and print initial stimulus configuration
		3 = read, print, and fix initial stimulus configuration
INITXC	21–24	This is applicable only to rectangular data
		0 = compute initial column stimulus configuration
		1 = compute and print initial column stimulus configuration
		2 = read and print initial column stimulus configuration
		3 = read, print, and fix initial column stimulus configuration
INITW	25–28	0 = compute initial subject weights.
		1 = compute and print initial subject weights
		2 = read and print initial subject weights
		3 = read, print, and fix initial subject weights
INITWS	29–32	0 = compute initial stimulus weights
		1 = compute and print initial stimulus weights
		2 = read and print initial stimulus weights
		3 = read, print, and fix initial stimulus weights

Card 5. This gives the data format in FORTRAN notation.

Card 6. Data are entered here unless accessed elsewhere (column 16 of card 4). All the data for Subject 1 is entered first, then Subject 2 and so on. Symmetric matrices must be entered as the lower triangular half of the matrix without diagonal. Thus for n stimuli there will be $n-1$ rows of data for each matrix. Asymmetric and rectangular matrices must be entered in full. Zeros and negative numbers are treated as missing data. Thus, a number such as 1 must be added to correlations for analysis by ALSCAL. Zero data values should be entered as .01 or some other number which is appropriately small for the numerical range of the data.

These conclude the mandatory cards for analysis of similarities data. The remaining cards are required only if initial stimulus coordinates or weights are to be input.

Cards 7, 9, 11, or 13. These give the data formats in F notation for initial coordinates or weights.

If initial coordinates or weights are read in and solutions are requested in several dimensionalities coordinate or weight matrices must be provided for each dimensionality. Format cards must precede each set of matrices.

Cards 8, 10, 12, and 14. These contain the matrices for: initial row stimulus coordinates, initial column stimulus coordinates, initial subject weights, initial stimulus weights.

All data for a stimulus or subject are entered on the first card with, if necessary, a continuation card. Data for the second stimulus or subject go on the second card and so forth.

Additional analyses of the data may be made by repeating cards 1 through 14 as needed.

9.2. Understanding ALSCAL Output

We provide here an explanation of the most commonly used ALSCAL feature—the individual differences model for scaling dissimilarity data. The first page, Figure 9.2(a) shows JOB TITLE, DATA SPECIFICATIONS, ANALYSIS SPECIFICATIONS, and I/O OPTIONS. This serves as both a check that that job is set up as desired, and a record for the analyses that follow. These start with the highest-dimensionality solution called for, and proceed to the lowest. The next pages provide printed information about the solution. Those for the cola analysis are shown in Figure 9.2(b) and (c). They contain the following tables:

ITERATION HISTORY
STRESS AND SQUARED CORRELATION IN DISTANCES
CONFIGURATION DERIVED—STIMULUS COORDINATES
SUBJECT WEIGHTS
RELATIVE SUBJECT WEIGHT INDICES

ITERATION HISTORY shows the change in SSTRESS as the analysis proceeds. The formula for SSTRESS is described in Section 16.2. It is *not* Kruskal's STRESS formula. A message follows this table showing whether the iterations stopped because improvement is less than the minimum permitted (.001) or because the maximum number of iterations (30) has been exceeded.

STRESS and SQUARED CORRELATION (RSQ) IN DISTANCES shows these values for each subject (MATRIX). The STRESS shown in this table is Kruskal's stress formula 1 and is the square root of the proportion of total sums of squares of the optimally scaled data which is not accounted for by the model. The overall stress shown at the bottom of the table is the root mean square of these individual stress values. The squared correlations RSQ show the proportion of variance of the disparities accounted for by the MDS model. The overall RSQ is the simple average of the individual RSQ values. Since RSQ has a simple interpretation, it is the best indicator of how well the data fit the model. In several of the examples shown in this chapter, RSQ is a much better indicator of the appropriate dimensionality than STRESS. Finally, it should be noted that ALSCAL correlations are not calculated in the same way as INDSCAL correlations. This point is discussed in Chapter 16.

The next table, CONFIGURATION DERIVED, gives the stimulus coordinates. These are normalized on each dimension so that their sum is zero and their sum of squares equal to the number of stimuli.

SUBJECT WEIGHTS gives the calculated weight for each subject on each dimension, and the simple average of these weights on each dimension for all subjects. For matrix and row conditional data, subject weights are normalized for each subject so that the sum of squares across the dimensions equals that subject's squared correlation. Further the square of a subject's weight on a dimension gives the proportion of the variance of that subject's optimally scaled data which is accounted for by that dimension. We recommend using conditional data. The interpretation of subject weights for unconditional data is less straightforward.

RELATIVE SUBJECT WEIGHT INDICES is the final table in the printout and can be ignored by most users. These indices show how each subject differs from a typical subject in the relative importance of the dimension. They are sines of twice the angle of departure from the 45° line(s) in a (further normalized) weight space. For a fuller discussion of their calculation see the ALSCAL user's guide referenced in the Appendix. The indices will vary between ± 1.00. The extreme values represent extreme weighting by a subject on at least one dimension. These subject weight indices are calculated for each dimension versus the other highest dimensions. Thus, in a three-dimensional solution, relative indices are calculated for dimension 1 versus dimension 2 and versus dimension 3 and for dimension 2 versus dimension 3. This has a further advantage of allowing portrayal of some of the information concerning subjects' perceptual differences in a two- as opposed to a three-dimensional space. Figure 9.3 (from the cola analysis), shows subject weight indices for dimensions 1 and 2 relative to dimension 3. Subjects A and H who lie near the origin behave very much like the typical subject in the perceptions of the relative importance of dimensions

```
JOB TITLE: COLAS-TEN INDIVIDUAL MATRICES


DATA SPECIFICATIONS-

 NROW - NUMBER OF ROW STIMULI                          10   ROW STIMULI
 NCOL - NUMBER OF COLUMN STIMULI                       10   COLUMN STIMULI
 NS   - NUMBER OF MATRICES                             10   MATRICES
 NDTYP- MEASUREMENT LEVEL                               3 = ORDINAL
 NSIM - DATA TYPE                                       0 = SYMMETRIC-DISSIMILARITY
 NPS  - MEASUREMENT PROCESS                             2 = CONTINUOUS
 NWC  - MEASUREMENT CONDITIONALITY                      1 = MATRIX CONDITIONAL
 NDMX - NUMBER OF CELLS FOR TIED OBSERVATIONS         450   CELLS


ANALYSIS SPECIFICATIONS-

 NWE  - MODEL TYPE                                      1 = INDIVIDUAL DIFFERENCES (INDSCAL) MODEL

ALSCAL WARNING: INCONSISTENT CONTROL PARAMETERS.
ONE-DIMENSIONAL WEIGHTED MODELS NOT PERMITTED.
ANALYSIS CONTINUES WITHOUT A ONE-DIMENSIONAL SOLUTION.
 NDIM - NUMBER OF DIMENSIONS (MAXIMUM)                  5   DIMENSIONS (MAXIMUM)
 NDMN - NUMBER OF DIMENSIONS (MINIMUM)                  2   DIMENSIONS (MINIMUM)
 NNC  - NEGATIVE WEIGHTS PERMITTED                      0 = NEGATIVE WEIGHTS NOT PERMITTED
 MAXIT- MAXIMUM NUMBER OF ITERATIONS                   30   ITERATIONS (MAXIMUM)
 EPSI - CONVERGENCE CRITERION                   0.0010000 = MINIMUM SSTRESS IMPROVEMENT


I/O OPTIONS-

 NDT  - PRINT DATA, DISTANCES AND DISPARITIES           0 = DO NOT PRINT
 NPT  - PLOT RESULTS                                    1 = DO PLOT
 NPH  - PUNCH RESULTS                                   0 = DO NOT PUNCH
 INDATA- DATA INPUT UNIT NUMBER                         1 = READ DATA FROM CARDS
 INITX- INITIAL STIMULUS COORDINATES                    0 = COMPUTE
 INITC- INITIAL COLUMN STIMULUS COORDINATES             0 = COMPUTE
 INITW- INITIAL SUBJECT WEIGHTS                         0 = COMPUTE
 INITWS- INITIAL STIMULUS WEIGHTS                       0 = COMPUTE


INPUT DATA FORMAT-

    (2X,9F2.0)
```

Figure 9.2(a).   First page of ALSCAL printout from the cola analysis (three-dimensional, ordinal).

ITERATION HISTORY FOR THE 3 DIMENSIONAL SOLUTION
SSTRESS (IN SQUARED DISTANCES) FORMULA 1 IS USED.

ITERATION	SSTRESS	IMPROVEMENT
1	0.31796	
2	0.29565	0.02230
3	0.29275	0.00290
4	0.29197	0.00078

ALSCAL MESSAGE: ITERATIONS STOPPED BECAUSE SSTRESS IMPROVEMENT LESS THAN MINIMUM PERMITTED.

STRESS AND SQUARED CORRELATION (RSQ) IN DISTANCES
KRUSKALS STRESS FORMULA 1 IS USED.

MATRIX	STRESS	RSQ	MATRIX	STRESS	RSQ	MATRIX	STRESS	RSQ	MATRIX	STRESS	RSQ
1	0.220	0.477	2	0.217	0.490	3	0.194	0.690	4	0.186	0.621
5	0.208	0.594	6	0.189	0.658	7	0.229	0.531	8	0.181	0.651
9	0.188	0.606	10	0.229	0.477						

OVERALL   0.205   0.580

CONFIGURATION DERIVED IN 3 DIMENSIONS

STIMULUS COORDINATES

STIMULUS NUMBER	PLOT SYMBOL	DIMENSION 1	DIMENSION 2	DIMENSION 3
1	A	-1.0106	0.9008	-1.1669
2	B	0.9180	0.9635	-0.6669
3	C	0.3710	-0.8424	1.6072
4	D	0.7287	-1.8351	-1.0759
5	E	1.1432	0.3254	0.5443
6	F	0.6093	0.3082	1.3326
7	G	-0.8598	-1.6235	-0.8199
8	H	-1.4361	0.2804	1.0946
9	I	-0.9681	0.9942	-0.6981
10	J	-1.4319	0.5284	-0.1510

Figure 9.2(b). Second page of ALSCAL printout from the cola analysis (three-dimensional, ordinal).

```
SUBJECT WEIGHTS
                                    DIMENSION
        SUBJECT    PLOT        1            2            3
        NUMBER    SYMBOL

           1         A       0.5297       0.3065       0.3195
           2         B       0.4013       0.4147       0.3968
           3         C       0.2514       0.6758       0.4129
           4         D       0.6163       0.2577       0.4178
           5         E       0.6810       0.1828       0.3109
           6         F       0.7063       0.1809       0.3559
           7         G       0.3570       0.5766       0.2657
           8         H       0.4827       0.4951       0.4161
           9         I       0.5846       0.2686       0.4382
          10         J       0.3543       0.4824       0.3450

    AVERAGE                  0.4965       0.3841       0.3679



RELATIVE SUBJECT WEIGHT INDICES
(RELATIVE TO DIMENSION 2)
                                    DIMENSION
        SUBJECT    PLOT        1
        NUMBER    SYMBOL
           1         A       0.2826
           2         B      -0.2817
           3         C      -0.8470
           4         D       0.5478
           5         E       0.7851
           6         F       0.8025
           7         G      -0.6267
           8         H      -0.2747
           9         I       0.4786
          10         J      -0.5118



RELATIVE SUBJECT WEIGHT INDICES
(RELATIVE TO DIMENSION 3)
                                    DIMENSION
        SUBJECT    PLOT        1            2
        NUMBER    SYMBOL
           1         A       0.2031      -0.0844
           2         B      -0.2809       0.0008
           3         C      -0.6616       0.4216
           4         D       0.0888      -0.4825
           5         E       0.4497      -0.5184
           6         F       0.3676      -0.6169
           7         G      -0.0043       0.6241
           8         H      -0.1502       0.1299
           9         I      -0.0115      -0.4874
          10         J      -0.2667       0.2839
```

Figure 9.2(c).   Third page of ALSCAL printout from the cola analysis (three-dimensional, ordinal).

1 and 2 versus dimension 3. Subjects G and I do not differ in perception of dimension 1 versus dimension 3 but G weights 2 more than 3 whereas I weights 3 more than 2. These relative subject weight indices provide additional information, but as represented in Figure 9.3 do not show how well the subject fits the model. This comes from the squared correlations discussed previously.

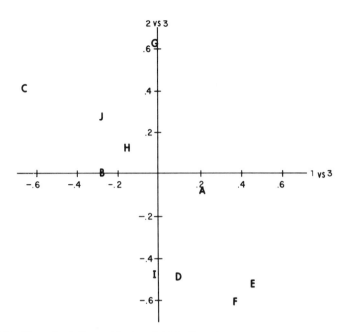

Figure 9.3. Plot of relative subject weight indices.

Following the two pages of printed information, ALSCAL provides the following two-dimensional plots:

Derived stimulus configuration—all pairs of dimensions (there will be 35 with six- through two-dimensional solutions): derived subject weights—all pairs of dimensions, scattergram—distances versus disparities, plot of transformations—disparities versus observations.

In the following sections, examples of each of these plots will be given.

9.3. Colas

This data set (Section 3.1) is from 10 subjects for 10 decarbonated commercial cola beverages. Since ALSCAL has the capability to analyze data in a variety of ways, we provide a number of analyses of the cola data here for comparison. In the next three subsections, ALSCAL solutions are shown using:

1. CMDS—externally averaged data—one single matrix of mean data
2. RMDS—replicated data—ten replications
3. WMDS—the individual differences model

Table 9.1
Typical Job Times on the IBM 370/155 and Pages of Printout for ALSCAL-4

Subjects	Number of stimuli	Dimensions	Measurement level	Time (min:sec)	Pages
1	10	3–1	I	0:21	14
1	10	3–1	O	0:23	20
1	14	5–1	I	0:38	34
1	14	5–1	O	0:42	44
10	10	5–2	I	1:09	58
10	10	5–2	O	1:11	63
12	19	5–2	I	1:44	58
12	19	5–2	O	2:27	62
32	14	5–2	I	2:18	63
32	14	5–2	O	3:15	67
46	11	5–2	I	2:25	67
46	11	5–2	O	2:21	71

In each treatment, data are considered at both the interval (metric) and ordinal (nonmetric) levels of measurement. In the ordinal analyses, two options—discrete (ties remain tied) and continuous (ties are broken)—are compared.

For the mean data there are only 45 data points so that the 10 stimuli cannot be analyzed in more than four-dimensional space. A five-dimensional solution has 50 coordinates for 10 stimuli which are more than the original number of data points. In the individual differences analyses, which require solutions for both distances and subject weights, analysis cannot be performed in less than two dimensions.

While job times depend on the particular computer installation, we show those required on the IBM 370/155 to provide some basis for comparison (see Tables 9.1 and 9.2).

Table 9.2
Job Times on the IBM 370/155 for Nine Different ALSCAL Analyses of Cola Data

	Interval	Ordinal, discrete	Ordinal, continuous
Mean data—CMDS			
(three through one dimensions)	0:20.5	0:23.8	0:22.9
Replicated data—RMDS			
(five through one dimensions)	0:58.4	0:55.8	0:57.2
Individual differences—WMDS			
(five through two dimensions)	1:09.0	1:10.2	1:10.6

Mean Data—CMDS

We provide here three analyses:

1. Interval level
2. Ordinal level—discrete (ties remain tied)
3. Ordinal level—continuous (ties are broken)

All three analyses provide very similar stimulus spaces. The differences lie in the stress and correlations. For three- through one-dimensional solutions these are:

	Changes in stress with dimensionality		
	Dimensions		
	1	2	3
Interval	.445	.263	.108
Ordinal, discrete	.459	.165	.073
Ordinal, continuous	.382	.198	.067

	Changes in squared correlations		
	Dimensions		
	1	2	3
Interval	.381	.671	.881
Ordinal, discrete	.492	.833	.941
Ordinal, continuous	.534	.800	.950

All three analyses show large reductions in stress and large increases in correlations as dimensionality is increased. As is to be expected the ordinal analyses show lower stress and greater correlations than the interval analysis. While the continuous analysis shows lower stress and higher correlations than the discrete analysis in the one- and three-dimensional solutions, this is not so for the two-dimensional solution. In general, continuous analyses allow for a little more data smoothing and thus better model fits.

The stimulus spaces show three clear dimensions: diet–nondiet, cherry cola–regular cola, and manufacturer flavor type. These are discussed in more detail in the individual differences analysis to be discussed shortly.

Replicated Data—RMDS

We provide here three analyses:

1. Interval level
2. Ordinal level—discrete (ties remain tied)
3. Ordinal level—continuous (ties are broken)

Like the mean data, all three analyses provide very similar spaces. The differences lie in the stress and correlations. For five- through one-dimensional solutions these are:

| | Changes in stress with dimensionality | | | | |
| | Dimensions | | | | |
	1	2	3	4	5
Interval	.549	.362	.233	.229	.137
Ordinal, discrete	.534	.340	.211	.166	.124
Ordinal, continuous	.484	.322	.206	.159	.121

| | Changes in squared correlations | | | | |
| | Dimensions | | | | |
	1	2	3	4	5
Interval	.198	.243	.303	.296	.255
Ordinal, discrete	.282	.354	.436	.430	.451
Ordinal, continuous	.336	.402	.459	.457	.477

Ordinal solutions provide less stress at a given dimensionality than the interval solution, and the continuous (tie-breaking option), slightly less stress than the discrete option. In all three analyses there are clear elbows in the stress versus dimension curves after the third dimension.

The squared correlations provide an even clearer indication of the appropriate dimensionality. They actually decrease for the fourth and fifth dimensions in the interval analysis. The low values for the squared correlations, particularly at the interval level analysis, while disturbing, do not necessarily mean that the solutions will be meaningless. They do indicate, however, that the data may be noisy, or reflective of considerable individual perceptual differences, or both.

Three-dimensional solutions appear appropriate for all three analyses. The two ordinal solutions provide very similar stimulus spaces. Dimension 1 separates diet and nondiet drinks, dimension 2 separates cherry and

Table 9.3

Squared Correlations for Each Subject in the Three-Dimensional Cola Spaces Achieved Using the Replicated Model

Subject	Interval	Ordinal, discrete	Ordinal, continuous
1	.324	.404	.445
2	.175	.430	.432
3	.204	.335	.358
4	.448	.486	.529
5	.288	.366	.386
6	.287	.395	.408
7	.329	.430	.460
8	.389	.556	.566
9	.408	.615	.659
10	.175	.344	.348
Overall	.303	.436	.459

regular colas, and dimension 3 provides further groupings by manufacturer. The interval solution provides the same overall interpretation except that here dimension 2 represents manufacturer flavor type while dimension 3 separates the cherry and regular colas. The reasons for this, while not clear from this analysis, are discussed in the next section covering individual differences.

Treating each data matrix as a replication allows determination of how well each subject's data fit the model. Values of stress and squared correlations are printed out for each subject. Squared correlations for the three-dimensional solutions are shown in Table 9.3. If a subject has low correlations, this shows up in all three analyses. The two subjects having particularly low correlations in the interval analysis, numbers 2 and 10, show the greatest improvement when their data are analyzed at the ordinal level.

Individual Differences Model—WMDS

We provide here three analyses:

1. Interval level
2. Ordinal level—discrete (ties remain tied)
3. Ordinal level—continuous (ties are broken)

All three analyses provide very similar stimulus spaces. The differences, as in the previous two examples, lie in the stress and correlations. For two-through five-dimensional solutions, these are:

	Changes in stress with dimensionality			
	Dimensions			
	2	3	4	5
Interval	.380	.228	.175	.135
Ordinal, discrete	.330	.210	.156	.119
Ordinal, continuous	.320	.205	.152	.115

	Changes in average squared correlation			
	Dimensions			
	2	3	4	5
Interval	.316	.420	.422	.437
Ordinal, discrete	.460	.550	.561	.609
Ordinal, continuous	.510	.580	.609	.641

There are several points to note here. As expected, analysis at the ordinal level provides solutions with lower stress, and higher average correlations than analysis at the interval level. For the two ordinal analyses the continuous option gives slightly lower stress and slightly higher correlations than the discrete option. The breaking of ties provides a little more "smoothing" of the data. While the elbows in the stress versus dimension plots occur after the third dimension, one might be tempted, from inspection of the stress values only, to interpret a fourth dimension. However, the squared correlations show very clearly that a fourth dimension does not improve the fit between the data and the model.

Each of the two-dimensional WMDS solutions (not shown) provides clear separations between diet–nondiet colas, and regular colas–cherry colas. Tab, Diet Pepsi, and Diet Rite are grouped in the top-left quadrant while Diet Dr. Pepper falls in the bottom left. Coca-Cola, Pepsi, RC, and Yukon are in the top-right quadrant while Dr. Pepper is in the bottom right. Shasta, also a nondiet cola, appears to fall between regular and cherry colas in terms of this attribute.

In the three-dimensional WMDS solutions, ordinal-continuous maintains dimension 2 as cherry cola–regular cola. However, this dimension is represented by dimension 3 in the ordinal-discrete and interval analyses. Thus, dimension 2 in these latter analyses is equivalent to dimension 3 in the ordinal continuous analysis. This flip–flop appears to be due to the fact that the average subject weights for dimensions 2 and 3 are very similar in each of the three analyses.

	Average subject weights in three-dimensional solutions		
	Dimension		
	1	2	3
Interval	.438	.326	.310
Ordinal, discrete	.497	.371	.356
Ordinal, continuous	.497	.384	.368

The second and third dimensions are thus of roughly equal importance and one or the other may come out first in the analysis. The equivalence of dimension 2 (ordinal-discrete or interval) and dimension 3 (ordinal-continuous) is shown by the locations of the stimuli on these dimensions:

	Stimulus rank orders	
Dimension 2 Interval	Dimension 2 Ordinal-discrete	Dimension 3 Ordinal-continuous
Coca-Cola	Yukon	Yukon
Yukon	Coca-Cola	Coca-Cola
Tab	Tab	Tab
Shasta	Shasta	Shasta
Diet Rite	Diet Rite	Diet Rite
RC Cola	RC Cola	RC Cola
Pepsi Cola	Pepsi Cola	Pepsi Cola
Diet Dr. Pepper	Diet Dr. Pepper	Diet Dr. Pepper
Dr. Pepper	Dr. Pepper	Dr. Pepper
Diet Pepsi	Diet Pepsi	Diet Pepsi

Having satisfied ourselves of the equivalence of the three stimulus spaces, the final question of interpretation is the nature of this second (or third) dimension. Figure 9.4(a) and (b) shows the plots of dimension 1 versus dimension 2 and dimension 2 versus dimension 3 for the ordinal-continuous analysis. Dimension 2 has already been identified as the cherry cola–regular cola dimension. From the reasonably close proximities of Coca-Cola and Tab, Diet Rite and RC Cola, Pepsi Cola and Diet Pepsi, and Dr. Pepper and Diet Dr. Pepper, it would seem that this dimension represents manufacturer flavor type. Similar interpretations were derived from analyses by the other algorithms described in earlier chapters as well as analysis of the mean and replicated data in this chapter.

In summary, for this data set, interpretable and basically equivalent stimulus spaces are provided whether the analysis is metric (interval) or non-

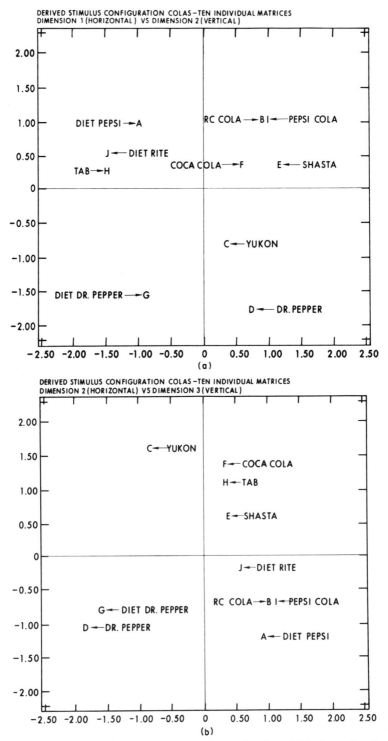

Figure 9.4. Plots of (a) dimension 1 versus dimension 2 and (b) dimension 2 versus dimension 3 for the stimuli in the three-dimensional ordinal-continuous individual difference analysis of cola data by ALSCAL.

metric (ordinal). Breaking of ties (continuous) provides solutions with slightly lower stress and slightly higher correlations.

Subject Differences

ALSCAL, like INDSCAL, allows for differences in perception of the importance of the various dimensions between subjects. The plots of the derived subject weights for the three-dimensional ordinal-continuous cola solution are given in Figure 9.5(a) and (b). Figure 9.5(a) plots dimension 1 versus 2; Figure 9.5(b) plots dimension 2 versus 3. The ratio of how a subject relatively weights a dimension is given in Figure 9.2(c) by the RELATIVE SUBJECT WEIGHT INDICES. Note that Subjects A, D, E, F, and I give relatively more weight to dimension 1 than 2, dimension 1 than 3, and relatively less weight to dimension 2 than 3. Furthermore, the reverse is true for the remaining five subjects. This split of the subjects into two groups corresponds to whether they taste PTC (A, D, E, F, and I) or not. The tasting of PTC is related to one's perception of sweetness. This split means that the analysis reflects individual physiological differences. We will see if these differences are statistically significant in Chapter 13.

To see if the program options affect subject weights we restrict ourselves here to an examination of the subject weights in the two-dimensional solutions.

Overall as shown by the average subject weights, dimension 1 is more important to the subjects than dimension 2:

	Average subject weights	
	Dimension 1 diet–nondiet	Dimension 2 cherry–regular
Interval	.446	.302
Ordinal, discrete	.540	.365
Ordinal, continuous	.537	.416

However for Subjects 3 and 10 the cherry–regular cola is the more important dimension in all three two-dimensional analyses. Their weights for the ordinal-continuous analysis are:

	Dimension weights for Subjects 3 and 10	
	Dimension 1	Dimension 2
Subject 3	.431	.577
Subject 10	.405	.639

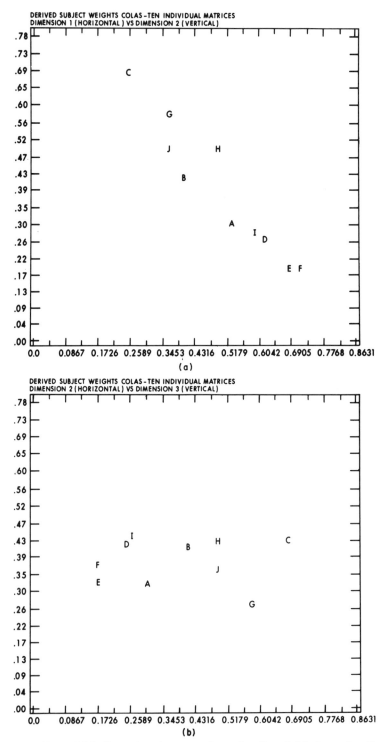

Figure 9.5. Plots of (a) dimension 1 versus dimension 2 and (b) dimension 2 versus dimension 3 for the weights in the three-dimensional ordinal-continuous individual difference analysis of cola data by ALSCAL.

On the other hand Subjects 5 and 6 attached a great deal of importance to dimension 1 but much less to dimension 2:

	Dimension weights for Subjects 5 and 6	
	Dimension 1	Dimension 2
Subject 5	.737	.211
Subject 6	.757	.225

One should note that from analysis of the similarity data alone it is not possible to say whether subjects like or dislike particular attributes. Subject weights only show the importance of various attributes in judging dissimilarities.

Again, as with the stimulus spaces, all three analyses provide similar differences in subject weights for each individual subject.

Comparison of Data Treatments

As will have become evident to the reader by this point, for this cola data set, ALSCAL has provided very similar stimulus spaces whether the data are externally averaged, treated as replications, or treated by the individual differences model. We compare here the three stimulus spaces derived from the ordinal discrete analyses. In each case dimension 1 separates diet and nondiet drinks. The diet drinks appear on the left in the individual differences analysis, on the right in the other two analyses. This is not important. For comparison of the positions of the stimuli along dimension 1, Table 9.4, the coordinates from the individual differences analysis have been multiplied by -1.

While the overall pattern is the same for the three analyses, there are some differences in location of certain stimuli. Replicated data represent Coca-Cola as much less diet-like and Dr. Pepper as much more diet-like than the individual differences analysis. Yukon which appears as least diet-like for externally averaged (mean) data occupies a middle ground in the other two analyses.

The cherry cola–regular cola dimension appears as dimension 2 for the externally averaged and replicated data, although with opposite signs, and as dimension 3 in the individual differences analysis. Positions along this cherry cola dimension are shown in Table 9.5. Apart from the Dr. Pepper drinks being at one extreme, agreement between the three analyses is poor. The individual differences analysis represents the Pepsi Cola drinks as being much less cherry-like than the Coca-Cola drinks whereas use of the replicated analysis portrays the reverse. In general, there is more agreement

Table 9.4
Coordinates for Colas on Dimension 1

	CMDS external averaging	RMDS replicated	WMDS individual differences model
Diet Rite	1.39	1.25	1.46
Tab	1.48	1.15	1.43
Diet Pepsi	1.17	1.07	1.02
Diet Dr. Pepper	1.28	1.29	.81
Yukon	− 1.22	− .67	− .37
Coca-Cola	− .70	− 1.10	− .59
Dr. Pepper	− .52	.33	− .63
RC Cola	− .92	− .87	− .94
Pepsi Cola	− .92	− 1.03	− 1.00
Shasta	− 1.03	− 1.41	− 1.18

in rank order for the mean or replicated data than between either of these and the individual differences model.

Agreement on the manufacturer flavor dimension, Table 9.6 is also fairly poor. While Yukon and Tab are at one extreme and Diet Pepsi is at the other in all three analyses, there are changes in order for the other beverages.

The most likely reason for this lack of agreement between the three spaces is somewhat different rotations for the three solutions. The individual differences analysis which solves for subject weights as well as stimulus coordinates is most likely to give the "true" dimensions. To determine if the three spaces are more equivalent than they appear to be at first sight,

Table 9.5
Coordinates for Colas on Cherry Cola Dimension

	CMDS dimension 2	RMDS dimension 2	WMDS dimension 3
Dr. Pepper	2.24	2.00	1.73
Diet Dr. Pepper	1.65	1.34	1.73
Yukon	− .31	.11	.88
Coca-Cola	− 1.35	− .93	− .22
Tab	− .58	− 1.01	− .36
Shasta	− .08	.45	− .48
Diet Rite	− .79	− .99	− .51
RC Cola	− .25	− .01	− .89
Diet Pepsi	− .47	− .77	− .89
Pepsi	− .05	− .19	− 1.00

Table 9.6
Coordinates for Colas on Manufacturer-Type Dimension

	CMDS dimension 3	RMDS dimension 3	WMDS dimension 2
Yukon	1.40	1.71	1.64
Coca-Cola	.20	.73	1.39
Tab	1.14	1.04	1.06
Shasta	.33	.01	.38
Diet Rite	− .11	− .08	− .12
Pepsi Cola	− .75	− 1.09	− .61
RC Cola	− 1.14	− 1.27	− .68
Diet Dr. Pepper	.25	.39	− .75
Dr. Pepper	.08	− .13	− 1.16
Diet Pepsi	− 1.25	− 1.31	− 1.16

the method of canonical correlation analysis (Chapter 12) can be applied. The results of such an analysis show that the replicated and externally averaged data sets provide spaces that are very highly correlated with those derived by individual differences analysis:

Canonical correlations with individual differences space		
Correlation	Externally averaged	Replicated
First	.996	.998
Second	.978	.996
Third	.897	.967

All correlations have significance reported to be .003 or better. However, the true significance is actually less than this because of lack of independence of the stimulus coordinates. Figures 9.6 and 9.7 show plots of the first and third canonical variables. These provide comparisons of the effects of rotating both spaces to see if better agreement in order along new dimensions can be achieved. In keeping with the high values of the correlation coefficients, much better rank order agreements appear although a few small differences remain.

What we want to illustrate here is that spaces derived by different data treatments or even different algorithms may appear to be more different than they are due to differences in rotation. The extent, or lack of agreement, can be examined by canonical correlation analysis, although a Procrustean rotation is somewhat more appropriate (Green & Carroll, 1976).

However, no amount of mathematical juggling with this data set is going to answer questions such as whether Coca-Cola or Pepsi Cola has more,

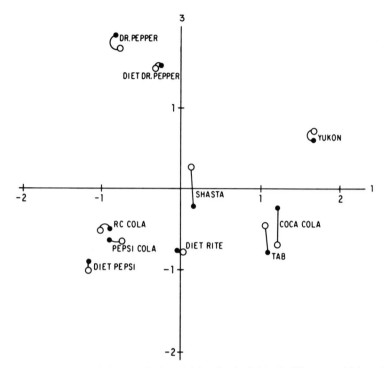

Figure 9.6. First and third canonical variables for individual differences (●) and replicated (○) ALSCAL cola solutions.

if any Dr. Pepper-like flavor. If we needed to get a better fix on this, we
would repeat the experiment with many more subjects than the current 10,
and with a larger number of stimuli.

9.4. Food Flavors

This data set (Section 3.2) is from 32 subjects (16 elderly, 16 young) for
14 food flavors. As with the strawberry-flavored drinks, we provide ordinal
and interval analyses for both mean data and the individual differences
models.

Mean Data—CMDS

Changes in stress and squared correlations with increasing dimensionality
are as follows:

	Change in stress with dimensionality				
	Dimensions				
	1	2	3	4	5
Interval	.321	.138	.087	.059	.047
Ordinal	.245	.108	.060	.035	.026

	Change in squared correlations with dimensionality				
	Dimensions				
	1	2	3	4	5
Interval	.747	.895	.942	.966	.975
Ordinal	.818	.937	.973	.988	.992

In terms of either reduction of stress or increase in squared correlation, a two-dimensional solution is the most called for.

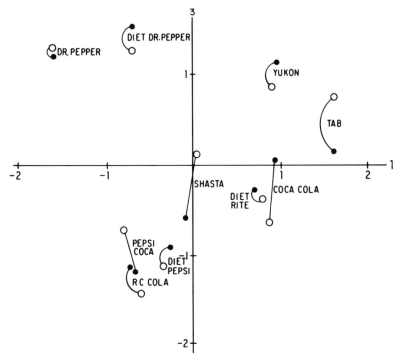

Figure 9.7. First and third canonical variables for individual differences (●) and externally averaged (○) ALSCAL cola solutions.

The ordinal and interval spaces, not reproduced here, are virtually identical. Fruit flavors are on the left of the space; butter, chocolate, and corn are top center; beef, bacon, and chicken are right center; and the three vegetables are in the bottom-right quadrant. The spatial representation, although sensible in terms of the stimuli grouped together, is otherwise unrevealing.

Individual Differences Analysis—WMDS

Changes in stress and squared correlations with increasing dimensionality are as follows:

| | Changes in stress with dimensionality | | | |
| | Dimensions | | | |
	2	3	4	5
Interval	.392	.292	.258	.226
Ordinal	.306	.210	.166	.135

| | Changes in squared correlations with dimensionality | | | |
| | Dimensions | | | |
	2	3	4	5
Interval	.223	.219	.196	.197
Ordinal	.439	.456	.466	.462

While stress decreases with increasing dimensionality, squared correlations *decrease* for analysis at the interval level and show little improvement at the ordinal level. Two-dimensional solutions only are therefore appropriate. Even though the squared correlations are miserable for the interval level analysis, the stimulus spaces are very similar for both analyses. The spatial arrangement for the ordinal level analysis is shown in Figure 9.8. Butter, chocolate, and corn are in the upper-left quadrant, bacon, chicken, and beef are in the upper right. Fruits are in the lower-left quadrant and vegetables are in the lower right. This space is similar to that derived from analysis of the mean data except for a rotation.

Weights for the elderly subjects are generally less than those for the young. Subject weights for the interval level analysis are shown in Figure 9.9 and for the ordinal level analysis in Figure 9.10. It is interesting to note that some of the elderly subjects show much greater weights at the ordinal

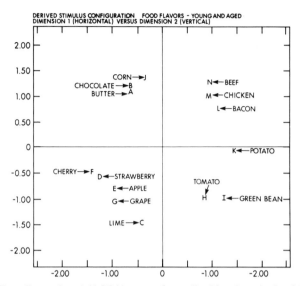

Figure 9.8. Two-dimensional ALSCAL space for ordinal level analysis of 14 food flavors using individual differences model.

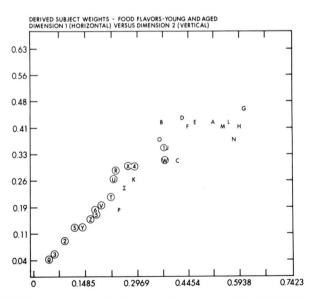

Figure 9.9. ALSCAL subject weights for food flavor space from interval level analysis; circles are elderly subjects.

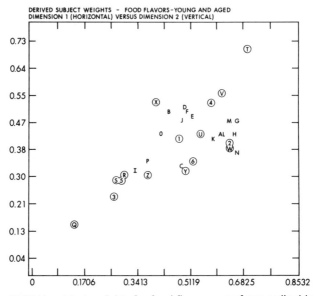

Figure 9.10. ALSCAL subject weights for food flavor space from ordinal level analysis; circles are elderly subjects.

level than the interval level, 2, V, and T for example, whereas the weights for young subjects are relatively unchanged. For the elderly subjects, there would appear to be two reasons for lack of fit to the model at the interval level of analysis. For some, such as Q and 3 discrimination is probably virtually nonexistent. Others, however, such as 2, V, and T tend to use the scale almost dichotomously and their data can be fitted much better at the ordinal level.

In summary, while both analyses give similar spaces, ordinal level data treatment can provide a much better fit. Analysis at the individual level serves to show which subjects can discriminate and which subjects cannot.

9.5 Strawberry-Flavored Beverages

This data set (Section 3.3) is for 11 strawberry-flavored beverages varying only in sweetness and depth of color. The 46 subjects were mothers of young children. We discuss here the CMDS analysis of externally averaged (mean data) and the WMDS analysis by the individual differences model. In each case the data are treated at the interval (metric) and ordinal (nonmetric) levels.

Mean Data—CMDS

The changes in stress and squared correlations with increasing dimensionality are as follows:

	Change in stress with dimensions				
	Dimensions				
	1	2	3	4	5
Interval	.159	.123	.096	.073	.044
Ordinal	.129	.088	.059	.032	.020

	Change in squared correlations with dimensions				
	Dimensions				
	1	2	3	4	5
Interval	.925	.932	.938	.954	.977
Ordinal	.949	.966	.978	.991	.995

It is clear that even in one dimension, either the interval or ordinal solution gives low stress and high correlations. At the very most no more than two dimensions should be considered. Both metric and nonmetric two-dimensional solutions are very similar. The first dimension ranks the stimuli in order of sweetness. The second dimension does not, however, rank the beverage in order of color. The ranking on dimension 2, ordinal analysis is:

Coordinates on dimension 2	Percentage color/percentage sweetness
.81	25/50
.79	225/50
.45	25/225
.21	100/225
.15	225/225
.12	100/50
− .01	150/75
− .30	150/150
− .47	75/150
− .77	100/100
−1.00	75/75

The interpretation of this dimension would appear roughly to be "like the normal drink (100/100)—not like the normal drink." Extremes of color or sweetness are at one end of the dimension while values closer to the normal are at the other.

Individual Differences Analysis—WMDS

The changes in stress and squared correlations with increasing dimensionality are as follows:

	Change in stress with dimensions			
	Dimensions			
	2	3	4	5
Interval	.290	.223	.173	.129
Ordinal	.249	.194	.145	.108

	Changes in squared correlations with dimensions			
	Dimensions			
	2	3	4	5
Interval	.555	.529	.537	.554
Ordinal	.673	.649	.668	.707

While the appropriate dimensionality is not necessarily clear from the reduction in stress, the squared correlations *decrease* in going from a two- to a three-dimensional solution. Thus two dimensions at most fit the data.

The stimulus spaces given by both analyses are very similar except for the location of stimulus 9 (150% red, 75% sweet) on dimension 2. Dimension 1 orders the stimuli in terms of sweetness. The coordinates on dimension 2 are as follows:

Ordinal	Interval	Stimulus (percentage color/percentage sweetness)
1.47	1.35	75/75
1.38	1.49	100/100
1.11	1.04	75/150
.85	.87	150/150

(cont'd.)

Ordinal	Interval	Stimulus (percentage color/percentage sweetness)
.16	−.32	100/225
−.48	−.65	100/50
−.53	.32	150/75
−.69	−.73	225/225
−.76	−1.02	225/50
−.92	−.88	25/225
1.59	−1.46	25/50

Apart from the fairly large difference for the 150/75 stimulus, the only other differences in rank order are minor flip–flops for 75/75 with 100/100 and 225/50 with 25/225. As in the analysis of the mean data the dimension seems to represent "like the normal drink" and "very different from the normal drink" with extremes of color or sweetness well separated from the 100/100 and 75/75 beverages. This dimension is of much less importance than the sweetness dimension. Average subject weights are .68 for dimension 1 and only .26 for dimension 2 in the interval analysis; .77 and .26, respectively, in the ordinal analysis. No subject in either analysis showed a higher weight on dimension 2 than dimension 1.

In summary, any of the four analyses give quite acceptable results with no major differences in interpretation. However, there were no major perceptual differences, and sweetness can probably be judged at the interval level.

Job times on the IBM 370/155 for the four jobs expressed as minutes and seconds were:

Mean, interval	0:36.1
Mean, ordinal	0:41.5
Individual differences, interval	2:24.7
Individual differences, ordinal	2:20.8

9.6. Odor of Chemicals—WMDS

This data set (Section 3.7) consists of odor dissimilarities among 19 pure chemicals. The 12 subjects (6 male, 6 female) were nonsmoking undergraduates at Duke University. We discuss here two individual differences analyses, one at the interval (metric) level and the other at the ordinal level.

Changes in stress and squared correlations with increasing dimensionality are as follows:

	Changes in stress with dimensionality			
	Dimensions			
	2	3	4	5
Interval	.376	.291	.235	.199
Ordinal	.346	.277	.223	.189

	Changes in squared correlations with dimensionality			
	Dimensions			
	2	3	4	5
Interval	.350	.377	.398	.399
Ordinal	.438	.482	.518	.532

Although stress is reduced by the inclusion of a third dimension the small increases in squared correlations do not justify examination of a three-dimensional space. In addition, no new relationships are revealed by a third dimension.

The two-dimensional stimulus spaces derived by either the ordinal or interval level analyses are virtually identical. Figure 9.11 shows the space from the interval analysis. The more pleasant smelling chemicals fall on the right, the unpleasant ones on the left. Chemicals with sharp, pungent

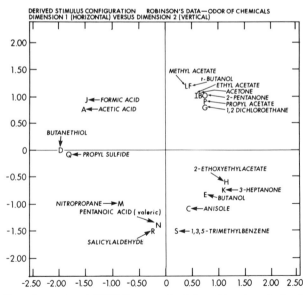

Figure 9.11. Two-dimensional ALSCAL space for interval level analysis of 19 chemicals using individual differences model.

odors are in the top of the figure while those at the bottom have aromatic rather than pungent odors.

Overall, and indeed for all but three subjects, dimension 1 is somewhat more important than dimension 2:

	Average subject weights	
	Dimension 1	Dimension 2
Interval	.443	.367
Ordinal	.509	.405

In summary this data set provides interpretable and very similar stimulus spaces whether analyzed at the interval or ordinal level. Job times for the two- through five-dimensional solutions were 1 min 44 sec and 2 min 27 sec, respectively. The spatial arrangement derived by ALSCAL-4 in Figure 9.11 is identical to the published version derived by ALSCAL-3 (Schiffman, Robinson, & Erickson, 1977) although it is rotated by 180°.

9.7. Musk Odors

This data set (Section 3.5) is from 20 subjects for the odors of 14 musks. These are difficult stimuli to differentiate from one another and a typical subject indicated "no difference" in about half of the 91 paired comparisons. Section 5.7 describes how this type of data may be averaged to develop a meaningful stimulus space with MINISSA. Section 8.6 discusses the failure of INDSCAL to develop a solution. We examine here the effect of the ALSCAL continuous and discrete options for individual differences analysis at the ordinal level.

The data contain a considerable number of tied observations. The discrete option maintains these ties whereas the continuous option unties tied data. Since ALSCAL treats zeros as missing data, it was necessary to enter no difference observations as a small number. The range of data values ran from 0 to 100 so zeros were entered as .1.

Values of stress and squared correlations for each of the two- and three-dimensional solutions are as follows:

	Stress		Squared correlations	
	Dimensions		Dimensions	
Process type	2	3	2	3
Continuous	.395	.303	.444	.499
Discrete	.378	.278	.081	.088

It is immediately apparent from the correlations that maintenance of the ties (DISCRETE) provides an extremely poor fit to the data whereas untying ties produces a three-dimensional model which accounts for about half the variance in the data. This is not apparent from the stress values and reemphasizes the value of squared correlations as a measure of fit.

While the three-dimensional solution may well be appropriate for analysis, and indeed was in the MINISSA treatment, we consider here only the two-dimensional stimulus spaces. These are shown in Figure 9.12(a) and (b). The differences are as striking as the differences in squared correlations.

The continuous option, which provides the much better fit, collapses the stimuli into three groups. The discrete option, which provides virtually no fit (RSQ = .08), arranges the stimuli in a rough circle. Even so the order of the stimuli around the circle in the discrete space follows the three groupings in the continuous space, and both models provide the same separation of stimuli on dimension 1. The stimulus arrangements also correspond with the chemical groupings discussed in the MINISSA analysis even though the squared correlations for the discrete analysis are so low.

It is probably helpful at this point to review what we have found so far before discussing further how ALSCAL has treated the data. We started with a noisy data set containing a large number of "no difference" observations. If we insist that these ties cannot be broken (discrete), ALSCAL arranges the stimuli in a rough circle but with a very poor fit. If we allow ties to be broken (continuous), the fit improves dramatically but the stimulus space collapses into three clusters and is what is called a *degenerate* solution.

An understanding of what is happening can be gained from comparison of the scattergrams and plots of transformations. The scattergram and transformation plots for the continuous solution are shown in Figure 9.13(a) and (b). The vertical axis of the scattergram represents the distances in the stimulus space, the horizontal axis represents the transformed data (disparities). The scattergram for the continuous solution shows three clusters of points. Note the large number of zero or small distances associated with large disparities in the bottom right corner. The plot of transformations, Figure 9.13(b) shows that many of the tied "no difference" observations have been transformed into large disparities. That many are also left as small disparities is less obvious—the character M represents multiple points. We can see from the transformation plot that untying the data has provided transformed values that are either basically zero or approximately uniform but large numbers. Distances can then be reasonably well fit to this transformed data (disparities) by clustering the stimuli as shown in Figure 9.12(a). These are the most extreme examples we have encountered and we recommend that you regard similar solutions with extreme caution.

Turning now to the transformation arising from the discrete option, Figure 9.14(a) and (b), we see the reason for the extremely poor fit. The disparities

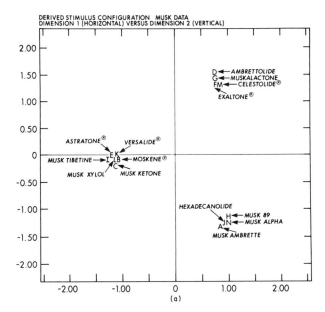

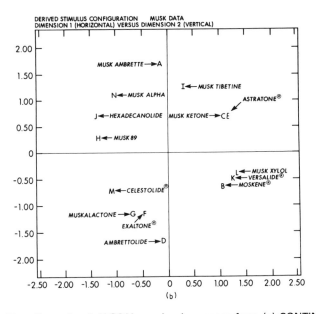

Figure 9.12. Two-dimensional ALSCAL musk odor spaces from (a) CONTINUOUS and (b) DISCRETE analyses.

SCATTERGRAM (PLOT OF LINEAR FIT) MUSK DATA
DISTANCES (VERTICAL) VS DISPARITIES (HORIZONTAL)

(a)

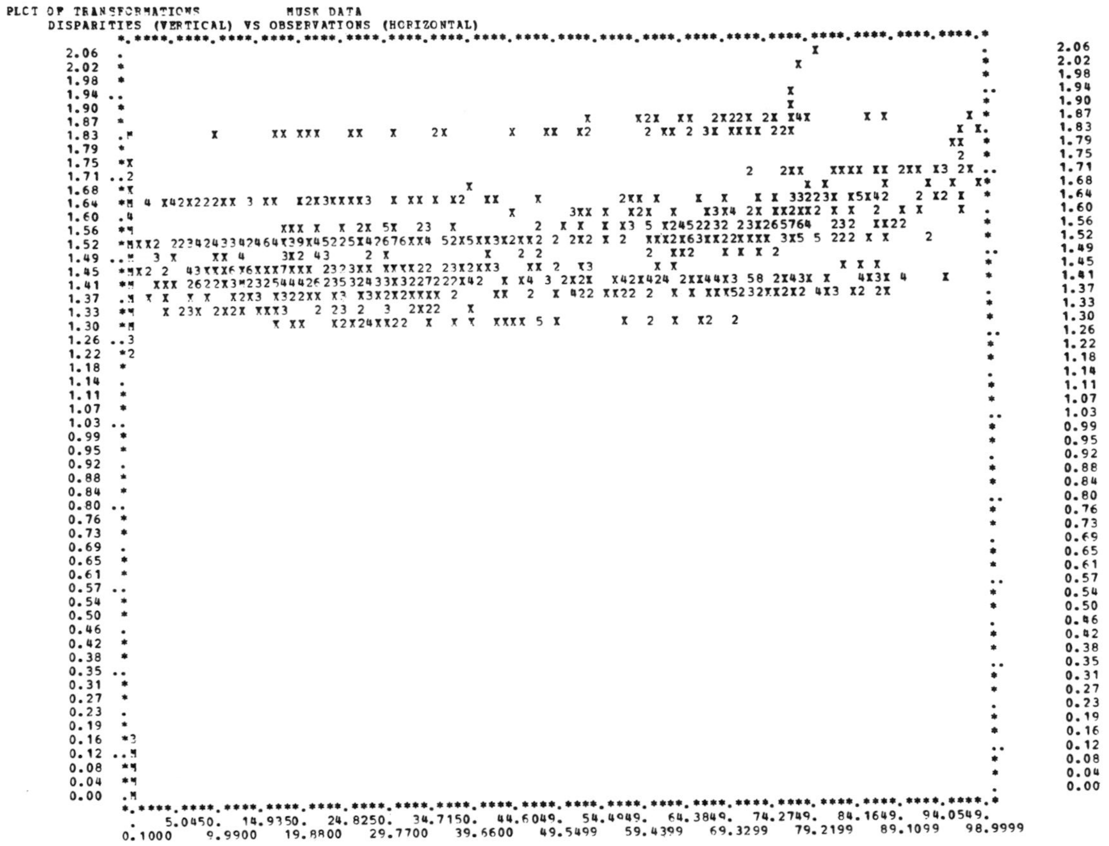

PLCT OF TRANSFORMATIONS
MUSK DATA
DISPARITIES (VERTICAL) VS OBSERVATIONS (HORIZONTAL)

Figure 9.13. ALSCAL (a) scattergram and (b) transformation plot for CONTINUOUS analysis.

(b)

SCATTERGRAM (PLOT OF LINEAR FIT), MUSK DATA
DISTANCES (VERTICAL) VS DISPARITIES (HORIZONTAL)

0.4441   0.5076,   0.5711   0.6347,   0.6982   0.7617,   0.8252   0.8887,   0.9523   1.0158,   1.0793   1.1428,   1.2063   1.2699,   1.3334   1.3969,   1.4604   1.5239,   1.5874   1.6510,   1.7145

(a)

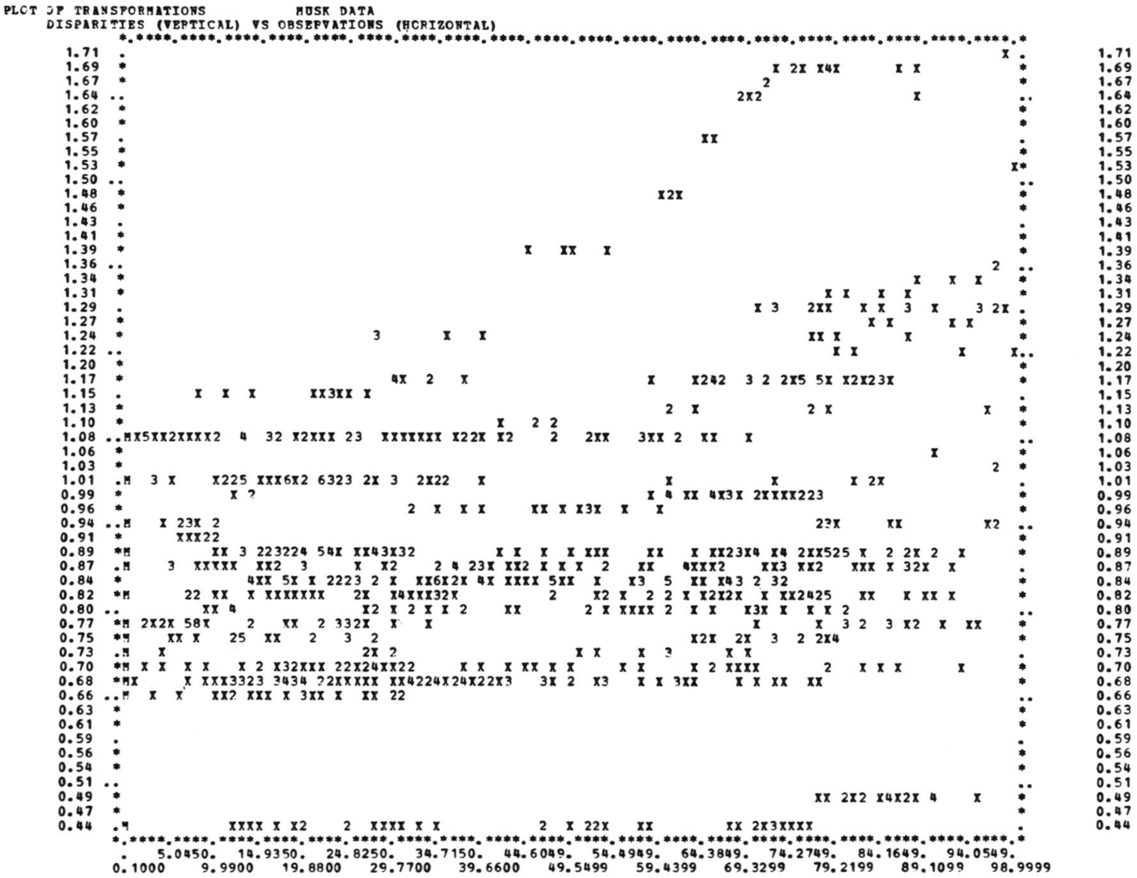

Figure 9.14. ALSCAL (a) scattergram and (b) transformation plot for DISCRETE analysis.

are literally all over the map when compared with both the distances and the observations.

The interval level analysis is, by its nature, discrete. The data are not subjected to monotone transformations so the question of how to treat tied observations does not arise. Having seen an extremely poor fit from the discrete ordinal analysis, we would expect an even worse fit from the interval analysis. This is indeed so; the squared correlations are only .042 and .043 for the two and three-dimensional solutions. The two-dimensional stimulus space, Figure 9.15 nevertheless provides the same arrangement of the stimuli as the discrete ordinal analysis which itself had some correspondence with the meaningful MINISSA space derived from averaged data.

We conclude therefore that the ALSCAL individual differences analyses of this data set are providing stimulus spaces with some meaning. At the very least they are providing a rigorous analysis of the observations to show which musks have very similar odors and which do not. Because of the large number of "no difference" observations, however, DISCRETE analysis provides a poor fit while CONTINUOUS analysis, which provides a better fit, clusters the stimuli. If you encounter similar data, our advice is not to *overinterpret* the solutions. If the stimulus spaces seem to make sense from what is known about the stimuli, well and good. But do not try to give precise meaning to stimulus positions or apply property fitting algorithms.

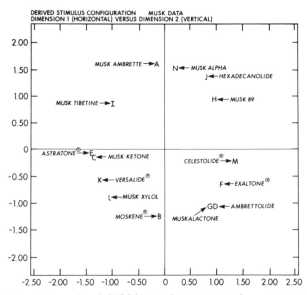

Figure 9.15. Two-dimensional ALSCAL musk odor space from INTERVAL analysis.

9.8. General Comments

ALSCAL provides the user with a great deal of flexibility in analysis. In particular, when similarity judgments from a number of subjects are available they may be treated as simple replications or by an individual differences model; analysis can be either ordinal or interval; ordinal analysis can be either discrete or continuous.

In most of the examples we have described the stimulus spaces are affected little by the analysis option used. Musk odors are the main exception and the data set here is somewhat unusual in that it contains so many "no difference" observations. For the other data sets stress is lowered and correlations are increased by ordinal continuous analysis but the stimulus spaces are unchanged.

Individual differences, as reflected by subject weights, are again for the most part preserved whatever the analysis option used. The actual weight on a given dimension for a particular subject though will be larger for ordinal-continuous than for ordinal-discrete than for interval. This was particularly so for the food flavors (Section 9.4) where some elderly subjects' data, which fitted the interval level model poorly, improved markedly at the ordinal level. This was not so, however, for all elderly subjects. Scale use, ability to discriminate, and actual dimensional perceptual differences all contribute to individual differences. ALSCAL is unique in that it allows the data to be analyzed under a variety of assumptions which thus provide some understanding of the reasons for the subject differences.

ALSCAL also provides a new concept, relative subject weights, for comparing individual differences. Whereas the squared correlations show how well a subject fits the model overall, relative subject weights show individual perceptual differences compared to the average subject for each dimension regardless of fit.

References

Green, P. E., & Carroll, J. D. *Mathematical tools for applied multivariate analysis.* New York: Academic Press, 1976.
Helwig, J. T., & Council, K. A. *SAS user's guide.* Raleigh, N.C.: SAS Institute, 1979.
Reinhardt, P. S. *SAS supplemental library user's guide.* Raleigh, N.C.: SAS Institute, 1980.
Schiffman, S., Robinson, D. E., & Erickson, R. P. Multidimensional scaling of odorants: Examination of psychological and physicochemical dimensions. *Chemical Senses and Flavor,* 1977, *2,* 375–390.

10

How to Use MULTISCALE

10.1. Setting Up a MULTISCALE Job

MULTISCALE is unique among MDS programs in that it provides output which permits the user to apply some statistical hypothesis tests. This feature represents an advance in the art and science of multidimensional scaling. The main decisions to make in using MULTISCALE are which of the four models to choose and the amount of graphical output required. Only dissimilarity data may be analyzed. If similarities have been collected, they may, of course, be transformed to dissimilarities for analysis by MULTISCALE. The maximum number of subjects is 100, of stimuli is 50, and of dimensions is 10. Additionally, the total number of observations for models M1, M2, and M4 must not exceed 15,000. For model M3 the total number of observations must not exceed 5000, and the product of the number of subjects and number of dimensions must not exceed 500. All analyses are metric. Each of the four models has its own program, and so model selection is made by a job control card which calls for program MLMDS1, MLMDS2, MLMDS3, or MLMDS4 (see Appendix).

Model M1 corresponds to metric, unconditional RMDS. It does not allow for differences in scale use or individual differences in dimensional saliences. The distance denoted by d_{ijr}^* between points i and j for replication r is calculated by:

$$d_{ijr}^* = \left[\sum_{m=1}^{k} (x_{im} - x_{jm})^2 \right]^{1/2},$$

211

where x_{im} and x_{jm} are the coordinates for points i and j on dimension m, respectively. While we do not discuss model M1 further, its mathematical form provides the basis for the more elaborate models M2, M3, and M4.

Two *response* parameters are added to model M1 to yield model M2, which is a metric, matrix conditional RMDS model. For each subject r, two response parameters, a regresson coefficient v_r and an exponent p_r, are added to allow for differences in scale use. Model M2 then has the form:

$$d_{ijr}^* = v_r \left[\sum_{m=1}^{k} (x_{im} - x_{jm})^2 \right]^{p_r/2}.$$

The response parameters are discussed more fully in the later sections of this chapter. In brief, the exponent p_r is a consequence of assuming that a subject's dissimilarities have a power law relationship with the group distances but that this power law will vary from subject to subject. Typically, the mean of the p_r values is approximately .7. The regression coefficients v_r are scale factors and have no intrinsic meaning. This model is also available in POLYCON.

Model M3 is a metric, matrix conditional WMDS model which introduces weights w_{rm} for subject r on dimension m. Model M3 has the form:

$$d_{ijr}^* = v_r \left[\sum_{m=1}^{k} w_{rm} (x_{im} - x_{jm})^2 \right]^{p_r/2}.$$

While MULTISCALE weights show the relative importance of the dimensions for each subject, they do not have the same overall interpretation as INDSCAL or ALSCAL weights. The latter weights provide an indication of how well subjects' data, or transformations of the data, fit the solution. MULTISCALE provides other measures of error. MULTISCALE weights are adjusted so that their average is one for each subject and for each dimension; that is, they are both row and column normalized.

Model M4, rather than building on model M3, extends model M2 in a different way. While model M2 provides a common standard error σ, model M4 computes variable standard errors σ_{ij} for coordinate positions, and is a metric, matrix conditional RMDS model. The standard error σ_{ij} for each stimulus pair is assumed to be made up of two parts, one for each stimulus i and j, and is related to the common standard error by:

$$\sigma_{ij} = \sigma \left[\frac{(\alpha_i^2 + \alpha_j^2)}{2} \right]^{1/2}.$$

Coefficients α_i and α_j are weighting factors for stimuli i and j and are referred to as standard error weights. This model provides a measure of cognitive uncertainty for each stimulus point.

As stated previously, the model selection is made by a job control card. That is, there is a separate program for each model. Figure 10.1 shows the deck setup for analysis of 10 colas by 10 subjects using model M2. The deck contains three types of cards, control cards, data cards, and label cards. Many of the algorithm parameters such as stepsize and acceleration parameter have default values and do not need to be specified by the average user.

Control Cards

Card 1. This is a single mandatory title card containing any title information.

Card 2. Integer parameter card in 7I3 format. The first three integers show the number of stimuli, N, number of dimensions to be used, K, and number of subjects, NS. Thus, the program must be rerun for solutions of different dimensionality.

Four other integers, not shown in the example, have default values. These are:

ITERMX: Maximum number of iterations allowed, default 200.

     IC: This is related to the stepsize parameter; its default, 0, causes the program to estimate the appropriate value. As the solution tends to convergence the stepsize is internally reduced by the program.

IFILE: The FORTRAN file number for the data, default 5.

JFILE: The FORTRAN file number for the labels, default 5.

Card 3. Floating point parameter card in 7F10.3 format. If all the default options are used, as in this example, a blank card must be included. The parameters on this card control aspects of the algorithm such as convergence criteria and acceleration parameters. If required they are entered in the following order:

CONV: The convergence criterion to be achieved before iterations terminate, default .0001. This is defined in terms of the relative change in the coordinates.

  DEX: An exponent for the data, default 1.0. Similarities may be converted to dissimilarities by setting DEX to -1.0, for example.

$\theta(T)$: The initial acceleration parameter for the configuration matrix, default 1.5. This is modified internally by the program after each third iteration to speed up or slow down the rate of

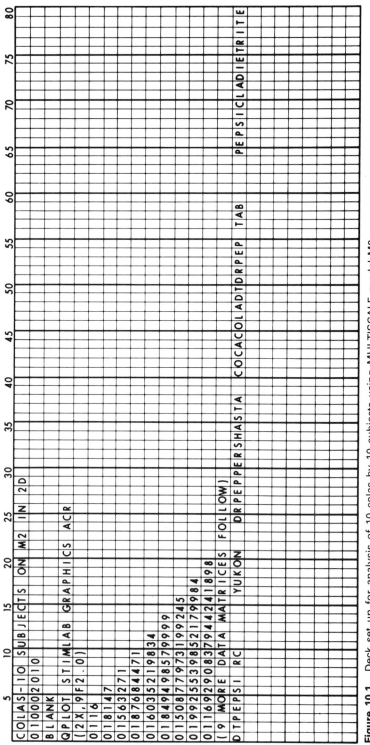

Figure 10.1. Deck set up for analysis of 10 colas by 10 subjects using MULTISCALE model M2.

214

change in coordinates. It is usually not necessary for the user to change this.

TLM: The upper limit on the acceleration parameter for the configuration matrix, default 100.

ϕ(TA): The initial acceleration parameter for the weight matrix in model M3, or the standard error weights in model M4; the defaults are .999 and .5, respectively.

TLA: Lower limit on the acceleration parameter ϕ; defaults are .9 and .0 for models M3 and M4, respectively.

TLWT: Lower limits for subject weights or standard error weights, default .0. J. Ramsay now recommends setting TLWT to .01 in both M3 and M4.

Card 4. This card contains control words described below. In this example, Figure 10.1, we use QPLOT, STIMLAB, GRAPHICS, and ACR. If none are used, insert a blank card. Only one card may be used. Control words can appear in any order with any or no spacing. Only spelling is critical. The control words are:

DIAGONAL: The dissimilarity matrix contains diagonals. This means that if a half matrix is input, the first card contains the first diagonal entry.

COMPLETE: A full square dissimilarity matrix is entered. The diagonal is ignored, and the two half matrices are analyzed independently. If neither DIAGONAL nor COMPLETE appear, the data are assumed to be a lower corner dissimilarity matrix without diagonal.

VECTOR: Allows data to be read in as a vector rather than a matrix. This saves on data cards.

ORDER: Controls input of integers to reorder data entered as VECTOR. If ORDER is present, VECTOR can be omitted.

QPLOT: Provides three pages of output for each subject. These are a plot of dissimilarities against distances, a plot of normalized residuals, and a listing of dissimilarities, model values, and normalized residuals.

NO PLOT: Suppresses configuration plots.

PUNCH: Punches out configuration, dimension weights (M3) and standard error weight (M4) matrices.

RANDOM: Causes the program to generate random data according to specifications that are input.

OLD DATA: Causes reanalysis of last data set.

INITIAL: Indicates that initial configuration or dimension weight or standard error weight matrices will be input.

LIST DATA: Provides list of input data.

EJECT: Separates each section of the printout onto a new page.

STIMLAB: Allows stimulus labels to be input, up to eight characters each.

SUBLAB: Allows subjects' labels to be input, up to eight characters each.

SUPRESS: Suppresses output from each iteration which appears under history of computation.

ACR: Computes standard error estimates for the coordinates of the points.

GRAPHICS: Directs output of configuration to a plotter. In conjunction with ACR provides elliptical 95% confidence regions round each point. In conjunction with STIMLAB labels each point.

A final note is that the single space between the two words in the control phrases NO PLOT, OLD DATA, and LIST DATA is essential.

Data Cards

Card 5. FORTRAN format specification. For dissimilarity matrices this will be the maximum number of entries in a row for a subject.

Card 6. This is only used if ORDER is specified as a control. Reordering indices are entered in 25I3 format. As many indices as data entries for each subject are required. If the *i*th reordering integer is *j*, then the *j*th element of the reordered vector is the *i*th input element.

Next Cards

Data sets for each subject are entered in sequence. Note that zeros or negative numbers are treated as missing data as in ALSCAL. Next come STIMULUS and/or SUBJECT LABEL cards. Labels must be eight characters long, with 10 per card. As many cards as necessary will be read.

If INITIAL is a control word, the configuration and/or weight matrices are entered after the dissimilarity data. The first card shows the FORTRAN format specification. Matrices are read in row by row. For M3 the sequence is: (*a*) configuration format, (*b*) configuration, (*c*) weights format, use one blank card if no weights, (*d*) weights. Both configuration and standard error weights are required for M4. For multiple analyses of the same data set, repeat all cards including the title card, using the control phrase OLD DATA on card 4.

10.2. Understanding MULTISCALE Output

As described earlier, the MULTISCALE package comprises four basic models:

M1:   Metric scaling of a single dissimilarity matrix (CMDS) or replicated matrices (RMDS). This is not discussed here.

M2:   The power model in which a subject's dissimilarities are assumed to be approximately a power function of the group distance (CMDS and RMDS).

M3:   The individual differences model (WMDS).

M4:   This model calculates standard errors for each stimulus point (CMDS and RMDS).

The output from models M2, M3, and M4 is discussed in this section, taking each model in turn.

Understanding M2 Output

Single or replicate matrices may be analyzed by M2. We show here analysis of 10 colas by 10 subjects. The output is divided into eight sections:

Section	Output
1	PROBLEM DEFINITION AND INPUT QUANTITIES
2	HISTORY OF COMPUTATION
3	FINAL CONFIGURATION ESTIMATE
4	SOME USEFUL SUMMARY RESULTS
5	WITHIN-SUBJECT STATISTICS
6	CONFIGURATION PLOTS
7	WITHIN-SUBJECT PLOTS AND RESIDUAL ANALYSES
8	ASYMPTOTIC RESULTS

Section 1 gives PROBLEM DEFINITION AND INPUT QUANTITIES (shown in Figure 10.2). The problem definition lists the number of objects, dimensions, and subjects. This is followed by the options called:

QPLOT: Gives three pages of output for each subject in Section 7 of the printout. This is discussed below.

STIMLAB: Means that stimulus labels were read in.

GRAPHICS: Directs output to a plotter.

ACR: Causes the standard errors for the coordinates of the points to be computed and, in conjunction with GRAPHICS, provides elliptical 95% confidence region plots around each point.

```
COLAS - 10 SUBJECTS ON M2 IN 2D

    THE DATA WILL BE ANALYZED USING MODEL M2.

SECTION 1.   PROBLEM DEFINITION AND INPUT QUANTITIES

        NUMBER OF SCALED OBJECTS =   10

        NUMBER OF DIMENSIONS =   2

        NUMBER OF SUBJECTS =   10

        THE FOLLOWING CONTROL LINE WAS READ IN:

            QPLOT STIMLAB GRAPHICS ACR

        MAXIMUM ITERATIONS FOR MAIN PROGRAM =   200

        CONVERGENCE CRITERION FOR LARGEST RELATIVE COORDINATE CHANGE =    0.1D-07

        INITIAL ACCELERATION PARAMETER FOR CONFIGURATION =    1.5

        INITIAL CONFIGURATION ESTIMATED BY CLASSICAL METRIC SCALING TECHNIQUE.

        THE NUMBER OF DATA ENTRIES TREATED AS MISSING IS    1

        INITIAL CONFIGURATION

            1   DTPEPSI   -0.362D+06   -0.116D+06
            2   RC         0.325D+06   -0.798D+05
            3   YUKON      0.248D+06   -0.374D+05
            4   DRPEPPER   0.203D+06    0.695D+06
            5   SHASTA     0.345D+06   -0.862D+05
            6   COCACOLA   0.198D+06   -0.354D+06
            7   DTDRPEP   -0.395D+06    0.477D+06
            8   TAB       -0.411D+06   -0.203D+06
            9   PEPSICLA   0.279D+06   -0.100D+06
           10   DIETRITE  -0.431D+06   -0.195D+06

                  INITIAL REGRESSION COEFFICIENTS                  INITIAL EXPONENTS
            1                  2.05                                       0.25
            2                  3.45                                       0.20
            3                  4.33                                       0.20
            4                  1.42                                       0.28
            5                  0.02                                       0.57
            6                  0.15                                       0.43
            7                  4.56                                       0.21
            8                  0.31                                       0.38
            9                  1.08                                       0.30
           10                  4.04                                       0.20
```

Figure 10.2. Section 1 of MULTISCALE M2 output: PROBLEM DEFINITION AND INPUT QUANTITIES.

The next four items are algorithm parameters, which have been discussed in Section 10.1. Since MULTISCALE reads zeros or negative numbers as missing data, the line THE NUMBER OF DATA ENTRIES TREATED AS MISSING should be checked and, if a large number appears, refer back to the data deck. The remainder of Section 1 shows the initial configuration, derived by the Torgerson technique (1958), and initial regression values and exponents. The meaning of these parameters is discussed below.

Section 2 of the output, not illustrated here, shows the progress of the computation. The ACCELERATION PARAMETER which speeds up or slows down the rate of convergence is modified internally by the program after each third iteration. Standard errors and log likelihoods (see following) are listed for each iteration. The convergence criterion, in this example .0001, is also listed and was achieved after 124 iterations.

Section 3 is the FINAL CONFIGURATION ESTIMATE, Figure 10.3. Coordinates are given to three decimal figures, rounded to integers, and in polar coordinate form. The coordinates for each dimension are constrained to sum to zero.

SECTION 3. FINAL CONFIGURATION ESTIMATE

IN ALL OF THE ENTRIES TABLED BELOW THE DECIMAL POINT
HAS BEEN MOVED 1 PLACES TO THE LEFT.

RESULTS ROUNDED TO THREE DECIMALS

1	DTPEPSI	-23.063	-7.571
2	RC	15.284	-4.929
3	YUKON	15.309	34.924
4	DRPEPPER	27.346	-45.167
5	SHASTA	32.892	7.503
6	COCACOLA	26.242	19.692
7	DTDRPEP	-37.896	-25.479
8	TAB	-46.562	15.203
9	PEPSICLA	29.782	-2.762
10	DIETRITE	-39.334	8.586

RESULTS ROUNDED TO INTEGERS

1	DTPEPSI	-23	-8
2	RC	15	-5
3	YUKON	15	35
4	DRPEPPER	27	-45
5	SHASTA	33	8
6	COCACOLA	26	20
7	DTDRPEP	-38	-25
8	TAB	-47	15
9	PEPSICLA	30	-3
10	DIETRITE	-39	9

RESULTS IN POLAR COORDINATE FORM:
THE FIRST VALUE IS DISTANCE FROM THE ORIGIN.
THE OTHER VALUES ARE ANGLES FROM FIRST DIMENSION

1	DTPEPSI	24.3	198
2	RC	16.1	-17
3	YUKON	38.1	66
4	DRPEPPER	52.8	-58
5	SHASTA	33.7	13
6	COCACOLA	32.8	37
7	DTDRPEP	45.7	214
8	TAB	49.0	161
9	PEPSICLA	29.9	-5
10	DIETRITE	40.3	167

Figure 10.3. Section 3 of MULTISCALE M2 output: FINAL CONFIGURATION ESTIMATE.

Section 4, SOME USEFUL SUMMARY RESULTS, Figure 10.4, shows the key statistics. The LOG LIKELIHOOD by itself does not provide an indication of significance. However, in conjunction with the LOG LIKELIHOOD value for a solution of different dimensionality or a model of different complexity, a significance test can be performed. A chi-square value is given by twice the difference between the log likelihood values:

$$\chi^2 = 2 (L_2 - L_1),$$

where L_2 is the log likelihood for the more general model (i.e., higher complexity or higher dimensionality) and L_1 is the log likelihood of the more specialized model. Examples of the usefulness of this statistic are given below. The FINAL STD. ERROR ESTIMATE is the final maximum likelihood estimate of σ. The UNBIASED STD. ERROR ESTIMATE uses the number of degrees of freedom for error as the divisor rather than the number of observations, and this makes it less sensitive to the number of

SECTION 4. SOME USEFUL SUMMARY RESULTS

LOG LIKELIHOOD = 6.078

TOTAL ITERATIONS = 124

FINAL STD. ERROR ESTIMATE = 0.598

UNBIASED STD. ERROR ESTIMATE = 0.624

NUMBER OF PARAMETERS = 36

NUMBER OF DEGREES OF FREEDOM FOR ERROR = 413

SECTION 5. WITHIN-SUBJECT STATISTICS

	FINAL REGRESSION COEFFICIENTS	FINAL EXPONENTS	WITHIN-SUBJECT UNBIASED STD. ERROR ESTIMATES	EXPONENTS ORDERED BY SIZE		STD. ERRORS ORDERED BY SIZE	
1	1.28	0.62	0.48	10	0.24	4	0.45
2	8.27	0.28	0.97	3	0.26	1	0.48
3	12.05	0.26	0.61	2	0.28	5	0.49
4	0.83	0.69	0.45	7	0.35	3	0.54
5	0.01	1.30	0.63	1	0.62	10	0.61
6	0.04	1.12	0.49	4	0.69	6	0.62
7	7.72	0.35	0.63	8	0.77	5	0.63
8	0.38	0.77	0.66	9	0.78	7	0.63
9	0.44	0.78	0.54	6	1.12	9	0.66
10	12.18	0.24	0.62	5	1.30	2	0.97

Figure 10.4. Sections 4 and 5 of MULTISCALE M2 output: SOME USEFUL SUMMARY RESULTS and WITHIN-SUBJECT STATISTICS.

dimensions or model employed. Its use is therefore recommended. The value in this example, .624, is relatively high due to the fact that the colas are perceptually quite similar. Roughly 60% of the data, in terms of the model, is error.

Section 5, WITHIN-SUBJECT STATISTICS, is also shown in Figure 10.4. The FINAL REGRESSION COEFFICIENTS have no interpretive value although they are generally negatively correlated with FINAL EXPONENTS. The exponents show the power to which the group distances are raised to fit the subject's data. Typical values are about .7, and values from .3 to 1.0 are not unusual. Small exponent values have the effect of compressing large distances in the stimulus space to fit the subject's data. This means that the subject's data do not fit the model well. The program internally fixes a minimum exponent value of .2 for each subject. An exponent of 1.0 represents classical metric scaling. Exponents greater than 1.0 are an indication of conservative subjects who are perhaps unwilling to show large dissimilarities.

Exponents should be looked at in conjunction with WITHIN-SUBJECT UNBIASED STD. ERROR ESTIMATES. These standard error estimates show how many parts out of one are error. Thus in the example shown, virtually all, 97% of Subject 2's data, is error from the perspective of the model. A low standard error value by itself is not, however, sufficient to say that the subject's data fit the model. The exponent must also be reasonably large. Section 5 also contains EXPONENTS ORDERED BY SIZE AND STD. ERRORS ORDERED BY SIZE. These are useful tabulations for a quick review of the results.

Section 6 contains the configuration plot, not shown here.

Section 7, which is printed only if QPLOT is specified, contains three pages of output for each subject. The first, Figure 10.5, is a plot of dissimilarity judgments against distance. This should be a scatter of points around the 1:1 line (plotted by zeros) whose dispersion increases with distance. The plot, which is for Subject 2, portrays the poor fit of that subject's data to the model. The second page, Figure 10.6, contains the quantile plot itself. This plot shows the degree of adherence to aspects of the log normal distribution. The normalized residuals (log d − log d^*)/σ are ordered and plotted against equal area boundaries (quantiles) of the standard normal density function. Ideally, the residuals will follow the straight line (plotted as zeros). Our poor Subject 2 shows large negative and positive deviations from the log normal distribution assumption. The third page, Figure 10.7, presents, as a lower corner matrix, the dissimilarity data, the model values, and the normalized residuals. Normalized residuals greater than 3.0 are underlined to call attention to possible outliers. The QPLOT section in this example contains 30 pages of output, 3 for each of 10 subjects.

Section 8 is ASYMPTOTIC RESULTS (not shown here). This is a calculation of standard error of estimate for the coordinates. From these a

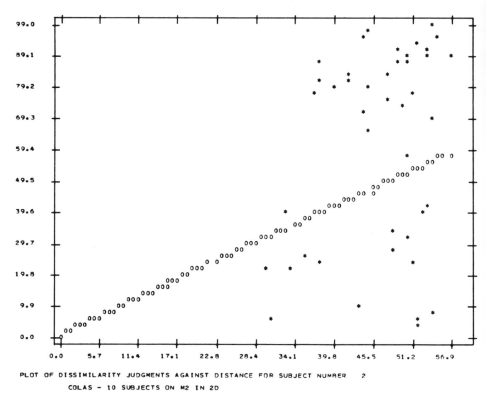

PLOT OF DISSIMILARITY JUDGMENTS AGAINST DISTANCE FOR SUBJECT NUMBER   2
COLAS - 10 SUBJECTS ON M2 IN 2D

Figure 10.5. Section 7 of MULTISCALE M2 output: DISSIMILARITY JUDGMENTS AGAINST DISTANCE.

plot may be generated, Figure 10.8, showing the 95% confidence regions for the location of each point. These are elliptical regions which have a probability of .95 of containing the population stimulus point. Therefore, these regions indicate the precision with which these points are estimated.

Understanding M3 Output

M3, the individual differences model (WMDS), is an elaboration of the power model M2. The main addition to the output is the table of subject weights. Two points need to be stressed about MULTISCALE weights. First, they do not indicate how well the subject's data fit the model. ALSCAL and INDSCAL weights provide a measure of how well data or some transformation of the data fit the model. MULTISCALE fit is described in terms of standard error and the exponent. Second, MULTISCALE weights are row and column normalized. Across a row, dimension weights

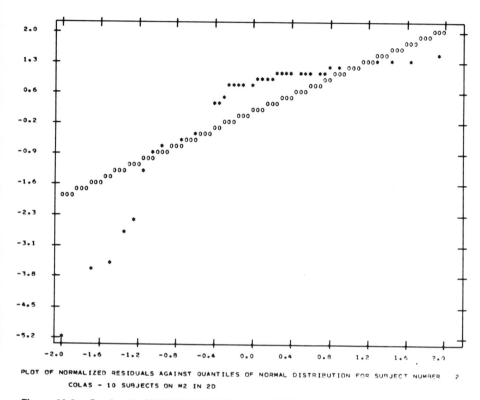

PLOT OF NORMALIZED RESIDUALS AGAINST QUANTILES OF NORMAL DISTRIBUTION FOR SUBJECT NUMBER   2
COLAS - 10 SUBJECTS ON M2 IN 2D

Figure 10.6.   Section 7 of MULTISCALE M2 output: NORMALIZED RESIDUALS AGAINST QUANTILES OF NORMAL DISTRIBUTION.

for a subject sum to the number of dimensions. Thus, for a three-dimensional solution each subject's weights will sum to 3.0. The weights in any column have an average of one. The weights do, of course, show the relative importance of each of the dimensions to the subject.

Understanding M4 Output

Model M4 is an elaboration of model M2. Neither of these models is an individual differences model. The difference between the models is that M2 assumes the dispersion σ_{ij} between points is constant. M4 allows σ_{ij} to vary by providing standard errors for each coordinate. The dispersion is then defined by

$$\sigma_{ij} = \sigma\left[(\alpha_i^2 + \alpha_j^2)/2 \right]^{1/2},$$

TABLE OF OBSERVATIONS, MODEL VALUES, AND NORMALIZED RESIDUALS FOR SUBJECT NUMBER   2

THE TOP ENTRY IN EACH CELL IS THE DISSIMILARITY OBSERVATION TAKEN TO INPUT POWER,
THE MIDDLE ENTRY IS THE BEST FITTING MODEL VALUE,
AND THE BOTTOM ENTRY IS THE NORMALIZED RESIDUAL.

IF A DISSIMILARITY OBSERVATION HAS BEEN TREATED AS MISSING,
ITS PLACE IS FILLED BY ASTERISKS AND ITS RESIDUAL SET TO ZERO.

IF A RESIDUAL MIGHT BE CONSIDERED AS UNUSUALLY LARGE, IT IS UNDERLINED.

```
 2    9.0
      44.0
     -2.55

 3   90.0   70.0
     49.3   44.5
     0.97   0.73

 4   87.0   65.0    6.0
     50.6   45.2   54.3
     0.87   0.58  -3.53

 5   87.0   77.0   83.0   83.0
     49.4   37.4   42.0   48.2
     0.91   1.16   1.09   0.87

 6   33.0   79.0   25.0   89.0   39.0
     49.0   39.9   36.0   51.0   33.1
    -0.54   1.10  -0.58   0.89   0.26

 7   86.0   86.0   99.0   22.0   90.0   40.0
     38.2   49.2   54.2   51.7   53.8   53.8
     1.30   0.89   0.97  -1.37   0.83  -0.48

 8   81.0   30.0   57.0   88.0   69.0   39.0   97.0
     42.1   51.1   51.0   56.9   54.1   52.7   45.0
     1.05  -0.85   0.18   0.70   0.39  -0.48   1.23

 9   74.0   20.0   94.0   78.0    5.0   81.0   92.0   88.0
     48.2   33.6   44.7   45.3   30.8   38.0   52.4   53.8
     0.69  -0.83   1.19   0.87  -2.91   0.90   0.79

10   23.0   26.0   72.0   94.0    2.0   76.0   81.0   20.0    5.0
     38.1   49.0   50.1   55.2   52.6   51.4   42.6   30.0   52.1
    -0.81  -1.02   0.58   0.85  -5.24   0.63   1.03  -0.65  -3.76
```

Figure 10.7. Section 7 of MULTISCALE M2 output: OBSERVATIONS, MODEL VALUES, AND NORMALIZED RESIDUALS.

where σ is the common standard error; α_i and α_j indicate the relative variability of judgment specific to stimuli i and j, respectively. The average value of $\alpha^2 = 1$. These are referred to in the output as standard error weights.

The output of M4 is similar to the output of M2 except that (a) HISTORY OF ITERATIONS contain convergence criteria for standard error weights, and (b) Section 4 contains standard error weights for each stimulus in NATURAL ORDER and ORDERED BY SIZE. It should be noted that if two or more standard error weights become zero, the program terminates and the resultant solution may be poor. This problem can be cured by setting a small positive lower limit to these weights using program parameter TLWT.

10.3. Colas

This data set (Section 3.1) is from 10 subjects for 10 decarbonated commercial colas. The analyses described here use the chi-square capability

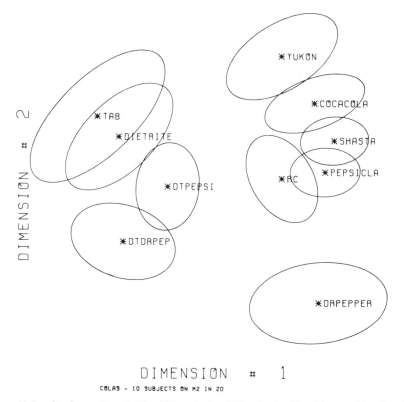

COLAS - 10 SUBJECTS ON M2 IN 2D

Figure 10.8. Configuration plot for M2 analysis of 10 colas by 10 subjects with ellipsoids showing 95% confidence regions for each point.

of MULTISCALE to determine the appropriate model and dimensionality. The chi-square calculations provide an indication of the significance of changing to a more complex model or higher dimensionality.

The questions to be answered from the 10 sets of cola dissimilarities are:

1. What is the appropriate dimensionality for model M2 (no subject weights)?
2. Does model M3 (with subject weights) give a better fit than M2 at its best dimensionality?
3. If M3 gives a better fit than M2, what is the best dimensionality for M3?

Analyses for M2 were run in one, two, and three dimensions; for M3, in two and three dimensions. The key results from these analyses, log likelihood and unbiased standard error estimate, are summarized in Table 10.1. Chi-square tests of dimensionality and models are shown in Table 10.2. Chi-square is calculated as twice the difference between two log

Table 10.1
Log Likelihoods and Unbiased Standard Error Estimates for Various Cola Analyses

Model	Dimensions	Log likelihood	Unbiased standard error estimate	Number of degrees of freedom for error
M2	1	− 41.1	.686	421
M2	2	6.1	.624	413
M2	3	11.8	.621	406
M3	2	83.3	.532	403
M3	3	106.8	.516	385

likelihoods, with degrees of freedom being the difference between the number of degrees of freedom for error in each analysis.

The standard errors for the M2 analyses are .686, .624, and .621 for one, two, and three dimensions, respectively. The three-dimensional solution does not therefore appear to represent an improvement over the two-dimensional solution. This is confirmed by the chi-square values which show a significant improvement in moving from one to two dimensions, but not from two to three.

The standard errors for the M3 analyses are .532 and .516 for two and three dimensions, respectively. Introduction of the individual differences model is thus providing an appreciable reduction in standard error. The chi-square values, Table 10.1, show significant improvments in fit for (*a*) model M3 in two dimensions over model M2 in two dimensions and (*b*) model M3 in three dimensions over model M3 in two dimensions.

The individual difference model M3 in three dimensions appears most appropriate therefore for interpretation. It is worth noting that it only takes a few minutes to assemble the data from the printouts and to develop and examine chi-square values such as are shown in Table 10.2. The rest of this section is devoted to further analysis of the three-dimensional M3 printout.

The stimulus spaces, Figures 10.9 and 10.10, provide clear separations between diet and nondiet colas, dimension 1, and cherry and regular colas, dimension 2. Dimension 3 is less clear-cut but appears related to manufacturer flavor type: Note the closeness of Tab and Coca-Cola, and the two

Table 10.2
Chi-square Tests for Cola Models

Test	χ^2	Degrees of freedom	p
M2,1D versus 2D	94.7	8	.001
M2,2D versus 3D	11.4	7	.25
M2 versus M3,2D	154.4	10	.001
M3,2D versus 3D	47.0	18	.001

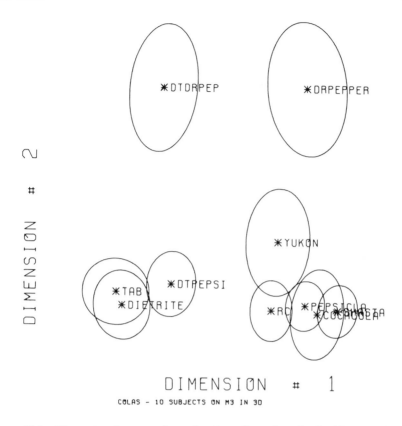

Figure 10.9. Dimension 1 versus dimension 2 configuration plot for M3 analysis of 10 colas by 10 subjects with ellipsoids showing 95% confidence regions for each point.

Dr. Pepper beverages. While the space is interpretable, the fit, in terms of unbiased standard error estimate, .516, is not impressive. One can say that the three-dimensional individual model only accounts for about half the variation in the data. The within-subject unbiased standard error estimates range from .38 to .65.

The subject weights, Table 10.3, indicate considerable individual variation among subjects. Subjects 2, 3, 7, and 10 appear insensitive to the diet–nondiet dimension 1; Subjects 3 and 10 are much more conscious than other subjects of the cherry cola dimension; Subjects 2 and 7 put more emphasis on the flavor dimension. Subjects 4, 5, 6, and 9 pay scant attention to the cherry–regular cola dimension 2 but perceive the diet–nondiet dimension as very important. Only Subjects 1 and 8 appear perceptive of all three dimensions in making their judgments. It is interesting to note that the subjects who weight dimension 1 heavily (1, 4, 5, 6, and 9) are tasters of a compound called PTC which is bitter to some persons. The remaining

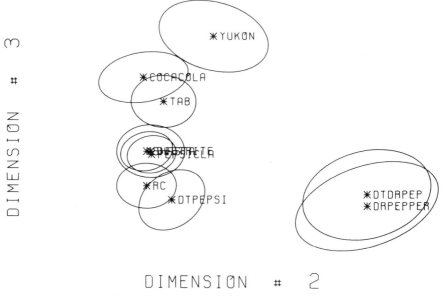

DIMENSION ⌗ 2

COLAS - 10 SUBJECTS ON M3 IN 3D

Figure 10.10. Dimension 2 versus dimension 3 configuration plot for M3 analysis of 10 colas by 10 subjects with elliposoids showing 95% confidence regions for each point.

five subjects, who, with the exception of Subject 8, give virtually zero weight to dimension 1, are nontasters of PTC.

The within-subject regression coefficients, v_r, and exponents, p_r, show considerable response variation among subjects (Table 10.4). Regression coefficients range from .04 to 16.86; exponents range from .29 to 1.33. Regression coefficients have no interpretive value as such. They scale the

Table 10.3
Subject Weights for M3 Cola Analysis

	Dimension		
Subject	1	2	3
1	1.84	.67	.49
2	.0	.56	2.44
3	.0	3.00	.00
4	1.47	.01	1.52
5	2.24	.21	.55
6	2.49	.15	.36
7	.10	.70	2.20
8	.74	1.58	.68
9	1.12	.15	1.73
10	.0	2.98	.02

Table 10.4
Within-Subject Statistics for M3 Cola Analysis

Subject	Regression coefficient	Exponent	Unbiased standard error
1	1.88	.65	.49
2	1.69	.70	.65
3	16.86	.29	.42
4	1.49	.71	.46
5	.04	1.33	.64
6	.17	1.06	.49
7	1.53	.76	.44
8	.54	.84	.63
9	.16	1.12	.49
10	14.11	.31	.38

distances after the power transformation and are therefore negatively correlated with exponents. The low exponents for Subjects 3 and 10, .29 and .31, suggest that these subjects' data do not fit the model as well as their standard errors, .42 and .38, would otherwise indicate. However, Subject 2, who had virtually no fit with model M2, standard error .97 and exponent .28, fits this individual differences model with standard error .65 and a typical exponent of .70. Subject 2 weights dimension 3 heavily and is not sensitive to dimension 1. In summary, the individual differences model M3 appears appropriate for analysis of this data set and reveals three interpretable dimensions. However, the standard error is high and indicates that about half the variation in the data may be noise.

10.4. Food Flavors

This data set (Section 3.2) is from 32 subjects (16 elderly, 16 young) for the odors of 14 food flavors. Analysis is restricted to the M2 model, which allows for differences in scale use but not for differences in dimensional saliences.

Tables 10.5 and 10.6 show the key results for analyses in one, two, and three dimensions. The chi-square tests indicate that a two-dimensional solution is significantly better than a one-dimensional solution and that possibly a three-dimensional solution is preferable to a one-dimensional solution. However, there is no real reduction in standard error in going from two to three dimensions. Therefore, only a clear interpretation of a three-dimensional solution can justify its retention.

We discuss first the two-dimensional solution shown in Figure 10.11. The ellipsoids represent the 95% confidence regions for the coordinates. It is

Table 10.5
Log Likelihoods and Unbiased Standard Error Estimates for M2 Analyses of
Food Flavors

Dimensions	Log likelihood	Unbiased standard error estimate	Number of degrees of freedom for error
1	−909.7	.846	2778
2	−817.3	.820	2766
3	−803.0	.818	2755

Table 10.6
Chi-square Tests for M2 Dimensionality of Food Flavors

Test	χ^2	Degrees of freedom	p
2D versus 1D	164.8	12	.001
3D versus 2D	28.6	11	.005

clear that, with the exception of cherry, grape, and apple, the stimuli are clearly separated from each other. The stimuli are grouped basically according to type. Proceeding counterclockwise from the left of Figure 10.11, we see fruits, vegetables, meats, and finally corn–chocolate–butter.

The within-subject statistics indicate that the elderly as a group are responsible for the high standard error. Their mean is .86 compared with .64 for the young subjects. While some of the elderly subjects performed as well in terms of standard error than some of the young subjects, seven had standard errors near 1.0 or greater. This suggests lack of discrimination by these elderly subjects. Further, the remaining nine elderly subjects with more reasonable standard error values all have exponent values lower than .3 and the program itself contains a lower cutoff of .2:

Elderly subject number	Exponent	Standard Error
17	.20	.59
20	.20	.16
31	.20	.34
29	.20	.49
25	.20	.44
28	.21	.98
22	.21	.60
32	.24	.65
21	.25	.93

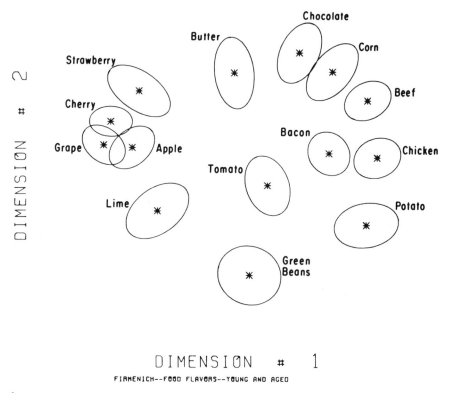

DIMENSION   #   1

FIRMENICH--FOOD FLAVORS--YOUNG AND AGED

Figure 10.11. Dimension 1 versus dimension 2 configuration plot for M2 analysis in two dimensions of 14 food flavors by 32 subjects with ellipsoids showing 95% confidence regions for each point.

None of the young subjects have such low exponent values. Indeed, the mean exponent value for the young subjects is .73, which is considered typical in MULTISCALE analyses of dissimilarities.

While it is possible that some of their data can fit better into a third dimension, the situation actually deteriorates with a three-dimensional model. Figures 10.12 and 10.13 show the 95% confidence regions around the stimuli. Not only is there now overlap between many of the stimuli in the dimension 1–dimension 2 plane, but also considerable overlap on dimension 3.

In summary, a two-dimensional model is appropriate for this data set. However, the data from the elderly subjects hardly fit the model. Elderly subjects have either excessively low exponents or very high standard errors. These results are generally consistent with those developed by the other algorithms.

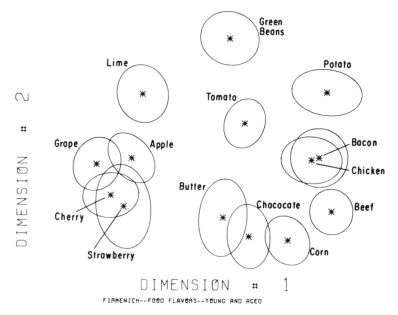

Figure 10.12. Dimension 1 versus dimension 2 configuration plot for M2 analysis in three dimensions of 14 food flavors by 32 subjects with ellipsoids showing 95% confidence regions for each point.

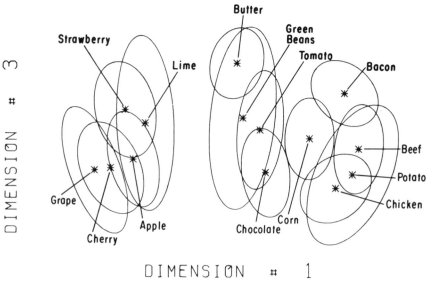

Figure 10.13. Dimension 1 versus dimension 3 configuration plot for M2 analysis in three dimensions of 14 food flavors by 32 subjects with ellipsoids showing 95 % confidence regions for each point.

10.5. Strawberry-Flavored Beverages

This data set (Section 3.3) is for 11 strawberry-flavored drinks varying only in sweetness and depth of color. The 46 subjects were mothers of young children. Since the stimuli are known to vary in only two physicochemical dimensions, the stimulus space should be readily interpretable. As will be seen, this is not entirely so.

The analyses discussed here are in terms of the M2 model only. That is, allowance is made for difference in scale use but not for differences in dimensional salience.

Tables 10.7 and 10.8 show the key results for analyses in one, two, and three dimensions. In all cases the standard error is high and is virtually unchanged between the two- and three-dimensional solutions. The chi-square test shows, in fact, that the three-dimensional solution provides no significant improvement over the two-dimensional solution. However, the two-dimensional solution is significantly better than the one-dimensional solution despite the small, .78 to .74, change in standard error.

The two-dimensional solution is shown in Figure 10.14. Dimension 1 orders the beverages by sweetness. There is a clear separation by sweetness level irrespective of color:

Sweetness/Color	Coordinates on dimension 1
225/25	37
225/100	37
225/225	44
150/75	21
150/150	24
100/100	1
75/75	−20
75/150	−25
50/25	−39
50/100	−40
50/225	−43

Interpretation of dimension 2 is less obvious. The stimuli are not ranked by color depth:

Color	Coordinates on dimension 2
225	2, −6
150	1, 3
100	−8, −2, 4
75	−13, −8
25	10, 15

Table 10.7
Log Likelihoods and Unbiased Standard Error Estimates for M2 Analysis of
Strawberry-Flavored Beverages

Dimensions	Log likelihood	Unbiased standard error estimate	Number of degrees of freedom for error
1	− 575.1	.779	2406
2	− 435.3	.738	2397
3	− 425.6	.736	2389

Table 10.8
Chi-square Tests for M2 Dimensionality of Strawberry-Flavored Beverages

Test	χ^2	Degrees of freedom	p
2D versus 1D	79.6	9	.001
3D versus 2D	19.4	8	.025

The stimulus order is, however, roughly compatible with the hypothesis that dimension 2 represents similarity to the standard (100/100 sweetness–color) commercial beverage. Extremes of color and/or sweetness lie at the top of Figure 10.14; sweetness–color combinations close to the 100/100 standard lie at the bottom of Figure 10.14.

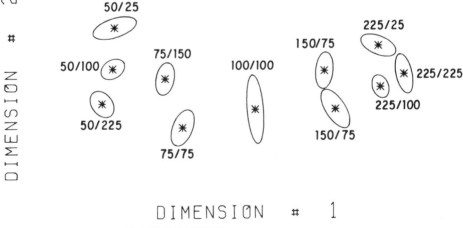

Figure 10.14. Dimension 1 versus dimension 2 configuration plot for M2 analysis in two dimensions of 11 strawberry-flavored beverages by 32 subjects with ellipsoids showing 95% confidence regions for each point.

The within-subject statistics show standard errors ranging from .41 to 1.22 and exponents ranging from .21 to 1.64. If one wished to perform further analyses on these data, subjects with high standard errors (greater than 1.0) or low exponents (less than .3) would be omitted.

Finally, despite the high standard error of the analysis, .74, the standard errors of estimates for the coordinates are such that the stimuli are well separated. The ellipsoids in Figure 10.14 show the 95% confidence regions and no overlap.

10.6. General Comments

In the examples discussed in this chapter, MULTISCALE has provided clearly interpretable stimulus configurations, two from taste data and one from odor data. Differences in scale use and dimensional saliences are demonstrated. MULTISCALE provides an elegant way of accommodating differences in scale use. MULTISCALE, with its power transformation, can in one sense be considered as lying between classical metric scaling (where the exponent is one) and nonmetric scaling. The problem with nonmetric procedures is that the number of degrees of freedom that they use is not fixed; it varies from one set of data to another. This makes it impossible to test hypotheses with any precision. It is here that MULTI-SCALE shows its greatest strength. Acceptance of a log normal distribution for distances about their error values allows development of chi-square tests for comparisons of dimensionality and model complexity. It also provides a measure of standard error. The size of the standard errors are at first disconcerting for the data examined. In the examples provided in this chapter, the models were unable to fit some 50 to 70% of the variability in the data. Nevertheless, with sufficient subjects, interpretable configurations were developed.

MULTISCALE is the only program discussed in this book which is still in the process of development. New packages with new options can be expected to be made available.

11

Comparison of Programs

11.1. Overview

The main purpose of this chapter is to compare the solutions provided by the six programs. It is certainly fair to ask which is the best one to use. Our reply has to be that there is no best one. The most important criterion is to develop good data. Access to and familiarity with a specific program may dictate your choice.

MINISSA is the easiest to use, and seems to give aberrant solutions least frequently. On the other hand, it is relatively expensive with regard to machine time, and it is time consuming comparing individual spaces for a large number of subjects. MINISSA is limited to nonmetric CMDS.

POLYCON overcomes the problem of a large number of individual spaces via the replicated data option. It has many useful options for treatment of data and for this reason can consume large amounts of computer time and requires more familiarity with the various options to use. POLYCON provides metric or nonmetric CMDS and RMDS but not WMDS.

KYST is very similar to POLYCON. It is a little easier to use and faster to run but accepts less data points, 1760 versus 4000; it also has less options than POLYCON, but provides metric or nonmetric CMDS and RMDS.

INDSCAL and SINDSCAL provide readily interpretable individual differences spaces provided the input data are not excessively noisy. They are limited to metric WMDS analyses.

ALSCAL, with its variety of options, is the only one of the programs that allows metric or nonmetric CMDS, RMDS, and WMDS analyses.

MULTISCALE provides an individual differences model which also allows for differences in scale use. MULTISCALE has the further advantage of allowing performance of statistical hypothesis tests.

All of the programs give similar stimulus spaces for most of the data sets. In general, we have found ALSCAL and INDSCAL to give similar subject and stimulus spaces when the metric option of ALSCAL is used to view the data as being at the interval level. At the nonmetric level, ALSCAL tends to compress the differences among both stimuli and subjects.

In the following sections we compare first CMDS of mean data by MINISSA, POLYCON, KYST, ALSCAL, and MULTISCALE. Next we examine RMDS solutions from POLYCON, KYST, ALSCAL, and MULTISCALE. Finally, we compare and contrast the individual differences models, WMDS, provided by ALSCAL, INDSCAL, and MULTISCALE. Only ALSCAL and MULTISCALE provide CMDS, RMDS, and WMDS options.

11.2. CMDS by MINISSA, POLYCON, KYST, ALSCAL, and MULTISCALE

CMDS analysis by these five programs for three different data sets provides in most cases very similar stimulus spaces. We consider first the mean dissimilarities for the odors of 14 food flavors. The solutions discussed for POLYCON, KYST, and ALSCAL are nonmetric and CONTINUOUS. The MULTISCALE model used is M2. Three of the stimulus spaces are shown in earlier chapters: MINISSA, Figure 5.6; POLYCON, Figure 6.6; and KYST, Figure 7.5. Apart from 180° rotations about one or both axes, the five stimulus spaces are all very similar. Values for Kruskal's stress are .096, MINISSA; .101, both KYST and POLYCON; and .108, ALSCAL. The unbiased standard error estimate for the MULTISCALE solution is .111, which also indicates a good fit to the data. The exponent is .55, which is a little low perhaps by virtue of averaging in the data for many poorly discriminating elderly subjects.

Figure 5.9 contains the MINISSA stimulus space for 11 strawberry-flavored drinks. All five programs give solutions which order the beverages along dimension 1 in terms of sweetness. Values for Kruskal's stress are .078, both MINISSA and KYST; .080, POLYCON; and .088, ALSCAL. The unbiased standard error estimate for the MULTISCALE solution is .15 and the exponent is quite typical at .84. In all analyses of this data set, the second dimension is weak, and there are some differences between the solutions in terms of rank order. However, the main feature, separation of extremes of color and sweetness from the typical commercial beverage, is shown by all.

The major difference between the programs arises in analysis of the cola data. Here, the KYST, POLYCON, ALSCAL trio provides interpretable three-dimensional solutions using CMDS, whereas MINISSA and MULTISCALE M2 do not. This data set is fairly noisy and there are some considerable differences between individual's perceptions which are of course lost when the data are averaged. All five of the programs clearly differentiate diet from nondiet drinks and cherry from regular colas. However, a 45° rotation of the MULTISCALE solution is necessary to place diet–nondiet as dimension 1 as found by the other programs. Since the individual differences programs WMDS, including MULTISCALE M3, support the existence of a third dimension, the best solution for the colas using CMDS is found by KYST, POLYCON, and ALSCAL. The reductions in stress with the addition of a third dimension are all large, and the Kruskal's stress values are .061, .061, and .067, respectively, for the three-dimensional solutions.

In summary, provided the data are not too noisy, similar stimulus spaces are provided by the CMDS options of the five programs. With noisier data POLYCON, KYST, or ALSCAL seem more capable of extracting order. Nevertheless, MINISSA and MULTISCALE M2 still show the more important features of the stimulus space. In general, however, we recommend individual differences analysis, WMDS, over CMDS whenever possible. The examples in this book show considerable differences in the way individuals respond and if data are collected from a number of subjects, as they should be, CMDS overly compresses the information.

11.3. RMDS by POLYCON, KYST, ALSCAL, and MULTISCALE

These are the only four of the six programs we discuss that allow RMDS. Each program can provide some measure of how well a given subject's data fit the model. POLYCON and ALSCAL provide stress values for each subject, while MULTISCALE gives both standard error estimates and exponents for each subject. Since POLYCON, KYST, and ALSCAL share some common heritage, their solutions are indeed generally similar. The real interest therefore lies in the comparison of these programs with the quite different model and computation strategy of MULTISCALE. We compare first, however, the RMDS solutions from KYST, POLYCON, and ALSCAL for the cola data. The comparison between KYST and POLYCON is for a nonmetric analysis; between POLYCON and ALSCAL for a metric analysis.

KYST and POLYCON both provide a clear separation of diet and nondiet drinks on dimension 1. However, dimensions 2 and 3 from the POLYCON analysis emerge fairly clearly as cherry–regular cola and manufacturer flavor type but less so from the KYST analysis. Even so, there is a general correspondence as comparison of Figures 6.5(b) and 7.4(b) will show. Indicative, however, of the fact that identical solutions were not reached is the small difference in stress (formula 1) which was .213 for POLYCON and .199 for KYST.

ALSCAL RMDS analysis of several matrices using the SIMPLE EUCLIDEAN MODEL is equivalent to POLYCON using REPLICATIONS. The analyses compared here use the "ties remain tied" measurement process (SECONDARY in POLYCON, DISCRETE in ALSCAL) and are conducted at the interval level.

Both provide a measure of Kruskal's stress for each subject which allows a comparison of these values as well as the stimulus spaces. The ALSCAL analysis terminated because of negative stress improvement. Stress was minimized in the POLYCON analysis. The root mean square of the individual stress values was .237 for POLYCON and .233 for ALSCAL. Thus despite the ALSCAL warning, the solutions may be comparable.

Inspection of the stimulus spaces reveals that dimension 1 separates the diet and nondiet colas in either analysis. However, whereas POLYCON separates the cherry and regular colas on dimension 2, ALSCAL provides this separation on dimension 3. Dimension 2 ALSCAL is equivalent to dimension 3, manufacturer flavor. Overall, the stimulus spaces are similar and all subjects have stress values within the range .20 to .26 so that further comparison is unnecessary.

We compare next analysis of the replicated cola data for 10 subjects using a metric version of POLYCON and MULTISCALE model M2. MULTISCALE model M2 allows for differences in response bias by means of exponents and regression coefficients for each subject. The metric version of POLYCON only allows for differences in response bias by means of regression coefficients for each subject.

Neither in terms of POLYCON stress (formula 2) nor MULTISCALE standard error estimate do the data fit either model well:

	Dimensions		
	1	2	3
POLYCON stress	.893	.853	.816
MULTISCALE standard error	.686	.624	.621

The minute change in MULTISCALE standard error between the two- and three-dimensional solutions indicates that a third dimension is improbable for this model. Indeed, the chi-square test applied to the MULTI-

SCALE results, Section 10.3, shows that its third dimension is not an improvement; neither is its third dimension interpretable. The POLYCON third dimension is interpretable as manufacturer flavor type. This dimension is lost with MULTISCALE M2, although not with model M3 (see the next section).

Both programs provide clear separation in two dimensions of diet and nondiet and cherry and regular cola. The two-dimensional solutions may, therefore, be compared with regard to how well each subject's data fit the respective models. With POLYCON the individual values of stress formula 2 may be used. With MULTISCALE it is necessary to examine both standard error and exponent. These values are shown in Table 11.1. Exponents below .3 can lead to apparently good fits in terms of standard error which are not justified.

The subjects with highest POLYCON stress (2, 3, and 7) all have dangerously low MULTISCALE exponents, indicating that their data are not fitting the model, although only subject 2 shows exceptionally high standard error. The subjects with lowest POLYCON stress (1, 4, 5, 6, and 8) combine exponents of .6 or greater with average standard errors. Thus POLYCON and MULTISCALE are providing, in general, similar information about the subjects. However, as in the case of CMDS, MULTISCALE M2 is apparently unable to extract quite as much order from this data set as the other programs.

If replicated data are available, it seems more sensible to perform individual differences analyses, WMDS, rather than RMDS.

11.4. WMDS by INDSCAL, ALSCAL, and MULTISCALE

The computation strategies for the three WMDS programs (Chapter 16) are quite different. Further, INDSCAL provides analysis only at the interval

Table 11.1
Comparison of POLYCON and MULTISCALE Subject Fits

Subject	POLYCON STRESS 2	M2 Exponent	M2 Standard error
1	.799	.62	.48
2	.975	.28	.97
3	.936	.26	.61
4	.801	.69	.45
5	.776	1.30	.63
6	.786	1.12	.49
7	.904	0.35	.63
8	.755	0.77	.66
9	.884	0.78	.54
10	.880	0.24	.62

level. ALSCAL provides either interval or ordinal analyses. MULTI-SCALE can be considered to lie somewhere between metric and nonmetric scaling. ALSCAL and INDSCAL subject weights can be interpreted in generally the same way and both provide some measure of fit. MULTI-SCALE subject weights are simply row and column normalized and provide no measure of fit; MULTISCALE uses its standard error as the main measure of fit.

We compare first INDSCAL and ALSCAL solutions for colas, food flavors, and strawberry drinks using the metric version of ALSCAL. This is followed by comparison of the MULTISCALE solution for the cola data with INDSCAL and nonmetric ALSCAL solutions.

Colas (INDSCAL and ALSCAL)

Although the INDSCAL dimension 2 is equivalent to the ALSCAL dimension 3 and the INDSCAL dimension 3 is equivalent to the ALSCAL dimension 2, both programs provide similar stimulus spaces. In both cases, dimension 1 separates diet and nondiet drinks, with Tab and Diet Rite being most diet-like and Shasta, RC, and Pepsi being least diet-like.

The orders on the cherry–regular cola dimension for INDSCAL and ALSCAL, as shown in Table 11.2, are identical except for Diet Rite and Diet Pepsi which are, in any case, extremely close to each other. The manufacturer flavor dimension has the same general order from each program (Table 11.3), but some stimuli differ in rank by as much as two places.

While the stimulus spaces are thus extremely similar, and the diet–nondiet dimensions most important, the two programs suggest different importance for the cherry–regular and manufacturer flavor dimensions. The approximate proportion of the total variance accounted for (in the scalar cross-

Table 11.2
Stimulus Order on Cherry–Regular Cola Dimension

INDSCAL (2)	ALSCAL (3)
Dr. Pepper	Dr. Pepper
Diet Dr. Pepper	Diet Dr. Pepper
Yukon	Yukon
Coca-Cola	Coca-Cola
Tab	Tab
Shasta	Shasta
Diet Pepsi	Diet Rite
Diet Rite	Diet Pepsi
RC	RC
Pepsi Cola	Pepsi Cola

Table 11.3
Stimulus Order on Manufacturer Flavor Dimension

INDSCAL (3)	ALSCAL (2)
Diet Pepsi	Diet Pepsi
RC	Dr. Pepper
Dr. Pepper	Diet Dr. Pepper
Pepsi	RC
Diet Dr. Pepper	Pepsi
Diet Rite	Diet Rite
Shasta	Shasta
Coca-Cola	Tab
Tab	Coca-Cola
Yukon	Yukon

cross-products) on each dimension by INDSCAL when compared with the average subject weights on each dimension from ALSCAL shows:

	INDSCAL "variance"	ALSCAL average weights
Diet–nondiet	.288	.438
Cherry–regular	.233	.310
Manufacturer flavor	.108	.326

Thus INDSCAL indicates that cherry–regular flavor is overall of greater importance than manufacturer flavor whereas ALSCAL suggests they are of equal importance.

We also see differences when comparing some of the individual subject weights (Table 11.4). Although the highest weighted dimension for a subject by INDSCAL is also the highest weighted by ALSCAL, this is not necessarily so for the lowest weighted dimension, Subjects 1 and 10. Further,

Table 11.4
Comparison of ALSCAL and INDSCAL Subject Weights[a]

Subject	Diet	Cherry	Manufacturer
1 INDSCAL	.64	.34	.25
1 ALSCAL	.43	.25	.28
3 INDSCAL	.20	.74	.30
3 ALSCAL	.28	.55	.38
4 INDSCAL	.67	.25	.43
4 ALSCAL	.57	.24	.37
10 INDSCAL	.20	.69	.22
10 ALSCAL	.32	.37	.30

[a] Underbar indicates lowest weighted dimension.

the INDSCAL weights often indicate greater relative importance between dimensions for a subject than do the ALSCAL weights (see, for example, Subject 10). As discussed in Chapter 16, the ALSCAL program separates differences in response style from differences in perception. INDSCAL does not. This accounts for some of the differences between and within subject weights found between the programs.

Food Flavors (INDSCAL and ALSCAL)

INDSCAL and ALSCAL both provide similar stimulus spaces in which there are four clusters of stimuli: fruits, meats, vegetables, and butter–chocolate–corn. Dimension 1 separates meats and vegetables from fruits and butter–chocolate–corn. Dimension 2 separates fruits and vegetables from the other stimuli. Both data sets include 16 elderly subjects as well as 16 young subjects, and neither solution fits the data well. The mean square correlation (in distances) for ALSCAL is .22. The mean square correlation (in scalar cross-products) for INDSCAL is .35. Both solutions indicate that the elderly provide a much poorer fit to the models than the young (Figure 11.1). Squared correlations are:

	INDSCAL	ALSCAL
Young	.27–.66	.09–.58
Elderly	.05–.41	.00–.26

One elderly subject fitted both models quite well, and two young subjects fitted both models quite poorly (Figure 11.1).

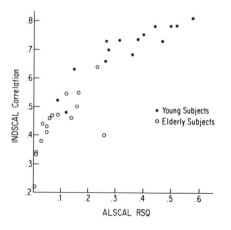

Figure 11.1. Comparison of INDSCAL correlations and ALSCAL squared correlations for food flavors.

In summary, the same general and specific conclusions are reached by the application of either algorithm to this data set. However, it should be noted that an ordinal ALSCAL analysis (Section 9.4) modified this conclusion somewhat.

Strawberry Drinks (INDSCAL and ALSCAL)

As discussed in Section 8.5, we were unable to develop sweetness as the first dimension when using INDSCAL, although the beverages were ranked according to sweetness on the second dimension. ALSCAL does provide sweetness as the first dimension. The order of the stimuli on the weak nonsweetness dimension is only roughly similar, although the same interpretation, "like standard beverage–not like standard beverage" may be drawn from either analysis.

Colas (INDSCAL and MULTISCALE)

Despite their differences both programs give solutions which have the same overall interpretation. Dimension 1 clearly separates diet from nondiet drinks. Dimension 2 separates regular from cherry colas. Dimension 3 may be related to manufacturer flavor type. There are, however, some differences in the order of the stimuli along the dimensions. INDSCAL, for example, provides no separation on dimension 1 between RC, Pepsi Cola, and Shasta and places these three stimuli as more nondiet than Coca-Cola, Yukon, and Dr. Pepper. MULTISCALE separates RC, Pepsi Cola, and Shasta on this dimension and indicates Coca-Cola to be more nondiet than RC or Pepsi Cola. On dimension 3, Table 11.5, Pepsi Cola, Dr. Pepper,

Table 11.5
Cola Coordinates on Dimension 3

Cola	INDSCAL	MULTISCALE
Yukon	− .56	102
Tab	− .39	41
Coca-Cola	− .38	64
Shasta	− .07	− 5
Diet Rite	.05	− 5
Diet Dr. Pepper[a]	.12	− 46
RC	.23	− 37
Dr. Pepper[a]	.29	− 56
Pepsi Cola[a]	.31	− 8
Diet Pepsi	.38	− 50

[a] Vary by two or more positions in rank order.

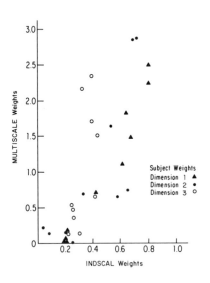

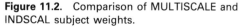

Figure 11.2. Comparison of MULTISCALE and INDSCAL subject weights.

and Diet Dr. Pepper vary by two or more positions in rank order along the dimension. It is fruitless to argue which program is more correct. Both indicate considerable noise in the data which leads to uncertainty in stimulus positions. The MULTISCALE unbiased standard error estimate is .53. The unexplained variance in the INDSCAL model is .37.

Comparison of subject weights between the two programs is more difficult because MULTISCALE weights for a subject are normalized to the number of dimensions, which is not the case for INDSCAL. The sum of squares of INDSCAL weights for a subject provides a measure of fit. MULTI-SCALE's measure of fit lies mostly in its unbiased standard error estimate. Nevertheless, there is a reasonable correspondence (Figure 11.2). In particular, the five subjects who have INDSCAL dimension 1 weights of .6 or greater have MULTISCALE dimension 1 weights of 1.0 or greater. These five subjects who find this diet–nondiet dimension important are PTC tasters. The remaining five subjects are not. The greatest differences exist on dimension 3 where four subjects show MULTISCALE weights greater than one yet have INDSCAL weights around .4. Further, two of the subjects show reversal in importance of the dimensions (Table 11.6).

Table 11.6
Reversal in Importance of Dimensions as Indicated by Subject Weights

	INDSCAL		MULTISCALE	
Subject	2	3	2	3
2	.58	.39	.65	2.34
7	.65	.32	.74	2.16

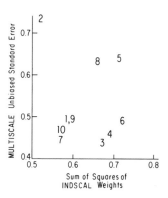

Figure 11.3. Comparison of MULTISCALE unbiased standard error with INDSCAL squared subject weights.

Subject 2 has the highest unbiased standard error estimate in the MUL-TISCALE analysis and may have particularly noisy data. However, there is no indication in either analysis that Subject 7 is unusual. The ALSCAL analysis provides equal weights for Subject 2 on dimensions 2 and 3 but sides with INDSCAL for Subject 7! Personally, we would obtain more data if it became important to resolve these differences.

The agreement between MULTISCALE unbiased standard error for each subject and INDSCAL sums of squares of subject weights is modest (Figure 11.3) at best. There should be an inverse correlation. Subjects 3, 4, and 6 fit both models well, and Subject 2 fits both models poorly. However, Subjects 5 and 8 show better fit than Subjects 1, 7, 9, and 10 for INDSCAL but the reverse for MULTISCALE. The MULTISCALE power transformations undoubtedly offer greater flexibility in fitting data to distances than the INDSCAL program. However, more work is needed to determine if this approach improves our understanding of subjects' perceptual behavior.

Colas (MULTISCALE and ALSCAL)

The ALSCAL solution used in this comparison is the weighted Euclidean model with ordinal scaling, matrix conditional. This is the most appropriate comparison since MULTISCALE may be considered to be somewhere between ordinal and metric scaling, and since matrix conditional allows for differences in scale use between subjects.

Both programs provide the same overall interpretation. Dimension 1 separates diet from nondiet drinks. Dimension 2 separates cherry from regular colas. Dimension 3 may be associated with manufacturer flavor type. There are, however, some differences in order along the dimensions, although as shown in Figure 11.4 these are minor for dimensions 1 and 2. The coordinates on dimension 3 are shown in Table 11.7. Only RC and Pepsi Cola show rank order reversal. These stimulus spaces are in fact remarkably similar.

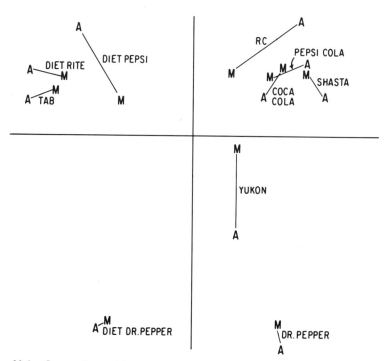

Figure 11.4. Comparison of first two dimensions of ALSCAL, A, and MULTISCALE, M, three-dimensional solutions for colas.

There is reasonable agreement between the two programs in how well subjects' data fit the model (Figure 11.5). ALSCAL provides two measures of fit, STRESS and RSQ (the squared correlation in distances). As fit improves, STRESS decreases and RSQ increases. The main measure of fit in MULTISCALE, unbiased standard error, decreases as fit improves. Figure 11.5 shows concordance for six of the subjects but lack of agreement

Table 11.7
Cola Coordinates on Dimension 3

Cola	ALSCAL	MULTISCALE
Yukon	1.61	102
Coca-Cola	1.33	64
Tab	1.09	41
Shasta	.54	− 5
Diet Rite	− .15	− 5
RC	− .67	− 37
Pepsi Cola	− .70	− 8
Diet Dr. Pepper	− .82	− 46
Diet Pepsi	−1.17	− 50

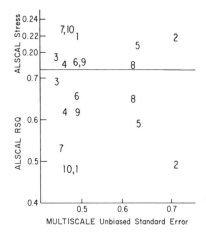

Figure 11.5. Comparison of ALSCAL and MUL-
TISCALE fits.

for Subjects 1, 7, and 10. The MULTISCALE power transformation of the distances improves the fit of data for Subjects 1, 7, and 10 in a way that the ALSCAL monotone transformations do not. At the present time more work is needed to determine if the improvement in fit actually represents an improvement in our understanding of subjects' perceptions. Conceptually, the idea is very attractive, but we do not have enough data to give the model our unqualified support.

It is not possible to compare subject weights directly between the two programs. The normalization procedures are quite different. MULTI-SCALE weights are simply row and column normalized so that the weights for each row, subject, add up to the number of dimensions, and the weights for each column, dimension, add up to the number of subjects. ALSCAL weights, like INDSCAL weights, include a measure of variance accounted for. In an overview of these two analyses for the cola data (Figure 11.6), large ALSCAL weights are mostly associated with large MULTISCALE weights. There are, also, some striking differences. ALSCAL weights in the .2 to .4 range are mostly associated with MULTISCALE weights of .0 to .6. However, one ALSCAL weight of .34 is associated with a MUL-TISCALE weight of 2.16. Other differences, not quite as extreme, appear on inspection of the figure.

Of the three individual differences programs, MULTISCALE provides the greatest apparent within-subject differences in dimensional saliences for this data set. There are also some reversals within subjects for the relative saliences of the dimensions (Table 11.8), although the overall agreement is good. ALSCAL indicates that for Subjects 2 and 7 dimension 3 is least important whereas MULTISCALE indicates it to be most important. INDS-CAL also disagreed with MULTISCALE in the analysis of these subjects' data, and it is possible that the fault lies in the data rather than the programs.

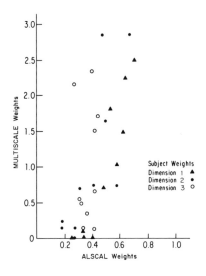

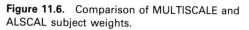

Figure 11.6. Comparison of MULTISCALE and ALSCAL subject weights.

Table 11.8
Comparison of ALSCAL and MULTISCALE Dimension Saliences for Each Subject in Cola Analyses

Subject	Program	Order of dimension saliences				
1	A	1		3	≈	2
1	M	1		2	≈	3
2	A	2	≈	1	≈	3
2[a]	M	3		2		1
3	A	2		3		1
3	M	2		3		1
4	A	1		3		2
4	M	3	≈	1		2
5	A	1		3		2
5	M	1		3		2
6	A	1		3		2
6	M	1		3		2
7	A	2		1		3
7[a]	M	3		2		1
8	A	2	≈	1		3
8	M	2		1	≈	3
9	A	1		3		2
9	M	3	≈	1		2
10	A	2		1	≈	3
10	M	2		3	≈	1

[a] Rank order changes.

11.5. Summary

We recommend use of individual differences programs (INDSCAL, ALS-CAL, or MULTISCALE M3) whenever possible. Since dissimilarity data are normally collected from several subjects, there is generally little point in compressing this information by external averaging and then applying CMDS procedures. Similarly, although the programs with RMDS options (POLYCON, KYST, ALSCAL, and MULTISCALE M2) allow for differences in scale use, it again seems more appropriate in most instances to use individual differences models.

With regard to the three individual differences programs, we have much more experience with INDSCAL and ALSCAL than MULTISCALE M3. Our comments, therefore, should be considered with this limitation in mind.

All three programs will provide similar solutions when the data are not excessively noisy. As the noise level rises, INDSCAL is the first to break down. Warning signs include low subject weights and clustering of the stimuli around the origin of the stimulus space. In spite of, or perhaps because of, these reasons, we recommend inclusion of INDSCAL in your MDS portfolio. If INDSCAL develops sensible solutions, they probably are meaningful and the data set reasonably robust.

We like the statistical hypotheses testing available with MULTISCALE but wish to point out the importance of checking for low values of the exponent. Low exponents can make a subject's data appear to fit the model (in terms of standard error) better than they really do. On the other hand, use of a power function has considerable psychophysical precedent and is an attractive alternative to the more traditional monotone transformation procedures. We would like to see wider use of MULTISCALE. Our present evidence suggests that in the CMDS or RMDS modes it is less capable of extracting information from noisy data than KYST, POLYCON, or ALS-CAL. We do not have enough information to compare the performance of model M3 on noisy data with ALSCAL, however.

In the WMDS situation ALSCAL seems to extract more information from noisy data than INDSCAL. For CMDS or RMDS, ALSCAL seems just as capable as KYST or POLYCON. However, some judgment must be exercised when examining ALSCAL solutions. Relaxation of the interval measurement level assumption improves fit, but may worsen interpretability, particularly for subjects who may use the scale almost dichotomously (see Section 9.4). With data containing a large number of tied observations (see Section 9.7), use of the DISCRETE option may give a rather different stimulus space than the CONTINUOUS option. It is actually quite helpful to be able to analyze data under a number of different assumptions as ALSCAL allows. For this reason, and because ALSCAL-4 is available with dynamic core allocation allowing entry of large data sets, we recommend its acquisition.

12

Interpreting Stimulus Spaces

12.1. Overview

After doing an MDS analysis (by using any of the programs discussed in Chapters 5 through 10), you will want to interpret the resulting stimulus and (if WMDS) weight spaces. Sometimes this is possible by simple visual inspection. The case of diet–nondiet colas or the sweetness order of the strawberry-flavored drinks are two examples. However, in some cases the analysis is completely exploratory, and you may have no idea what the results mean by simple visual inspection. On the other hand you may know what you expect from the MDS, but you cannot see it by looking at the space. Finally, you may have a specific theoretical model which you wish to relate to the results. In all of these latter cases mathematical analysis is needed to help you interpret the results.

This chapter and Chapter 13 deal with mathematical methods for interpreting the spaces derived by an MDS program. This chapter shows how to use preference analysis, property fitting, and canonical regression to help interpret the stimulus space. Chapter 13 shows how to use direction statistics to interpret the weight space.

For most of these interpretation aids it is necessary to have information about the stimuli (and subjects) in *addition* to the similarity information used in the basic MDS analysis. Thus, to perform a preference analysis it is necessary to have obtained preference ratings of the stimuli from the subjects. To do property fitting it is necessary to have some sort of information about the properties of each stimulus (i.e., physicochemical properties or psychological attribute ratings). To use direction statistics it is necessary to have additional information about the subjects (e.g., their weight, age, sex).

In the first part of this chapter preference and property analysis are discussed. We present two different preference and property models that have often been found useful. These models are related to multiple regression; in addition, it is shown how these models can be fit to ordinal or quantitative data.

In the next part of this chapter we show how to use PREFMAP, a program specifically designed to do preference and property analysis, indicating how it can fit both of the models to either ordinal or quantitative data. Examples of how to input data to this program and how to interpret the results are given as well.

In the final portion of this chapter use of canonical regression is discussed as an interpretation aid when the properties are multidimensional.

12.2. Preference and Property Models

In this section we discuss models for interpreting the stimulus configuration provided by MDS. These models relate additional information about the stimuli to the configuration. This additional information may be preferences for the stimuli as judged by several subjects, or it can be physical properties or psychological perceptions of physical properties of the stimuli.

The preference models try to determine the preferred mix of characteristics for a set of stimuli. Since individual preferences vary widely, it is important to perform preference analyses at the individual level. Analysis of average preferences is rarely informative. Preference models do not explain the process by which a person makes a choice. Instead, they fit preference ratings to a stimulus space.

The property models try to find out which properties of the stimuli were important to the subjects while they were making their similarity judgments. That is, property models attempt to identify the attributes the person used to structure the stimulus domain. These properties can be either *objective* physical characteristics of the stimuli (i.e., their molecular weight), or they can be *subjective* judgments of stimulus characteristics (i.e., their sweetness).

Property models can tell us when a property was *not* used, but they cannot really tell us that a specific property *was* used. They can only identify properties that *are like* those used in the similarity judgments. They may have identified the attributes actually used by the subjects, but we do not know for certain. Thus, property analysis does not necessarily identify the actual properties used by the subjects. Note that it is often reasonable to assume that homogeneous subjects use the same properties, so property analysis can be performed on ratings averaged over these subjects as well as on individual ratings.

Two models for preference and property analysis are discussed here. Both models can be used for both kinds of analysis. The models differ in their basic assumption about the nature of an individual's preferences, or about the way properties contribute to similarity judgments. The two basic assumptions are:

1. The more, the better. This is the *vector* model.
2. Some amount is ideal. This is the *ideal point* model.

The vector model is generally most useful when the stimulus set does not contain stimuli which have either too much or too little of each characteristic. Suppose that subjects are asked to taste several brands of coffee which vary in strength and sweetness. Also suppose that they received none strong enough and sweet enough for their tastes. Here the *more is better* vector model is the appropriate model of preference.

The ideal point model is generally most useful when the stimulus set does contain stimuli which have either too much or too little of at least one characteristic. Suppose that the coffee in the experiment did in fact vary from exceedingly weak to overbearingly strong. Then, for each subject it is probably true that there is some *ideal* strength. Here the *ideal point* model is most appropriate.

Whichever model is used, it is vital that the stimulus space contain dimensions which pertain to the attributes. This is why stimulus spaces derived by scaling similarity judgments are superior to spaces derived from adjective ratings. In the latter case the relevant scales may not have been included in the experiment by the experimenter, so the subjects do not make the relevant ratings, and the relevant attributes are not present in the stimulus space.

Before discussing these two models in detail we need to introduce some terminology. The word *attribute* will refer collectively to preference, to a psychological property, to a physical property, or to any other aspect which may be relevant to the stimulus configuration. We will often refer to the *degree* of attribute possessed by the stimulus as a shorthand way of referring to either the amount of some physical characteristic of the stimulus, the psychological perception of the amount of some property, or the degree of preference a subject has for the stimulus. We do not mean to imply that the psychological property or the subject's preference is actually "possessed" by the stimulus; this is simply a shorthand reference. Thus, we refer to the direction through the stimulus space as the *attribute direction*, and we represent it by an *attribute vector*, and we say that stimuli have certain *amounts* of an attribute.

The Vector Model

Let us now take a detailed look at the vector model (see Figure 12.1). What the model does is to find a direction through a stimulus space which is the direction that corresponds to increasing amounts of the attribute (preference, property) in question. The model assumes that the stimulus space has already been determined by some one of the MDS programs; only the direction is to be identified.

The attribute vector is the line through the space on which the projection of each stimulus corresponds with the degree of attribute possessed by the stimulus, as nearly as possible. In Figure 12.1 five stimuli are portrayed by the points labeled with the capital letters A–E. Also an attribute is portrayed by the heavy vector (arrow). The projection of each point onto the attribute vector is shown by the dashed vector from each point. These

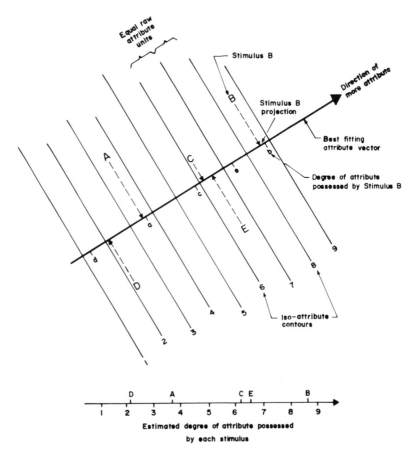

Figure 12.1. Vector model, metric.

projections are reproduced at the bottom of the figure on the horizontal scale. Finally, the lower case letters a–e located along the attribute vector show the actual degree of attribute contained by each stimulus.

Note that the lower case letters represent the actual amount of the attribute possessed by the stimulus (the rating of preference or the judged degree of sweetness, or the actual molecular weight of each stimulus), whereas the projections of each stimulus onto the vector represent an *estimate* from the MDS stimulus configuration of the amount of the attribute used in the similarity judgment process.

In Figure 12.1 we also present several lighter lines that are parallel. These lines are called *iso-attribute* contours because all stimuli located on one of these contours project onto the same spot on the attribute vector. Thus, they would have equal (iso)attribute estimates. They represent, in the raw units that the attribute is measured in, the amount of attribute actually possessed by each stimulus.

In Figure 12.1 there are nine contours, labeled 1–9. These contours could represent, for example, ratings of the sweetness of the five stimuli on a scale of 1–9, averaged over a group of subjects. Or, they could represent one subject's ratings (again on a scale of 1–9) of his or her degree of preference for the five stimuli. The location of the lower case d on the attribute vector shows that stimulus D had, say, an average sweetness rating of 1.3 units. The best estimate, from the MDS space, of the degree of sweetness of stimulus D is 2.2, as determined by the location of the arrowhead from stimulus D. This says that the similarity judgments imply that stimulus D is just a bit sweeter than the sweetness ratings suggest.

If the attribute in question is strongly related to the stimulus space then the stimulus projections will coincide very closely with the attribute values. Also, the correlation between the projections and the attribute values will be quite large. When the attribute is not strongly related to the stimulus space, the projections will not fall near the attribute values, and the correlation between the two will be low.

Note, in Figure 12.1, that the attribute vector is labeled "best fitting." This is because the procedure used to determine the direction of the attribute vector is multiple regression. This procedure finds the direction for the attribute vector such that the correlation between the stimulus projections and the attribute values is as large as possible. This correlation is, of course, the familiar multiple correlation coefficient.

The value of the correlation coefficient tells us how strongly the attribute in question is related to the stimulus space. If the value is *low,* then we conclude that the subjects were not using the attribute when they were making their similarity judgments. If the value is *high,* then we conclude that the subjects were using the attribute, or some other attribute which is strongly related to it.

We cannot, however, use the significance test associated with multiple regression in the usual way. The problem is that the observations, which, in our case, are the stimulus coordinates, are not independent. Thus, the significance levels are inflated: That is, they tell us that the relationship is more significant than it actually is. This means that we can use the significance tests if we are *very conservative* about the levels. If the test tells us that the relationship is not significant then it most certainly is not significant. If we are told that the relationship is *very* significant (.001 or .0001), then we might conclude that the attribute (or something like it) is being used by the subjects in their similarity judgments.

In Figure 12.2 we present some of the details for the *nonmetric* version of the vector model. The nonmetric version is appropriate when the attribute is measured at the *ordinal* level. The model is just the same as the metric

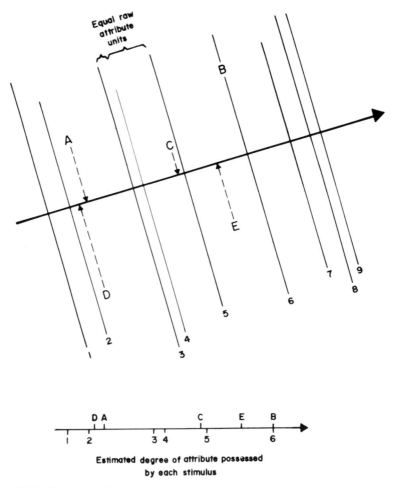

Figure 12.2. Vector model, nonmetric.

one discussed in Figure 12.1 (which assumes the attribute is at the interval level), except that we think of the attribute scale as being "rubbery." Thus, we are free to stretch it in some places and shrink it in others. Therefore, we wish to stretch and shrink the scale, as well as to find the best location of the vector.

We can see, in the figure, that the iso-similarity contours are no longer equally spaced. Note that the contours are still numbered in raw attribute units, but that now the differences in units are not preserved. This reflects the fact that we have stretched and shrunk the attribute scale due to its ordinal nature. This is the only difference from Figure 12.1, where the equal spacing reflects the assumption that the attribute is at the interval level of measurement.

Procedures used to fit the nonmetric vector model adjust the values on the attribute scale and simultaneously determine the direction of the vector so that the multiple correlation coefficient is optimized. The advantage of this approach is that it allows us to treat the attribute as being ordinal. This is sometimes the appropriate assumption as, for example, when the subject has been asked to give his or her preference rank order. The disadvantage is that there are now no significance tests. It is also more difficult to determine what a large correlation is, since the optimal correlation is often .95 or greater.

The Ideal Point Model

The ideal point model is used to find a point in a stimulus space which is most like an attribute. If the attribute is a subject's preferences for the stimuli, then this point is interpreted as the subject's ideal stimulus. It is the hypothetical stimulus which, if it existed, the subject would prefer most. If the attribute is a property, then the ideal point is the place which is most like the property. It is the hypothetical stimulus which, if it existed, would contain the maximum amount of the attribute.

Since every point in a stimulus space represents a unique combination of stimulus characteristics, the ideal point represents the optimal combination of stimulus characteristics for the attribute in question. Any other combination corresponds to a point which is less like the attribute.

The notions of the ideal point model are portrayed in Figure 12.3. The notions are completely parallel to those discussed for the vector model, but the geometry is different. As with the vector model, we assume that the stimulus space has already been determined. In Figure 12.3 we portray five stimuli with the letters A–E.

Whereas in the vector model we determined the direction through the space which was most like increasing amounts of the attribute, with the ideal point model we determine the point in the stimulus space which is

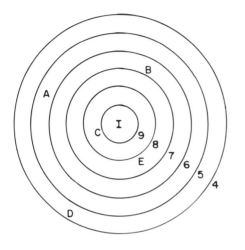

```
4   5   6   7   8   9  I0
L___L___L___L___L___L
D   A   B  E   C    I
```

Figure 12.3. Ideal point model, metric.

most like the attribute. A hypothetical ideal point is represented in the figure by the letter I.

Whereas with the vector model we had iso-attribute contours which were parallel lines, with the ideal point model we have circular iso-attribute contours. The contours are concentric, the ideal point being their center.

Since the ideal point is the point at which the attribute reaches its maximum, the amount of attribute falls off in all directions from the ideal point. This is shown in the figure by the numbering of the contours. Contour 9 represents more attribute than contour 8, and 9 is closer to the ideal point than 8.

At a fixed distance from the ideal point, the degree of attribute is a constant, regardless of direction. Thus, if we go one unit of distance from I in any direction we have an estimated amount of attribute of 9. If we go farther we have a smaller estimate. The distance between the ideal point and a stimulus point is the *best estimate,* from the MDS space, of the amount of attribute contained in each stimulus. This aspect of the ideal point model corresponds to the stimulus projection aspect of the vector model.

The amount of attribute estimated for each stimulus is given by the scale at the bottom of the figure. Each stimulus is represented on this scale, as is the ideal point. Each stimulus is located on this scale so that its distance from the ideal point equals the corresponding distance in the stimulus space. We see that stimulus E is located between the 8 and 7 contours in the stimulus space, and between the 8 and 7 on the scale.

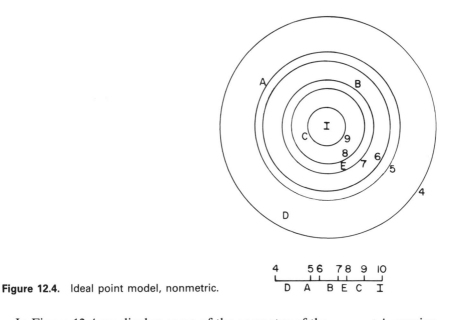

Figure 12.4.   Ideal point model, nonmetric.

```
4       5 6  7 8  9  IO
L___I___I__I___I__I
D   A   B E  C   I
```

In Figure 12.4 we display some of the geometry of the *nonmetric* version of the ideal point model. There is no reason to go into this model in great detail since it combines the nonmetric notion with the ideal point notion, both of which have already been discussed. The important difference from the metric ideal point model (Figure 12.3) is that the iso-similarity contours are no longer equally spaced. This is exactly the same as the relationship between the metric and nonmetric vector models (Figures 12.1 and 12.2).

The procedure used to locate the ideal point is a special kind of multiple regression proposed by Carroll (1972) and used for response surface regression by Cochran and Cox (1957). This procedure correlates the attribute values with the stimulus coordinates *and* a dummy variable constructed from the *sum of squares* of the coordinates for each point. Carroll proved that this procedure finds the point that maximizes the correlation between the attribute values and the squared distances between ideal and stimulus points. The nonmetric ideal point procedure simply combines this procedure with the nonmetric notions mentioned earlier.

Since multiple correlation is used we can interpret the correlation coefficient in the usual way. A *low* correlation means the attribute is not strongly related to the solution, a *high* correlation means it is. The significance tests, however, are even less appropriate than with the vector model since we now have dependence between variables as well as between observations. Thus, in general, significance tests should be avoided, or should be taken with a grain of salt.

There is an interesting relationship between the vector and ideal point models. The geometry of their relation is shown in Figure 12.5. Specifically,

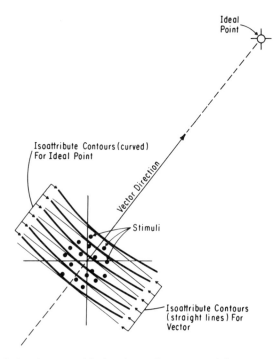

Figure 12.5. Relation between ideal point and vector models.

the vector model corresponds with the ideal point model when the ideal point is moved far away from the swarm of stimuli in the direction of the vector. When the ideal point is far outside of the swarm of stimuli, as is shown in the figure, then the iso-attribute arcs transecting the stimulus swarm look like lines that are almost straight. The farther away the ideal point moves, the straighter the arcs become. Finally, when the point is infinitely far away, the arcs are straight lines. Thus, the two models are equivalent when the ideal point is located at infinity.

Algebraically, the relation between the two models is as follows: The vector model involves performing a multiple regression between the attribute values and the several stimulus space dimensions. The ideal point model involves the same regression except that the dummy variable of sums of squares is included with the dimensions. Since the point model uses precisely the same information in the regression except for the additional dummy variable, the two models become the same when the regression weight for the dummy variable is zero.

Carroll suggests a significance test to see if the dummy variable accounts for additional variance beyond that accounted for by the dimensions. He states that if it does, then the ideal point model is appropriate. If it does not, the vector model is appropriate. We find such tests to be useful as an aid in trying to decide which model is best. We prefer not to rely on such tests alone, but find them useful as one aid among many in trying to decide which model is appropriate. It is important, of course, to use the meaningfulness of the regression as a central aid in this decision.

Finally, Carroll (1972) suggests two variants on the ideal point model (see Figure 12.6). One of these has elliptical iso-attribute contours instead of circular ones, with the axes of the ellipses being parallel with the dimensions of the space. The other also has elliptical contours, but the axes of the ellipse are rotated from parallelism with the dimensions. In the figure, ideal point I has circular contours, ideal point II has elliptical contours whose axes parallel the dimensions, and ideal point III has elliptical contours whose axes have been rotated.

The elliptical model implies that the dimensions of the space contribute to the strength of the attribute in question, but that they are not equal in their impact. The relation between axis length and impact is counterintuitive. The *longest* axis corresponds with the *least* important dimension, since it takes greater variation in this dimension to produce a given change in attribute strength. The shortest axis is the most important, since small changes in this dimension yield large changes in attribute strength. The rotated elliptical model implies that several characteristics contribute to the strength of the attribute, that the characteristics do not contribute equally, and that they do not correspond directly with the dimensions of the stimulus space.

As might be suspected, Carroll suggested a special multiple regression procedure for fitting each of these models. It turns out that the circular model is a special case of the elliptical one, and the elliptical model is a

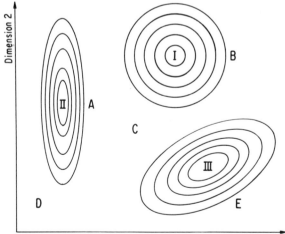

Figure 12.6. Variants on the ideal point model. I, phase III PREFMAP; II, phase II PREFMAP; III, phase I PREFMAP.

special case of the rotated elliptical one. That is, each more general model involves variables used in the less general models plus additional dummy variables. Thus, Carroll suggests significance tests to see if the more general models account for significantly more variance than the less general ones. Again, we find these significance tests to be useful as one criterion among many in deciding which model is best.

Mathematical Foundations[1]

As mentioned earlier, the vector and ideal point models for relating preferences and properties to an MDS stimulus space are based on multiple regression when the data are quantitative, and on optimal multiple regression, when the data are ordinal. In this section we briefly present the mathematical details of these procedures.

First, we present some notation. Let us denote a specific value for stimulus i on the attribute by p_i. We use p_i because the attribute is either a *property* or a *preference*. If there are n stimuli there are np_i values, p_1, p_2, etc., up to p_n. We denote the coordinates of stimulus i on dimension a by the symbol x_{ia}. If there are r dimensions, then for each stimulus i we have r coordinates x_{i1}, x_{i2}, etc., up to x_{ir}. Since there are n stimuli, we have n sets of r coordinates, or nr in total.

For the metric vector model we just have ordinary multiple regression. That is, we set up the equation

$$p_i \cong \bar{p}_i = b_0 + b_1(x_{i1}) + \cdots + b_r(x_{ir}).$$

In summation notation this equation is

$$p_i \cong \bar{p}_i = b_0 + \sum_a^r b_a(x_{ia}).$$

The values b_1, b_2, etc., are *regression weights* (b_0 is the intercept) whose values are to be solved for by the multiple regression. There are $r+1$ b_a values, one for each of the r dimensions and one for the intercept.

This equation takes p_i (the attribute value for stimulus i) and x_{i1}, x_{i2}, etc. (the coordinates of point i in the stimulus space), and weights b_a (determined by the multiple regression) to compute $\bar{p}_i$. This new symbol, $\bar{p}_i$, is the algebraic equivalent of the geometric projection of stimulus i onto the vector shown in Figure 12.1. The projection $\bar{p}_i$ is the *best estimate*, from the stimulus coordinates x_{ia}, of the attribute value p_i.

The equation is for one particular stimulus, stimulus i. However, there are n stimuli. Thus, there are n of these equations. Each equation projects one of the stimuli onto the attribute vector. Each of these equations involves

---

[1] This section may be skipped with no loss of continuity.

the same unknown values that we wish to solve for (b_1, b_2, etc.), and different attribute values p_i and coordinates x_{i1}, x_{i2}, etc. Each equation generates a different projection $\tilde{p}_i$.

If we have fewer dimensions than we have stimuli (if $r < n$), we can solve the system of n equations in r unknowns for values of b_a. These values, called the regression coefficients, maximize the correlation between $\tilde{p}_i$ and p_i.

After completing the regression analysis, the attribute vector may be drawn in the stimulus space by the following steps. First, compute the *standardized* regression weights β_1, β_2, etc. These are commonly called beta weights. Second, if the stimulus space is two dimensional, find the point in the stimulus space whose coordinates are the standardized regression weights β_1, β_2. Call this point the β point. Third, draw a line through the origin of the stimulus space and through the β point. (This is correct only if the mean coordinate is zero on each dimension. If not, find the means on each dimension, locate the mean point in the stimulus space, and draw the line through it and the β point.) The length of this line is arbitrary, but it is informative if it is made proportional to the squared correlation coefficient since that length tells us how well the attribute fits the space. Fourth, put an arrowhead on the end of the vector in the direction of the β point. If the stimulus space is more than two dimensional, plot the appropriate pairs of β_a values in each two-dimensional stimulus plot, draw the line from the origin through the plotted β point, but make the length proportional to the sum of squared β_a values being plotted.

For the nonmetric vector model we use optimal multiple regression (Young, de Leeuw, & Takane, 1976) to solve the equation

$$p_i \overset{m}{=} p_i^* \cong \tilde{p}_i = b_0 + b_i(x_{i1}) + b_2(x_{i2}) + \cdots + b_r(x_{ir}),$$

or, in summation notation,

$$p_i \overset{m}{=} p_i^* \cong \tilde{p}_i = b_0 + \sum_a^r b_a(x_{ia}).$$

The new symbol, p_i^*, is the *optimally scaled* value of stimulus i on the attribute. It is required to be monotonically equal to ($\overset{m}{=}$) the raw values p_i and to have a least-squares relation ($\cong$) to the projection $\tilde{p}_i$. That is, the symbol $\overset{m}{=}$ means that the order of the values p_i^*, p_j^*, etc., is the same as the order of values p_i, p_j, etc.:

$$\text{If } \quad p_i < p_j \quad \text{then} \quad p_i^* \leqslant p_j^*.$$

Once we have solved for p_j^* and the regression weights b_0, b_1, b_2, etc., we use the beta weights in the same fashion as described earlier.

For the metric (or nonmetric) circular ideal point model we introduce one new term into the metric (or nonmetric) vector model equation. The term is the sum of the squared coordinates:

$$s = x_{i1}^2 + x_{i2}^2 + \cdots + x_{ir}^2 = \sum_a^r x_{ir}^2.$$

Thus, for the metric circular ideal point model we have the regression equation

$$p_i \cong \bar{p}_i = b_0 + \sum_a^r b_a(x_{ia}) + b_{r+1}\left(\sum_a^r x_{ir}^2 \right)$$

which has, in addition to the $r+1$ regression weights b_0, b_1, b_2, ... , b_r, the new regression weight b_{r+1}. All other symbols in this equation are defined as before. Also as before, there are n of these equations, one for each of the n stimuli.

After solving for the $r+2$ regression coefficients that maximize the correlation between $\bar{p}_i$ and p_i (by multiple regression), the ideal point is found in the stimulus space as follows: We simply form the ratio of regression weights

$$q_a = -b_a/2b_{r+1}$$

for each dimension $a = 1, ... , r$. These values, q_1, q_2, etc., are the coordinates of the ideal point in the stimulus space. Thus, we simply find the spot corresponding to these coordinates and place a symbol there to represent the ideal point. Note that a negative sign for b_{r+1} (negative ideal point) means the point is *least* preferred or *least* like the attribute.

Finally, it should be clear how the nonmetric circular ideal point model is represented. We simply introduce p_i^*, the optimally scaled attribute notion, into the regression equation for the ideal point, perform the optimal regression, and calculate the coordinates q_a as earlier.

12.3. PREFMAP

PREFMAP is a computer program (see Appendix) which will perform preference and property analysis using any of the models discussed in the preceding section. It can do the analyses metrically or nonmetrically, and can use the vector model or any of the three point models.

PREFMAP consists of four phases. The phases correspond to the four preference–property models, as follows:

Phase	Model
IV	Vector model
III	Ideal point model (circular)
II	Elliptical ideal point model
I	Elliptical ideal point model with rotation

The models are performed in numerical order (that is, phase I is done before phase II, etc.) starting and stopping as the user wishes. We recommend, especially when using the program for the first time, that you consider only phases III and IV. We also recommend that you select the metric option. And, we recommend that phase I not be used with the WMDS situation. (Note that when phase I is used phases II through IV are based on the *rotated* stimulus space, but when phase I is not used phases II through IV are based on the unrotated stimulus space.)

Following our suggestions helps to decide whether the vector or (circular) ideal point model is best for your data. When there is a borderline decision we would come down in favor of the vector model, especially if the ideal point is negative ideal (see explanation following). On the other hand, ideal points are sometimes intuitively more reasonable than extreme values for stimulus qualities. Only if the fit is poor in phase III would we consider a phase II analysis. It is usually not worthwhile to perform phase I analysis on stimulus spaces developed by WMDS programs (ALSCAL, INDSCAL, and MULTISCALE M3), since they already have determined the optimum rotation for the stimulus space. The experiences of Carroll (1972) and Huber (1975) support this view.

Setting Up a PREFMAP Job

Setting up a PREFMAP job is straightforward. The analysis parameters described are entered in coded form on card 1. The maximum number of stimuli, dimensions, and subjects allowed depends on the version as shown:

Version	Maximum number of		
	Stimuli	Dimensions	Subjects
PREFMAP 0	100	5	49
PREFMAP	20	5	119
PREFMAP 2	40	10	499

If PREFMAP is used for property fitting then the number of properties is the number of subjects. Figure 12.7 shows the input deck for a liqueur analysis.

Card 1. The parameter card contains 17 parameters in I4 format. These are:

Identifier	Columns	
N	1–4	Number of stimuli.
K	5–8	Number of dimensions.
NSUB	9–12	Number of subjects (or properties).

(cont'd.)

Identifier	Columns	
ISV	13–16	0 Small scale value represents greater preference.
		1 Large scale value represents greater preference.
NORS	17–20	1 Normalize scale values for each subject to length = 1. (Use this.)
		0 Do not normalize scale values.
IPS	21–24	Enter 1,2,3, or 4 for starting phase.
IPE	25–28	Enter 1,2,3, or 4 for ending phase.
		IPS must be less than or equal to IPE.
		For vector property fitting IPS and IPE are both 4.
IPLOT	29–32	0 provides ideal point for average subject only.
		1 provides ideal point for average subject and function plots for each subject.
		2 provides ideal point plots and function plots for each subject.
MDV	33–36	0 Ideal points plotted without axes.
		1 Ideal points plotted with axes showing rotation and weights.
MLIP	37–40	0 Label ideal points with numbers.
		1 Label ideal points with letters.
MIDEN	41–44	0 The program generates sequential numbers for labeling stimuli.
LFITSW	45–48	0 Linear or metric fitting. We recommend this option.
		1 Nonmetric, no ties in preferences.
		2 Nonmetric, use when ties in preferences (primary approach).
		3 Nonmetric, use when ties in preferences (secondary approach).
IAV	49–52	0 Average subject's scale values are computed in the starting phase and remain the same.
		1 Average subject's scale values are computed for each new phase.
		IAV is irrelevant and set to 0 when LFITSW = 0.
IRX	53–56	0 Stimulus coordinates are punched on a card for each stimulus. (Use this.)
MAXIT	57–60	The preferred value for maximum number of iterations is 15.
IRWT	61–64	If IPS is 3, weights, one for each dimension, may be read in by setting this parameter at 1. 0 is the usual option.
ISHAT	65–68	0 Use scale values from the previous phase. (Use this.)
		1 Use original scale values for each phase.

Card 2.   This gives the criterion for stopping iterations on a monotone fit and should be set at .001 in F7.3 format. For the metric procedure, LFITSW = 0 insert instead a blank card.

Card 3.   The title may use 80 characters but only one card.

Card 4.   F Format for reading in the coordinates.

Card 5.   Cards containing the stimulus coordinates. There should be *N* of these.

Card 6.   Only if weights are read in, F Format of weights for card 7.

Card 7.   Values of weights for *K* dimensions.

Card 8.   F Format for reading in scale values on card 9.

```
        5      10     15     20     25     30     35     40     45     50     55     60
    7      2      9      0      1      2      4      2      1      1      0      0      0      0    15
METRIC PREFERENCE MAPPING FOR 9 SUBJECTS AND 7 LIQUEURS
( 2 F 5 . 0 )
- 0 . 0 7   0 . 0 7
- 0 . 6 2   0 . 1 4
- 0 . 2 1   0 . 7 2
  0 . 6 2   0 . 1 4
- 0 . 2 0 - 0 . 3 8
  0 . 3 5 - 0 . 1 8
  0 . 1 4 - 0 . 5 1
( 7 F 2 . 0 )
1 0 3 7 2 1 2 5 2 6 1 6 2 2
4 8 7 5 6 1 1 6 5 0 2 6 3 3
2 2 4 1 3 1 1 2 2 7 2 4 3 3
1 9 3 7 2 9 1 6 3 3 2 8 3 1
2 4 3 6 2 7 1 1 2 9 2 1 3 5
5 1 6 0 5 6 1 2 4 3 1 9 2 9
1 2 3 1 2 8 2 1 2 9 1 7 2 4
3 6 2 4 3 3 4 9 3 1 3 9 2 5
4 2 1 5 2 9 6 4 4 1 6 1 5 3
```

Figure 12.7. Input deck for PREFMAP.

Card 9. Scale values for subjects or properties. Use one card for each subject. There should be NSUB cards each containing N scale values.

Card 10. A blank card which terminates the analysis. Cards 1 through 8 may be repeated for further analyses.

Understanding PREFMAP Output

PREFMAP output consists of two main sections:

1. The results for each phase of the analysis.
2. A summary table showing correlations and F ratios for all phases analyzed.

SUMMARY TABLE

This summary table appears as the last page of the printout and is a good place to start inspecting the results. An example is shown as Figure 12.8. The table contains, for each subject, correlations and F ratios for each phase and between phase F ratios. These are only valid if the data are analyzed metrically. For nonmetric analysis they should be considered no more than an indication of improvement.

The root mean square correlations for each phase are shown at the bottom of the table. In the example these increase, as might be expected, as the model complexity increases. The important question, however, is whether

CORRELATION (PHASE)

DF SUBJ	R1	R2	R3	R4
1	0.9958	0.9928	0.8460	0.4874
2	1.0000	0.9995	0.9993	0.9993
3	0.9996	0.9764	0.9268	0.8568
4	0.9451	0.9431	0.9123	0.8090
5	0.9876	0.9876	0.9163	0.8856
6	0.9923	0.9898	0.9878	0.9763
7	0.9767	0.9451	0.9311	0.5705
8	0.9876	0.9876	0.9163	0.8856
9	0.9985	0.9965	0.9926	0.9880
AVE	0.9916	0.9916	0.9916	0.8680

F RATIO (PHASE)

DF SUBJ	F1 5 1	F2 4 2	F3 3 3	F4 2 4
1	23.6769	34.3844	2.5171	0.6233
2	1000.0000	461.6821	688.6824	1454.2920
3	1000.0000	10.2250	6.0917	5.5207
4	1.6729	4.0226	4.9623	3.7891
5	7.9064	19.7361	5.2311	7.2719
6	12.8333	24.1699	40.1935	40.7717
7	4.1337	4.1805	6.5109	0.9651
8	7.9058	19.7365	5.2312	7.2719
9	66.9451	70.6290	66.8561	82.1305
AVE	11.8226	29.5589	59.1131	6.1094

F RATIO (BETWEEN PHASE)

DF SUBJ	F12 1 1	F13 2 1	F14 3 1	F23 1 2	F24 2 2	F34 1 3
1	0.7111	16.4720	30.0062	37.6740	52.1916	5.0443
2	1000.0000	1000.0000	1000.0000	0.6806	0.2695	-0.1585
3	1000.0000	1000.0000	1000.0000	4.0493	4.7043	2.6577
4	0.0353	0.2853	0.7451	1.0341	2.1250	3.1796
5	0.0015	2.7524	2.5810	10.9903	7.7301	1.0323
6	0.3208	0.2910	0.6824	0.3955	1.3071	2.7786
7	1.3148	0.9425	4.5385	0.4926	5.3140	12.1984
8	0.0014	2.7521	2.5808	10.9905	7.7303	1.0323
9	1.3600	1.9738	2.3270	2.1929	2.3818	1.8393
AVE	-0.0001	0.0	4.6085	0.0002	13.8268	41.4769

ROOT MEAN SQUARE

PHASE	
1	0.9871
2	0.9800
3	0.9376
4	0.8465

A F - VALUE OF 1000.0 IN THE ABOVE TABLE INDICATES
A POSSIBLE DIVISION BY ZERO. I.E. R IS VERY CLOSE TO 1.00

Figure 12.8. Last page of PREFMAP output, phases I to IV.

the more complex models are justified. The within- and between-phase F ratios help establish this.

In this particular example there are only seven stimuli so we conservatively choose 1% critical values of F rather than 5% critical values. For phase IV the 1% critical value of F is 18.00, a value met only by Subjects 2, 6, and 9. For phase III the 1% F value of 29.46 is met by Subjects 2, 6, and 9 also, but not by any other subjects. For the average subject, however, the Phase III model with an F value of 59.1 is significant. The root mean square correlation also increases from .85 to .94, and the between-phase F ratio of 41.48 is greater than the 1% critical value of 34.12. However, for none of the individual subjects is phase III a better fit than phase IV.

The phase II model incorporates individual weights for the dimensions. The 1% critical F value for this phase in this example is 99.25. This is met only by Subject 2, who seems to fit all models well. The 5% critical value of 19.30 is met by six of the nine subjects and by the average subject. However, the between-phase F ratios do not support the phase II model over either phase III or phase IV except for Subject 1.

While the phase I model with its rotating and weighting produces very high correlations for all subjects, the within- and between-phase F ratios do not support its consideration.

Overall, therefore, the review of this data set is not very encouraging. We would rerun such an analysis starting at phase II to eliminate the rotation of the stimulus space. This will not change the correlations or F values for the Phase IV vector model but will change them for phases II and III. More importantly, though, the analysis will maintain the original dimensions developed by the WMDS procedure used to generate the stimulus space.

We turn now to a description of the printout for each phase. The printouts contain some information whose meaning is not clear without reference to the original literature. The best source is the article by Carroll (1972). The key information is, however, clearly labeled and it is not necessary for the average user to understand the precise meaning of regression coefficients and transformation matrices.

We start with the simple vector model, phase IV, and proceed through to the most general model, phase I.

PHASE IV OUTPUT

The printout consists of the following:

1. X MATRIX. This gives the coordinates input for the stimuli unless the analysis commenced with phase I. In that case the coordinates shown and used are those generated from the phase I analysis.

2. For each subject and for the average subject:

a. S (VECTOR OF SCALE VALUES). These are the input preferences (or properties) for the stimuli normalized so that their sum is zero and their sum of squares is one.

b. BETA. These are the unstandardized *b* coefficients for the regression of the scale values on the stimulus coordinates (p. 264) not β values (p. 265). The first BETA value listed in the printout is for the intercept. Since the vector passes through the origin of the stimulus space, this term, except for rounding error, should be zero. The remaining BETA values, of which there are as many as dimensions, are used to calculate the direction of the vector.

c. *R* (CORRELATION). This is the correlation for the regression. It is the product moment correlation, not the Spearman rank order correlation.

d. PROJECTIONS ON THE FITTED VECTORS. These are the projections of each stimulus onto the fitted vector. They are normalized so that their sum is zero, the sum of squares is equal to one. They should correspond fairly well with the VECTOR OF SCALE VALUES, which correspondence the routine maximizes.

3. STIMULI COORDINATES. This is a repeat of the X matrix.

4. A plot of the stimulus space which also contains points showing where to draw the preference vectors for each subject and the average subject.

5. DIRECTION COSINES OF FITTED SUBJECT VECTORS. These are calculated from the BETA values and are proportional to them. Either the BETAs or the direction cosines may be used as the coordinates to position the subject vectors due to their proportionality. The dimension 1 cosine is the cosine of the angle between the preference vector and dimension 1.

PHASE III PREFMAP OUTPUT

PREFMAP phase III is the circular ideal point model in which preference decreases with the square of the distance from the ideal point. There is, however, provision for negative ideal points. Preference increases with the square of the distance from negative ideal points.

The printout for a metric analysis consists of the following:

1. X MATRIX. These are the stimulus coordinates specified as described earlier.

2. For each subject and for the average subject:

a. S (VECTOR OF SCALE VALUES). These are the input preferences normalized as described earlier.

b. BETA. These are unstandardized regression coefficients *b* for the scale values on the stimulus coordinates. The first BETA value is for the intercept term. The *sign* of the last BETA value shows whether the ideal point is a positive or a negative ideal point. The intermediate BETA values, and there are as many of these as there are dimensions, provide, together with the value of the last BETA, the coordinates for the ideal point, as described in the section entitled "Mathematical Foundations" on page 266.

c. R (CORRELATION). This is the correlation for the model.

d. DSQ. These are the squares of the distances from the ideal point for each stimulus.

If the data are analyzed nonmetrically, the printout shows these values for each iteration. It also provides a plot of DSQ versus scale values after the first iteration and the final iteration.

e. IDEAL POINT WITH RESPECT TO OLD AXES. These are the coordinates for the ideal point.

f. IMPORTANCES OF NEW AXES. These numbers are the same as the last BETA value listed. Only their sign is important in the phase III analysis. If positive, the ideal point is positive. If negative, the ideal point is negative. The size of the number in the phase III analysis does not have a bearing on dimension weights.

3. Tables of STIMULI COORDINATES, COORDINATES OF IDEAL POINTS, and WEIGHTS OF AXES. The WEIGHTS OF AXES TABLE is titled misleadingly. These are the same numbers described above as IMPORTANCES OF NEW AXES and serve only to show whether the ideal point is positive or negative.

4. A plot showing the ideal points for each subject and the stimulus coordinates.

In analyzing a phase III printout, the first criterion, of course, is that the model is significant for some of the subjects. This is determined from a review of the summary table as discussed earlier. We do not necessarily believe that phase III has to represent a "significant" improvement over phase IV since phase III is conceptually an appealing model. However, unless there is a physical interpretation of a negative ideal point (as in lukewarm tea), we would not consider it useful. Finally, in inspecting the ideal point plot we would retain ideal points only within or close to the bounds of the stimulus domain. If an ideal point lies much beyond the bounds of the stimulus domain, that subject's data are better represented by the vector model, as discussed in the section entitled "The Ideal Point Model" on page 259.

PHASE II PREFMAP OUTPUT

Phase II provides the generalization of individual weights for each subject and positive–negative ideal weights. This is the eliptical ideal point model. In most respects the output is similar to Phase III. As before the printout provides for each subject:

> S (VECTOR OF SCALE VALUES)
> BETA
> R (CORRELATION)
> DSQ
> IDEAL POINT WITH RESPECT TO OLD AXES
> IMPORTANCES OF NEW AXES

Only BETA and IMPORTANCES OF NEW AXES differ in interpretation from phase III. The final BETA (unstandardized b) coefficients listed are dimension weights which are repeated under the heading IMPORTANCES OF NEW AXES. There are as many of these as there are dimensions. Both the sign and the magnitude of these are now important. The signs show whether the ideal point is positive, negative, or positive–negative and so on. The magnitude is related to the importance of the dimension as a component of preference. A large weight means that a small movement along a dimension can have a large effect on preference. A small weight means that larger changes can be made in the properties represented by the dimension without having much effect on preference.

We apply basically the same criteria for the analysis of a phase II printout as for phase III. Is the model itself significant in terms of the F ratio for that subject for that phase? If the ideal point contains negative components, can some interpretable meaning be attached to them? Do the ideal points lie within the general bounds of the stimulus domain?

In addition, we must treat mixed positive–negative points with care since they have *hyperbolic* iso-preference contours, not elliptical ones. This aspect makes them difficult to interpret. Carroll (1972) has discussed this point and should be consulted.

PHASE I PREFMAP OUTPUT

Phase I is the most general form of the model. It contains provision for rotation of the axes of the stimulus space in addition to positive–negative ideal points and differential weighting of the dimensions. This is the elliptical ideal point model with rotation. The printout provides for each subject:

S (VECTOR OF SCALE VALUES)
BETA
R (CORRELATION)
DSQ
DIRECTION COSINE OF NEW AXES WITH RESPECT TO OLD
COMPOSITE TRANSFORMATION MATRIX
TRANSFORMED X
IDEAL POINT WITH RESPECT TO NEW AXES
IDEAL POINT WITH RESPECT TO OLD AXES
IMPORTANCES OF NEW AXES

The key part of the printout is the table showing DIRECTION COSINE OF NEW AXES WITH RESPECT TO OLD. If the value of this cosine is greater than .9, there is in fact very little rotation of the axes and one may confidently begin the analysis with phase II.

The calculation of ideal points and dimension weights from the BETA ("b") values is a bit complicated. We refer the interested reader to Carroll (1972).

Preferences for Liqueurs

This data set is for the preferences of nine subjects for seven liqueurs. The details of this experiment are provided in Chapter 15 where the derivation of the stimulus space is also discussed. In this section we will take you through PREFMAP analyses in all four phases and compare metric and nonmetric solutions for phases III and IV.

The summary table for the four phases analyzed metrically, Figure 12.8, was discussed in the previous section. The phase I analysis did not represent a significant improvement over the less general models. Note that phase I analysis rotates the stimulus space and the stimulus space derived for the average subject is used for subsequent phases of the analysis. The data were therefore reanalyzed commencing at phase II. The summary table for these analyses is given in Figure 12.9.

The within- and between-phase critical F values taken from a table of F values are:

	Phase(s)											
	Within phase						Between phase					
	F2		F3		F4		F23		F24		F34	
Degrees of freedom	4	2	3	3	2	4	1	2	2	2	1	3
5%	19.3		9.3		6.9		18.5		19.0		10.1	
1%	99.3		29.5		18.0		98.5		99.0		34.1	

Using the conservative 1% critical F value we see from the results in Figure 12.9 that for the average subject phase III is significant, and that the move from phase IV to phase III, $F = 33.9$, is very nearly so as well. While phase II is significant at the 5% level, $F = 27.8$, the move from phase III to phase II, $F = 0.275$, is not at all.

We are, however, more interested in results for individual subjects. Significance of within-phase results are:

	Within phase		
Subject	2	3	4
1	—	—	—
2	1%	1%	1%
3	—	—	—
4	—	—	—
5	—	—	5%
6	5%	1%	1%
7	—	—	—
8	—	—	5%
9	1%	1%	1%

CORRELATION (PHASE)

DF SUBJ	R1	R2	R3	R4	F RATIO (PHASE) F1 5 1	F2 4 2	F3 3 3	F4 2 4
1	0.0000000000	0.9814	0.8943	0.6874	0.000000000	113.0638	346.9946	0.6233
2	0.0000000000	0.9909	0.9044	0.8563	0.000000000	1000.0412	840.7857	145.6717
3	0.0000000000	0.9122	0.9126	0.8560	0.000000000		44.15461	53.5207
4	0.0000000000	0.9317	0.9054	0.8856	0.000000000	2.6329387		37.7810
5	0.0000000000	0.9544	0.9454	0.8655	0.000000000	2.613037	4.93601	
6	0.0000000000	0.9653	0.9424	0.5705	0.000000000	6.3991	7.5613	407.7201
7	0.0000000000	0.9531	0.9936	0.9880	0.000000000	150.6657	77.5613	86.1096
8	0.0000000000	0.9961	0.9899	0.8680	0.000000000	127.6362	48.6176	
AVE	0.0	0.9951	0.9899	0.8680				

F RATIO (BETWEEN PHASE)

DF SUBJ	F12 1 1	F13 2 1	F14 3 1	F23 1 3	F24 2 2	F34 1 3
1	-0.9631	-0.3999	-0.0792	8.8621	19.6821	0.4244
2	-0.9966		-0.3329	1000.46017	1000.94046	0.5024
3	-0.8635	-0.4161	-0.2442			1.75225
4	-0.8275	-0.4108	-0.2821	0.97565	1.34765	2.5805
5	-0.6573	-0.4896	-0.1617	2.07566	11.02365	15.5804
6	-0.6473	-0.4906	-0.1085	2.10765	1.97655	150.5804
7		-0.4996	-0.3544	2.01763	1.5691	33.6013
8	-0.9624			6.10751		
AVE	-0.9624	-0.4990	-0.2551	6.2752	12.9770	33.659

ROOT MEAN SQUARE

PHASE	
1	0.0
2	0.9664
3	0.9386
4	0.8465

A F - VALUE OF 1000.0 IN THE ABOVE TABLE INDICATES
A POSSIBLE DIVISION BY ZERO. I.E. R IS VERY CLOSE TO 1.00

Figure 12.9. Last page of PREFMAP output, phases II to IV.

276

In general the fit to the models is poor. Four subjects (1, 3, 4, and 7) fit none of the models at the 5% significance level. Subject 1 does show an improvement in correlation between phase III, .89, and phase IV, .49, as does Subject 7, .94 and .57. The phase III model represents an improvement over phase IV at the 5% level for Subject 7, $F = 15.1$, and almost so for Subject 1, $F = 8.4$. We will therefore review the phase III results for these subjects despite their lack of strict statistical significance. For none of the subjects does phase II represent a significant improvement over phase III.

To summarize at this point, Subjects 2, 5, 6, 8, and 9 may fit the vector model. The data for Subjects 1, 2, 6, 7, and 9 will also be examined with the ideal point model. Even though the between-phase F ratios are not significant for any of the subjects except Subject 7, the ideal point model may have merit provided the ideal points are positive and lie within the bounds of the stimulus domain.

We find, however, on inspection of the phase III output that Subjects 6 and 9 have negative ideal points. Further, the ideal point for Subject 2 lies way outside the stimulus domain. Therefore, only Subjects 1 and 7 should be considered for this model. That leaves Subjects 2, 5, 6, 8, and 9 as candidates for the vector model and Subjects 3 and 4 as fitting neither model.

Figure 12.10 summarizes the results. Preference vectors are shown for all the subjects and also the ideal points for Subjects 1 and 7 and the average Subject A. Most of the preference vectors lie in the direction of sweeter and more alcohol. The preference vectors for Subjects 3 and 4 who did not fit the model well also ran in this direction. This suggests that while they may have been somewhat inconsistent in their judgments, they probably like the same liqueur composition as the majority. An alternative explanation for their poor fit is that the stimulus space does not contain the dimensions of their preference. Only two subjects (8 and 9) show preference vectors in the direction of less sweetness. The ideal points for Subjects 1 and 7 and the average subject lie close to the center of the stimulus space but in the upper-right quadrant. This fact, together with the preference vectors, suggests that liqueur 4 is probably close to the optimum composition.

We turn now to the nonmetric analysis. We expect to see an apparent better fit, but the important question is whether it materially alters the preceding conclusions. The F values increase dramatically in the nonmetric analysis. Only three subjects have F values below 18 in phase IV, only one below 29.5 in phase III, and the between phase F values are all greater than the 5% critical value of 10.1. However, these values are not really meaningful.

A more interesting question is whether ideal points change sign or position or whether the directions of the preference vectors materially alter. In fact they do not. Irrespective of statistical significance, all subjects with positive

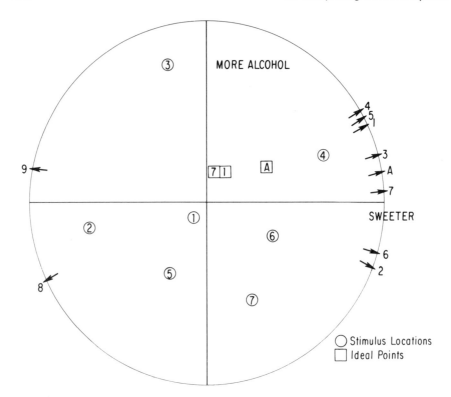

Figure 12.10. Preference vectors and ideal points on stimulus space.

ideal points in the metric analysis have positive ideal points in the nonmetric analysis. Likewise, subjects with negative ideal points in one analysis also have them in the other. Further, the coordinates of the ideal points occur in the same general region of the stimulus space. For the two subjects (1 and 7) considered as best fitting the ideal point model, we have:

	Coordinates on dimension			
	1		2	
Subject	Metric	Nonmetric	Metric	Nonmetric
1	.09	.04	.17	.14
7	.12	.13	.13	.16

In the phase IV model we find only Subjects 8 and 9 with less sweet preference vectors for metric or nonmetric analyses. Similarly, both analyses show sweeter but less alcohol preference vectors for Subjects 2 and 6. Since statistical power is lost with nonmetric analysis, and the conclusions are not altered, we recommend using metric analysis of preference.

This view is supported by Huber (1975) who examined a number of preference models at the metric and nonmetric levels.

Preferences for Strawberry-Flavored Beverages

Hedonic ratings for the 11 strawberry-flavored beverages (Section 3.3) were developed from the mean of three scales:

good–bad
like–dislike
pleasant–unpleasant

The perceptual space used for the preference analysis was that developed with ALSCAL (Section 9.5). The hedonic ratings were fit at the metric level using both phase IV and phase III of PREFMAP. The critical F values for the phase IV vector model, 2 and 8 d.f., are 4.46 (5%) and 8.65 (1%). Of the 46 subjects, 22 fit the model at the 1% level and 11 more at the 5% level. Thirteen of the subjects do not have a significant fit. The majority of the subjects fitting the vector model have preference vectors closely arranged around the sweetness dimension. Only two subjects (5 and 46) have preference vectors in the direction of less sweetness. Two other subjects (22 and 31) have preference vectors roughly perpendicular to the sweetness direction and toward the standard commercial beverage color.

None of the 13 subjects failing to fit the phase IV model fit the phase III model either. However, 5 of the subjects fitting phase IV show a significant improvement in fit for the ideal point phase III model. Correlations for phase III and phase IV are:

	Correlation	
Subject	Phase III	Phase IV
10	.95	.84
24	.96	.87
27	.98	.95
32	.93	.81
46	.88	.77

All except Subject 46 have positive ideal points located along the first dimension of the stimulus space in the direction of greater sweetness. Thus, even for these few subjects whose data are better fitted by the ideal point model, the conclusion arrived at from phase IV is unchanged. More sweetness than found in the standard beverage is preferred.

It is unlikely that invocation of the more general phase II model would provide a fit to the data of the 13 subjects not fitting the phase IV model.

It is more probable that their preference data are inconsistent. Subject 1, for example, also gave a poor fit to the ALSCAL stimulus space and is probably a poor discriminator. Her preference vector in the lower-right quadrant of the stimulus space stands alone. Two of the other subjects have preference vectors in the unpopular "less sweet" direction.

Fitting Chemical Properties to a Taste Space

PREFMAP is a general property fitting algorithm and as such may be used to relate adjective ratings or physico-chemical properties to a perceptual space. Two physicochemical properties found to be highly related to the MINISSA "taste of chemical" space (Section 5.6) are molecular weight and departure from pH 7. The rank order correlations are .78 and .80, respectively. Figure 12.11(a) shows the plane in the taste space defined by these two dimensions. Additionally, a hedonic dimension may be projected through the taste space. The mean of the subjects' ratings for good–bad on each stimulus provides a dimension which lies at 47° to the molecular weight dimension, Figure 12.11(c), and at 81° to the pH 7 dimension, Figure 12.11(b). The rank order correlation for the stimuli along the hedonic dimension is .78.

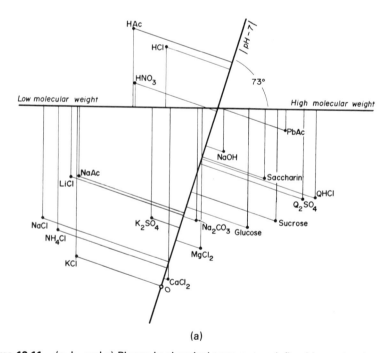

(a)

Figure 12.11. (a, b, and c) Planes in chemical taste space defined by molecular weight, departure from pH 7, and mean hedonic ratings. (Parts b and c on page 281.)

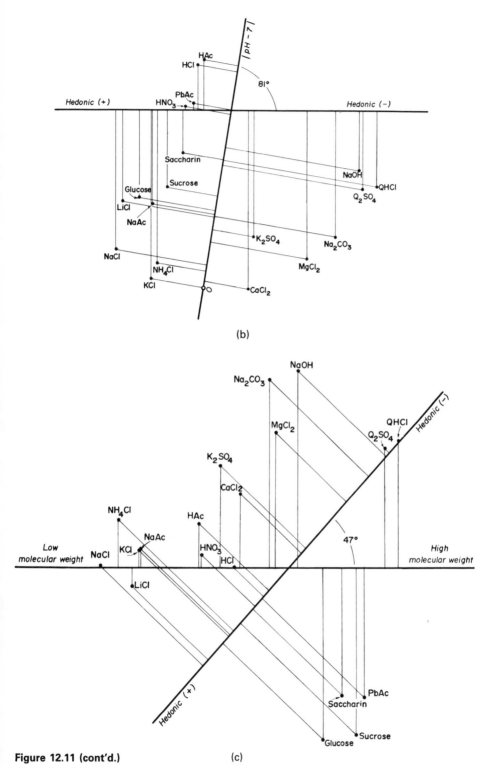

Figure 12.11 (cont'd.)

(c)

When a number of properties are expressed in completely different units, it is more appropriate to examine the correlation of each separately with the stimulus space than to apply the method of canonical correlations (Section 12.4). Linear combinations of pH (a negative logarithm of a concentration), with molecular weight (a relative mass), and goodness (an ordinal perception), make little intuitive sense.

12.4. Canonical Regression

Overview

In Sections 12.2 and 12.3 we reviewed models and methods for relating preferences and properties to MDS stimulus spaces. Those sections concentrated on relating a *single* set of preference or property ratings to the space. If there were, actually, many sets of preference or property ratings, then we had to perform many analyses, one for each set of ratings. The results of these many analyses would be many attribute vectors or ideal points, one point or vector for each attribute.

In this section we discuss two models which parallel the vector and ideal point models discussed earlier. The essential difference in our present discussion is that we now look at procedures which let us *simultaneously* relate several sets of preference or property rating scales to an MDS stimulus space. In *one* analysis we can take *several* sets of preference or property ratings and find a *few* attribute vectors or ideal points, which are most like the several attributes.

The procedure which is used to do this is canonical regression. Programs for canonical vector analysis are available in all of the popular statistical systems. Addition of a dummy variable (see next section) is necessary to perform canonical ideal point analysis. (There is no special purpose program like PREFMAP to do this.) Following the terminology of canonical regression, we call the attribute vector the *canonical attribute vector,* and the ideal attribute point the *canonical ideal attribute point.* There can be more than one vector or point, in which case the one accounting for the most variance is called the *first* canonical vector or ideal point, the next is called the *second,* etc. While canonical vector analysis is treated in a number of multivariate analysis texts, this is the first published discussion, to our knowledge, of canonical ideal point analysis.

Let us look at the example in which subjects are asked to make similarity and preference judgments of several kinds of coffees which vary in their strength and sweetness. As we saw, the methods discussed in Section 12.2

and 12.3 find preference vectors for each subject. However, there will be a number of subjects who like unsweetened coffee and a number who like sweetened coffee. Thus, there will be a cluster of vectors on the unsweetened side of the MDS space, and a cluster on the sweetened side.

Using canonical regression we can find the first canonical vector. This is the direction which represents the type of coffee most preferred by our group of subjects. If most of the subjects like unsweetened coffee then the first canonical vector will be on that side of the space. If most subjects like sweetened coffee it will be on the other side.

Furthermore, in the same analysis we can find the *second* canonical vector. If, in our example, the first canonical vector is near the sweetened coffees, the second will be near the unsweetened ones. Thus we have two canonical vectors, instead of many individual vectors. These two canonical vectors represent the two common patterns of preference found in our sample of subjects. They have just the same characteristics as the vector in Figure 12.1. Note that the canonical analysis also tells us how strongly each subject's preferences are related to each of the two vectors, as we will see.

The nature of the canonical ideal point model should be clear. If, in our example, most subjects find strong coffee desirable, then the first canonical point would be on that side of the space. If nearly all subjects shared this preference function, then the second canonical point would account for very little variance, and would probably not be interpretable. The interpretation procedures for each canonical point, regardless of how many are used, would be the same as for Figure 12.3. As with the canonical vector model, the canonical point model tells us how strongly each subject's preferences are related to each canonical preference point.

Thus, the interpretation of each canonical vector or point exactly follows the discussion in Section 12.2, and the geometry is exactly like Figures 12.1 and 12.3. The main new aspect is that each vector or point now represents a *weighted sum* of several attributes instead of representing a single attribute. For each attribute there is a weight for each vector or point. The weight tells us how strongly each attribute is related to each canonical vector or point.

Let us return to our example of the canonical vector analysis of coffee preferences where we found two vectors, the first for sweetened, the second for unsweetened. If a particular subject has a large weight for the first canonical vector and small for the second, she prefers sweetened coffee. The opposite pattern of weights implies preference for unsweetened coffee. Two small weights imply dislike for all coffees, and two large weights imply liking for both types, but no preference of one over the other.

As in Section 12.2, the mathematical basis of the canonical vector and point models permits an analysis that maximizes a correlation index. For the vector model the correlation is between the weighted sum of the attributes and the projections of the stimuli onto the canonical vector. There is such a correlation for each vector. The correlation for the first canonical vector is greater than for the second, etc. The squared correlation tells us the proportion of variance in the MDS space accounted for by the first canonical vector. The second says the same for the second vector. The sum of squared correlation coefficients is the total proportion of MDS variance accounted for. The analysis actually maximizes this sum.

For the ideal point model the correlations are between the weighted sum of attributes and the squared distances between the stimuli and ideal point. There is a correlation for each canonical point, and it is interpreted as in the preceding (as is the sum).

The mathematical basis of the analysis is called canonical regression and the correlations are called canonical correlation coefficients. While there is a significance test for these coefficients, a number of its assumptions are violated in our application, and we prefer to use the test *very* conservatively. That is, if it indicates that a correlation is not significantly different from zero, then we can be *very* sure that there is no relationship between the attributes and the MDS space. Significance, on the other hand, must be *very* great to reach the conclusion that there is a relationship.

Mathematical Foundations

The canonical vector and canonical ideal point models are based on the mathematics of canonical regression analysis. Canonical regression is a way of finding linear relationships between two sets of variables. It is similar to multiple regression which seeks a relation between a single variable and a set of variables. The equations for canonical regression involve defining several pairs of linear combinations. There is one pair for each canonical vector or point. The equations, for the vector model, are:

$$\tilde{y}_{ki} = a_{k0} + a_{k1}(y_{i1}) + \cdots + a_{kr}(y_{ir}),$$

and

$$\tilde{x}_{ki} = b_{k0} + b_{k1}(x_{i1}) + \cdots + b_{kr}(x_{ir}),$$

where the values x_{i1}, x_{i2}, etc., are the values of stimulus i on dimensions 1, 2, etc., of the MDS space (as in the multiple regression equations), and where y_{i1}, y_{i2}, etc., are ratings of stimulus i on several attribute scales, preferences for stimulus i from several subjects, etc.

For the ideal point model the second equation is modified just as in the section entitled ''Mathematical Foundations'' on page 264. That is, we define the sum of squared stimulus coordinates s:

$$s = x_{i1}^2 + \cdots + x_{ir}^2,$$

and append this dummy variable to the set of dimension variables in the preceding equation.

In the first two equations given above, the coefficients a_{k0} and b_{k0} are intercepts and a_{k1}, b_{k1}, etc., are canonical regression weights. There is a complete set of regression weights and intercepts for each of the k canonical vectors or points. For each canonical vector or point there are always two intercepts, one regression weight for each attribute, one for each dimension, and for the point model, an additional regression weight for the dummy variable.

While the regression weights may be taken as an index of the relationship between an attribute and the canonical vectors or points, a better index is available. The relative contribution of the attributes to each canonical vector or point is shown by the canonical factor structure matrix, a matrix that contains entries called canonical variable loadings. An element of this matrix gives the correlation between a particular attribute (a set of preference ratings from a particular subject, for example) and a particular canonical vector or point. This correlation can be used in the usual descriptive fashion.

In the equations just given, the intercepts and weights are solved for so that the correlation between $\bar{y}_{ki}$ and $\bar{x}_{ki}$ is as large as possible, given that all $\bar{y}_{ki}$ are mutually uncorrelated, and that all $\bar{x}_{ki}$ are also mutually uncorrelated. Thus, the first canonical vector or point (i.e., when $k = 1$) involves the linear combination of attributes and dimensions which gives the maximum possible correlation between the two sets. The second canonical vector or point ($k = 2$) involves the linear combination with the next largest correlation under the restriction that the projections onto the new vector or point are uncorrelated with the first projections.

With large data sets several canonical vectors or points are possible. However, the maximum number of vectors or points is constrained. The constraint is that the number of stimuli must exceed the total number of variables in both sets combined, including the dummy variable for the point model. Thus, if the number of dimensions and attributes is, say, 10, there must be at least 11 stimuli for the canonical vector model and 12 for the canonical ideal point model. However, it is strongly recommended that there be many more than this minimum number of stimuli to obtain robust estimates of the regression weights.

There is no restriction on the number of variables in either set. However, the smallest set of variables places a limit on the number of canonical vectors or points possible (i.e., the maximum value of k). If, for example, the MDS space is three dimensional and there are 10 sets of preferences (and at least 14 stimuli), there can be at most three canonical vectors, or points.

The common terminology for these concepts is as follows. The stimuli are usually called observations, cases, etc. The dimensions are the set of variables in one of the sets, the attributes the variables in the other set. Note that when attributes correspond to subject preferences, that the subjects are the variables in that set, not the observations. Generally, the two sets of variables are called dependent and independent variables, criterion and predictor variables, left and right variables, etc. The canonical vectors or points are called canonical factors, and the regression coefficients are often called canonical factor coefficients.

Canonical Regression Analysis Using BMD6PM

The examples in the following sections were analyzed using BMD6PM and are limited to the vector model. The job set-ups are clearly described in the Biomedical Computer Programs manual published by the University of California Press and will not be shown here.

The key parts of the BMD output for users of this book are three pages labeled CORRELATIONS, CANONICAL VARIABLES, and CANONICAL VARIABLE LOADINGS. These provide all the information necessary to determine the significance and redundancy of the analysis, and to plot spaces in terms of both left-hand and right-hand variable sets. Examples are shown in Figures 12.12, 12.13, and 12.14.

CORRELATIONS gives the correlation coefficients and their significance for each of the canonical correlations. Significance is determined as follows: Test statistics, Bartlett's λ_i, are defined for a total of r correlations by:

$$\lambda_i = \prod_{i=1}^{i=r}(1 - R_i^2).$$

Thus if $r = 3$

$$\lambda_1 = (1 - R_1^2)(1 - R_2^2)(1 - R_3^2),$$

$$\lambda_2 = (1 - R_2^2)(1 - R_3^2),$$

$$\lambda_3 = (1 - R_3^2).$$

Chi-square values are then calculated from λ by

$$\chi^2 = -\left[N - 1 - \frac{(P_1 + P_2 + 1)}{2}\right] \ln \lambda$$

for $(P_1 + 1 - i)(P_2 + 1 - i)$ degrees of freedom, P_1 being the number of variables in the first set and P_2 the number of variables in the second set. The BMD program calculates χ^2 and gives the significance for each correlation.

CANONICAL VARIABLES provides coordinates for plotting spaces.

CORRELATIONS

	X(3) 3	X(4) 4	X(5) 5	X(6) 6	X(7) 7	X(8) 8
X(3) 3	1.000					
X(4) 4	-0.209	1.000				
X(5) 5	-0.980	0.677	1.000			
X(6) 6	-0.548	0.230	0.062	1.000		
X(7) 7	0.044	-0.421	0.069	-0.745	1.000	
X(8) 8	0.044	0.287	-0.064	-0.642	0.220	1.000

SQUARED MULTIPLE CORRELATIONS OF EACH VARIABLE IN SECOND SET WITH ALL OTHER VARIABLES IN SECOND SET

VARIABLE NUMBER	NAME	R-SQUARED
5	X(5)	0.3772
6	X(6)	0.80073
7	X(7)	0.67944
8	X(8)	0.56407

SQUARED MULTIPLE CORRELATIONS OF EACH VARIABLE IN FIRST SET WITH ALL OTHER VARIABLES IN FIRST SET

VARIABLE NUMBER	NAME	R-SQUARED
3	X(3)	0.04359
4	X(4)	0.04359

EIGENVALUE	CANONICAL CORRELATION
0.75872	0.87105
0.36626	0.60519

NUMBER OF EIGENVALUES	BARTLETT'S TEST FOR REMAINING EIGENVALUES		
	CHI-SQUARE	D.F.	SIGNIFICANCE
0	21.60	8	0.00572
1	5.25	3	0.15469

BARTLETT'S TEST ABOVE INDICATES THE NUMBER OF CANONICAL
VARIABLES NECESSARY TO EXPRESS THE DEPENDENCY BETWEEN THE
TWO SETS OF VARIABLES. THE NECESSARY NUMBER OF CANONICAL
VARIABLES IS THE SMALLEST NUMBER OF EIGENVALUES SUCH THAT
THE REST OF THE REMAINING EIGENVALUES ARE NON-SIGNIFICANT.
FOR EXAMPLE, IF THE A REMAINING EIGENVALUES WERE DESIRED,
THEN 1 VARIABLE WOULD BE CONSIDERED NECESSARY.
HOWEVER, THE NUMBER OF CANONICAL VARIABLES OF PRACTICAL
VALUE IS LIKELY TO BE SMALLER.

Figure 12.12. CORRELATIONS output from BMD6PM.

CANONICAL VARIABLES (CASE NUMBERS REFER TO DATA BEFORE DELETION OF CASES)

LABEL	CASE NO.	WEIGHT	CNVRF1	CNVRF2	CNVRS1	CNVRS2
ACETONE	1	1.0000	-1.0350	-0.4331	-1.2639	-0.7106
ANISOLE	2	1.0000	1.1238	-0.3363	1.1574	0.6203
1-BUTANE	3	1.0000	-0.2914	2.3799	-0.4163	2.0203
TER-BUTA	4	1.0000	-1.2065	-0.1272	-0.9938	-0.6037
1,2-DICH	5	1.0000	-0.6761	-0.5703	0.0090	1.4828
2-ETHOXY	6	1.0000	0.6097	-1.1414	0.7905	-1.0226
ETHYLACE	7	1.0000	-0.9307	-0.3196	-0.9914	-0.4055
3-HEPTAN	8	1.0000	0.7332	-1.1478	0.3566	-0.2070
METHYLAC	9	1.0000	-1.0926	-0.0737	-1.4234	-0.2786
1-NITROP	10	1.0000	0.9771	0.7702	0.3877	-0.7446
2-PENTAN	11	1.0000	-1.0542	-0.3133	-0.5010	-0.5094
PROPYLAC	12	1.0000	-0.9019	-0.4993	-0.5593	-0.5323
PROPYLSU	13	1.0000	-0.0108	2.1575	0.1492	1.6540
SALICYLA	14	1.0000	1.3627	0.2751	2.3900	-1.0522
1,3,5STR	15	1.0000	1.4203	-0.0842	0.8283	0.9038
1-BUTANO	16	1.0000	0.9721	-0.5364	0.0804	-0.6148

NUMERICAL CONSISTENCY CHECK

THE FOLLOWING VARIANCES OF CANONICAL VARIABLES SHOULD ALL BE EQUAL TO ONE

CANONICAL VARIABLE	VARIANCE	RELATIVE ERROR
CNVRF1	0.100000D 01	0.804912D-15
CNVRF2	0.100000D 01	0.666134D-15
CNVRS1	0.100000D 01	0.160982D-14
CNVRS2	0.100000D 01	0.133227D-14

Figure 12.13. CANONICAL VARIABLES output from BMD6PM.

An example is shown in Figure 12.13. This is from the odor space–Laffort parameter analysis (see the following section, on page 290). The column labeled CNVRF1 provides the coordinates for the *F*irst (or left-hand) variable on dimension *1*. Similarly CNVRS2 provides the coordinates for the *S*econd variable on dimension *2*.

CANONICAL VARIABLE LOADINGS (Figure 12.14) shows the correlations between the original variables and the canonical factors. Large absolute values indicate a large contribution to the factor. Canonical variable loadings show the extent to which the total analysis accounts for the variance of each variable. This is the sum of the squares of the loadings for a given variable across all correlations. These are analogous to the communalities of factor analysis. Canonical variable loadings are also used to calculate redundancies. Redundancies show how much of the data in the dependent or first set are explained by the data in the predictor or second set. One way to view redundancy is to consider two circles representing all the information contained in the two data sets.

The smaller circle here represents the dependent variable information, the larger the predictor variable information. The shaded overlap between the circles represents the amount of information that can be deduced about each set from the data in the other. In the cola example (see the section beginning on page 293) 87% of the information in the similarity space is explained by information from the adjectives. On the other hand, information in the stimulus space only accounts for 70% of the information in

CANONICAL VARIABLE LOADINGS (CORRELATIONS OF CANONICAL VARIABLES WITH ORIGINAL VARIABLES)

		$CNVRF1_1$	$CNVRF2_2$
X(3)	3	0.051	0.999
X(4)	4	0.987	0.158

		$CNVRS1_1$	$CNVRS2_2$
X(5)	5	0.799	-0.108
X(6)	6	-0.181	-0.781
X(7)	7	-0.391	0.878
X(8)	8	0.328	0.048

IN THE BIVARIATE PLOTS WHICH FOLLOW, A = 10 CASES, B = 11 CASES, ..., AND * = 20 OR MORE CASES.

3 PLOTS ARE TO BE MADE

VARIABLE NO. NAME	VARIABLE NO. NAME	PAGE NUMBER
9 CNVRF1	11 CNVRS1	10
10 CNVRF2	12 CNVRS2	10
11 CNVRS1	12 CNVRS2	11

Figure 12.14. CANONICAL VARIABLE LOADINGS from BMD6PM.

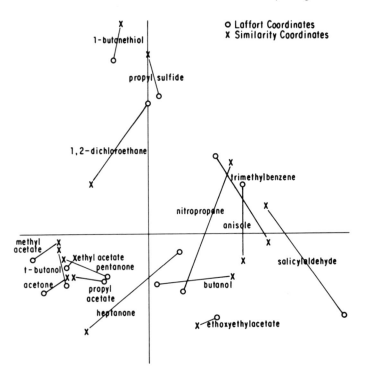

Figure 12.15.   Odor space and Laffort parameters.

the adjective set. This is not surprising. Adjective measures included may not be relevant to the stimulus space. Or they may be noisy. Therefore one would not expect to be able to predict all their values from similarity information. However, if less than half the information in the criterion set is explained by information in the predictor set the analysis obviously has little value. Calculation of redundancies for the canonical factors for each data set for each correlation run as follows:

1. Calculate proportion of variance extracted by the canonical factor. This is the sum of the squares of the canonical variable loadings in each set divided by the number of variables in that set.
2. Determine the redundancy as the product of the proportion of variance extracted and the square of the correlation coefficient.

Odor of Chemicals (Physicochemical Properties)

This example shows an attempt to match with physicochemical properties an odor space derived by MDS of similarity judgments. The experimental details are not given in this book but may be found in Schiffman, Robinson, and Erickson (1977). The odor space is for 16 pure chemicals, Table 12.1,

Table 12.1
Laffort Parameters for Sixteen Chemicals

	Alpha	Rho	Epsilon	Pi
Acetone	0.77	1.83	−0.02	−0.37
Anisole	2.23	0.91	0.85	0.15
1-Butanethiol	1.35	0.30	1.02	0.03
1-Butanol	1.65	0.59	0.07	1.17
Ter-butanol	1.31	0.90	−0.16	0.62
1,2-Dichloroethane	0.88	0.11	1.04	0.78
2-Ethoxyethylacetate	2.83	1.78	0.02	−0.26
Ethyl acetate	1.60	1.53	−0.06	−0.34
3-Hepatanone	2.60	1.61	0.24	−0.53
Methyl acetate	1.00	1.54	0.0	−0.35
1-Nitropropane	1.46	1.64	0.33	0.05
2-Pentanone	1.74	1.73	0.06	−0.46
Propyl acetate	2.20	1.52	−0.12	−0.33
Propyl sulfide	2.44	0.49	0.81	−0.18
Salicylaldehyde	3.45	1.17	0.31	0.68
1,3,5-Trimethyl benzene	3.03	0.74	0.62	−0.09

and was developed by ALSCAL analysis of similarity judgments made by 12 nonsmoking Duke University undergraduates. The physicochemical properties, also given in Table 12.1, are Laffort parameters (Dravnieks & Laffort, 1972). A brief explanation of these is:

Alpha   an apolar factor proportional to molecular volume
Rho   a proton receptor factor
Epsilon an electron factor high in unsaturated compounds
Pi   a proton donor factor

For the canonical correlation analysis the stimulus coordinates in the two-dimensional odor space provide the left-hand or first variable set. The four Laffort parameters provide the right-hand or second variable set. The number of canonical correlations is limited to two, the number of variables in the left-hand set. Since there are 16 cases (number of stimuli) and only six total variables there is no need to make any selection of the Laffort parameters. If there are more variables than cases, as in the cola example (see pages 293–297), then some selection must be made.

The canonical correlations given by BMDP6M analysis between the two stimulus coordinates and the four Laffort parameters are:

Canonical correlation	Correlation coefficient	Significance
First	.871	.006
Second	.605	.155

The first correlation coefficient is reasonably high, and very significant. The second correlation is low, but possibly meaningful.

The next step in examining the output is to calculate the redundancies. These will show how much of the stimulus space is explained by the Laffort parameters and, of lesser concern, how much of the information contained in the Laffort parameters can be derived from the stimulus space. Redundancies for each correlation are the product of the square of the correlation coefficient and the mean of the sum of the squares of the canonical variable loadings. These are as follows:

	Correlation	Redundancy	Total redundancy
Left-hand set	First	.37	
(odor space)	Second	.19	.56
Right-hand set	First	.18	
(Laffort)	Second	.13	.31

What this means is that 56%, just over half, of the information in the odor space is contained within the Laffort parameters. However, only 31% of the information contained in the Laffort parameters can be derived from the odor space. This latter point is not surprising since the Laffort parameters contain a great deal of information about the molecules, some of which may not be relevant to, or even contained within, this two-dimensional odor space. On the other hand it is pleasing that the Laffort parameters provide a reasonable amount of information about the odors. It is worthwhile therefore to continue examining the output to see how the parameters are used to describe the odor space. This is done by inspection of the canonical variable loadings which are:

	Canonical variable loadings	
Laffort parameter	First correlation	Second correlation
Alpha	.799	−.108
Rho	−.181	−.781
Epsilon	.391	.878
Pi	.328	.048

By far the greatest contribution to the first correlation comes from alpha. Both rho and epsilon contribute to the second correlation. Pi contributes little to the correlations.

Figure 12.15 provides a graphic representation of the analysis. The coordinates in the stimulus space (after some rotation and standardization) are plotted as X. The coordinates for the variables derived from the Laffort parameters are plotted as O. The lines joining the two sets of coordinates show that the greatest differences are on the vertical dimension. This corresponds to the second canonical correlation which is rather weak. The order on the first dimension from the odor space is fairly well preserved by the first correlation.

While remembering that only 37% and 19%, respectively, of the information in the two dimensions of the odor space is contained in the canonical variables based on the Laffort parameters, it is interesting to see what is being represented. Alpha, which is proportional to molecular volume and surface area is the major contributor to the first dimension, and the larger molecules are on the right in Figure 12.15. Rho (negatively) and epsilon are the major contributors to the vertical dimension. Rho is high for oxygenated compounds while epsilon is high for compounds containing divalent sulfur. Propyl sulfide and butane thiol are in the upper half of the figure while the oxygenated compounds are in the lower.

In summary, canonical correlation analysis applied to this data set shows that the Laffort parameters provide a partial explanation of perceived dissimilarities between the odor of chemicals. In examining the output from the analysis the following steps are important:

1. Examine size and significance of the correlation coefficients.
2. Calculate the redundancies using the squared correlation coefficients and the canonical variable loadings.
3. Examine the contributions of variables, given by the canonical variable loadings, to each of the correlations.
4. If all of these seem sensible, plot out the values given in the table of canonical variables.

Colas (Adjective Ratings)

This example shows an attempt to match (from adjective ratings) a stimulus space derived by MDS of similarity judgments. The stimulus space used is that developed by INDSCAL for 10 colas (Section 8.3). The space contains three dimensions:

diet–nondiet

cherry cola flavor–regular cola flavor

Pepsi Cola company flavor–Coca-Cola company flavor

Subsequent to the similarity judgments subjects provided ratings on 13 adjectives for each of the 10 colas.

The first step in the analysis is to obtain the mean adjective ratings over subjects. These are shown in Table 12.2.

Since there are more total variables than cases the number must be reduced before a meaningful canonical correlation can be attempted. Spe-

Table 12.2
Mean Adjective Ratings for the Ten Colas

1	2	3	4	5	6	7	8	9	10	11	12	13	14	15	16	17	18	19	20	21	22	23	24	25	26	Cola
5	8	6	9	5	6	5	3	7	4	8	4	8	4	6	2	6	2	6	8	6	7	4	5	4	2	DIET PEPSI
5	φ	5	8	3	2	8	3	8	7	7	2	8	5	7	5	8	2	7	9	5	4	5	8	6	5	PEPSI COLA
7	4	4	4	6	9	3	3	3	6	5	3	5	9	3	6	3	5	2	3	5	8	4	1	3	7	YUKON
3	8	3	6	1	6	8	9	8	6	2	φ	6	1	6	8	6	8	7	6	3	4	6	9	4	2	DR PEPPER
7	3	3	2	5	8	3	6	4	7	7	2	6	4	3	1	3	4	4	7	7	5	3	1	4	4	SHASTA
6	2	3	4	4	7	5	4	6	4	7	φ	6	3	4	2	4	3	5	φ	6	6	4	φ	4	3	COCA COLA
6	5	3	2	4	3	5	8	5	5	4	2	6	3	4	8	4	φ	3	4	6	4	3	5	3	5	DIET DR P
8	φ	3	5	7	1	2	6	2	5	7	1	7	3	4	5	3	9	3	6	7	7	3	2	4	7	TAB
4	8	4	6	2	1	7	3	6	8	4	2	7	3	6	φ	7	9	7	9	6	φ	6	1	4	9	RC
7	7	3	2	8	1	2	5	3	6	7	7	6	8	3	2	2	6	3	3	8	2	2	1	2	9	DIET RITE

Adjective labels (read vertically): GOOD, STRONG, SWEET, BITTER, SOUR, FRUITY, SPICY, COATS, SHARP, PUCKERS, FRESH, CHEMICAL, COMPLEX

cifically since we are trying to place 10 stimuli in three dimensions we must use no more than six adjectives. While a trial and error approach could be used, one way to decide which adjectives to eliminate is to examine the correlations between adjective ratings. If several show high intercorrelations only one of that group need be used. The correlations between the adjectives are shown in Table 12.3.

Good, sweet, bitter, and sharp were eliminated because of their high positive (or negative) correlations with sour, fresh, and puckers mouth. Coats mouth was eliminated as it correlated with puckers mouth and chemical. Complex and strong were eliminated for a different reason. Both showed relatively small standard deviations indicating that they were poor discriminators. While spicy also showed a low standard deviation, it was retained as a possibly useful flavor descriptor.

The six adjectives retained for the canonical correlation were: sour, fruity, spicy, puckers mouth, fresh, and chemical. With three variables in the left-hand set there may be up to three canonical correlations.

The canonical correlations between the six adjectives (the right-hand set of variables) and the three stimulus coordinates (the left-hand set) are:

Table 12.3
Correlations between Adjectives Used for Rating Colas

	Good	Strong	Sweet	Bitter	Sour	Fruity	Spicy	Coats mouth	Sharp	Puckers mouth	Fresh	Chemical	Complex
Good													
Strong	-.38												
Sweet	.94	-.18											
Bitter	-.97	.33	-.96										
Sour	-.93	.51	-.84	.93									
Fruity	.56	.32	.67	-.56	-.30								
Spicy	-.22	.80	-.09	.23	.37	.52							
Coats mouth	-.85	.63	-.77	.87	.85	-.30	.59						
Sharp	-.88	.63	-.83	.87	.84	-.29	.58	.94					
Puckers mouth	-.89	.54	-.81	.84	.88	-.20	.55	.85	.93				
Fresh	.84	-.21	.80	-.84	-.72	.75	.12	-.69	-.65	-.56			
Chemical	-.94	.41	-.91	.92	.82	-.63	.19	.86	.90	.82	-.90		
Complex	-.45	.48	-.50	.54	.52	.10	.62	.66	.74	.67	-.31	.55	

Canonical correlation	Correlation coefficient	Significance
First	.973	.08
Second	.956	.13
Third	.850	.27

The first two correlations seem meaningful, the third dubious.

The next step in the analysis is to calculate the redundancies for each variable set. These are as follows:

		Correlation	Redundancy	Total redundancy
Left-hand set	First	.33		
(cola space)	Second	.29		.62
	Third	.25		.87
Right-hand set	First	.33		
(adjective ratings)	Second	.14		.47
	Third	.23		.70

Considering first the left-hand variable set we see that 87% of the information in the cola space can be derived from the adjectives. Although the third correlation was of dubious statistical significance it is apparently conveying a good deal (25%) of information about the cola space. The acid test of course is whether this information seems to make sense. This is discussed in the following.

Looking at the redundancy for the right-hand variable set we see that 70% of the information contained therein can be derived from the cola space. While this is also a high figure it is reasonable for it to be less than the redundancy for the left-hand variable set. Subjects may give ratings on adjectives which are not relevant to the judgments they made when determining dissimilarities. Inspection of canonical variable loadings can show whether this is the case.

The three canonical variables of the right-hand set are correlated with the six adjectives as follows:

Adjective	Canonical variables			Sum of squares
	1	2	3	
Sour	−.433	−.428	−.700	.86
Fruity	.862	−.141	.146	.78
Spicy	.500	−.650	−.229	.72
Puckers mouth	−.150	−.509	−.814	.94
Fresh	.775	−.066	.480	.61
Chemical	−.524	−.133	−.697	.78

The last column in the table shows the overall contribution of each adjective to the three canonical correlations. In each case these are quite large indicating that all are providing information concerning the cola space.

At this point it is now appropriate to determine if the canonical correlation analysis has preserved the original cola space in development of the left-hand set of variables. Again this is done by inspection of the variable loadings. Correlations of the three canonical variables of the left-hand set with the original dimensions of the MDS stimulus space are:

	Canonical variables			
Original dimension	1	2	3	Sum of squares
1 (diet)	.191	− .499	.846	1
2 (cherry)	.945	− .085	− .316	1
3 (manufacturer)	.316	− .835	.452	1

As shown by the values of unity for the sum of squares all the information is retained. However the space has been rotated somewhat.

Comparing now the right-hand variables with the new left-hand variables we see that the first variable with its high loading on fruity and fresh relates to the cherry cola–regular cola left-hand variable. The second variable (company flavor type) is mostly associated with sour, spicy, and puckers mouth. However sour and puckers mouth are more strongly associated with the third variable which is largely but not entirely diet–nondiet. The adjective ratings while capturing some features of the MDS stimulus space are not recovering it entirely. This is not unexpected.

References

Carroll, J. D. Individual differences and multidimensional scaling. In R. N. Shepard, A. K. Romney, & S. B. Nerlove (Eds.), *Multidimensional scaling. Theory and applications in the behavioral sciences.* New York: Seminar Press, 1972.

Cochran, W. G., & Cox, G. M. *Experimental designs,* 2nd Ed. New York: John Wiley and Sons, 1957.

Green, P., & V. Rao *Applied multidimensional scaling: A comparison of approaches and algorithms.* New York: Holt, Rinehart & Winston, 1972.

Huber, J. Predicting preferences on experimental bundles of attributes: a comparison of models. *Journal of Marketing Research,* 1975, *12,* 290–297.

Schiffman, S., Robinson, D. E., & Erickson, R. P. Multidimensional scaling of odorants: Examination of psychological and physicochemical dimensions. *Chemical Senses and Flavor,* 1977, **2,** 375–390.

Young, F. W., de Leeuw, J., & Takane, Y. Multiple (and canonical) regression with a mix of qualitative and quantitative variables. *Psychometrica,* 1976, **41,** 505–530.

13

Interpreting Subject Spaces

In this chapter we discuss some methods to help interpret the subject spaces obtained when INDSCAL, ALSCAL, or MULTISCALE are used with the WMDS model.

Unlike the methods for interpreting stimulus spaces, the methods presented in this chapter are not standard statistical methods like regression analysis. In fact, the methods presented are part of a new branch of statistics called *directional statistics,* an area of the statistical literature that has only recently come to the attention of psychometrics. There are very few, if any, applications of these methods to assist in interpreting MDS subject spaces, though, as we will see, they are ideally suited for the purpose.

The reason that subject spaces need relatively novel interpretation procedures, while stimulus spaces need standard procedures, is that there is a crucial difference in the fundamental nature of the two MDS spaces:

A stimulus space contains *points,* one point for each stimulus.

A subject space contains *vectors,* one vector for each subject.

An important aspect of stimulus *points* is their *linear* separation (i.e., the *distance* between them), whereas the corresponding aspect of subject vectors is their *angular* separation (i.e., the *angle* between them). This point was discussed in Section 4.3 and is illustrated in Figure 4.4.

As we have mentioned a number of times, there are two important aspects of a subject's weight vector—its direction and its length. We have also mentioned that the meaning of the length of a subject's weight vector (i.e., the square root of the sum of squared weights for the subject) depends on which MDS program has been used. With INDSCAL and ALSCAL the length reflects the degree of fit between the subject's data and personal space (see Section 4.3, "Weighted MDS (WMDS)" for definition of personal space). For MULTISCALE, on the other hand, the vector length does not reflect goodness of fit.

In this chapter we are not concerned with vector length; instead, we are only concerned with interpreting the *direction* of the weight vectors.

You will recall that the direction of a subject's vector tells us, for each subject, the relative importance the subject attaches to each of the stimulus space dimensions. Two vectors that point in the same direction tell us that the two subjects do not differ in the importance they attach to the several dimensions. Two vectors with different orientations correspond to two individuals who do differ in dimensional salience.

Thus, the statistical methods for interpreting subject spaces presented in this chapter enable us to look at the way individuals vary in the way they use the dimensions of a particular stimulus space. We will discuss a method that allows us to test whether one group of subjects uses the dimensions in a way significantly different from the way another group uses them. The same test is appropriate to test if several groups differ in their use of the dimensions of a space, or whether an experimental manipulation has a significant effect on dimensional salience. We will also present a simple algebraic manipulation of the subject weights that lets us use methods like MDS and cluster analysis to get a simplified view of the structure of individual differences. At the end of this chapter we list a computer program that performs these analyses.

It is important to point out that the material in this chapter assumes that the subject weights all refer to the same stimulus space. When we describe subjects as being in several groups, we do *not* mean that the weights come from several separate analyses. Rather, we mean that we have combined the several groups of subjects together and subjected their data to one unified WMDS analysis.

For example, the cola data described in Chapter 3 involve two groups of subjects, 5 PTC tasters and 5 nontasters. However, when these data were subjected to WMDS (Chapters 8, 9, and 10) the 10 subjects were combined together into a single individual differences analysis. In this chapter we will analyze the subject weights from each chapter's analysis to demonstrate the methods discussed here and to see if PTC tasters differ significantly from nontasters in the way they use the dimensions of the stimulus space.

13.1. Mean and Variation

All of the statistical methods discussed in this chapter focus on the direction of each subject's weight vector. They do not look at the length of the vectors. Thus, the first step in all analyses is to equate the lengths of all vectors. This preliminary step, called *normalization,* is done by computing the square root of the sum of squared weights for a subject, and then dividing each of this subject's weights by the computed value. That is, we determine

$$C_k = \left(\sum_{a=1} W_{ka}^2 \right)^{1/2},$$

where W_{ka}^2 is the squared weight that subject k applies to dimension a. Thus we compute the normalized weights

$$W_{ka}^* = W_{ka}/C_k.$$

It is easy to show that the normalized weights have the characteristic

$$\left(\sum_{a=1}^{r} W_{ka}^{*2} \right)^{1/2} = 1.$$

Since the square root of the sum of squares represents the distance of the end of the weight vector from the origin, we have made all vectors have a length of 1. Thus, in two dimensions the vector tips all fall on a circle whose radius is 1; in three dimensions they fall on a sphere with radius 1; and in more than three dimensions they fall on a *hypersphere* with radius 1.

The geometry and algebra of the normalization is shown in Figure 13.1. We have taken the weights from the example used in Chapter 4 (Figure 4.4) and have normalized them. Note that the vectors are all equally long. In particular note that Subjects 3 and 4, whose vectors differed in length before normalization are identical after normalization.

In the remainder of this chapter we *only* are concerned with normalized weights. But, to simplify the notation, we drop the * from W_{ka}^*. Thus, in the rest of this chapter W_{ka} refers to a *normalized* subject weight.

Mean

The *mean direction* of a set of vectors is the simple mean that we are all familiar with. That is,

$$W_{.a} = \frac{1}{m} \sum_{k=1}^{m} W_{ka}$$

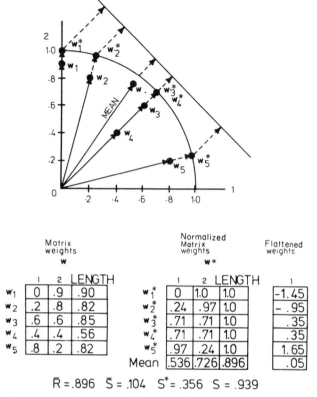

Matrix weights W				Normalized Matrix weights w*				Flattened weights
	1	2	LENGTH		1	2	LENGTH	1
w_1	0	.9	.90	w_1^*	0	1.0	1.0	-1.45
w_2	.2	.8	.82	w_2^*	.24	.97	1.0	- .95
w_3	.6	.6	.85	w_3^*	.71	.71	1.0	.35
w_4	.4	.4	.56	w_4^*	.71	.71	1.0	.35
w_5	.8	.2	.82	w_5^*	.97	.24	1.0	1.65
				Mean	.536	.726	.896	.05

$$\bar{R} = .896 \quad \bar{S} = .104 \quad S^* = .356 \quad S = .939$$

Figure 13.1. Geometry and algebra of the normalization.

gives the coordinate, on dimension a, of the mean direction. The mean direction is drawn in Figure 13.1 and the coordinates $W_{.a}$ are given at the bottom of the normalized weights matrix in the figure. The mean direction has two important properties that parallel properties of the ordinary mean: (a) The orientation of the mean direction does not depend on the choice of the zero direction, and (b) the sum of the angular deviations about the mean direction (in radians) is zero. Note that the mean direction is *not* defined on the raw weights: It is defined on the *normalized* weights. Furthermore, these two possible definitions are *not* equal.

It is important to note that the length of the mean direction is *not* 1. The length, denoted $\bar{R}$ and called the *mean resultant length,* is calculated according to the formula

$$\bar{R} = \left(\sum_{a=1}^{r} W_{.a}^2 \right)^{1/2}$$

where $W_{.a}$ is the mean direction coordinates defined earlier. For the example in Figure 13.1, $\bar{R} = .896$, as shown.

Variation

The mean resultant length is of more than passing interest. It is, in fact, intimately related to a useful index of variation of a set of directed vectors. The index, discussed by Mardia (1972)[1] and called the index of *angular variation,* is, surprisingly enough, simply $1 - \bar{R}$. That is, if we denote the angular variation by the symbol $\bar{S}$, then

$$\bar{S} = 1 - \bar{R}$$

$$= 1 - \left(\sum_{a=1}^{r} W_{.a}^2 \right)^{1/2}$$

$$= 1 - \frac{1}{m} \left[\sum_{a=1}^{r} \left(\sum_{k=1}^{m} W_{ka} \right)^2 \right]^{1/2}.$$

$\bar{S}$ is adopted as an index of angular variation because it has several desirable properties. First one can easily demonstrate that the length of the mean direction depends on the degree of clustering of the subject vectors. At one extreme, when all the subjects have identical vector directions (i.e., equal normalized weights), the mean direction coincides with all of the individual directions and has length 1. Thus, $\bar{S} = 0$ when there is no variation. Second, when negative weights are allowed, the opposite extreme occurs when half the subject vectors point in the opposite direction from the other half. This and other patterns of vectors are the maximum variation pattern. The mean direction has no length and zero coordinates. Thus, for maximum variation $\bar{S} = 1$.

$\bar{S}$ has several desirable statistical properties. First, it is invariant under change of zero direction. Also, the angular variation is minimized relative to the mean direction, and $\bar{S}$ reflects this fact. However, the most important property of $\bar{S}$ is a property that parallels the analysis of variance property of the usual variance index, namely, that the total angular variation is separable into within and between components. More will be said on this later.

Unfortunately, when the weights are positive, as they usually are,[2] the

---

[1] Our definition of angular variation as $\bar{S} = 1 - \bar{R}$ corresponds to Mardia's (1972) definition (pp. 22 and 219), but differs slightly from that given by Mardia *et al.* (1979, p. 427) who define $\bar{S} = 2(1 - \bar{R})$. The first definition gives $\bar{S}$ a range [0,1] whereas the second has a range [0,2]. We see no justification for the second definition.

[2] It is important to note that the definitions of $\bar{S}$ assume that the subject weights are distributed on the range $[-1, +1]$. This assumption would appear to be violated since the weights are nearly always positive for INDSCAL and (by default) are restricted to being positive by ALSCAL and MULTISCALE.

However, it is important to note that negative weights are possible in INDSCAL and when the restriction is removed in ALSCAL and MULTISCALE. The reason that negative weights

maximum value of $\bar{S}$ is not 1. In fact, the maximum value is dependent on the dimensionality of the subject space. It can be shown that the maximum value of $\bar{S}$, when the weights are nonnegative, is $1 - (1/r)^{1/2}$ when the space is r dimensional. This value occurs when $(1/r)$th of the subjects use only dimension 1, another $(1/r)$th use only dimension 2, etc. (in this case the mean direction has coordinates of $1/r$ on each dimension, and a length of $(1/r)^{1/2}$).

Clearly, we can construct an index that varies between 0 and 1 when the weights are restricted to being nonnegative. We can do this by defining

$$S^* = \frac{\bar{S}}{1 - (1/r)^{1/2}} = \frac{1 - \bar{R}}{1 - (1/r)^{1/2}},$$

leaving S^* with all of the important properties of $\bar{S}$ except that it no longer equals $1 - \bar{R}$.

Of course, S^* varies between 0 and 1 whereas the familiar standard deviation varies between 0 and ∞. For this reason Mardia (1972, p. 24) proposed a transformation to yield values with the desired range. The transformation is

$$S = [-2 \, \mathrm{Log}_e \, (1 - S^*) \,]^{1/2}$$

which is called the circular standard deviation index. The values of S^* and S are given for the example in Figure 13.1. As noted by Mardia (1972) S is "somewhat analogous to the ordinary sample standard deviation on the line [p. 24]." However, he also notes that $\bar{R}$ and $\bar{S}$ are "more useful" than S for theoretical reasons. As we will see, $\bar{R}$ and $\bar{S}$ are useful in the inferential procedure discussed later, whereas S is not. The reason is that S does not have the analysis of variance property possessed by $\bar{R}$ and $\bar{S}$. We can, however, interpret S as being roughly analogous to the familiar standard deviation.

Examples

We use the cola data to illustrate the mean direction, mean resultant length, and standard deviation. We use these data for several reasons. First,

---

are infrequent, even with unrestricted ALSCAL and MULTISCALE, lies in the basic nature of similarities data, *not* in the weights themselves.

Thus, we do not use the modified definition of $\bar{S}$ given by Mardia (1972, pp. 69–71) which applies to restricted angular distributions (see also Mardia, 1975).

We are, then, assuming that subject vectors are distributed in all regions of a hypersphere, albeit with low probability in the nonpositive orthants (quadrants, octants, etc.). This view is somewhat less appropriate for ALSCAL and MULTISCALE than for INDSCAL because of their default restrictions. However, this restriction, which, when activated, results in precisely zero weights, is *very* seldomly activated in either program. The user may, of course, remove the restriction if desired, although we see no reason to do so, and the results will seldom yield negative weights.

they have been analyzed by all three WMDS programs. Second, we have reported the weights (Tables 8.2, 9.2, and 10.3) and have subjectively interpreted them in each chapter. Third, the subjects fall into two categories (PTC tasters and nontasters) giving us an opportunity to look at individual differences and, later in the chapter, to statistically test whether there are significant differences between the two types of subjects in the salience they attach to the stimulus space dimensions.

In Table 13.1 we present the mean directions, mean resultant lengths $\bar{R}$, and standard deviations S for the subject weights derived by INDSCAL, ALSCAL, and MULTISCALE from the cola data. These statistics are presented separately for the 5 PTC tasters (Group 1) and 5 nontasters (Group 2) and for all 10 subjects combined.

We hypothesize a difference in the weights for the tasters and nontasters because the ability to taste PTC is related to one's perception of artificially sweetened drinks. (Four of the colas are artificially sweetened.)

Table 13.1
Descriptive Statistics

INDSCAL

Group	N	Resultant lengths	Standard deviations	Mean directions (dimension coordinates)		
				1	2	3
1	5	.983	.283	.871	.240	.389
2	5	.987	.250	.316	.834	.424
Total	10	.897	.745	.593	.537	.407

ALSCAL

Group	N	Resultant lengths	Standard deviations	Mean directions (dimension coordinates)		
				1	2	3
1	5	.994	.176	.811	.315	.480
2	5	.988	.237	.495	.702	.489
Total	10	.959	.452	.653	.509	.484

MULTISCALE

Group	N	Resultant lengths	Standard deviations	Mean directions (dimension coordinates)		
				1	2	3
1	5	.936	.573	.821	.112	.436
2	5	.820	1.052	.088	.674	.459
Total	10	.749	1.342	.454	.393	.448

We see that all three programs display the same general pattern of results. Furthermore, the pattern supports our hypothesis (and the conclusions reached in Chapters 8, 9, and 10) that the two groups of subjects do not have the same pattern of saliences for the three stimulus space dimensions.

The resultant lengths and standard deviations show that there is much less variation in dimensional salience within each group than there is in the entire group of subjects. This effect is most pronounced for INDSCAL, and least pronounced for MULTISCALE. (The significance of this effect will be tested later.) Also, we see the greatest subject variation in the MULTISCALE solution, and the least in ALSCAL's.

The mean directions indicate, for all three solutions, that PTC tasters (Group 1) find dimension 1 more salient than dimension 2, whereas non-tasters have the opposite pattern. Note that dimension 1 separates diet and nondiet drinks. We also see that dimension 1 is more salient to tasters than nontasters, and that dimension 2 has the reverse pattern. Dimension 3 does not differentiate the two groups. These effects are most pronounced for MULTISCALE, least for ALSCAL.

The effects we can see in Table 13.1 hold up for all three programs. INDSCAL and ALSCAL show remarkable agreement, while MULTI-SCALE shows greater separation of the two mean vectors, but less separation of the distribution of individual vectors. That is, with MULTI-SCALE the ratios of mean weights on dimension 1 and 2 are more extreme for both groups than with ALSCAL or INDSCAL (greater separation of mean vectors), but the group standard deviations are closer to the total standard deviation (less separation of individual vector distributions).

13.2. Analysis of Angular Variation (ANAVA)

We mentioned that one important property of the mean resultant length $\bar{R}$ and the angular variance $\bar{S}$ (but *not* of the standard deviation S) is that they have a property called *separability*. We can now explain more fully just what that means.

Actually, the most useful index to use at this point is the resultant length R, *not* the mean resultant length $\bar{R}$, where, simply,

$$R = m\bar{R}$$

(m being the number of subjects). It follows that we can define

$$m\bar{S} = m(1 - \bar{R})$$
$$= m - m\bar{R}$$
$$= m - R,$$

which is the total sum of squared angular deviations of the observed vectors

about the mean direction. It is important to note that $m\bar{S}$ has a property
known as separability. That is

$$m\bar{S} = \left(m - \sum_i R_i\right) + \left(\sum_i R_i - R\right),$$

where R_i is the resultant length for those subjects who are in the ith group.
This shows that we can separate the total sum of squares $m\bar{S}$ into within-
group sum of squares $m - \Sigma_i R_i$ and between-group sum of squares $\Sigma_i R_i - R$.
Furthermore, the degrees of freedom of each source of variation are known,
and the distribution of the ratio of the between to within mean squares
approximates the F distribution when the distribution of the normalized
subject weight vectors approximates an $r - 1$ von Mises distribution and
when $\bar{R} > .67$ (see Mardia, 1975b; Stephens, 1962). The analysis of angular
variation (ANAVA) table is presented in Table 13.2. Unfortunately, there
is no ANAVA analogue of two-way or multiple-way ANOVA. If we wish
to perform a multiple-way ANAVA we must perform several separate one-
way ANAVAs. This forces us to assume that there is no interaction between
the several ways, and there is no way to check the validity of this assumption. The F-test for the ANAVA also assumes that the angular variation within groups is homogeneous. An approximate test of homogeneity
of angular variation can be found in Mardia (1972). The results of the F-
test are conditional on the normalization of the stimulus space used by the
MDS program that performed the analysis. If the normalization, which is
arbitrary, is changed the weights will be changed in ways which *do not*
preserve within-group variation relationships. Work by De Soete and Young
(1981) circumvents this problem.

Finally, as in ordinary ANOVA, the significance level of the ANAVA
F-test is accurate only when the *observations* (i.e., the subject weights)
are independently distributed. This assumption is not met in our situation:
If the data for one subject are changed, then the stimulus space will change,
and the weight for *all* subjects will change. Thus the significance levels will
be too optimistic, and we should be cautious in interpreting the results.

However, the weights are *conditionally independent*. That is, for a *given*

Table 13.2
Analysis of Angular Variation[a]

Source	SS	Degrees of freedom	mS
Between	$\sum_i R_i - R$	$(r-1)(q-1)$	$(\sum_i R_i - R)/(r-1)(q-1)$
Within	$m - \sum_i R_i$	$(r-1)(m-q)$	$(m - \sum_i R_i)/(r-1)(m-q)$
Total	$m - R$	$(r-1)(m-1)$	

[a] Note: r dimensions, m subjects, and q groups.

stimulus configuration the weights for each subject are independent from those for every other subject. If the data for one subject are changed, and if the stimulus configuration is held constant, then the weights for only that one subject will change. The weights for other subjects will remain unmodified. Thus, the weights are independent *conditional* upon a given, unchanging stimulus configuration.

This situation occurs when the stimulus configuration is not derived by analyzing some data, but obtained in some other way. For example, if we have a theoretical structure for some stimuli, we could use it to construct a hypothetical stimulus space, and to then compute weights. These weights would be conditionally independent and the significance levels of the ANAVA F-test would be appropriate, conditional on the hypothesized stimulus structures.

The weights from the three cola analyses were submitted to the ANAVA, the results being reported in Table 13.3. We see that all three programs derive weights which are significantly different for the PTC tasters and nontasters ($F > 6.25$ for $p < .001$). Thus, we conclude that the two groups of subjects do not use the three dimensions of the stimulus space in the same fashion. Note that the effect, while clear for all three programs, is strongest for the INDSCAL analysis and weakest for the MULTISCALE analysis.

Table 13.3
Analysis of Angular Variance (ANAVA) Table

INDSCAL

Source	SS	Degrees of freedom	mS	F
Between groups	.877	2	.439	47.56
Within groups	.148	16	.009	
Total	1.025	18		

ALSCAL

Source	SS	Degrees of freedom	mS	F
Between groups	.319	2	.160	28.03
Within groups	.091	16	.006	
Total	.410	18		

MULTISCALE

Source	SS	Degrees of freedom	mS	F
Between groups	1.292	2	.646	8.48
Within groups	1.218	16	.076	
Total	2.510	18		

13.3. Scaling Subjects

The final aid for interpreting subject spaces that we discuss is a way to apply MDS to distances computed between subject weight vectors. Once the distances are computed they are submitted to a CMDS analysis to obtain a "stimulus" space which contains points for subjects. This analysis, then, converts the vector representation of the subjects into a point representation which can be interpreted using the procedures discussed in Chapter 12.

The distances that are most appropriate in the present situation are not the familiar Euclidean distances discussed in Chapter 4. Rather, the most appropriate distance is the *arc distance*.

As you recall, we have normalized all of the subject vectors so that they are of unit length. Thus, they all terminate at a point which is exactly one unit from the origin. In two dimensions these points all lie on a quarter circle which has a radius of one unit (see Figure 13.1). The arc distance between two points which lie on a circle is the length of the segment of the circle between the two points. In three dimensions the arc distance between two points on the surface of a sphere is the shortest circular segment between the two points. In r dimensions the arc distance between two points on the surface of a hypersphere is still the shortest circular segment between the two points.

The formula for calculating the arc distance between points for subjects g and h which lie on the surface of an r-dimensional hypersphere is

$$d_{gh}^* = \cos^{-1}\left[\sum_{a=1}^{r} W_{ga} W_{ha}\right].$$

To understand this formula we must realize that the term inside the brackets (the *cross-product* of the weights for Subjects g and h) is the cosine of the angle between the two weight vectors. We also need to know that the inverse cosine function ($\cos^{-1}$ or ARCOSINE) gives us the angle, in radians, of its argument. Thus, the distance d_{gh} is defined as the angle, in radians, between the two vectors.

Now, it is the case for a hypersphere of unit radius, that the arc length equals the angle in radians. This follows from the definition of the circumference of a circle, $C = 2\pi r$, which, when the radius is 1 becomes $C = 2\pi = 6.28$, the number of radians in a 360° angle. Thus, for a unit radius circle the angle of 360°, when converted to radians, equals the entire distance around the circle. It follows that any angle in a unit circle, when expressed in radians, equals the distance around the circle between the two points.

Finally, because the weight vectors lie in the positive quadrant (octant, orthant) the maximum distance is a quarter circle, which is $\frac{1}{4}(2\pi) = \pi/2$ radians (for a unit circle). Therefore, we define the normalized arc distances as

$$d_{gh} = 2\cos^{-1}\left[\sum_{a=1}^{r} W_{ga}W_{ha}\right]\bigg/ \pi,$$

which range from zero to one. (Negative weights *may* result in distances greater than 1.0.)

These distances, of course, are between points in r dimensions. However, we know that the points reside on the surface of an r-dimensional hypersphere, and that we have measured the distance between points on the surface. These r-dimensional arc distances are monotone with $(r-1)$-dimensional Euclidean distances. Thus, nonmetric MDS in $r-1$ dimensions will "flatten" the r-dimensional hypersphere surface into a space with one less dimension.

Thus, an MDS of the arc distances computed from a two-dimensional subject weight space will yield a one-dimensional subject point space; a three-dimensional subject weight space will be flattened into a two-dimensional point space; etc. This characteristic is diagrammed in Figure 13.1. The process is equivalent to projecting the points from the circle (sphere, hypersphere) orthogonally onto a line (plane, hyperplane) tangent to the circle. What we see as a result of the MDS is the position of the points as projected onto the line (plane, hyperplane).

Naturally, we can do this for the means (and group means, if any) computed from the weights as well (the means must first be normalized to a length of 1 before computing distances). In Figure 13.1 the "flattened" weight values are those derived by an ALSCAL ordinal analysis of the intersubject arc distances, including the mean subject.

Interpreting the flattened weight space is a bit tricky. First of all, the dimensions of the flattened space are not meaningful. Instead, there are other aspects to be interpreted. These aspects are shown in Figure 13.2 for a two-dimensional flattened weight point space (i.e., a three-dimensional weight vector space).

All subject weight points must fall either inside or on the perimeter of the figure shown in Figure 13.2. No subject weight points will be outside of the figure. Subjects in the interior use all three dimensions, those on the perimeter do not (they have zero weights on at least one dimension).

The three vertices of the figure represent one-dimensional subjects. The labeling of these vertices refers to the values of each subject's normalized squared weights. Thus, the left vertex (1,0,0) is a subject who only uses dimension 1; the right vertex (0,1,0) is a subject who uses just dimension 2; and the bottom vertex is a subject who uses only dimension 3.

The perimeter of the figure is for subjects who are two-dimensional. Those on the top edge use dimensions 1 and 2, but have a zero weight on

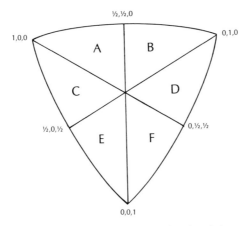

Figure 13.2.   Schematic of a flattened three-dimensional weight vector space.

dimension 3. Those on the left edge do not use dimension 2; and those on the right edge do not use dimension 1.

The midpoint of each edge is for subjects who use the two dimensions of the edge equally. Thus, the midpoint of the top edge is labeled $(\frac{1}{2}, \frac{1}{2}, 0)$ to show that such a subject has equal squared normalized weights of $\frac{1}{2}$ for the first two dimensions, and zero weight on dimension 3. Points on the top edge which are on the left of the midpoint are for subjects who use dimension 1 more than dimension 2, but who do not use dimension 3 at all.

A subject who falls in the interior of the figure uses all three dimensions. Those subjects who fall along a line connecting a vertex to a midpoint use two dimensions equally and also use the third dimension. Subjects who weight all three dimensions equally fall at the center of the figure.

The six sectors of the space (labeled A through F) represent the six possible orders of the values of the three weights. Subjects in sector A are typical subjects since they weight dimension 1 more than dimension 2 more than dimension 3. Those in sector F have the reverse order. They find dimension 3 most important and dimension 1 least. Subjects in sectors A and B use dimension 3 least and those in E and F use dimension 3 the most. Subjects in C and E use dimension 2 the least and those in B and D use dimension 2 the most.

For a two-dimensional weight vector space the flattened one-dimensional weight point space is interpreted as we interpret the top edge of the figure in Figure 13.2. That is, the left is for subjects who use one of the two dimensions (1,0); the right is for subjects who only use the other dimension (0, 1); and the midpoint is for subjects who weight both dimensions equally $(\frac{1}{2}, \frac{1}{2})$.

For a four-dimensional weight vector space the flattened three-dimensional figure is a solid whose faces look like Figure 13.2. Any subject in a face is at most three-dimensional. Any subject inside the solid uses all four dimensions.

Example. We computed arc distances between the subject weight vectors (including means) for the weights derived by INDSCAL, ALSCAL, and MULTISCALE from their analyses of the cola data. These three sets of arc distances were then submitted to ALSCAL for three ordinal CMDS analyses. The subject configurations are presented in Figures 13.3 (INDS-CAL), 13.4 (ALSCAL), and 13.5 (MULTISCALE).

These figures reveal strong agreement between INDSCAL and ALSCAL, and less agreement with MULTISCALE. The two groups of subjects show greatest separation in the INDSCAL and ALSCAL analyses. We also notice greater stability across the three solutions among the PTC tasters (Subjects A, D, E, F, and I) than among the nontasters, with the spread of the nontasters changing across the three solutions more than among the tasters. These results agree closely with the ANAVA, as is necessarily the case.

It is instructive to compare these figures with the subject weight spaces presented in Chapters 8, 9, and 10. Clearly, it is easier to grasp the structure of the subjects from the present analysis than from the weight spaces.

It is also instructive to compare the ALSCAL space presented here (Figure 13.4) with the plot of ALSCAL relative subject weight indices presented in Figure 9.3. We see essentially the same structure, except that the separation among the two groups is clearer for the present analysis. We tend to prefer the present analysis since it is based on geometric ideas

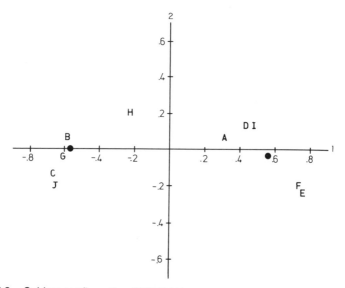

Figure 13.3. Subject configuration (INDSCAL).

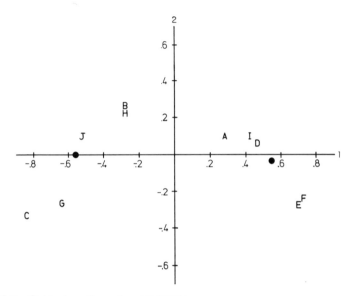

Figure 13.4.   Subject configuration (ALSCAL).

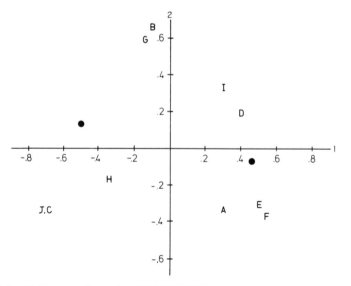

Figure 13.5.   Subject configuration (MULTISCALE).

which tend to be simpler. The present analysis also presents a genuinely two-dimensional view of the original three-dimensional weight space, whereas the structure in Figure 9.3 is based on pairing pairs of weight dimensions.

Appendix A: Subject Statistics Program Listing

```
c
c Program:       SUBJSTAT
c Version:       1.01
c Date:          July, 1980
c Copyright:     1980, Forrest W. Young
c
c Program to perform statistical analysis of subject weights using the
c procedures discussed in section 6.4 and 9.5 of Mardia, K.V.,
c Statistics of Directional Data, New York, Acedemic Press (1972)
c
c The program requires an input file structured as follows:
c
c       Card 1:        Parameter Card
c
c       This card must specify the number of subjects (NSUB) in columns
c       1 and 2, number of dimensions (NDIM) in columns 3 and 4, and
c       number of groups (NGR) in columns 5 and 6.  Each number must be
c       right justified in its columns.  Maximum number of subjects = 50,
c       maximum dimensionality = 9, maximum number of groups = 10.
c
c       Card 2:        A title card
c
c       The information on this card is used to title the output.
c       Any alphanumerics are permitted.
c
c       Card 3:        A format card
c
c       This card specifies the format of the data cards that follow.
c       First variable must be in I format, remainder in F format.
c
c       Data Cards:
c
c       Following the three control cards comes the data.  There is
c       one data card (or set of cards) for each subject.  Each card
c       contains NDIM+1 values.  The first value (an integer) specifies
c       the group the subject belongs to.  This is coded with an integer
c       between 1 and NGR, inclusive.  The remaining values are the
c       weights for the subject, one weight for each dimension.
c       There are NDIM weights, and they are floating point.
c       The data are punched in the format specified on Card 3.
c
c
c       The dimension statements can be changed to allow for
c       more subjects (NSUB), dimensions (NDIM), or groups (NGR).
c       The desired dimensions can be determined from the following:
c       w          (NSUB+NGR+1 , NDIM)
c       direct     (NGR+1 , NDIM)
c       r          (NGR+1)
c       sd         (NGR+1)
c       arcdis     (NSUB+NGR+1 , NSUB+NGR+1)
c       iclass     (NSUB)
c       ifreq      (NGR+1)
c
        dimension w(61,9),direct(11,9),r(11),sd(11),fmt(20)
        dimension arcdis(61,61),title(20)
        integer*2 iclass(50),ifreq(11),betdf,witdf,totdf,in,udf
```

```
c
c          The input and punch units can be changed by
c          changing the following two statements.
c
           in=5
           ipunch=6
c
c Get input parameters and data
c Determine group frequencies.
c
           read(in,2)nsub,ndim,ngr
2          format(3i2)
           nspng1=nsub+ngr+1
           if(ngr.eq.1)nspng1=nspng1-1
           ngrp1=ngr+1
           rndim=1.0/float(ndim)
           do 3 i=1,ngr
3          ifreq(i)=0
           ndimm1=ndim-1
           read(in,4)title
           read(in,4)fmt
4          format(20a4)
           write(ipunch,4)title
           write(ipunch,986)
986        format('(10F8.5)')
           do 5 i=1,nsub
           read(in,fmt)iclass(i),(w(i,j),j=1,ndim)
           if(iclass(i).gt.ngr)go to 900
           if(iclass(i).lt.1)go to 900
           j=iclass(i)
5          ifreq(j)=ifreq(j)+1
           ifreq(ngrp1)=nsub
c
c Normalize length of each subject's vector to one.
c
           do 6 j=1,ndim
           do 6 i=1,ngrp1
6          direct(i,j)=0.0
           do 20 i=1,nsub
           rms=0.0
           do 10 j=1,ndim
10         rms=rms+w(i,j)**2
           rms=sqrt(rms)
           do 20 j=1,ndim
20         w(i,j)=w(i,j)/rms
c
c Compute Mean Directions for each group and overall
c
           do 50 j=1,ndim
           do 40 i=1,nsub
           k=iclass(i)
           direct(k,j)=direct(k,j)+w(i,j)
40         direct(ngrp1,j)=direct(ngrp1,j)+w(i,j)
           do 50 k=1,ngrp1
50         direct(k,j)=direct(k,j)/ifreq(k)
```

```
c
c Normalize mean directions for later distance computation
c
        do 54 i=1,ngrp1
        k=i+nsub
        rms=0.0
        do 52 j=1,ndim
52      rms=rms+direct(i,j)**2
        rms=sqrt(rms)
        do 54 j=1,ndim
54      w(k,j)=direct(i,j)/rms
c
c Compute Resultants and "Standard Deviations"
c
        do 70 i=1,ngrp1
        r(i)=0.0
        do 60 j=1,ndim
60      r(i)=r(i)+direct(i,j)**2
        r(i)=sqrt(r(i))
        sstar=(1.0-r(i))/(1.0-sqrt(rndim))
70      sd(i)=sqrt(-2.0*alog(1.0-sstar))
        if(ngr.eq.1)go to 168
c
c Perform ANAVA calculations
c
        totdf=(ndim-1)*(nsub-1)
        witdf=(ndim-1)*(nsub-ngr)
        betdf=totdf-witdf
        totss=nsub*(1.0-r(ngrp1))
        witss=0.0
        do 80 i=1,ngr
80      witss=witss+(ifreq(i)*(1.0-r(i)))
        betss=totss-witss
        betms=betss/betdf
        witms=witss/witdf
        f=betms/witms
c
c Calculate Hyperspherical Arc-Distances between subjects
c (arc-distances between subjects on the surface of a hypersphere)
c
168     do 169 i=1,nspng1
        do 169 j=1,nspng1
169     arcdis(i,j)=0.0
        halfpi=1.57079
        nsubm1=nspng1-1
        do 180 i=1,nsubm1
        ip1=i+1
        do 180 j=ip1,nspng1
        do 170 k=1,ndim
170     arcdis(i,j)=arcdis(i,j)+(w(i,k)*w(j,k))
        arcdis(i,j)=acos(arcdis(i,j))/halfpi
180     arcdis(j,i)=arcdis(i,j)
```

```
c
c Print Results
c
          print 90,title
90        format('1'///' ',20a4
     *    ///' Descriptive Statistics'/)
          print 100,(i,i=1,ndim)
100       format(' Group    N    Resultant    Standard    Mean Directions'/
     *    '              lengths   deviations  (dimension coordinates)'
     *    /30x,9i9)
          if(ngr.eq.1)go to 122
          do 110 i=1,ngr
110       print 120,i,ifreq(i),r(i),sd(i),(direct(i,j),j=1,ndim)
120       format(i4,i6,3x,f7.3,f11.3,1x,9f9.3)
122       print 125,ifreq(ngrp1),r(ngrp1),sd(ngrp1),
     *              (direct(ngrp1,j),j=1,ndim)
125       format(' Total',i4,3x,f7.3,f11.3,1x,9f9.3)
          if(ngr.eq.1)go to 1776
          print 130
130       format(///'0Analysis of Angular Variance (ANAVA) Table'//
     *    ' Source              SS     DF     MS        F'/)
          print 140,betss,betdf,betms,f
          print 150,witss,witdf,witms
          print 160,totss,totdf
140       format(' Between groups',f8.3,i5,f8.3,f8.2)
150       format(' Within  groups',f8.3,i5,f8.3)
160       format(' Total',9x,f8.3,i5)
1776      print 1777,(i,i=1,nspng1)
1777      format(////' Arc-Distances Between Subjects',
     *    ' (Group distances are based on Mean Direction coordinates)'//
     *    ' Subject       Subject'/
     *    (4x,15i7))
          k=0
          nsubp1=nsub+1
          do 190 i=1,nspng1
          im1=i-1
          if(i.ne.1)write(ipunch,876)(arcdis(i,j),j=1,im1)
          k=k+1
          if(i.ne.nsubp1)go to 190
          k=1
          print 220
220       format('0 Group')
190       print 200,k,(arcdis(i,j),j=1,i)
          print 240,k
240       format('0Group',i2,' is all subjects combined.')
200       format(i5,(t8,15f7.3))
876       format(10f8.5)
          stop
900       print 901
901       format('1The groups are not coded properly.'/
     *    'They must be coded with values between 1 and '/
     *    'the total number of groups (inclusive).')
          stop
          end
```

Input to SUBJSTAT for ALSCAL Cola Weights

```
10 3 2
Alscal Analysis of Cola Data
(i1,3f6.4)
1 .5297 .3065 .3195
2 .4013 .4147 .3968
2 .2514 .6758 .4129
1 .6163 .2577 .4178
1 .6810 .1828 .3109
1 .7063 .1809 .3559
2 .3570 .5766 .2657
2 .4827 .4951 .4161
1 .5846 .2686 .4382
2 .3543 .4824 .3450
```

Output from SUBJSTAT

Alscal Analysis of Cola Data

Descriptive Statistics

Group	N	Resultant lengths	Standard deviations	Mean Directions (dimension coordinates)		
				1	2	3
1	5	0.994	0.176	0.811	0.315	0.480
2	5	0.988	0.237	0.495	0.702	0.489
Total	10	0.959	0.452	0.653	0.509	0.484

Analysis of Angular Variance (ANAVA) Table

Source	SS	DF	MS	F
Between groups	0.319	2	0.160	28.03
Within groups	0.091	16	0.006	
Total	0.410	18		

Arc-Distances Between Subjects (Group distances are based on Mean Direction coordinates)

Subject	Subject												
	1	2	3	4	5	6	7	8	9	10	11	12	13
1	0.000												
2	0.169	0.000											
3	0.384	0.228	0.000										
4	0.087	0.217	0.444	0.000									
5	0.156	0.321	0.540	0.118	0.000								
6	0.156	0.316	0.539	0.105	0.026	0.000							
7	0.292	0.189	0.147	0.370	0.442	0.447	0.000						
8	0.157	0.039	0.229	0.218	0.312	0.310	0.164	0.000					
9	0.090	0.195	0.423	0.031	0.149	0.135	0.357	0.200	0.000				
10	0.231	0.089	0.153	0.295	0.388	0.387	0.105	0.077	0.276	0.000			
Group													
1	0.087	0.241	0.465	0.038	0.084	0.075	0.380	0.236	0.068	0.313	0.000		
2	0.242	0.099	0.143	0.306	0.398	0.397	0.098	0.088	0.287	0.011	0.324	0.000	
3	0.082	0.089	0.304	0.146	0.237	0.235	0.226	0.075	0.132	0.152	0.162	0.163	0.00

Group 3 is all subjects combined.

References

Mardia, K. V. *Statistics of directional data*. New York: Academic Press, 1972.

Mardia, K. V. Statistics of directional data (with discussion). *Journal of the Royal Statistical Society (B)*, 1975, *37*, 349–393. (a)

Mardia, K. V. Distribution theory for the von Mises–Fisher distribution. In G. D. Patil, S. Kotz, & J. K. Ortz (Eds.), *Statistical distributions in scientific work* (Vol. 1). Dordrecht, Holland: Reidel, 1975 Pp. 113–130. (b)

Mardia, K. V., Kent, J. T., & Bibby, J. M. *Multivariate analysis*, New York: Academic Press, 1979

Stephens, M. A. Exact and appropriate tests for directions, I. *Biometrica*, 1962, *59*, 463–477.

de Soete, G., & Young, F. W. A statistical test of group differences in individual differences multidimensional scaling. Psychometric Laboratory Report 165, University of North Carolina, Chapel Hill, North Carolina.

14

Treating Rectangular Matrices by Multidimensional Scaling

14.1. Overview

We prefer to develop stimulus spaces from a square matrix of pairwise similarity judgments. However, there are occasions when it is necessary or expedient to develop spaces from rectangular matrices. Two common examples are:

1. Attribute ratings across a number of stimuli from a number of subjects
2. Neural firing patterns in response to a number of stimuli

The classical approach to data reduction of rectangular matrices is factor analysis. As with all multivariate techniques there are pitfalls for the unwary, with less cases than variables being the most common. Furthermore, unless specialized three-mode factor analysis (Tucker, 1972) is employed, individual differences are lost.

A second method of classification is cluster analysis (Johnson, 1967). While this approach does not provide a stimulus space in the traditional sense, it can show interconnections between clusters. The basic difficulty with cluster analysis is determination of what weightings or transformations to apply to variables to derive an appropriate distance measure.

Our purpose in this chapter is to present two alternative strategies for analysis of rectangular matrices, although we would like to emphasize that there is no procedure at present which is entirely satisfactory for developing spaces from them. The first strategy, transformation of the rectangular matrix to a square matrix of distances, suffers from the problems inherent in cluster analysis, that is, what weighting or transformation should be applied to derive a sensible distance measure? However, once a distance matrix is derived it may be analyzed by any of the MDS algorithms. INDSCAL, ALSCAL, and MULTISCALE obviously allow for individual differences. The second strategy, analysis of the raw data themselves, does not suffer from this problem. Nevertheless, most published algorithms which are based on Coombs (1964) unfolding method give degenerate solutions so frequently that they are not recommended. We describe in this chapter an alternate model developed by Schiffman and Falkenberg (1968) for the analysis of rectangular matrices that yields a multidimensional vector space.

14.2. Blended Foods—Transformation of a Rectangular Matrix

This data set (Section 3.8) is from 43 subjects (27 normal weight, 16 obese) who made ratings of 26 blended foods on 51-adjective scales. The transcriptions on the adjective scales were used to develop dissimilarity measures among all pairs of food stimuli for each subject. The dissimilarity measures were computed in the following way:

$$d_{ijs} = \left[\sum_{k=1}^{51} \left(a_{iks} - a_{jks} \right)^2 \right]^{1/2},$$

where d_{ijs} = distance between stimulus i and stimulus j for subject s, a_{iks} = numerical transcription for subject s on adjective scale k for stimulus i, a_{jks} = numerical transcription for subject s on adjective scale k for stimulus j.

An example shows how this works. Suppose we wanted to compute a measure of dissimilarity between two stimuli for a given subject (Subject 1) whose ratings are

	Stimulus 1: blended apple	Stimulus 2: blended broccoli
Good	15	44
Bitter	20	54
Sour	23	81
Sweet	36	87

The measure of dissimiarity d_{121} would be computed as follows:

$$d_{121} = [(15\text{-}44)^2 + (20\text{-}54)^2 + (23\text{-}81)^2 + (36\text{-}87)^2]^{1/2}.$$

Forty-three 26 × 26 dissimilarity matrices were derived in this manner from the adjective data with one matrix for each subject. Two multidimensional scaling procedures, SINDSCAL (see Chapter 8) and the nonmetric option of ALSCAL (see Chapter 9), were applied to the dissimilarity measures. The arrangements of the stimuli in the blended foods spaces resulting from the two procedures were virtually identical, although the SINDSCAL solution was rotated 45° relative to the ALSCAL solution. The fact that the arrangements were virtually identical indicates that the solution was stable over various levels of assumed measurement type. The rotation achieved by the ALSCAL was more interpretable because the first dimension or axis in this space correlated highly with the rank order of the mean stimulus ratings on the following scales: good–bad (.94), flavorous–not flavorous (.93), repulsive–not repulsive (−.87), and obnoxious–not obnoxious (−.84).

In both SINDSCAL and ALSCAL, the weights for obese and normal weight subjects were clearly separated from one another. However, the interpretation of the weights for the SINDSCAL solution was more difficult because of the 45° rotation of the stimulus space. Because the ALSCAL rotation was more readily interpretable, this rotation was used as input for a second application of SINDSCAL in accordance with the instructions given in Chapter 8. The two-dimensional arrangement utilized in the second application of SINDSCAL (i.e., the ALSCAL rotation) is shown in Figure

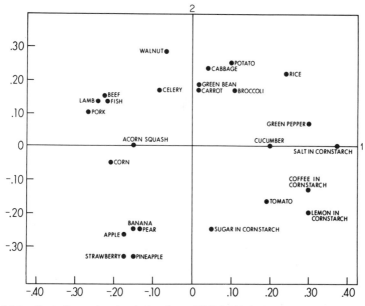

Figure 14.1. Two-dimensional solution from SINDSCAL (using ALSCAL rotation) which represents the communalities among 16 obese subjects and 27 normal weight individuals for 26 blended foods. (From Schiffman *et al.*, 1978.)

14.1. This space indicates the relative arrangements which were common to 16 obese subjects and 27 normal weight individuals.

The individual weights found by SINDSCAL using the ALSCAL rotation are given in Figure 14.2. The weights for obese subjects are labeled O; those for male and female normal weight subjects are labeled M and F, respectively.

It can be seen that all the obese subjects (and one normal weight male) found dimension 1 relatively more important than dimension 2. Thus, their perception of the blended foods would be similar to Figure 14.1, but stretched out in an elliptical fashion along the first dimension. Both male and female normal weight individuals tended to find the two dimensions equally important or weighted the second dimension more than the first.

Thus, by applying an individual differences model to a square matrix of dissimilarities created from a rectangular matrix of the adjective by stimulus form, the conclusion can be drawn that obese subjects find meats and fruits relatively more pleasant and flavorous than vegetables and cornstarch standards. The elliptical stretching of the perceptual space along the first dimension by obese subjects also suggests a tendency for obese subjects to

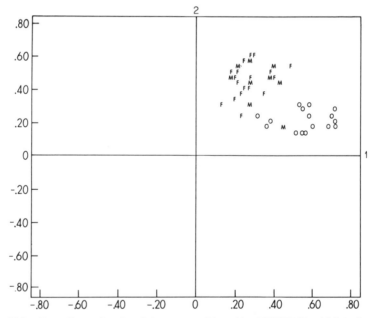

Figure 14.2. Two-dimensional weight space achieved by SINDSCAL which indicates the salience of the two-dimensions in Figure 14.1 for both the normal weight (labeled M for male and F for female) and obese (labeled O) subjects. It can be seen that dimension 1, which is a hedonic-flavorous dimension, received relatively greater weight from obese subjects when compared with normal weight subjects. (From Schiffman *et al.*, 1978.)

rate foods with high caloric density as relatively more pleasant than those with low caloric density when compared to normal weight subjects.

14.3. Taste of Chemicals

This data set (Section 3.4) is based on ratings on 45 scales by four subjects for tastes of 19 chemical stimuli. Eleven scales (listed in Part 4 of Table 3.9) were removed because they did not differentiate the stimuli from each other. The dilute scale was also eliminated as the data were incomplete. Mean adjective ratings over subjects on the remaining 33-adjective scales were developed to give a 19 × 33 matrix of the stimulus by adjective-category form. This matrix was analyzed by the Schiffman–Falkenberg procedure (see Section 14.5) resulting in the two-dimensional solution illustrated in Figure 14.3.

As in spaces found by applying multidimensional scaling procedures to similarity data, the two dimensions found here are artifacts of the mathematical analysis and only gain meaning if meaning can in fact be assigned to them. In the solution in Figure 14.3, the first axis seems to be related to the hedonic qualities of the stimuli since good, foodlike, and pleasant are located at one end of the continuum and repulsive, obnoxious, and bitter at the other end. The second axis bears some relationship to the caustic quality of the stimuli.

Dimensionality when rectangular matrices are analyzed can be altered depending on the number of scales or stimuli used as input. In this example, two solutions were initially determined for each of the four individual subjects as well as for their mean data. One solution was based on 44 scales (with the dilute scale eliminated); the other solution was based on 33 scales (with the 12 eliminated in Part 4 of Table 3.9). The dimensionalities for these solutions found by the Schiffman–Falkenberg procedure, based on either 44 scales or 33 scales for both individual subjects and the mean (i.e., composite) solution are shown in Table 14.1.

The problem that arises at this point is what is the "correct" dimensionality of the semantic differential space. We can only say that both the dimensionality and arrangement of stimuli in semantic differential solutions are functions of the number and type of scales on which the stimuli are rated; as a result they are thus much more susceptible to bias by the experimenter who chooses the adjectives than spaces found from similarity judgments. In addition to differing in dimensionality because of scale type and number, the two-dimensional arrangement of the 19 chemical stimuli in Figure 14.3 based on semantic differential judgments differs from the three-dimensional arrangement achieved from similarity judgments among

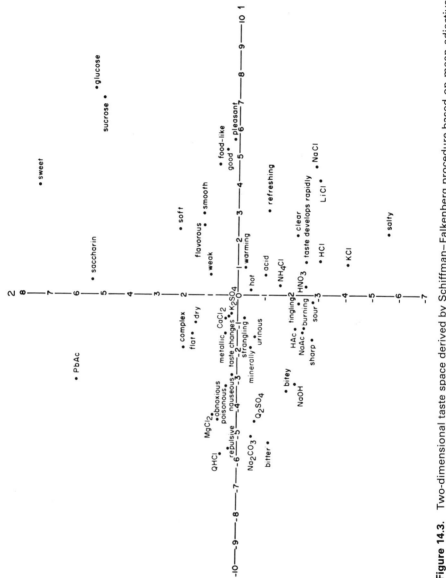

Figure 14.3. Two-dimensional taste space derived by Schiffman–Falkenberg procedure based on mean adjective data for 33 scales. (From Schiffman & Erickson, 1971.)

Table 14.1

Dimensionality of Solutions for Individual Subjects and Composite Based on Both Thirty-Three and Forty-Four Semantic Differential Scales[a]

	Dimensions retrieved	
Subject	Thirty-three scales	Forty-four scales
1	5	4
2	3	2
3	4	3
4	2	2
Composite	2	1

[a] From Schiffman and Erickson, 1971.

the same stimuli in Figure 5.10 both in dimensionality and relative location of stimuli.

In the semantic differential space, PbAc and saccharin are not grouped as closely with glucose and sucrose as they are in the similarity space. This is most likely due to the fact that all of the stimuli, including PbAc, saccharin, glucose, and sucrose, were rated on only one sweet scale but were rated on numerous hedonic, tactile, and temperature scales. Thus, the single sweet scale was not powerful enough to keep PbAc, saccharin, glucose, and sucrose tightly grouped as the other scales such as hedonic ones spread them apart. The four sweet-tasting stimuli would most likely have been more tightly grouped in the semantic differential space if the stimuli had been rated on more sweet-type scales, such as sugary or syrupy, and less on the other hedonic scales.

Comparison of the arrangements of these 19 chemical stimuli in multi-dimensional spaces achieved from both similarity data and semantic differential data illustrates the strengths and weaknesses of both approaches. PbAc is judged on adjective scales to have sour and bitter components. The similarity space indicates by its placement of PbAc close to the other sweet substances that when sweet stimuli are scaled with a group of taste stimuli which range widely in quality that the sweet taste seems to override any other components. (Subsequent studies [Schiffman, Reilly, & Clark, 1979] indicate that when a set of stimuli, all of which have sweet components, are scaled by themselves, the multidimensional sweetener space based on similarity judgments clearly reflects all the components in the sweeteners.) The important strength of similarity judgments is that it does not introduce experimenter bias in recovering the underlying structure among tastes because it does not require a priori assumptions about the dimensions relevant to the stimuli. A space based on adjective ratings can be useful when the experimenter has a clearly specific purpose in mind for his or her choice of semantic differential scales. However, it cannot yield an unbiased arrangement of the stimuli because the number and type of scales which are assumed to be relevant to the stimuli must be chosen in advance.

The two-dimensional solution shown in Figure 14.3 accounts for 99% of the variance of the data. The points in the figure represent the length of adjective and stimulus vectors. The space, hence, is a vector space in which the scalar cross-product of a vector from the origin to a stimulus with a vector from the origin to an adjective represents the relative importance for that stimulus on that adjective as given by the experimental ratings. Adjectives, represented by points falling distant from the origin (e.g., bitter and salty) are important in differentiating stimuli from one another. Adjectives falling close to the origin (e.g., hot and weak) are not important in differentiating stimuli from one another.

14.4. Color Vision Data

This example is the one used by Schiffman and Falkenberg (1968) in their original paper. The data set (Table 14.2) is the absorption of light at various wavelengths by cones in goldfish retina. The Schiffman–Falkenberg procedure applied to these data provides a three-dimensional solution which accounts for 99% of the variance. The first dimension is an intensity dimension. A plot of the second and third dimensions is shown in Figure 14.4. The stimuli are arranged in what is basically a color circle. The receptors are grouped close to the colors to which they are most sensitive; numbers 1, 2, and 3 next to blue; numbers 4, 5, and 6 next to green; and 8, 9, 10, and 11 next to red. Number 7 represents an aberrant double cone.

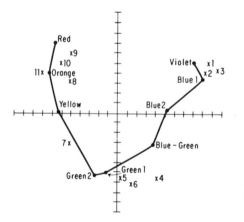

Figure 14.4. Arrangement of stimuli and neurons in the dimension 2 versus dimension 3 cross section of the solution achieved for Marks' data on spectral absorption by cones in the goldfish retina. (From Schiffman & Falkenberg, 1968.)

Table 14.2
Data Derived from Marks' Curves with Stimuli and Receptor Orders Randomized [a,b]

Receptor	Green 530	Yellow 585	Red 660	Blue *I* 458	Blue-green 498	Blue 485	Green 540	Orange 610	Violet 430
7	97	137	45	2	52	46	106	92	14
4	154	93	0	101	140	122	153	44	99
1	12	0	0	153	57	89	4	0	147
5	152	116	26	85	127	103	148	75	46
9	86	139	146	59	52	58	79	153	87
6	151	109	0	78	121	85	154	57	73
8	84	151	120	65	73	77	102	154	44
3	14	0	0	152	100	125	0	0	145
2	32	23	0	154	75	110	24	17	153
11	55	120	132	0	39	40	62	147	0
10	56	136	111	27	24	23	72	144	60

[a] From Schiffman and Falkenberg, 1968.
[b] The cell entries represent the measured height of the ordinate for the particular spectral frequency.

14.5. Mathematical Description of the Schiffman–Falkenberg Procedure

The Schiffman–Falkenberg program was written for the use of its developers and is not available for public distribution. However, it can be programmed by the interested reader from the following mathematical description.

The purpose for its development was to circumvent the problems inherent in unfolding procedures (Coombs, 1964) which generally yield degenerate spaces, for example, the adjectives and stimuli are not appropriately melded together in a meaningful way in the solution.

The purpose of this program is to take the **F** matrix (the empirical data matrix of ratings) where f_{ij} is an element of the **F** matrix which gives the ratings for a stimulus on a given attribute

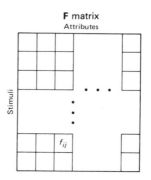

and divide it into two matrices which are a statement of the stimuli and adjectives in component form:

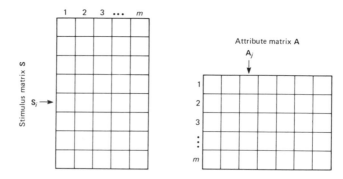

Any given stimulus S_i is a row vector and any given attribute A_j is a column vector. Theoretically, we can express the observed f_{ij} as follows:

$$f_{ij} = S_i A_j, \tag{14.1}$$

that is, the scalar product of two vectors. Thus,

$$f_{ij} = \sum_m s_{im} a_{mj} \qquad (14.2)$$

and

$$\mathbf{F} = \mathbf{SA}, \qquad (14.3)$$

that is, this is the formally precise statement of the model. Hence, if m is equal to 2

$$f_{ij} = s_{i1} a_{1j} + s_{i2} a_{2j}\,.$$

Thus, this program takes a matrix of ratings and yields attribute and stimulus vectors which can ultimately be plotted in the same multidimensional space. A two-dimensional space, for example, would look like this:

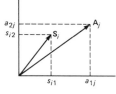

Several points should be made at this time:

1. The closeness of the homogeneous elements represents their similarity in that: (*a*) Close stimuli have similar attribute ratings, and (*b*) close attributes have similar ratings for the same stimulus.
2. The closeness of the nonhomogeneous elements represents the importance of an attribute in describing the properties of a given stimulus. The length of the vector specifically represents its sensitivity in describing a stimulus.

These vectors, $\mathbf{S}_i$ and $\mathbf{A}_j$, are derived as follows. The rectangular matrix $\mathbf{F}$ can be expressed as:

$$\mathbf{F} = \mathbf{U}\,\beta\,\mathbf{V}, \qquad (14.4)$$

where $\mathbf{U}$ and $\mathbf{V}$ are orthonormal matrices composed of principal vectors[1] and β is a diagonal matrix of roots.

From Equation (14.4):

$$\mathbf{F}\mathbf{F}^{\mathrm{T}} = \mathbf{U}\beta\mathbf{V} \cdot \mathbf{V}^{\mathrm{T}}\beta\mathbf{U}^{\mathrm{T}}. \qquad (14.5)$$

---

[1] The conditions for the **U** matrix:

to be orthonormal are: (*a*) that the sums of the squares of the elements of a column (principal vector) equals 1, and (*b*) that the matrix is orthogonal, that is, the sums of the cross-products is 0 or $\mathbf{U}_1\mathbf{U}_2 = 0$, implying that the columns are independent. (This holds for the **V** matrix as well, but the principal vectors are rows.)

However, for orthonormal matrices

$$\mathbf{VV}^T = \mathbf{I},$$

where $\mathbf{I}$ is an identity matrix. Thus:

$$\mathbf{FF}^T = \mathbf{U}\beta^2 \mathbf{U}^T, \tag{14.6}$$

where $\mathbf{F}^T$ and $\mathbf{U}^T$ are the transposed $\mathbf{F}$ and $\mathbf{U}$ matrices.

$\mathbf{U}$ and β can be determined from Hotelling's (1933) method. In order to determine $\mathbf{V}$, we return to Equation (14.4) and solve for $\mathbf{V}$:

$$\mathbf{U}^T\mathbf{F} = \mathbf{U}^T\mathbf{U}\beta\mathbf{V},$$
$$\mathbf{U}^T\mathbf{F} = \beta\mathbf{V},$$
$$\beta^{-1}\mathbf{U}^T\mathbf{F} = \beta^{-1}\beta\mathbf{V}^2,$$
$$\beta^{-1}\mathbf{U}^T\mathbf{F} = \mathbf{V},$$

where β^{-1} is the inverse of the β matrix.

$\mathbf{S}$ and $\mathbf{A}$ are then defined as:

$$\mathbf{S} = \mathbf{U}\beta^{1/2} (n_1/n_2)^{1/2} \tag{14.7}$$

and

$$\mathbf{A} = (n_2/n_1)^{1/2} \beta^{1/2}\mathbf{V}, \tag{14.8}$$

where n_1 is the number of stimuli and n_2 is the number of adjectives. The ratio of these two numbers is used to parcel out the variance to the $\mathbf{S}$ and $\mathbf{A}$ matrices.

The loadings of the stimulus and adjective vectors are the elements of the $\mathbf{S}$ and $\mathbf{A}$ matrices. When the stimulus and adjective vectors are plotted in the same space, it is generally found, empirically, that the first dimension is related to the row and column means and not to the structure inherent in the data. For example, in the data described in Section 14.4, the first dimension was related to intensity where the cones were ordered according to overall intensity in all stimuli and the stimuli were ordered in overall effectiveness in producing responses in all cones.

The extent to which this model is useful is settled empirically. It has been helpful in numerous experiments (Schiffman, 1977; Schiffman & Dackis, 1975; Schiffman & Engelhard, 1976; Schiffman, Moroch, & Dunbar, 1975) and will find a useful arrangement with a much higher probability of success than unfolding procedures.

A program which can perform an analysis similar to the Schiffman–Falkenberg approach has been independently developed by Carroll (1972). The analysis performed by this program, called MDPREF (see Appendix), is identical to that described above except for two differences.

---

[2] We wish to solve for $\mathbf{V}$, but since we cannot divide in matrix algebra, we instead multiply by the inverse (i.e., β^{-1}). $\beta\beta^{-1} = \mathbf{I}$, where $\mathbf{I}$ is a diagonal identity matrix.

First, MDPREF removes each subject's mean judgment prior to the analysis. This eliminates the first "mean" or "intensity" factor. When this centering is performed then the stimuli can be represented as points, but when the centering is not done they should be represented as vectors. In both cases the attributes are depicted as vectors.

The second difference is that the β term in Equation (14.6) is absorbed entirely into the **A** matrix (14.8) and not into **S** (14.7). This difference, which is arbitrary in either case, is not crucial.

References

Carroll, J. D. Individual differences and multidimensional scaling. In R. N. Shepard, A. K. Romney, & S. Nerlove (Eds.), *Multidimensional scaling: Theory and applications in the behavioral sciences.* New York: Academic Press, 1972.

Coombs, C. H. *A theory of data.* New York: Wiley, 1964. (Reprinted by Mathesis Press, Ann Arbor, Michigan, 1976.)

Hotelling, H. Analysis of a complex of statistical variables into principal components. *Journal of Educational Psychology,* 1933, *24,* 417–441.

Johnson, S. C. Hierarchical clustering schemas. *Psychometrika,* 1967, *32,* 241–254.

Marks, W. B. *Difference spectra of the visual pigments in single goldfish cones.* Unpublished doctoral dissertation, Johns Hopkins University, 1965.

Schiffman, H., & Falkenberg, P. The organization of stimuli and sensory neurons. *Physiology and Behavior,* 1968, *3,* 197–201.

Schiffman, S. S. Food recognition by the elderly. *Journal of Gerontology,* 1977, *32,* 586–592.

Schiffman, S. S., & Dackis, C. Taste of nutrients: Amino acids, vitamins, and fatty acids. *Perception and Psychophysics,* 1975, *17,* 140–146.

Schiffman, S. S., & Engelhard, H. H. Taste of dipeptides. *Physiology and Behavior,* 1976, *17,* 523–535.

Schiffman, S. S., & Erickson, R. P. A psychophysical model for gustatory quality. *Physiology and Behavior,* 1971, *7,* 617–633.

Schiffman, S. S., Moroch, K., & Dunbar, J. Taste of acetylated amino acids. *Chemical Senses and Flavor,* 1975, *1,* 387–401.

Schiffman, S. S., Musante, G., & Conger, J. Application of multidimensional scaling to ratings of foods for obese and normal weight individuals. *Physiology and Behavior,* 1978, *21,* 417–422.

Schiffman, S. S., Reilly, D. A., & Clark, T. B. Qualitative differences among sweeteners. *Physiology and Behavior,* 1979, *23,* 1–9.

Tucker, L. R. Relations between multidimensional scaling and three-mode factor analysis. *Psychometrika,* 1972, *37,* 3–27.

15

Use of Multidimensional Scaling in Product Development

15.1. Overview

There is usually a good deal of information on product composition in most companies, and many hypotheses concerning attributes which are important to the consumer. Frequently lacking is a demonstration of the relevance of these attributes, a means of eliciting them in a mutually understood language, and the relationship between composition and quality. Multidimensional scaling of similarity judgments identifies the more important dimensions of a product category. It does this without any prior assumptions about the attributes. Further, it avoids all problems of articulation and meaning. What does "strong" refer to, for example, in an alcoholic beverage? One of us has seen occasions whereby adjustment of flavor or sugar content provides a "stronger" coffee liqueur than another of higher actual proof. Derivation of the perceptual space from similarity judgments avoids language problems yet allows correlation of perceived qualities with composition and preference.

The positioning of a product in a relevant perceptual space containing competing products is a key step in determining if improvements are needed or if opportunities exist for line extensions or new entries. Further, if an image space is also developed for the same collection of products, again by MDS of similarity judgments, valuable direction for product or image modification can be derived. "Sell (i.e., advertise) them strong but make them mild" is a successful marketing dictum for certain goods. Comparison of product and image spaces can show where this is happening. Finally, a lot of products are not really that different and consumers frequently are not very discriminating. Experiments can be designed to determine who can discriminate and on what dimensions (see, for example, Section 8.7).

One thing that MDS of similarity judgments cannot do directly is provide novel products. With a little thought, this is obvious. The perceptual map is of course bounded by the domain of the stimuli from which it is derived. While different combinations of qualities may provide a product *modification* to fit a gap in this space, this product will not be *novel*. Fluoride toothpaste was not and could not be developed from a "toothpaste" space. Or, as Francis Bacon more eloquently wrote in his *Novum Organum* of 1620: "Thus, had anyone meditated on balistic Machines, and Battering Rams, as they were used by the Ancients, whatever application he might have exerted, and though he might have consumed a whole life in the pursuit, yet would he never have hit upon the Invention of Flaming Engines, acting by means of gunpowder." With this understood, MDS can be accepted and applied as a useful tool.

There remain some practical difficulties:

Number of stimuli to use
Removal of visual cues
Use situation

In Section 2.6, we recommended use of at least 18 stimuli for derivation of a three-dimensional perceptual map. Yet a product category may contain only four entries. The experimenter can perhaps provide some additional stimuli by modification of his or her own brand. However, the inclusion of the majority of stimuli in this way brings the danger of obscuring subtle features in competitive products. The space may collapse to the one dimension of ours–theirs. Thus, in practice it may sometimes be necessary to use fewer stimuli than were suggested in Section 2.6.

Reduction or elimination of visual cues presents another problem. Although color or brand names contribute hugely to the overall perception of a product, these must be disguised to uncover the relation between taste–odor qualities and composition. Whenever possible, repackaging or masking, dim lights and, as a last resort, blindfolds should be used.

Finally, the use situation provides an obvious criticism of the similarity judgment procedure. There are three aspects to this criticism:

1. Laboratory atmosphere as opposed to home or normal use
2. "Sip" testing instead of full consumption of the product
3. The abnormality of puffing on two cigarettes or tasting two foods or beverages

The first is easiest to defend. Differences between competing brands are often small. A laboratory atmosphere provides the setting needed to detect subtle dissimilarities. There are too many distractions in home use to allow the necessary concentration. This is not to say that home use of a product is not an integral step in its total evaluation, but rather that the elucidation of certain product qualities requires a laboratory setting. On the other hand, home use is often required to determine such elusive and ill-defined qualities of soft drinks and cigarettes as refreshment and satisfaction. Thus we do not defend the "sip" testing inherent in assessment of dissimilarities as the only facet for testing. Rather, we need its strengths and accept its limitations.

The following sections describe the use of MDS in examining two product categories—raspberry liqueurs and beer. In the first case, we discuss an exploratory experiment aimed at eliciting attributes and optimizing composition. The beer study is concerned with comparing taste images with taste experiences.

15.2. Case Study 1: Raspberry-Flavored Liqueurs

This example, though based on a real situation, uses reconstructed data and different stimulus descriptions to protect the source. The product category, raspberry-flavored liqueurs, was dominated in the United States by a European import sold at a high price with attractive packaging. There were, however, several other imported and a domestic product competing with it. Another company felt that there was an opportunity for a U.S. entry but was uncertain as to whether to try to match, as closely as possible, the leading import, or to try to develop a preferred formulation. An additional complication was the excise tax, which varies with alcohol content. Since the liqueurs consist basically of sugar, water, alcohol, and flavor, the possibility existed for attempting a match of perceived "strength," if that was indeed an important attribute, by manipulation of sugar, alcohol, and flavor level at a reduced price. The company's flavorists believed they had developed a good match for the qualities of the leading import.

The portion of the work described here investigates the hypothesis that strength is an important attribute and not dependent solely on alcohol content. This is achieved by developing a taste space for formulations varying in sugar, alcohol, and flavor content from dissimilarity judgments. We also show an attempt to relate (a) the formulas to the taste space by the method of canonical correlation analysis and (b) the preference ratings to the taste space (see Chapter 12).

Experimental Details

The stimuli (Table 15.1) are seven liqueurs differing only in alcohol and sugar content and the amount of raspberry-flavored concentrate added.
Nine subjects provided:

Table 15.1
Percentage Composition of Liqueurs

Stimulus	Sugar	Alcohol	Flavor
1	30	30	1.0
2	20	30	1.0
3	30	40	1.0
4	40	35	1.2
5	25	20	1.4
6	35	30	0.8
7	30	25	0.6

1. Measures of dissimilarity in taste–flavor for each of the 21 pairs
2. Judgments of overall liking for each drink

The following sections show:

1. The development of the taste–flavor space from INDSCAL analysis of the dissimilarity judgments
2. The relationship of this space to the chemical composition of the liqueurs via canonical correlation analysis
3. Analysis of each panelist's preference via PREFMAP using the INDS-CAL stimulus coordinates

INDSCAL Taste–Flavor Space

Figure 15.1 (identical to Figure 12.10) shows both the taste flavor space for the seven raspberry-flavored liqueurs and the results of the preference analysis. Dimension 1 is mainly a sweetness dimension. The liqueur with the lowest sugar content (20%) is on the extreme left. The sweetest liqueur, 40% sugar, is on the extreme right. Dimension 2 appears to be related to alcoholic strength. The liqueur with the highest alcohol content (40%), is at the top of Figure 15.1; the weakest, 20% and 25% alcohol, are at the bottom.

Reduction in alcohol content at constant sugar (stimuli 3, 1, and 7) increases perceived sweetness. Reduction in sugar content at constant alcohol (stimuli 6, 1, and 2) does not, however, lead to a consistent increase in perceived strength on the alcohol dimension. Stimulus 1 (30% sugar) not only appears to be stronger than stimulus 6 (35% sugar) but also stronger than stimulus 2 (20% sugar). Flavor levels do not explain the discrepancy. Indeed, they do not have any obvious explanatory value for the arrangement of the stimuli. We examine next, therefore, the relation of product composition to the taste space by canonical correlation analysis.

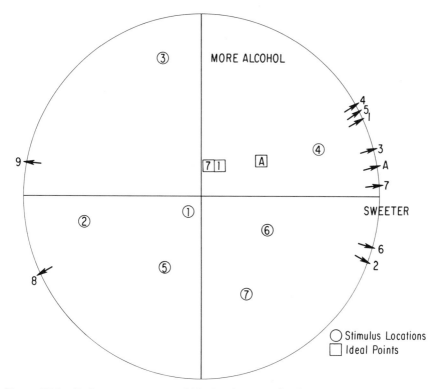

Figure 15.1. Preference vectors and ideal points on stimulus space.

Canonical Correlation Analysis

The stimuli vary in sugar, alcohol, and flavor content although their dissimilarities are represented in a two-dimensional stimulus space. While this space can be explained roughly in terms of alcohol and sugar content, it is of interest to see how flavor content affects–improves this interpretation.

The stimulus coordinates provide the two variables for the first or criterion set. The product compositions provide the three variables for the second or predictor set. Since there are only two criterion variables, only two canonical correlations may be developed. These are both highly significant:

Canonical correlation	Bartlett's chi-square	Degrees of freedom	Significance
.99985	35.51	6	.0000
.98792	11.19	2	.0037

Table 15.2
Canonical Variable Loadings

	First correlation	Second correlation
First set		
Sweetness coordinate	.716	−.698
Alcohol coordinate	.528	.849
Second set		
Sugar content	.878	−.478
Alcohol content	.771	−.589
Flavor content	.018	−.207

The canonical variable loadings which show the correlations of the canonical variables with the original variables are given in Table 15.2. The canonical variable loadings for the first set indicate a rotation of the stimulus space. Both the first and second canonical variables contain contributions from the sugar and alcohol dimensions. Likewise, the canonical variable loadings for the second set contain significant contributions from the alcohol and sugar contents. Disappointingly, the flavor concentration provides no contribution to the first correlation and precious little to the second.

The redundancies between the data sets are as follows:

	Correlation	Redundáncy
First set (stimulus coordinates)	First	.40
	Second	.59
Second set (chemical composition)	First	.46
	Second	.31

Virtually all the information (total redundancy is .99) in the taste space is provided by the chemical composition. However, only 77% of the chemical composition data is explained by the taste space. As we saw earlier, the flavor concentration provides little contribution to the canonical correlations.

Preference Analysis

Subjects rated each liqueur on an undifferentiated line scale anchored with "dislike very much" and "like very much." These ratings were used as the input to PREFMAP together with the stimulus coordinates for the two-dimensional INDSCAL space. Analyses were made using both the ideal point (phase III) and vector (phase IV) models.

This analysis has been discussed in detail in Chapter 12 and therefore only the highlights will be recapitulated here. Figure 15.1 shows the preference vectors for all subjects and the ideal points for Subjects 1 and 7, and the average Subject A. Except for subjects 8 and 9, the preference vectors lie in the direction of greater sweetness. The ideal points, however, suggest that 40% sugar is perhaps a little too much. Both the preference vectors and the ideal points indicate that alcohol content should be greater than 30%. Further work, therefore, would concentrate on a narrower stimulus domain, say 30–40% sugar and 30–40% alcohol. Moreover, in this phase some competitive products could be introduced to determine how closely the experimental products matched them, and if flavor differences gave rise to a third dimension.

The MDS of dissimilarity judgments to provide a stimulus space, canonical correlation analysis of composition with this space, and preference analysis of this space are the basic tools for understanding how to formulate products to maximize acceptance. Once the major variables are set, a further round of tests can be conducted on minor variables.

15.3. Case Study 2: Comparison of Taste Images and Taste Experiences

At the conclusion of a taste test it takes only a short while to gather data from subjects on taste perceptions using brand names as stimuli. It is worthwhile collecting both similarity judgments and preference rank orders. Comparison of product image data with product experience data is very helpful in determining what needs to be fixed to help a troubled brand. Is the product composition really at fault or has the brand developed an image over the years which is at odds with its actual quality? Regional beers and coupon cigarettes are two product types particularly susceptible to poor image problems. Their lower costs or "added value" are considered by all, except their loyal users, as an indication of reduced product quality. In fact, for the regional beers, transportation and advertising costs are usually less and corporate overheads probably lower. Coupon cigarettes use reduced advertising to cover coupon redemption costs.

A difficulty in collecting taste image data, however, is the tendency for subjects to make judgments in hedonic terms once confronted with brand names. Thus, the resultant space can be a multidimensional preference space revealing the dimensions of "liking" rather than "taste." Two brands which subjects think they like will be judged as similar, as will brands they think they dislike. In the extreme case the scaling of a subject's data will be unidimensional and reflect only preference rank order. We will show examples of this in the next section. This is more likely to happen where real product differences are small, as in domestic beer, as opposed to, say, breakfast cereals which cover a wide range of product differences.

Taste Images of Beers

A small group of 13 regular beer users provided dissimilarity judgments on their taste images of seven beers. Two of these beers were local, one had fairly wide regional distribution, and four were national. The two local brands and one of the national brands were sold at a lower price than the other four brands. The data were analyzed using ALSCAL at the ordinal level in three dimensions. Average subject weights for the three dimensions were .53, .36, and .33, suggesting that all three dimensions had meaning. However, inspection of individual subject weights showed some subjects using only dimension 1 and others only dimension 3. It is reasonable to suspect in such cases that these subjects' dissimilarity judgments are simply reflecting preference rank orders. It is possible although unlikely that one person would be thinking solely in terms of "body" and the other in terms of "bitterness" (if these were the dimensions) when making their judgments. Five of the 13 subjects shared this distinction of having weights of .9 or more on one dimension and .2 or less on the other two. Inspection of their preference rank orders showed that these matched closely, in one case perfectly, the stimulus orders on the heavily weighted dimension. The data set was therefore reanalyzed with their data excluded.

Average subject weights for the three dimensions in the new analysis were .44, .43, and .39, again giving credence to a three-dimensional solution. Moreover, only one subject excessively weighted one particular dimension. The other subjects' weights were spread across all three dimensions.

The second dimension gave a clear separation of national brands from local–regional brands. In one sense this is not very helpful since all we are learning is that in people's minds national beers taste more like each other than local beers. It reemphasizes the problem inherent, though, in developing a quality image for a local brand.

While, for proprietary reasons, the taste image space is not reproduced here, dimension 1 separated the beers in terms of perceived bitterness while dimension 3 separated them in terms of perceived body. Interestingly, the regional beer was separated from the two local beers on these dimensions. It was more "Miller-like" on dimension 1 and more "Budweiser-like" on dimension 3.

Taste Experiences of Beers

Prior to collection of the taste image data, the panelists provided pairwise dissimilarity judgments by sip testing all 21 pairs of the seven beers. The two-dimensional taste space separated the beers in terms of body and bitterness. The key finding was that one of the local beers which, in image terms, was low in body and very bitter, had, in fact, average bitterness and high body. This confirmed the management viewpoint that the problem which needed overcoming was the taste quality image rather than the actual taste quality. Blind preference testing had not indicated a product problem either. While beer seems to be sold more on user image than product image, in this instance, emphasis on enhancing product image seemed indicated.

15.4. Summary

This chapter has described the strengths and limitations of applying MDS procedures to product development. Analysis of similarity judgments is a powerful tool for determining the dimensions (attributes) of a product category most relevant to consumers. Care must be taken as in all MDS experiments, with selection of the stimulus set. There are sometimes practical difficulties in finding stimuli that are sufficiently different within a desired range. We show how to relate the derived stimulus space to product composition via canonical correlation analysis, and how to embed preference data in the stimulus space. We also suggest that it is useful at times to compare product image with product experience. This helps determine whether it is the product or the advertising that requires alteration. The skills and resources to collect and analyze similarity judgments should be part of the total product development–marketing research arsenal of any consumer goods company.

Part III

Theory

16

How Multidimensional Scaling
Programs Work

16.1. Overview

This chapter describes the way the six scaling programs discussed in this book work. All of the programs are iterative, that is, they all take the approach of trying over and over again to obtain the best possible solution. All of the programs have some special way to get the iterations started. This is called the *initialization routine*. They also have some way to stop the iterations, called the *termination routine*.

The initialization routine prepares an initial set of stimulus coordinates and (for WMDS) subject weights. For most of the programs the initial values are computed directly from the raw data. MINISSA uses an ordinal transformation of the data for this purpose. Except for this difference the programs are all fairly similar in the strategy used to get started. They all use some variant of Torgerson's classical proposal for the CMDS and RMDS cases, although there is not as much agreement in the WMDS case. The initial values are then modified by the iterations which follow.

The iterative routine, for most of the programs, consists of two steps, one that tries to estimate the best possible order-preserving transformation of the raw data, and one that tries to estimate the best possible stimulus coordinates and (for WMDS) subject weights. Once the iterative process is initialized these two steps are alternated back and forth until the program decides that it should terminate. Note that the programs differ in the way the parts of each iteration are constructed. MINISSA, KYST, POLYCON, and ALSCAL are fairly similar to one another. INDSCAL and MULTI-SCALE differ from each other and from the other four.

The termination routine, in all of the programs, involves making a decision as to how well the program is describing the data by the stimulus coordinates (and subject weights). Some programs calculate a measure of goodness of fit called *stress*. If the stress does not improve by very much from one iteration to the next, the program will stop. Sometimes the program stops because too many iterations have occurred. All of the programs use different measures of stress, and different definitions of very much and too many.

We turn to each program now.

16.2. ALSCAL

FORREST W. YOUNG

As described in Chapter 9, ALSCAL can perform CMDS, RMDS, and WMDS analyses of the type of data considered in this chapter. When there is only one matrix of data the unweighted Euclidean model must be used, resulting in the CMDS situation. When there is more than one matrix, the unweighted Euclidean model generates the RMDS situation and the weighted Euclidean model generates the WMDS situation. A detailed mathematical description of all aspects of ALSCAL is given by Takane, Young, and de Leeuw (1977) and Young, Takane, and Lewyckyj (1978).

Before turning to the step-by-step description, we remind the reader that ALSCAL, like all MDS programs, is an iterative program. As with many of the programs, each ALSCAL iteration consists of two major substeps, one of which transforms the data and the other of which estimates stimulus coordinates and subject weights. The authors of ALSCAL call the first substep *optimal scaling* and the second one *model estimation*. These two substeps are alternated until the program decides the solution has been obtained with sufficient accuracy. Since, in ALSCAL, each substep is a least-squares procedure, the overall algorithm is called an alternating least-squares (ALS) algorithm. This is where the acronym ALSCAL comes from: *A*lternating *L*east-*S*quares s*CAL*ing.

The optimal scaling step consists primarily of only one activity, the optimal scaling itself, which will be described shortly. However, the model estimation step is more complicated, and deserves a short overview now. The complication is because of the fact that this step involves two major substeps, estimation of stimulus coordinates and estimation of subject weights (the latter substep is skipped with the unweighted Euclidean model).

In the coordinate estimation substep, the coordinates for the points are estimated *one at a time* in such a way that the least-squares value for each coordinate is found. Specifically, the coordinate of one of the points (say point 1) on dimension 1 (or, in other words, the location of that point on dimension 1) is determined by least-squares methods, then the coordinate of that same point on dimension 2 is determined, then on dimension 3, etc., until all coordinates of the point have been estimated. Since the estimation of each of the point's coordinates depends on the values of all the other coordinates, it is necessary to iterate their estimation until the location of the point in multidimensional space stabilizes. When this happens we have moved the point to the best possible location, given that all the other points have remained unmoved. We then move on to the next point (number 2, say), repeating the same process.

When we have gotten through all n points, we then move on to the subject weight estimation substep. This substep provides us with least-squares estimates for each subject's weight on each dimension. However, since the weights are all independent of each other, it is not necessary to iterate their estimation. We simply estimate them once and then turn to the optimal scaling step. Note that the independence characteristic means that we can view the estimation of subject weights as taking place subject-by-subject, or simultaneously. Both views are equivalent.

Initial Configuration

1. The first step is to estimate an additive constant c_k which is added to the observed proximity measures, for example, o_{ijk}. Thus,

$$o_{ijk}^* = o_{ijk} + c_k$$

such that (*a*) for all triples the triangular inequality holds:

$$o_{ijk}^* + o_{j\ell k}^* \geqslant o_{i\ell k}^*$$

and (*b*) positivity holds

$$o_{ijk}^* \geqslant 0,$$

where o_{ijk}^* is the adjusted proximity between stimulus i and stimulus j for subject k, $o_{j\ell k}^*$ is the adjusted proximity between stimulus j and stimulus ℓ for subject k, and $o_{i\ell k}^*$ is the adjusted proximity between stimulus i and stimulus ℓ for subject k. The constant c_k which is added is as small as possible to estimate a zero point for the dissimilarity data, thus bringing the data more nearly in line with the ratio level of measurement. This step is necessary to make the $\mathbf{B}_k^*$ matrix, described later, positive semidefinite, that is, it has no imaginary roots.

2. The next step is to compute a scalar products matrix $\mathbf{B}_k^{**}$ for each subject k by double centering $\mathbf{O}_k^*$, the adjusted proximity matrix for each subject. An element of the $\mathbf{B}_k^{**}$ matrix b_{ijk}^{**} is computed as follows:

$$b_{ijk}^{**} = -\frac{1}{2}(o_{ijk}^{*2} - o_{i.k}^{*2} - o_{.jk}^{*2} + o_{..k}^{*2}),$$

where $o_{i.k}^*$ are the row means for the adjusted proximities for subject k, $o_{.jk}^*$ are the column means for the adjusted proximities for subject k, and $o_{..k}^*$ is the grand mean for subject k. Double centering to convert distances to scalar products is necessary because a scalar products matrix is required to compute an initial configuration utilizing the Young–Householder–Torgerson procedure.

3. Next the individual subject matrices are normalized so that they have the same variance. The normalized matrix $\mathbf{B}_k^*$ is found for each subject. The elements of the matrix are

$$b_{ijk}^* = \frac{b_{ijk}^{**}}{\left[\sum_i \sum_j (b_{ijk}^{**})^2/(n)(n-1)\right]^{1/2}},$$

where n = number of stimuli, and $(n)(n-1)$ = number of elements in the $\mathbf{B}_k^{**}$ matrix off the diagonal. The denominator is both the root mean square and the standard deviation of the unnormalized scalar products matrix $\mathbf{B}^{**}$. (It is both these things because $b_{..k}^{**} = 0$ due to double centering.) $\mathbf{B}_k^*$ is thus a matrix with elements b_{ijk}^* which are scalar products for individual subject k. Normalization of individual subjects' matrices equates the contribution of each individual to the formation of a mean scalar products matrix and thus the resulting initial configuration.

4. Next an average scalar products matrix $\mathbf{B}^*$ over the subjects is computed. The elements of this matrix are

$$b_{ij.}^* = \frac{\sum_k b_{ijk}^*}{m},$$

where m is the number of subjects.

5. The average $\mathbf{B}^*$ matrix in step 4 is used to compute an initial stimulus configuration using the classical Young–Householder multidimensional scaling procedure:

$$\mathbf{B}^* = \mathbf{XX}',$$

where $\mathbf{X}$ is an $n \times r$ matrix of n stimulus points on r dimensions, and $\mathbf{X}'$ is the transpose of the $\mathbf{X}$ matrix, that is, the rows and columns are interchanged. The $\mathbf{X}$ matrix is the initial configuration.

6. For the weighted ALSCAL model, initial weight configuration matrices W_k for each of the m subjects are computed. The initial weight matrices W_k are $r \times r$ matrices where r is the number of dimensions. Later the diagonals of W_k will form rows of the W matrix, which is an $n \times r$ matrix. The matrices W_k are determined such that

$$B_k^* = YW_kY',$$

where $Y = XT$ and $TT' = I$, and where T is an orthogonal rotation of the configuration X to a new orientation Y. T is computed by the Schönemann–de Leeuw procedure as discussed by Young, Takane, and Lewyckyj (1978). T rotates X so that W_k is as diagonal as possible (i.e., off-diagonal elements are as close to 0 as possible on the average over subjects). Off-diagonal elements represent a departure from the model (which assumes that subjects weight only the dimensions of the stimulus space).

Optimization Algorithm

The optimization algorithm is a series of steps which are repeated (iterated) until the final solution is achieved. The steps of the optimization algorithm are represented diagrammatically around the circle in Figure 16.1. The steps for the optimization algorithm are performed successively because disparities, weights, and coordinates cannot be solved for simultaneously.

DISTANCES

Distances are computed according to the weighted Euclidean model

$$d_{ijk}^2 = \sum_{a=1}^{r} w_{ka}(x_{ia} - x_{ja})^2,$$

where w_{ka} is the weight for subject k on a dimension a, x_{ia} is the coordinate of stimulus i on dimension a, and x_{ja} is the coordinate of stimulus j on dimension a. The first set of distances are computed from the coordinates and weights found in steps 5 and 6 (earlier). Subsequently, new distances are computed from new coordinates found in the iteration process (described later).

OPTIMAL SCALING

Optimal scaling for ordinal data uses Kruskal's least-squares monotonic transformation. This yields disparities that are a monotonic transformation of the data *and* which are as much like the distances (in a least-squares sense) as possible. Ideally, we wish that the distances were in exactly the same rank order as the data. But usually they are not. So we locate a new

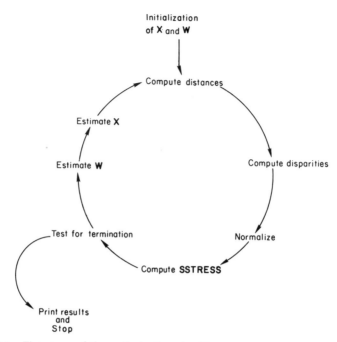

Initialization
of **X** and **W**

Compute distances

Estimate **X**

Estimate **W**

Compute disparities

Test for termination

Normalize

Compute **SSTRESS**

Print results
and
Stop

Figure 16.1. The steps of the optimization algorithm.

set of numbers, called disparities, which are in the same rank order as the data and which fit the distances as well as possible. When we see an order violation we replace the numbers that are out of order with a block of values which are the mean of the out of order numbers.

In Table 16.1 we present an example of what goes on. At the upper-left corner there is a hypothetical symmetric matrix of ordinal data about five stimuli. We rearrange the data into a vector of numbers sorted into ascending order. This is the order we want to reproduce.

Directly below this we have done the same thing with the matrix of distances. However, they have *not* been placed in ascending order. Rather, the numbers in the data and distance vectors come from corresponding cells in the data and distance matrices. For example, the fourth number in the distance vector (3.0) comes from the lower-left cell in the distance matrix; analogously, the fourth number in the data vector (4) comes from the lower-left cell in the raw data matrix. Thus, if the distances were in the right order (i.e., the data order) the numbers in the distance vector would be in ascending order. However, they are not. So we replace every sequence of two numbers which are not in ascending order with their mean. In the example, the distances 2.5 and 1.5 are out of order (as indicated by NG—"no good") so they are replaced with their mean, 2.0. Then this mean is used as the value for the two corresponding disparities, as shown at the

Table 16.1
Kruskal's Least-Squares Monotonic Transformation

	Raw data				*Raw data (sorted into ascending order)*

```
                                              Raw data
            Raw data                   (sorted into ascending order)
0
1   0
8   7   0          ───────────►  1   2   3   4   5   6   7   8   9   10
3   2   5   0
4  10   9   6   0                                  │
                                                   │
                                                   ▼

         Distances                            Distances
                                        (arranged in data order)
0.0
1.0  0.0
6.4  6.2  0.0      ───────────►  1.0  2.5  1.5  3.0  4.2  8.4  6.2  6.4  8.2  8.4
1.5  2.5  4.2  0.0
3.0  8.4  8.2  8.4  0.0
                             Least-squares monotonic transformation
```

```
              OK    NG       OK    OK   NG            OK
            ⌒  1  ⌒ 2 ↘    ⌒ 5 ↘ 6 ↘ 7 ↘          ⌒ 11 ↘
            1.0  2.5  1.5   3.0  4.2  8.4  6.2   6.4   8.2  8.4
            ▲         ▲     ▲              ▲       ▲
            └── 4 ────┘     3            7.3─── 8
                 2.0           ▲       10        NG        9
            OK          OK                ───── 7.0 ─────
                                        OK          OK
```

	Disparities (optimally scaled data)				

```
         Disparities
      (optimally scaled data)
0.0                                          Disparities
1.0  0.0
7.0  7.0  0.0  ◄───────  1.0  2.0  2.0  3.0  4.2  7.0  7.0  7.0  8.2  8.4
2.0  2.0  4.2  0.0
3.0  8.4  8.2  7.0  0.0
```

bottom of the table. Note that sometimes the mean of two distances is not in the correct order and we must form the mean of three (or more) distances, as happens in the example. Finally, we take the disparities out of their vector and put them back into matrix form. The sequence of the transformations is shown by the numerals in bold type.

When there are ties in the data the optimal scaling process is changed somewhat, but we do not go into the details here. However, Kruskal's primary and secondary procedures are used in ALSCAL-4.

NORMALIZATION

The disparities found in step 2 are now normalized for technical reasons related to the alternating least-squares algorithm. During the course of the optimization process, we want to minimize a measure of error called

SSTRESS. But the monotone regression procedure described above only minimizes the numerator of the SSTRESS formula. Thus, the following formula is applied to readjust the length of the disparities vector so that SSTRESS is minimized:

$$\mathbf{D}_k^{*N} = \mathbf{D}_k^*(\mathbf{D}_k'\mathbf{D}_k)(\mathbf{D}_k'\mathbf{D}_k^*)^{-1},$$

where $\mathbf{D}_k^*$ is a column vector with $n(n - 1)/2$ elements containing all the disparities for subject k, $\mathbf{D}_k$ is a column vector with $n(n - 1)/2$ elements containing all the distances for subject k, $\mathbf{D}_k'\mathbf{D}_k$ is the sum of the squared distances, and $\mathbf{D}_k'\mathbf{D}_k^*$ is the sum of the cross-products. The normalized disparities vector $\mathbf{D}_k^{*N}$ is a conditional least squares estimate for the distances, that is, it is the least-squares estimate for a given iteration. The previous $\mathbf{D}^*$ values are replaced by $\mathbf{D}^{*N}$ values, and subsequent steps utilize the normalized disparities.

SSTRESS

The Takane–Young–de Leeuw formula is used:

$$\text{SSTRESS(1)} = S = \left\{ \frac{1}{m} \sum_{k=1}^{m} \left[\frac{\sum_i \sum_j (d_{ijk}^2 - d_{ijk}^{*2})^2}{\sum_i \sum_j d_{ijk}^{*4}} \right] \right\}^{1/2},$$

where d_{ijk}^* values are the normalized disparity measures computed earlier, and d_{ijk} are computed as also shown earlier. Thus SSTRESS is computed from the normalized disparities and the previous set of coordinates and weights.

TERMINATION

The value of SSTRESS is compared to the value of SSTRESS from the previous iteration. If the improvement is less than a specified value (default equals .001), the iteration stops and the output stage has been reached. If not, the program proceeds to the next step. (This step is skipped on the first iteration.)

MODEL ESTIMATION

In ALSCAL the weights and coordinates cannot be solved for simultaneously, so we do it successively. Thus, the model estimation phase consists of two steps: (*a*) estimation of subject weights, and (*b*) estimation of stimulus coordinates.

Estimation of Subject Weights. (This Step Is Skipped for the Simple [i.e., Unweighted] Euclidian Model.) A conditional least-squares estimate of the weights is computed at each iteration:

$$\mathbf{W} \cong \mathbf{D}^*\mathbf{P}(\mathbf{P}'\mathbf{P})^{-1}.$$

This derivation of the computation formula is as follows:
We have found disparities such that:

$$d_{ijk}^* \cong d_{ijk}^2,$$

where

$$d_{ijk}^2 = \sum_{a=1}^{r} w_{ka}(x_{ia} - x_{ja})^2.$$

Let p_{ija} be the unweighted distance between stimuli i and j as projected onto dimension a, that is

$$p_{ija} = (x_{ia} - x_{ja})^2.$$

Then

$$d_{ijk}^{*2} \cong d_{ijk}^2 = \sum_{a=1}^{r} w_{ka}p_{ija}.$$

In matrix notation this is expressed as follows:

$$\mathbf{D}^* = \mathbf{WP}',$$

where $\mathbf{D}^*$ is now an $m \times [n(n-1)/2]$ matrix having one row for every subject and one column for each stimulus pair, $\mathbf{W}$ is an $m \times r$ matrix having one row for every subject and one column for each dimension, and $\mathbf{P}'$ has one row for every dimension and one column for every stimulus pair. We wish to solve for $\mathbf{W}$

$$\mathbf{WP}' \cong \mathbf{D},$$

which we do by noting that

$$\mathbf{WP'P(P'P)}^{-1} = \mathbf{D^*P(P'P)}^{-1}.$$

Therefore,

$$\mathbf{W} = \mathbf{D^*P(P'P)}^{-1}$$

and we have the conditional least-squares estimate for $\mathbf{W}$. We have in fact minimized SSTRESS at this point relative to the previously computed values for stimulus coordinates and optimal scaling. We replace the old subject weights with the newly estimated values.

Estimation of Stimulus Coordinates. This is done, one at a time, utilizing the previously computed values for $\mathbf{D}^*$ (disparities) and weights. Coordinates are determined one at a time by minimizing SSTRESS with regard to a given coordinate. Equation (16.2), which allows us to solve for a given coordinate $x_{\ell e}$, is derived as follows:

$$S = \text{SSTRESS} = \left\{ \frac{1}{m} \sum_k \left[\frac{\sum_i \sum_j (d_{ijk}^2 - d_{ijk}^{*2})^2}{\sum_i \sum_j d_{ijk}^{*4}} \right] \right\}^{1/2},$$

but $\Sigma_i\Sigma_j d_{ijk}^{*4}$ is constant with respect to $x_{\ell e}$, and can be written

$$c_k = \frac{1}{\sum_i \sum_j d_{ijk}^{*4}}$$

then

$$S = \left[\frac{1}{m}\sum_k c_k \sum_i \sum_j (d_{ijk}^2 - d_{ijk}^{*2})^2\right]^{1/2} = \left[\frac{1}{m}\sum_k c_k S_k\right]^{1/2},$$

where

$$S_k = \sum_i \sum_j (d_{ijk}^2 - d_{ijk}^{*2})^2.$$

Thus S is separated into a sum of functions S_k, each of which can be optimized with respect to $x_{\ell e}$.
But

$$d_{ijk}^2 = \sum_a w_{ka}(x_{ia} - x_{ja})^2.$$

Hence,

$$S_k = \sum_i \sum_j \left[\sum_a w_{ka}(x_{ia} - x_{ja})^2 - d_{ijk}^{*2}\right]^2.$$

This can be expanded and written as:

$$S_k = \sum_i \sum_j \left[\sum_{a \neq e} w_{ka}(x_{ia} - x_{ja})^2 + w_{ke}(x_{ie} - x_{je})^2 - d_{ijk}^{*2}\right]^2.$$

Now define

$$a_{ijke}^2 = \frac{\left[d_{ijk}^{*2} - \sum_{a \neq e} w_{ka}(x_{ia} - x_{ja})^2\right]}{w_{ke}}.$$

Thus

$$S_k = w_{ke}^2 \sum_i \sum_j \left[a_{ijke}^2 - (x_{ie} - x_{je})^2\right]^2$$
$$= w_{ke}^2 \sum_i \sum_j (a_{ijke}^2 - x_{ie}^2 + 2x_{ie}x_{je} - x_{je}^2)^2$$

but defining $b_{ijke}^2 = a_{ijke}^2 - x_{je}^2$ (the constant terms) we obtain

$$S_k = w_{ke}^2 \sum_i \sum_j (b_{ijke}^2 - x_{ie}^2 + 2x_{ie}x_{je})^2.$$

We have now isolated the constant terms (in b_{ijke}^2) from the variable terms x_{ie}.

Next the partial derivative of S with respect to a given coordinate $x_{\ell e}$ is found.

$$\frac{\partial S}{\partial x_{\ell e}} = \frac{\partial \frac{1}{m}\sum_k c_k S_k}{\partial x_{\ell e}}.$$

Thus

$$\frac{\partial S}{\partial x_{\ell e}} = \frac{1}{m}\sum_k c_k \frac{\partial S_k}{\partial x_{\ell e}}, \qquad (16.1)$$

$$\frac{\partial S_k}{\partial x_{\ell e}} = \partial_{x_{\ell e}}\left[w_{ke}^2 \sum_i \sum_j (b_{ijke}^2 - x_{ie}^2 + 2x_{ie}x_{je})^2 \right].$$

If

$$\gamma_{ijke} = (b_{ijke}^2 - x_{ie}^2 + 2x_{ie}x_{je}).$$

Then

$$\frac{\partial S_k}{\partial x_{\ell e}} = 2w_{ke}^2 \sum_i \sum_j \gamma_{ijke} \partial \gamma_{ijke x_{\ell e}}$$

$$= 2w_{ke}^2 \sum_i \sum_j \gamma_{ijke}\left[\partial_{x_{\ell e}} b_{ijke}^2 - \partial_{x_{\ell e}} x_{ie}^2 + \partial_{x_{\ell e}} 2x_{ie}x_{je} \right]$$

$$= 2w_{ke}^2 \sum_j \gamma_{\ell jke}[0 - 2x_{\ell e} + 2x_{je}]$$

$$= 4w_{ke}^2 \sum_j \gamma_{\ell jke}[x_{je} - x_{\ell e}]$$

$$= 4w_{ke}^2 \sum_j [b_{\ell jke}^2 - x_{\ell e}^2 + 2x_{\ell e}x_{je}][x_{je} - x_{\ell e}]$$

$$= 4w_{ke}^2 \sum_j [x_{\ell e}^3 - 3x_{\ell e}^2 x_{je} + 2x_{\ell e}x_{je}^2 + b_{\ell jke}^2 x_{je} - b_{\ell jke}^2 x_{\ell e}].$$

Rearranging terms we end up with

$$\frac{\partial S_k}{\partial x_{\ell e}} = 4w_{ke}^2 \sum_j \left[x_{\ell e}^3 - 3x_{\ell e}^2 x_{je} + 2x_{\ell e}x_{je}^2 - b_{\ell jke}^2 x_{\ell e} + b_{\ell jke}^2 x_{je} \right]. \qquad (16.2)$$

This can be substituted back into equation (16.1). This equation with one unknown, $x_{\ell e}$, is then set equal to zero and solved by standard techniques. All the other coordinates except $x_{\ell e}$ are assumed to be constant while we solve for $x_{\ell e}$.

Immediately upon solving for $x_{\ell e}$ we replace the value for $x_{\ell e}$ used on the previous iteration with the newly obtained value, and then proceed to estimate the value for another coordinate. We successively obtain values for each coordinate of point ℓ, one at a time, replacing old values with new ones. This continues for point ℓ until the estimates stabilize. We then move to a new point and proceed until new coordinates for all stimuli are estimated. We then return to the beginning of the optimization algorithm and start another iteration.

16.3. KYST and POLYCON

FORREST W. YOUNG

In this section we describe how the KYST and POLYCON programs work. We discuss these programs simultaneously because they are so similar. In fact, these two programs are more similar than any other pair of programs discussed in this text. We also compare POLYCON and KYST to ALSCAL, since these are the three most similar MDS programs discussed here. Note that these three programs share a common author, thus accounting for their strong similarity.

As described in Chapters 6 and 7, KYST and POLYCON can perform CMDS and RMDS, but not WMDS. When there is only one matrix of data both programs perform a CMDS analysis, and they perform RMDS when there is more than one matrix of data. In the description given here, we assume that there are several matrices of data. There are, however, only occasional differences when there is but one matrix, and these differences are noted in the description.

As with other MDS programs, KYST and POLYCON are iterative programs. Like ALSCAL and MINISSA, each iteration consists of two major substeps, one computing an order-preserving data transformation, the other computing stimulus coordinate values. These two steps are alternated until the iterative process terminates. Both programs are based on the same type of algorithm, called a *negative gradient* algorithm. Furthermore, they both optimize the same function, Kruskal's STRESS index.

Like ALSCAL, both POLYCON and KYST use a least-squares procedure to obtain the order-preserving data transformation. While all three programs are least squares, ALSCAL optimizes a different function than that optimized by KYST and POLYCON (SSTRESS, not STRESS), thus ALSCAL also differs from the others in this substep. The difference is that POLYCON and KYST are least squares in terms of *distances,* whereas ALSCAL is least squares in terms of *squared distances.*

The coordinate estimation substep in KYST and POLYCON is a bit complex, and has the following general structure. Each algorithm starts by determining a direction for moving each point in the configuration. When a point is moved a small amount in the indicated direction, the goodness of fit of the configuration improves. (This direction is called the *negative gradient,* hence, the name of the algorithm.) A direction is determined for each point prior to moving any of the points. Then, all points are moved by a small amount.

Unfortunately, we do not necessarily know how much a *small amount* is, and we may wind up moving the points too far, accidentally worsening the fit. In this case we have to try over again, taking a smaller step in the desired direction, shortening our step until it does result in a better fit. This problem is known as the *step size problem*. KYST has a number of mechanisms for trying to guess the step size, whereas POLYCON is rather primitive in this regard. Unlike ALSCAL the coordinate estimation substep in KYST and POLYCON is not least squares, thus KYST and POLYCON are not ALS procedures. This is probably the most critical difference between the three programs.

We now turn to a detailed description of the KYST and POLYCON negative gradient procedures.

Initial Configuration

1. The first step is to compute an average data matrix over all of the data matrices read in. This is done simply by obtaining the root mean square (RMS) mean, over data matrices O_k, for each element o_{ijk}. (Root mean square means that all values are squared before the mean is calculated, and then the square root of the mean is taken.) We denote the RMS data matrix as O^*.

2. The next step is to obtain the scalar products of the averaged data O^*. This is done by the formula

$$b_{ij.}^* = -1/2(o_{ij.}^{*2} - o_{i.}^{*2} - o_{.j}^{*2} + o_{..}^{*2}),$$

where the $o_{ij.}^{*2}$ are the squares of the elements of O^*, $o_{i.}^{*2}$, $o_{.j}^{*2}$, and $o_{..}^{*2}$ are the row, column, and grand means of the squared averaged data O^*, respectively. Steps 1 and 2 are equivalent to first converting each subject's data into scalar products and then averaging, as is done in the ALSCAL initialization steps 2 and 4.

3. Finally, the average scalar products B^* from step 2 are used to compute the initial stimulus configuration using the classical Young–Housholder multidimensional scaling procedure:

$$B^* = XX',$$

where X is an $n \times r$ matrix of n stimulus points on r dimensions, and X' is the transpose of the X matrix. Matrix X is the initial configuration. This initial configuration is essentially identical to the one prepared by ALSCAL, except for the lack (in POLYCON) of estimating an additive constant.

Optimization Algorithm

1. *Distances:* Distances are computed according to the (unweighted) Euclidean model

$$d_{ij} = \left(\sum_a^r (x_{ia} - x_{ja})^2 \right)^{1/2},$$

where x_{ia} and x_{ja} are the coordinates of stimulus i and j on dimension a. The first set of distances are computed from the coordinates obtained in step 3 of the initialization procedure. After that, the coordinates are obtained from step 3b of the iterative process (see the following). Note that POLY-CON and KYST compute *distances* at this point, whereas ALSCAL computes *squared distances*. Note also that ALSCAL permits the distances to be weighted, whereas POLYCON and KYST do not.

2. *Data transformation:* In KYST and POLYCON the order-preserving data transformation is Kruskal's least-squares monotonic transformation. This yields transformed data (called *disparities*) that are a monotonic transformation of the raw data and a least-squares fit to the distances. The procedure is *exactly* the same as that used in ALSCAL *except* that AL-SCAL obtains a transformation that is a least-squares fit to the squared distances, whereas POLYCON and KYST obtain transformations that are a least-squares fit to the (unsquared) distances (see Table 16.1). When there are ties in the data, both KYST and POLYCON provide the choice of untying the ties (with Kruskal's primary approach) or of leaving ties tied (with his secondary approach). This is identical to ALSCAL, again, except for the use of distances instead of squared distances.

3. *Model Estimation:* The model estimation step consists of several substeps which calculate the negative gradient, move the points, calculate STRESS, and when necessary, change the stepsize and move the points again. We describe each of these substeps below.

3a. The negative gradient is computed. This tells us the direction each point should be moved so that the distances between the moved points will be more like the disparities (transformed data) just computed in step 2. We do not, in this step, actually move the points, we only figure out the direction of optimal movement. The negative gradient direction is determined by computing the partial derivatives for point i on each dimension a. These derivatives are denoted g_{ia}, and are calculated, in both programs, by the formula:

$$g_{ia} = \sum_j^n (d_{ij} - d_{ij}^*)(x_{ia} - x_{ja})/d_{ij},$$

where d_{ij} is the distance between points i and j before they are moved (from step 1), d_{ij}^* is the disparity (transformed similarity) for stimuli i and j (from step 2), and x_{ia} and x_{ja} are the coordinates of points i and j on dimension a before movement (from step 3 of the initialization or step 3b).

The rationale of this formula, and its derivation has been explained geometrically by Young (1975). The vector going from point i through the point with coordinates g_{ia} is the negative gradient direction for point i, and is the direction in which point i will be moved.

3b. Next, the points x_{ia} are all moved a step along their negative gradient directions. This is done, for each point, by adding a proportion of g_{ia} to x_{ia}:

$$x_{ia}^+ = x_{ia} + s(g_{ia}),$$

where x_{ia} is the old (unmoved) coordinate of point i on dimension a, x_{ia}^+ is the new (moved) coordinate, g_{ia} is the gradient, and s is the *step size*. In POLYCON the step size s is set at $s = p(f/t)$ where $p = 1$ initially (it gets changed in step 3d); f is the value of STRESS on the previous iteration, and t is the numerator of STRESS on the previous iteration (on the first iteration STRESS is calculated prior to this step). In KYST, s is calculated as described in step 3d.

3c. The goodness-of-fit, STRESS, is calculated according to the formula:

$$\left[\sum_i^n \sum_j^n (d_{ij} - d_{ij}^*)^2 / \sum_i^n \sum_j^n (d_{ij}^2) \right]^{1/2}.$$

3d. We now modify the step size. The procedure for doing this differs in the two programs, KYST having a fairly sophisticated modification procedure, and POLYCON a fairly rudimentary one.

In POLYCON the current value of STRESS is compared to the value on the previous iteration. If the value has improved we do not change the step size. If the value has not improved, we cut the value of p in half, and we return to step 3b unless the value of p has become "too small," in which case we go to step 4. Of course, if this is the first iteration we have no previous value to compare to, so we do not change the step size.

KYST takes a different approach to determining the best step size. The procedure involves several factors, but is primarily dependent on the angle of the current gradient vector with the previous one. If the angle is nearly zero then we are continuing on in the same direction as before, and we should have taken a bigger step. On the other hand, if the angle is almost a right angle, then we probably have just about the right step size. Finally, if the angle is 180°, we are turning around and backing up, so the step size is clearly too big. KYST uses these notions to modify the step size in a continuous fashion as a function of the running average of such angles over several previous iterations.

4. *Termination:* We now check to see if we should terminate the iterations. The check involves seeing whether the value of STRESS is im-

proving by *too small* an amount, whether the stepsize is *too small,* whether the value of STRESS is *very small,* or whether the number of iterations is *too many.* There are default values given to each of these aspects, and each default can be overridden. The default values and precise definitions of each aspect differ in the two programs. If none of these conditions are met the program goes to step 1 of the iterative process and starts on another iteration. Otherwise, the current coordinates (from step 3b) are used to compute distances (using the procedure in step 1) and disparities (step 2). These values are printed, and the program terminates.

16.4. MINISSA[1]

EDWARD E. ROSKAM
JAMES C. LINGOES

We intend only to give a brief overview of some of the basic concepts involved in the *integrated* program known as MINISSA and what sets it apart from similar programs. But first, a short historical note is in order.

MINISSA was originally developed by J. C. Lingoes of the University of Michigan and E. E. Roskam of the University of Nijmegen in the fall of 1968. Its development is documented in several papers, namely, Roskam (1969a), Roskam and Lingoes (1970), Lingoes and Roskam (1971), and Lingoes and Roskam (1973). Since then, both Lingoes and Roskam elaborated the program further, but independently of each other, and various versions of the program now exist.

The program acronym stands for *M*ichigan–*I*srael–*N*ijmegen–*I*nte-grated–*S*mallest–*S*pace–*A*nalysis: Michigan for Lingoes, Israel for Guttman, and Nijmegen for Roskam, but we like to decode the *N* also as New Jersey to honor Kruskal at Bell Laboratories, whose work is, as much as Guttman's, at the basis of this program. Lingoes and Roskam chose to add the cipher I to the acronym to be in line with the naming convention of the Guttman–Lingoes series of nonmetric programs, thereby anticipating a MINISSA-II, a MINISSAR-II, and others. Such programs have indeed been developed at Nijmegen, but are known under other rubrics, namely MINICPA (paralleling SSA-II) and MINIRSA (paralleling SSAR-II) (see Lingoes, 1973, for a description of the Michigan extensive nonmetric program series).

Since computers usually have a dislike for long names, Roskam decided to abbreviate all the names in his set of programs, for example, MNCPAEX, referring to the experimental version of the MINI program for conditional proximity analysis. The original version of MINISSA is still available at

---

[1] An abbreviated and updated, modified version of *MINISSA Standard Version,* E. E. Roskam, 1973, Nijmegen Math. Psychol., Univ. of Nijmegen, Nijmegen, Holland.

Nijmegen (known as MNSSAOR). Roskam developed another version, incorporating Monte Carlo procedures, for further experimentation (known as MNSSAEX).

For routine applications, a simplified version was developed at Nijmegen, omitting many of the options which were available in the original and experimental versions. This shortened version is referred to in Nijmegen as the *standard version* or MNSSAST. MNSSAST was first made available in May, 1969, and underwent minor corrections and alterations in subsequent years. A major revision was made in 1973 and the present version has incorporated the options for either a Euclidean or city-block metric (in contrast, MNSSAOR includes all Minkowski metrics) and the option for the primary and secondary approaches to ties (which was absent from MNSSAOR).

Apart from these three Nijmegen versions, the Michigan version of the program was developed by Lingoes and is known and documented as MINISSA-I(M). In distinction, the Nijmegen family should be called MINISSA-I(N) and is so identified in Lingoes and Roskam (1973). The latter paper provides a detailed description of the options available in MINISSA-I(M). We shall confine our efforts here to describing features common to the Michigan and Nijmegen versions and, for convenience, shall simply refer to this method as MINISSA hereafter.

Description of the MINISSA Method

The following description applies to most MINI programs. Further details concerning the computational characteristics are presented in Lingoes and Roskam (1971, 1973). A mathematical discussion appears in Roskam (1969b), while a recent review of several MINI programs can be found in Roskam (1979) and Lingoes (1979).

PURPOSE

Given the rank order or ratings of the (dis)similarities among n objects (say, stimuli), the purpose of the algorithm is to find the coordinates of n points, representing the stimuli, in an m-dimensional space, such that the distances among these points are in approximately the same rank order as the data. Such can always be achieved perfectly in general in n-2 dimensions (Lingoes, 1971).

MEASUREMENT MODEL AND CRITERION FOR
GOODNESS OF FIT

Let the stimuli or points be indexed by $i, j, = 1, 2, \ldots, n$.
Let the coordinates be written as $x_{ia}, a = 1, 2, \ldots, m$.
The *distance* d_{ij} between two points is defined by:

$$d_{ij} = \{\sum_a |x_{ia} - x_{ja}|^u\}^{1/u} \quad (u = 1,2). \tag{16.3}$$

For $u = 2$, (16.3) is the familiar Euclidean distance metric and for $u = 1$ we have the so-called city-block metric.

Let the *dissimilarities* be symbolized by δ_{ij}. These can be either ranking numbers, for example, running from 1, 2, . . . , through $n(n-1)/2$ or any set of coefficients (given or derived), for example, as obtained from a judgment task or as calculated by some subroutine as would be correlations. These values have only an ordinal interpretation within the context of the MINISSA procedure. They are usually arranged as the elements of a lower-triangular data matrix (because of symmetry), but there exist many subroutines to handle other forms of input. The diagonal elements δ_{ii} (self-[dis]similarities) are either absent or ignored in the analysis.

We refer to the set of coordinates, x_{ia}, as the *configuration*.

The *stress* of the configuration is defined as:

$$S = \left[\left\{ \sum_{i>j} [d_{ij} - f(\delta_{ij})]^2 \right\} \Big/ \sum_{i>j} d_{ij}^2 \right]^{1/2} \quad \text{(SFORM 1),} \qquad (16.4)$$

where $f(\delta_{ij})$ is a real number assigned to the dissimilarity δ_{ij}, such that $f(\delta_{ij}) \geqslant f(\delta_{kl})$ whenever $\delta_{ij} \geqslant \delta_{kl}$.

There are basically two ways of obtaining the values of $f(\delta_{ij})$, namely, (a) Kruskal's *monotone regression procedure* ($\hat{d}_{ij}$ or *d*-hat) and (b) Guttman's *rank-image procedure* (d_{ij}^* or *d*-star).

Details of each of these procedures are given in the following.

The objective now is to *minimize the loss function, stress, in (16.4) by moving the configuration,* after first providing a well-chosen initial configuration (see p. 366).

An alternative to Kruskal's (1964) stress coefficient S is the Guttman–Lingoes *coefficient of alienation K* (Guttman, 1968). The latter loss function is defined in terms of an intermediate coefficient ϕ (Lingoes, 1966). When d^* is substituted for $f(\delta_{ij})$, the stress is approximately equal to the coefficient of alienation (Roskam, 1969a; Lingoes & Roskam, 1973).

The *raw stress,* which is equivalent to Guttman–Lingoes' *raw phi* is:

$$\phi_0 = S_0 = \sum_{i>j} [d_{ij} - f(\delta_{ij})]^2 \quad \text{(RAW PHI/STRESS),} \qquad (16.5)$$

and the coefficient of alienation K is:

$$K = \left[1 - \left\{ \sum_{i>j} d_{ij} \cdot f(\delta_{ij}) \right\}^2 \Big/ \sum_{i>j} d_{ij}^2 \cdot \sum_{i>j} \{f(\delta_{ij})\}^2 \right]^{1/2} \quad \text{(ALIENATION).} \qquad (16.6)$$

The following relations between these two coefficients can be derived: (a) if $f(\delta_{ij}) = \hat{d}_{ij}$ then $K = S = \sin(d_{..},\hat{d}_{..})$ and (b) if $f(\delta_{ij}) = d_{ij}^*$ then $K = S[1 - (.5S)^2]^{1/2} = \sin(d_{..},d^*_{..})$, by virtue of: (c) $\Sigma d_{ij}^2 = \Sigma d_{ij}^{*2}$ and $\Sigma \hat{d}_{ij}d_{ij} = \Sigma \hat{d}_{ij}^2$.

In both cases, S is strictly monotone with K, so that it does not matter whether we minimize either coefficient. Although S and K are thus equivalent, and even identical if $\hat{d}$ is used in (16.4) and (16.6), it has become customary to use S *in conjunction with* $\hat{d}$, Kruskal's monotone regression, and K *in connection with* d^*, Guttman's rank images. This usage is also adopted in the printed output of MINISSA: K is always calculated in terms of d^* and S is computed in terms of $\hat{d}$. One should, however, be aware that d^* and $\hat{d}$ are hardly ever identical (bounds relating these two coefficients based on their respective definitions are given in [Lingoes & Roskam, 1979]).

PLAYING PING-PONG

The iterative process for minimizing our loss functions is analogous to a game of ping-pong. We start with an initial set of monotone values (we simply take ranking numbers) and find a fairly adequate set of coordinates X. The configuration X generates its set of d's. We then determine the monotone values, $f(\delta)$, which match these d's, using either monotone regression or rank-image permutation. The latter is called the second phase of the process and we have then completed one cycle, after which we compute K or S. We now switch back to finding another set of coordinates X, whose distances fit best (or approximate a best fit) to the values $f(\delta)$, which is known as the first phase. The cycle thus consists of determining an optimal X (the first phase), computing a monotone transformation using either d^* or $\hat{d}$ (the second phase), and evaluating our loss function K or S. When our fit is deemed sufficiently low or the change in fit over iterations is minuscule or nil, the ping-pong game is concluded.

The iterative process is indexed by the superscript s, parenthesized. Thus, $X^{(s)}$ is the configuration matrix of points at iteration s. At each iteration, the first phase consists in finding an improved configuration $X^{(s+1)}$, which fits best to the monotone values, $f(\delta)^{(s)}$. After this, the second phase finds an improved set of monotone values $f(\delta)^{(s+1)}$ which fit to the distances $d^{(s+1)}$ obtained from $X^{(s+1)}$. After completing the second phase we compute the coefficient of alienation $K^{(s+1)}$ or stress $S^{(s+1)}$.

The fit at iteration $s + 1$ is compared to that of iteration s and a number of tests are performed. The most important one is to test if the fit has sufficiently decreased to warrant continuation of the iterations; if so, s is incremented by 1 and the cycling process is continued. Other tests are: Have at least a minimum number of iterations been performed? Have at most a maximum number of iterations been carried out? If our loss has increased (for example, in the rank-image approach), we then take steps to save the best configuration and alter our tactics from rank images to monotone regression values, and, hence, proceed.

The first phase in MINISSA is itself an iterative process nested within the s iterations. First phase iterations are similarly indexed by t. Further details about the iterative process will be given in the sections on the first phase and in the sections on the second phase (it should be noted that these designations are somewhat arbitrary).

The iterative process has to start somewhere; this calls for a procedure for determining an initial configuration. However, when the user has some reasonable hypothesis about the final configuration, for example, from a metric MDS or factor analysis solution, he or she should use this information as input and the iterative procedure will take off from there.

Finally, after convergence (which is assured by our procedure in MINISSA, see de Leeuw and Heiser [1979]) the configuration is normalized.

THE INITIAL CONFIGURATION

The initial configuration (when not supplied by the user) uses only the ordinal information in the data. It calculates $X^{(0)}$ by finding the principal components of a matrix C, defined by:

$$c_{ij} = \begin{cases} 1 - \Sigma_k \rho_{ik}/\ell & (i = j) \\ 1 - \rho_{ij}/\ell & (i \neq j) \end{cases}, \tag{16.7}$$

where ρ_{ij} is the rank number of δ_{ij} in the data (the smallest ρ corresponding to the [smallest]largest [dis]similarity) and ℓ is the largest ρ, that is, $n(n - 1)/2$. Details justifying this choice of initial configuration can be found in Lingoes and Roskam (1973).

THE FIRST PHASE IN MINISSA

S, given a set of monotone values, is minimized with respect to X by a method known as *steepest descent*. That is, we move the values of X and, hence, the d's along a direction where the d's will come closer to the monotone values $f(\delta)$ and, therefore, the stress will decrease. The gradient method consists of calculating:

$$x_{ia}^{(t+1)} = x_{ia}^{(t)} - \alpha_t \{\partial S/\partial x_{ia}\}^{(t)}, \tag{16.8}$$

where α is the (optimally chosen) step size. Application of the method of steepest descent calls for the calculation of the partial derivatives of S with respect to X. A slightly different way of obtaining basically the same formula consists in putting the partial derivatives simultaneously to zero and solving the resulting equations iteratively.

There are two variants implemented in MNSSAST for performing the steepest descent method. One is called the *hard squeeze*, while the other is termed the *soft squeeze* (terminology due to Guttman [1968]). The *hard squeeze* minimizes the normalized stress in (16.4), while the *soft squeeze* minimizes the raw stress in (16.5), the method of choice in MINISSA-I(M). Experience seems to favor the soft squeeze approach when the monotone transformation is in terms of rank images, while the hard squeeze is better, although more complicated, in conjunction with monotone regression values for $f(\delta)$.

Explicit expressions for (16.8), for the hard squeeze, minimizing S, and for the soft squeeze, minimizing raw stress and the formulae used to monitor the step size are given in Lingoes and Roskam (1973).

Here we must add a brief note about the method used in counting iterations. The initial configuration is denoted by $X^{(0)}$, that is, $s = 0$. Calculating the initial configuration is the first phase at iteration $s = 0$. After that, we compute the distances d_{ij} and we then enter the second phase to compute $f(\delta)$, the second phase, which is described later. This completes iteration $s = 0$. We now return to the first phase, which consists of one or more iterative improvements of $X^{(0)}$, which now places us in iteration $s = 1$. Hence, writing $X^{(s,t)}$ to indicate s iterations and first phase t iterations, we have the sequence:

$$X^{(1,0)} = X^{(0)}; X^{(1,1)}; X^{(1,2)}; \ldots; X^{(1,t)}; \ldots; X^{(1,t_{max})}.$$

Having thus completed the first phase of the first iteration, we perform the second phase of the first iteration and evaluate the stress or coefficient of alienation (testing for convergence). The second phase does not affect X. After the second phase, we increment s by 1 and then enter the first phase of the second iteration, producing the sequence:

$$X^{(2,0)} = X^{(1,t_{max})}; X^{(2,1)}; \ldots; X^{(2,t)}; \ldots; X^{(2,t_{max})}.$$

In general, $X^{(s+1,0)} = X^{(s,t_{max})}$. In MINISSA, t^{max} is set at 5 when rank images are used and to 1 when monotone regression values are employed for defining $f(\delta)$. In the latter case, t is redundant.

THE SECOND PHASE IN MINISSA

As indicated, we can choose between two possibilities for defining the monotone values $f(\delta)$, namely, monotone regression or rank-image permutation. Experience has indicated that the rank-image method is more efficient computationally and tends to be more robust (in diminishing the chances of a local minimum solution or of degeneracy). Therefore, MINISSA performs first a number of iterations which minimize the raw stress (soft squeeze) using the rank-image transformation and then performs a series of iterations to minimize the normalized stress (with the hard squeeze for MNSSAST, but with a continuation of the soft-squeeze for MINISSA-I(M) after an appropriate normalization) using the monotone regression transformation. Of course, when the fit is perfect, that is, S or $K = 0$, there is no point in switching to $\hat{d}$.

Monotone Regression: $\hat{d}$. Imagine an (arbitrary) configuration X from which we compute distances by (16.3). How well do X's distances fit the data, that is, how well does the rank order of the d's correspond to the rank order of the δ's given as input?

Kruskal's (1964) approach to this question consists in finding a set of values, $\hat{d}$, which are monotone with the data and, at the same time, minimize the sum of squares $\Sigma(d_{ij} - \hat{d}_{ij})^2$ ($i > j = 1, 2, \ldots, n$). In other words: The $\hat{d}$'s are a monotone transformation of the data, such that they best match the d's among the n points in a least-squares sense.

The algorithm for finding the values for $\hat{d}^{(s)}$, given $d^{(s)}$, is called, somewhat unspecifically, the *fitting algorithm*. It can briefly be described as follows:

First, put the pairs of subscripts $\langle i,j \rangle$ in the order of (dis)similarities as given by the data, the (smallest)largest (dis)similarity coming first and the (largest)smallest (dis)similarity coming last. Taking this order of the subscripts, arrange the d's accordingly, that is, the d_{ij} that belongs to the (smallest)largest (dis)similarity is written first and the d_{ij} that belongs to the (largest)smallest (dis)similarity is written last. If the fit were perfect, the d's would now show an order of (increasing)decreasing magnitude. Usually they do not show this order.

Next, we start with the first d (the d for the [smallest]largest [dis]similarity), and unless the next d is (larger)smaller, we replace it and its successor by their common average; we then check if the d coming third in sequence is (larger)smaller than this average. If it is, the average is said to be *up-satisfied*, but if it is not, we calculate the average of the three d's (*not* the average of the current d and previous d's which are represented by averages). In general, for every d or average of d's we test if it is (larger)smaller than the preceding d or average of d's (and when this condition is met our algorithm is said to be *down-satisfied*). We then test for up-satisfaction, that is, does the current d or new average d have the proper order with respect to the next d in the sequence? If the d is not down-satisfied, we merge with the preceding d or d's and compute a new average. If it is not up-satisfied we merge with subsequent d and compute the average. This process of testing for upward and downward satisfaction, merging and averaging whenever the conditions are not met, is continued until we have worked ourselves through all the d's. The result of this procedure is a set of non-(decreasing)increasing values of the averages of *blocks* of d's, where a block can consist of one or more d's which have been averaged. Each average is now the $\hat{d}$ value for those elements $\langle i,j \rangle$ belonging to the block which comprise it. If the fit is perfect, each block consists of a single element, but if the fit is the worst possible, there will be but one block consisting of the average of all the d's (which could happen if the choice of initial configuration was poor, yielding d's which were antimonotone with the data, for example). For further details on the fitting algorithm, the reader should consult Kruskal (1964) and for a worked out example, see Roskam (1979, p. 334).

Rank-Image Permutation: d^*. Quite another way of defining a set of values which are monotone with the data and which can serve to express the goodness of fit of the coordinates' distances to the data is Guttman's (1968) rank-image principle. The array of rank images is simply a permutation of the array of distances. The procedure is as follows: Imagine the pairs of subscripts ordered according to the data (low to high for dissimilarity data and high to low for similarity data). Let d_{kl} be the smallest distance (where k,l may or may not correspond with the i,j occupying the first position in the sequence of subscript pairs for the data) and place d_{kl} in the first position. The next smallest distance is put in the next position, etc., until we have all the distances in the same order as the data (ignoring the identifying subscripts of the d's, thus, for example, d_{13} may occupy the position of δ_{27}). The d_{kl} is said to be the rank image of d_{ij} if they have the *same* position in the sequence and we write $d_{ij}^* \equiv d_{kl}$ to denote this. The d^*'s are ordered low to high and are monotone with the data. The d's, however, in this sequence may be in any order and retain their identifying subscripts (thus, d_{ij} corresponds with δ_{ij}).

The rank images d^* do not in general minimize $\Sigma(d_{ij} - d_{ij}^*)^2$ *for a given set of d's*. This raises some problems in algorithm construction and for convergence, which are addressed in Roskam (1969a) and in Lingoes and Roskam (1973); see Roskam (1979) for a worked out example.

THE PRIMARY VERSUS THE SECONDARY APPROACHES TO TIES

When there are ties in the data, we have essentially two options for dealing with them. One option is the so-called *primary approach:* It is the simplest and it breaks the ties in such a way that the goodness of fit is optimized. This tie breaking is accomplished by simply defining the rank order among tied data elements, δ, as being the same as the rank order of the d's corresponding to them, which, of course, change with every s iteration. Consequently, there are never violations of monotonicity within a tied block when the primary approach is used. In the algorithm, the only thing we have to do to implement this approach for tied subsets is to permute the $\langle i,j \rangle$ subscript pairs to correspond with the appropriately ordered d's. After performing this permutation, we proceed as outlined in executing the monotone regression or rank image algorithms.

Our other option is called the *secondary approach* to ties. It consists in the requirement that tied data have equal distances, which is implemented by replacing the d's in any tied block by their average *prior* to executing the fitting algorithm in the case of monotone regression. In determining the $\hat{d}$'s, the entire block of tied values is treated as a unit in testing up and down sequence order and in merging and averaging if either test fails.

The secondary approach for ties is simpler for rank images: Replace the rank images in a tied block by their average.

NORMALIZATION

The matrix of coordinates X is normalized prior to each s iteration, that is, prior to the calculation of $f(\delta)$ in the second phase. The normalization consists in setting the mean for each coordinate to zero and then multiplying each element of X by a constant, such that the length or squared norm of X is unity (MINISSA-I(M)) or n (MNSSAST), yielding a sum of squares for the distances which is n or n^2, respectively, when the metric is Euclidean.

When we achieve our final configuration, $X^{(s=\max)}$, we rotate our configuration to a principal axes rotation, such that $\Sigma_i x_{ia} x_{ib} = 0$ (for all dimension
pairs a,b; where $a \neq b$; $i = 1, 2, \ldots, n$), but *only* when the metric is
Euclidean. Such an orientation of the axes implies that the different dimensions are uncorrelated. No such rotation is permitted, however, in the
case of the city-block metric. It can be easily shown that our normalizations
and rotations preserve the relative sizes of the distances and this is the only
important factor in measuring goodness of fit nonmetrically.

INTERPRETATION OF S OR K

No rigorous rules can be given as to what is a high stress or a high
coefficient of alienation (cf. the guidelines provided by Kruskal, 1964), but
Lingoes and Borg (1980) offer some *exact* procedures for assessing differences in fit, based on a linear prediction model, for *any* MDS procedure
(metric or nonmetric), which obviates the need for statistical simulations.

K is typically larger than S by a factor of about 1.4. One should remember,
however, that K is used with rank images only and that S is based on
monotone regression values and that MINISSA minimizes S in terms of
$\hat{d}$.

The use of d^* values serves both a tactical purpose in speeding up
convergence and in minimizing the risk of local minima entrapment. Over
and above these robust properties of rank images, the d^*'s define a loss
function in their own right and a stronger model than that based on $\hat{d}$'s.
Thus, the inequalities following (16.4) would need modification if we were
to use d^*'s exclusively, that is, $d_{ij} > d_{kl}$ whenever $d^*_{ij} > d^*_{kl}$ and $d^*_{ij} = d^*_{kl}$
whenever $d_{ij} = d_{kl}$ (*strong monotonicity*, when there are ties to be main-
tained in the data) and $d_{ij} \geq d_{kl}$ whenever $\delta_{ij} > \delta_{kl}$ (*semi-strong monotonicity*,
when there are no ties in the data). $\hat{d}$ values, on the other hand, may tie
the d's irrespective of whether ties exist or do not exist in the data, yielding
semi-weak monotonicity (if ties are to be maintained as in the secondary
approach) or *weak monotonicity* (if there are ties and the primary approach
is used to break ties). In general, maintaining or creating ties goes against
achieving the smallest space in which to embed one's points.

Additional properties of rank images are given in Lingoes (1981a), who
demonstrates, among other things, that r_s, Spearman's rank order correlation coefficient, is equal to μ_r, the mean of the Pearson product moment
correlation coefficients, over *all* possible monotone transformations of one's
data. It can also be shown that while it may be true that $\hat{d}$ is closer to d
than is d^* to d, that, similarly, d^* is closer to δ than is $\hat{d}$ to δ, which is
yet another way of saying that rank images are more robust than are
monotone regression values.

When the same data are analyzed in different dimensionalities, one should
expect lower stress with a higher dimensionality; sometimes this is not
what actually happens. Such contrary results may be caused by a local
minimum entrapment, or from the fact that convergence was not achieved

in terms of the number of iterations allowed, or a degeneracy occurred at a lower dimensionality. The secondary approach to ties will, in general, give a higher stress value than will the primary approach (if there are ties in the data, of course); if this is not found when both approaches are used, one should conclude that the anomalous result is due to a local minimum. Procedures for handling these difficulties are now available (as well as for testing structural hypotheses [see Lingoes & Borg, 1978; Borg & Lingoes, 1980]).

INTERPRETATIONS OF CONFIGURATIONS

The reader is referred to the three chapters in Lingoes *et al.* (1979) for some principles of interpretation *via* the use of *spatial directions, manifolds,* and *regions* (also see Lingoes, 1981b) for a particular emphasis on the latter mode of interpretation. For other than *unconditional proximity data* (addressed by MINISSA), there are approximately 30 models and designs incorporated in the Guttman–Lingoes Nonmetric Program Series (1973) and in the Roskam MINI-series (Roskam, 1979).

16.5. INDSCAL[2]

J. DOUGLAS CARROLL

INDSCAL (*IN*dividual *D*ifferences multidimensional *SCAL*ing) is (admittedly, but somewhat intentionally ambiguously) the name of a *model,* a *method,* and a particular *computer program* for three-way (or many-way) multidimensional scaling (MDS). The basic reference describing the INDSCAL model and method is the paper by Carroll and Chang (1970a). Horan (1969) contains the earliest published discussion of the weighted Euclidean model now widely known as the INDSCAL model. Horan's paper did not, however, provide a method for fitting the model to three-way proximities data, nor did he consider explicitly the exceedingly important property, here called *dimensional uniqueness,* which numerical analysts or statisticians might refer to as *identifiability* of the dimensions defined in the INDSCAL model. Other references bearing on different aspects of this model and method are Carroll (1972), Carroll and Wish (1974a,b) and Wish and Carroll (1974). For a recent general discussion of two-way, three-way, and many-way methods of multidimensional scaling for not only proximities data, but also dominance (e.g., preferences) and other types of data in terms of spatial, as well as nonspatial and hybrid (i.e., mixed spatial and nonspatial models) see Carroll and Arabie (1980).

[2] The figures in this section are from *Contemporary Developments in Mathematical Psychology,* Volume II, edited by D. H. Krantz, R. C. Atkinson, R. D. Luce, and P. Suppes. W. H. Freeman and Company. Copyright © 1974.

The INDSCAL *model* is a particular model for individual differences similarities or dissimilarities or other three-way *proximities* data, that assumes these data arise via a process that relates them closely (via linear, monotonic, or other well specified functions) to weighted Euclidean distances defined in a certain way on a common (or *group*) space underlying the stimuli or other entities on which the proximities are defined. Specifically, the INDSCAL model can be expressed in the form:

$$F_i[\delta_{jk}^{(i)}] \cong d_{jk}^{(i)},\qquad(16.9)$$

where

$$d_{jk}^{(i)} = \left[\sum_{t=1}^{r} w_{it}(x_{jt} - x_{kt})^2\right]^{1/2},\qquad(16.10)$$

where $\delta_{jk}^{(i)}$ is the dissimilarity (say) between stimulus (or other objects) j and k for subject (or other data source) i, while the functions F_i will generally be considered to be linear, in the metric case, monotonic in the nonmetric case, or other specified functional forms in other cases. It is important to note, however, that a different F_i is assumed, in general, for each separate individual, so that INDSCAL is (in that sense) a matrix *conditional* model. Essentially, then, INDSCAL generalizes two-way Euclidean MDS by substituting a *weighted* Euclidean metric for the ordinary (unweighted) Euclidean metric. Different patterns of weights and different functions relating distances to data are allowed for each individual or other data source. The symbol $\cong$ can be taken here (again, somewhat intentionally ambiguously) as meaning "equals, except for error terms whose distribution form and other characteristics are not further specified."

Figures 16.2 and 16.3 contrast the type of data and resulting output of two-way MDS (shown in Figure 16.2) with that for the INDSCAL model and method of three-way MDS (shown in Figure 16.3). As can be seen the

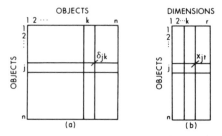

Figure 16.2. The typical (a) input and (b) output for two-way MDS. The input is a single $n \times n$ square symmetric matrix (or half matrix) of proximities (similarities or dissimilarities) data. $\delta_{jk} \equiv$ proximity of stimuli, or other objects, j and k. Symmetry implies $\delta_{kj} = \delta_{jk}$, for all j, k, so only a half matrix is required in most instances. Diagonals may be present or absent. The MDS output is a single $n \times r$ matrix of coordinates of the n stimuli in r dimensions ($x_{jt} \equiv$ coordinate of jth stimulus on the tth dimension).

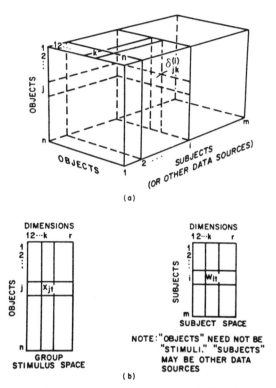

(a)

(b)

GROUP
STIMULUS SPACE

SUBJECT SPACE

NOTE:"OBJECTS" NEED NOT BE
"STIMULI." "SUBJECTS"
MAY BE OTHER DATA
SOURCES

Figure 16.3. Schematic diagrams of typical (a) input and (b) output for three-way MDS. The input is a set of m (≥ 2) $n \times n$ square symmetric data matrices (or half matrices), one for each of m subjects or other data sources. $\delta_{jk}^{(i)}$ is the proximity of objects j and k for Subject i. Symmetry implies $\delta_{kj}^{(i)} = \delta_{jk}^{(i)}$ for all i, j, k. The output is comprised of two matrices, an $n \times r$ matrix of coordinates of the n objects on r dimensions (group stimulus space) and an $m \times r$ matrix of weights of m subjects on the same r dimensions (subject space). Both of these can be plotted graphically. A private space for each subject can also be constructed (as illustrated in Figure 16.4) by applying (square roots of) the subject weights to stimulus (object) dimensions (according to equation [16.13.]).

input for INDSCAL (along with other methods of three-way MDS of proximities data, such as those described and discussed in Carroll and Wish, 1974b) comprises a three-way (e.g., stimuli × stimuli × subjects) data array of similarities, dissimilarities, or other *proximities* data symmetric in two of its indices (e.g., the two that correspond to stimuli). Each two-way slice (in the plane of the page in Figure 16.3) is simply an ordinary two-way square symmetric matrix of proximities data. Thus, the input to two-way MDS, each matrix representing data from a different subject or other data source corresponding to the third way.

While the output for two-way MDS is (generally speaking) a single matrix of stimulus coordinates (which can, of course, be plotted graphically in various ways) the output of INDSCAL is *two* matrices—one defining the coordinates of the group stimulus (or object) space, the other defining what is usually called the subject space (in which the weights for different subjects or other data sources are plotted).

A more geometric interpretation of the INDSCAL model is provided by Equation (16.11). Recall that x_{jt} is the tth coordinate of the jth stimulus in what we call the *group stimulus space*. We may furthermore conceive of each individual (or other data source) as having what we may call a *private perceptual space* whose general coordinate we will designate as $y_{jt}^{(i)}$. The $y^{(i)}$'s, however, are derived from the x's by the very simple relation expressed in Equation (16.11)

$$y_{jt}^{(i)} = w_{it}^{1/2} x_{jt}.$$ (16.11)

The distances for individual i are simply ordinary Euclidean distances computed in that subject's own private stimulus space, as in Equation (16.12)

$$d_{jk}^{(i)} = \left[\sum_{t}^{r} (y_{jt}^{(i)} - y_{kt}^{(i)})^2 \right]^{1/2}.$$ (16.12)

It can easily be seen that by substituting Equation (16.11) into (16.12) we get (16.10). Thus (16.11) and (16.12), which together provide an alternate interpretation of the weighted generalization of the ordinary Euclidean metric defined in (16.10), express the INDSCAL model in terms of a particularly simple class of transformations of the common space followed by computation of the ordinary Euclidean metric. The class of transformations can be described algebraically as linear transformations, with the transformation matrix constrained to be diagonal (sometimes called a strain transformation). More simply, it amounts to simply rescaling each dimension (by the square root of that particular subject's weight for that dimension). Geometrically we can think of this as differentially stretching or shrinking each dimension by a factor proportional to the square root of the weight (only the relative sizes of the weights are important, here, however).

Hypothetical Example Illustrating the INDSCAL Model

This more geometric interpretation of the model is illustrated in Figure 16.4. The group stimulus space in the upper left shows nine stimuli, A through I, in a lattice configuration; the subject space in the upper right shows the weights, or perceptual saliences, of the dimensions for nine hypothetical subjects. These weights can be thought of as stretching factors that are applied to the dimensions of the group stimulus space.

We may think of the effect of these differential weights as producing, for each subject, a private perceptual space by rescaling (stretching and

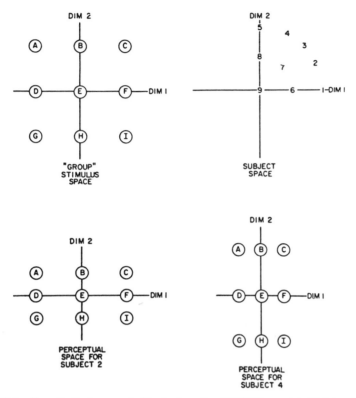

Figure 16.4. Hypothetical example illustrating the INDSCAL model. Weights from the subject space are applied to the dimensions of the *group* stimulus space to produce private perceptual spaces for Subjects 2 and 4. (While technically it is the square roots of the weights that are applied, the first power weights have been used in this illustration to accentuate the effects of differential weighting.)

contracting) the dimensions of the group stimulus space. In the illustration, for example, Subject 3 has equal weights for the two dimensions; that subject's private perceptual space would therefore look exactly the same as the group stimulus space (except for an overall scale factor that could stretch or contract both dimensions uniformly, leaving their relative saliences unchanged).

The private spaces for Subjects 2 and 4 are shown in the lower left-hand and right-hand corners of Figure 16.4, respectively. Subject 2, who weights dimension 1 more highly than dimension 2, has a perceptual space *compressed* along the dimension 2 axis (or what amounts to the same thing, stretched in the dimension 1 direction). The reverse applies to Subject 4, who has a higher weight on the second than on the first dimension.

An important property of INDSCAL is one often called *dimensional uniqueness*. This means that, unlike ordinary (two-way) MDS, the dimensions are uniquely determined, and cannot be rotated or otherwise transformed without changing the solution in an essential way. Psychologically this means that INDSCAL dimensions are assumed to correspond to fundamental physiological, perceptual, or conceptual processes whose strength, or salience, may differ from individual to individual (whether because of genetic or environmental differences, or simply because of differing interpretations of instructions, or the like). Mathematically, a rotation or other transformation of coordinate system will change the family of permissible transformations of the group stimulus space, and thus the family of possible individual metrics. (This can be seen quite clearly in the hypothetical example by noting that, say, a 45° rotation would change the family of private perceptual spaces from one of different rectangles to one of different rhombuses.) Statistically, a rotation or other transformation of axes will generally deteriorate the fit of the data to the INDSCAL model (except in certain special cases, to be detailed later). In the metric case, to be described later, the goodness of fit is measured by the root mean square correlation (over subjects) between scalar products derived from the input similarities or dissimilarities and scalar products computed from the solution. The solution is, of course, designed to optimize the measure of fit. The property of dimensional uniqueness proves to be one of the most important aspects of INDSCAL, as it obviates the problem of rotation of axes in almost all cases. This problem is one that (particularly in the case of higher-dimensional solutions) frequently complicates and often attenuates the utility of MDS analysis. The value of this property should become clearer in the discussion of applications.

Distance of a subject from the origin in the subject space is roughly a measure of the proportion of the variance of the data for that subject accounted for by the multidimensional solution (comparable to the concept of communality in factor analysis). Although Subjects 3 and 7 have the same pattern of dimension weights, a higher proportion of the variance in Subject 3's data could be accounted for by the hypothetical INDSCAL solution. The data for subjects closer to the origin are generally less well accounted for by the INDSCAL analysis, so that the dimensions of the group stimulus space in toto are less salient for them. The lower *communality* for subjects closer to the origin may be due to idiosyncratic dimensions not uncovered in the r-dimensional solution or to lower reliability (more random error) in their data.

Subject 9, who is precisely at the origin, is completely "out of" this analysis. Either he or she is responding completely randomly or is simply "marching to a different drummer" (responding reliably to a completely different set of dimensions).

The possibility of zero weights allows as a special case the situation in which two or more groups of subjects have completely different perceptual spaces, with no necessary communality between them. This situation can be accommodated by defining a group stimulus space whose dimensions are the sum total of the dimensions for the two different groups of subjects— each subgroup has nonzero weights on only one subset of dimensions.

For example, if one group perceives the stimuli in terms of dimensions A and B while the second perceives them in terms of C and D, we may accommodate these two completely different "points of view" (to use Tucker & Messick's, 1963, terminology) by assuming a four-dimensional space comprised of dimensions A, B, C, and D. Thus, the Tucker and Messick points of view model can be accommodated as a special case of INDSCAL. INDSCAL is, of course, more interesting and appropriate when there is some communality in perception among the subjects (which is usually the case).

The Metric INDSCAL Method of Analysis of Three-Way Proximities

The INDSCAL method of analysis for the metric version of the IND-SCAL model is a direct generalization of the "classical" two-way MDS method described in Torgerson's (1958) book. As in the classical method, each (two-way) symmetric matrix of proximities is first converted to dissimilarities (i.e., if the initial data are similarities the scale is reversed by multiplying the values by -1 or subtracting them from the largest value; if the initial data are already dissimilarities no transformation would be done at this point).

The next step, as in the classical metric two-way MDS procedure, is to convert the *dissimilarities* (interpreted as estimates of *comparative distances,* that is, values related to estimated distances by a positive linear function) to estimated distances. This is the process usually referred to as *estimation of the additive constant.*

Under metric assumptions we may assume, without loss of generality, that

$$d_{jk}^{(i)} \cong \delta_{jk}^{(i)} + c^{(i)}. \tag{16.13}$$

Dropping the (i) superscript for now, the smallest constant c guaranteeing satisfaction of the *triangle inequality* $(d_{j\ell} \leq d_{jk} + d_{k\ell})$ *for all triples* (j,k,ℓ) *can be shown to be*

$$c_{\min} = \max_{(j,k,\ell)} (\delta_{j\ell} - \delta_{jk} - \delta_{k\ell}). \tag{16.14}$$

(Note: $c_{\min}$ *may* be negative.)

This is the additive constant method, for converting comparative distances (i.e., interval scale distance estimates) into absolute distances (i.e., ratio scale distance estimates) described in Torgerson's (1958) book as the "one-dimensional subspace" scheme (assuming at least three points lie exactly on a straight line in the space). It is in many respects the simplest and most straightforward technique for additive constant estimation, and is the one used in the metric INDSCAL procedure.

CONVERSION OF ESTIMATED DISTANCES TO ESTIMATED SCALAR PRODUCTS

If $\mathbf{x}_j = (x_{j1}, x_{j2}, \ldots, x_{jr})$ and $\mathbf{x}_k = (x_{k1}, x_{k2}, \ldots, x_{kr})$ are two vectors in r-dimensional space, their *scalar product*, usually written as $\mathbf{x}_j \cdot \mathbf{x}_k$ (which we shall also call b_{jk}) is defined as:

$$b_{jk} \equiv \mathbf{x}_j \cdot \mathbf{x}_k \equiv \sum_{t=1}^{r} x_{jt} x_{kt}. \tag{16.15}$$

Geometrically, the scalar product can be interpreted as the cosine of the angle between the two vectors multiplied by the product of their lengths. Actually, however, this geometric fact is not really necessary for our purposes. Rather, it is quite sufficient to deal with the algebraic definition in Equation (16.15).

In most applications of MDS, the *origin* of the space is not of any importance, and thus may be arbitrarily fixed. This is because a shift in origin (defined by adding the same constant vector to all points) leaves (Euclidean) distances unchanged. It has therefore become conventional to place the origin at the *centroid*, or generalized mean, of all the points.

While *distances* remain unchanged with a shift in origin, *scalar products* do not, since the vectors whose lengths and angles are involved are the vectors *from* the origin to the particular point. We can resolve this indeterminacy of scalar products, however, by dealing always with scalar products from an origin at the centroid of all the points. We will henceforth assume that the origin is at the centroid, and will use the symbol b_{jk} to represent scalar products of vectors about such an origin.

As shown by Torgerson (1958), Euclidean distances may be converted into scalar products of vectors about an origin placed (arbitrarily) at the centroid of all the points by Equation (16.16):

$$b_{jk} = -\frac{1}{2}(d_{jk}^2 - d_{.k}^2 - d_{j.}^2 + d_{..}^2), \tag{16.16}$$

where

$$d_{.k}^2 = \frac{1}{n}\sum_{j} d_{jk}^2, \tag{16.17}$$

$$d_{j.}^2 = \frac{1}{n}\sum_{k} d_{jk}^2, \tag{16.18}$$

$$d_{..}^2 = \frac{1}{n}\sum_{j}\sum_{k} d_{jk}^2. \tag{16.19}$$

This is equivalent to *doubly centering* the matrix of $-\frac{1}{2}$ times the *squared* interpoint distances (i.e., subtracting grand mean and row and column main effects, in the analysis of variance sense). A derivation of Equation (16.16) is given as follows.

Given

$$d_{jk}^2 = \sum_{t=1}^{r} (x_{jt} - x_{kt})^2. \qquad (16.20)$$

Assume

$$\sum_{j=1}^{n} x_{jt} = 0 \qquad \text{for all } t = 1, 2, \ldots, r. \qquad (16.21)$$

(We may do this without loss of generality, since the origin of the x space is arbitrary, and this just fixes it at the centroid of all n points.) Expanding (16.20)

$$\begin{aligned}
d_{jk}^2 &= \sum_{t} (x_{jt}^2 - 2x_{jt}x_{kt} + x_{kt}^2) \\
&= \sum_{t} x_{jt}^2 - 2 \sum_{t} x_{jt}x_{kt} + \sum_{t} x_{kt}^2 \\
&= \ell_j^2 + \ell_k^2 - 2b_{jk},
\end{aligned}$$

where

$$\ell_j^2 \equiv \sum_{t} x_{jt}^2, \qquad (16.23)$$

$$b_{jk} \equiv \sum_{t} x_{jt}x_{kt} \qquad \text{(the scalar product).} \qquad (16.24)$$

Because of (16.21)

$$b_{.k} = b_{j.} = b_{..} = 0 \qquad (16.25)$$

from (16.22) and (16.25), we have

$$d_{.k}^2 = \ell_{..}^2 + \ell_k^2, \qquad (16.26)$$
$$d_{j.}^2 = \ell_j^2 + \ell_{..}^2, \qquad (16.27)$$
$$d_{..}^2 = 2\ell_{..}^2, \qquad (16.28)$$

where

$$\ell_{.}^2 = \frac{1}{n} \sum \ell_j^2, \qquad (16.29)$$

then (16.22), (16.26), (16.27), and (16.28) together imply that

$$d_{jk}^2 - d_{.k}^2 - d_{j.}^2 + d_{..}^2 = -2b_{jk}; \qquad (16.30)$$

multiplying both sides of (16.30) by $-\frac{1}{2}$ gives the desired result in (16.16).

By analogy to this *exact* formula for converting distances to scalar products (about an origin at the centroid), we may apply the same formula to $\hat{d}$'s ($\hat{d}_{jk} = \delta_{jk} + c$ min) to get $\hat{b}$'s (estimated scalar products). (In matrix terms, $\hat{\mathbf{B}}$ is $-\frac{1}{2} \hat{\mathbf{D}}^{(2)}$ after double centering, where $\hat{\mathbf{D}}^{(2)} \equiv \|\hat{d}_{jk}^2\|$). We shall generally use a hat (^) over a variable to indicate an estimate of the corresponding unhatted variable.

At this point, the classical (two-way) metric MDS procedure à la Torgerson (1958) would simply *factor* this matrix $\hat{\mathbf{B}}$ into a product of the form

$$\hat{\mathbf{B}} \cong \hat{\mathbf{X}}\hat{\mathbf{X}}' \qquad (16.31)$$

to get estimates of the coordinates $\hat{x}_{jt}$. ($\hat{\mathbf{X}}$ is just the $n \times r$ matrix $\|\hat{x}_{jt}\|$ containing these estimated coordinates, while the matrix equation [16.31] is equivalent to the *scalar* equation $\hat{b}_{jk} = \Sigma \, \hat{x}_{jt}\hat{x}_{kt}$, the analogue of [16.15], but with estimates replacing exact values.)

This factorization usually is done by methods closely related to principal components analysis (Hotelling, 1933) or factor analysis (Harman, 1967). Perhaps the best way to describe this is in terms of the procedure described by Eckart and Young (1936) for least-squares approximation of an arbitrary matrix by a product of two matrices of smaller rank. When applied to a square symmetric matrix such as $\hat{\mathbf{B}}$ presumably is, the Eckart–Young procedure results in two matrices (such as $\hat{\mathbf{X}}$ and $\hat{\mathbf{X}}'$) that are simply the transposes of one another. (This statement is true so long as appropriate normalizing conventions are observed, and so long as the largest [in absolute value] r *eigenroots* of $\hat{\mathbf{B}}$ are nonnegative, which is generally true in practice.) Details of this can be found in Torgerson (1958).

THE INDSCAL MODEL IN SCALAR PRODUCT FORM

By applying the procedures described (for converting estimated dissimilarities into estimated scalar products) to each two-way proximities matrix, we arrive at a three-way array of estimated scalar products, whose general entry is $\hat{b}_{jk}^{(i)}$ (for Subject i and stimuli j and k). We now need to make an analogous conversion of the INDSCAL *model* into scalar product form.

By definition, the (true) scalar products for Subject i are defined as:

$$b_{jk}^{(i)} = \sum_{t} y_{jt}^{(i)}y_{kt}^{(i)}, \qquad (16.32)$$

where the $y^{(i)}$'s are defined as

$$y_{jt}^{(i)} = w_{it}^{1/2}x_{jt} \qquad \text{(Equation [16.11])}.$$

Substituting (16.11) into (16.32), we have

$$b_{jk}^{(i)} = \sum_{t} w_{it}x_{jt}x_{kt} \qquad (16.33)$$

which is the desired *scalar product form* of the INDSCAL model.

Equation (16.33) can easily be seen to be a *special case* of what we have called the CANDECOMP (for *CANonical DECOMPosition* of *N*-way tables) model of the form (for $N = 3$):

$$z_{ijk} = \sum_t a_{it} b_{jt} c_{kt}. \tag{16.34}$$

We get the INDSCAL model (16.33) as a special case of the three-way CANDECOMP model (16.34) by imposing the constraints:

$$z_{ijk} = b_{jk}^{(i)}, \tag{16.35}$$

$$a_{it} = w_{it}, \tag{16.36}$$

$$b_{jt} = c_{jt} = x_{jt}. \tag{16.37}$$

For the INDSCAL special case of this CANDECOMP (three-way) model, we may, however, ignore the symmetry constraint of (16.37) and fit the model in its general form. It turns out that the symmetry of the basic data is ordinarily sufficient to guarantee that (after appropriate normalization of the solution) b_{jt} will *in fact* equal c_{jt}.

THE ALGORITHM FOR FITTING THE CANDECOMP
MODEL IN THE THREE-WAY CASE

Given the model

$$\hat{z}_{ijk} \cong \sum_t a_{it} b_{jt} c_{kt} \tag{16.38}$$

(Equation [16.34] with $\hat{z}_{ijk}$ replacing z_{ijk} and $\cong$ replacing $=$) and current estimates of the two sets of parameters (say the b_{jt}'s and c_{kt}'s), we can find an *exact least-squares* estimate of the third set by linear regression methods. This can be seen by reformulating the problem as

$$\hat{z}_{is}^* \cong \sum_t a_{it} \hat{g}_{st}, \tag{16.39}$$

where

$$\hat{z}_{is}^* = \hat{z}_{i(jk)} \tag{16.40}$$

and

$$\hat{g}_{st} = \hat{b}_{jt} \hat{c}_{kt} \tag{16.41}$$

($\hat{b}_{jt}$ and $\hat{c}_{kt}$ are *current* estimates of b_{jt} and c_{kt}, respectively, while s is a subscript that is a function of j and k, and ranges over all $n_j.n_k$ values of j and k).

By this simple notational device, we have converted this original *trilinear* model into a *bilinear* model. This can be expressed in matrix notation as:

$$\hat{\mathbf{Z}}^* \cong \mathbf{A}\hat{\mathbf{G}}'. \tag{16.42}$$

Note that the matrix $\hat{\mathbf{G}}$ incorporates both the $\hat{b}$'s and $\hat{c}$'s, while $\mathbf{A}$ is the matrix containing the a's. The $\cong$ can be taken to mean, in the present context, that we seek the $\mathbf{A}$ providing the best least-squares approximation to $\mathbf{Z}^*$. This proves to be a standard problem, essentially equivalent to least-squares multiple linear regression. In matrix notation, the least-squares estimate of $\mathbf{A}$ is:

$$\hat{\mathbf{A}} = \mathbf{Z}^*\hat{\mathbf{G}}(\hat{\mathbf{G}}'\hat{\mathbf{G}})^{-1}. \tag{16.43}$$

(This amounts to postmultiplying both sides of [16.42] by the right *pseudoinverse* of $\hat{\mathbf{G}}'$. See Green [with Carroll], 1976, for a discussion of pseudoinverses, other generalized inverses, and related aspects of linear algebra relevant to this discussion.)

We use a general estimation scheme called by Wold (1966) a NILES (for *N*onlinear *I*terative *LE*ast *S*quares) procedure. In the present case this amounts to iterating this least squares estimation procedure; that is, estimating the a's (with b's and c's fixed) by least-squares methods, then the b's (with a's and c's fixed), and so on round the iterative cycle until convergence occurs. While there is no guarantee this process will converge to the *overall* least-squares estimates of all three sets of parameters, it does seem to do so in most cases. There is a mild local minimum problem (tendency to converge to estimates such that no *small* change can improve the fit, although a *large* or global change can) but it seems to be very minor.

In practice the method seems almost always to converge to the global optimum solution. In any case the local minimum problem seems to be very slight in comparison with that in nonmetric two-way MDS, where the algorithms are generally based on a gradient, or steepest descent, method. Whether it is the difference in numerical procedures or the difference in the models that is critical is not known at present.

It might be noted that the CANDECOMP model and method itself has many applications other than this rather special application to fitting the INDSCAL model (although this is certainly its most widely used and currently most important application). These include a general approach to factor analysis of three-way data tables, closely allied to a method called PARAFAC by Richard Harshman (1970) and a nonsymmetric generalization of INDSCAL called "Three-Way Metric Unfolding" (DeSarbo & Carroll, 1979). CANDECOMP also generalizes to the many-way case. An interesting application of this is to analysis of three-way or many-way contingency tables via Lazarsfeld's latent class model (Carroll, Pruzansky, & Green, 1979). The many-way case of CANDECOMP could also be applied (possibly after suitable preprocessing) as a many-way factor analytic procedure (a generalization of the PARAFAC approach to the N-way case, for $N > 3$). It can (and has) also provided a many-way generalization of INDSCAL, to the case involving more than one data source (e.g., the case in which proximities data are provided by different subjects in each of a number of experimental conditions). The original INDSCAL program (see Chang & Carroll, 1972) allows many such N-way analyses.

It might be noted that this general iterative approach to least-squares fitting of complex nonlinear models that can be subdivided into simpler components (corresponding to subsets of parameters for which fairly simple numerical procedures provide *conditional* least-squares estimates) to which Wold (1966) applied the general term NILES (as mentioned earlier) or more specifically, NIPALS (for *N*onlinear *I*terative *PA*rtial *L*east *S*quares), is the same general numerical procedure called ALS (for *A*lternating *L*east *S*quares) by Takane, Young, & de Leeuw's [1977] ALSCAL). Strictly speaking ALS is a misnomer if the iterative procedure involves more than two components (or subsets of parameters). J. W. Tukey (personal communication) has recently suggested renaming this approach *cyclical* least squares (which would include the case of two *or more* component steps, and would presumably be abbreviated CLS). Wold himself (personal communication) has recently suggested the somewhat simpler (than NILES or NIPALS) term *partial* least squares (to be abbreviated PLS). Since the procedure for fitting the three-way CANDECOMP model used in the INDS-CAL method entails three component conditional least squares estimation steps, (while the N-way CANDECOMP procedure entails N steps) it should perhaps be referred to as a CLS or PLS procedure.

NORMALIZING CONVENTIONS IN
THE INDSCAL PROCEDURE

By the nature of the INDSCAL model there is a basic scale indeterminacy; that is, the dimensions of the stimulus space could be rescaled by an arbitrary diagonal transformation, and the effect of this could be undone by rescaling the dimensions of the subject space by the inverse of the square of that diagonal transformation. (An arbitrary permutation of the dimensions of both the stimulus and subject space is also allowable, but this indeterminacy is generally—although not always—resolved by simply ordering the dimensions according to [approximate] overall variance accounted for.) This scale indeterminacy is resolved in the INDSCAL procedure by introducing the normalizing convention that the variance of stimulus coordinates of all dimensions be equal (to $1/n$, where n is the number of stimuli).

Also, as in any Euclidean distance model (including the weighted Euclidean model underlying INDSCAL) there is an indeterminacy of the origin of the coordinate system—due to the invariance of Euclidean distances under translation of coordinates. This indeterminacy is resolved very simply (as in almost all distance based two-way and three-way MDS procedures) by placing the origin of the coordinate system at the centroid of the stimulus points. Translated into simpler terms, the effect of these two normalizing conventions is that the mean of the coordinates on each dimension is zero, while the sum of squares of the coordinates (which, given that the mean is zero, is just n times the variance of the coordinates) is one.

It is because of the adoption of these conventions (particularly the one regarding the variance of stimulus coordinates) and the data normalization mentioned earlier (specifically, normalization of the sum of squared entries in each scalar product matrix to one) that the square of the distance of a subject point from the origin of the coordinate system in the subject space is interpretable (approximately) as proportion of variance accounted for in the (derived scalar products) data for that subject or other data source.

RECENT DEVELOPMENTS IN INDSCAL APPROACH

A not-so-recent development that is of great practical importance is Pruzansky's (1975) SINDSCAL (for *S*ymmetric *INDSCAL*) program, which is much more efficient (in both data storage and running time) than the older INDSCAL program, but is restricted to the case of three-way symmetric data. SINDSCAL is described in detail elsewhere in this book.

Some *recent* developments that bear mentioning include use of a linearly constrained version of CANDECOMP (called CANDELINC, for *CAN*onical *DE*composition with *LIN*ear *C*onstraints) instead of standard CANDECOMP to provide an INDSCAL analysis with linear constraints on the INDSCAL parameters (stimulus coordinates and/or subject weights). A paper by Carroll, Pruzansky, and Kruskal (1979) describes this approach in detail. A particularly promising application of this involves a way of using the linearly constrained version of INDSCAL (called LINCINDS, for *LIN*early *C*onstrained *INDS*cal) to provide a *rational start* for the standard version of INDSCAL. The virtue of the resulting procedure, called SINDSCAL-LS (for *SINDSCAL-L*incinds *S*tart) is that it can be enormously faster, particularly for very large data matrices, than SINDSCAL (which in turn is much faster, as mentioned, than the older INDSCAL program). This approach is described in a paper by Carroll and Pruzansky (1979).

NONMETRIC, QUASI-NONMETRIC, AND OTHER VERSIONS OF FITTING THE INDSCAL MODEL

While a fully nonmetric version of the INDSCAL method is not currently available, Carroll and Chang (1970b) have developed a quasi-nonmetric version (i.e., an approximation to a fully nonmetric version). This is implemented by alternating the metric version of INDSCAL, as just described, with the use of least-squares monotone regression (using Kruskal's, 1964, MFIT routine) in an iterative fashion. Given data values $\delta_{jk}^{(i)}$, we first estimate additive constants $c^{(i)}$ to convert to $_0\hat{d}_{jk}^{(i)}$. Then, the Ith iteration of this outer iterative process (metric INDSCAL provides an inner iterative process) can be described as follows:

Given $\delta_{jk}^{(i)}$ and $_{(I-1)}\hat{d}_{jk}^{(i)}$.

Phase 1. (*a*) Convert $_{(I-1)}\hat{d}_{jk}^{(i)} \rightarrow _{(I-1)}\hat{b}_{jk}^{(i)}$ via Equation (16.16); (*b*) apply CANDECOMP to the three-way matrix of $\hat{b}$'s, and normalize, to get

$$_I\mathbf{X} = \|_I x_{jt}\| \quad \text{and} \quad _I\mathbf{W} = \|_I w_{it}\|. \tag{16.44}$$

Phase 2. (*a*) Use the weighted Euclidean distance formula of (16.10) to calculate $_I d_{jk}^{(i)}$, for all i,j,k. (*b*) Use the least-squares monotone regression routine (MFIT) to find

$$_I \hat{d}_{jk}^{(i)} = M_i^I(\delta_{jk}^{(i)}) \cong _I d_{jk}^{(i)} \tag{16.45}$$

(where $\cong$ implies a least-squares fit, and M_i^I is a monotone nondecreasing function).

Increment I by 1 and return to the beginning of Phase 1. Continue iteratively until no further improvement in fit occurs. Badness of fit, in this case, is measured by a generalization of Kruskal's STRESSFORM2, namely,

$$\text{STRESS} = \left\{ \sum_i \left[\frac{\sum_j \sum_k (d_{jk}^{(i)} - \hat{d}_{jk}^{(i)})^2}{\sum_j \sum_k (d_{jk}^{(i)} - \bar{d}^{(i)})^2} \right] \right\}^{1/2} \tag{16.46}$$

which is essentially a root mean square over subjects of STRESSFORM2 computed separately for each subject. STRESS^2 is the measure actually printed out in what is called the NINDSCAL program, as implemented by Chang (1972).

Typically STRESS will go down for several outer iterations, but will ultimately go up again. This is because the two phases of the algorithm are not optimizing the same criterion. Phase 1 is least squares in the (derived) *scalar products,* while Phase 2 is least squares in *distances.*

To make the procedure fully nonmetric, both phases should be optimizing the same criterion. One way is to make Phase 1 least squares in distances. Another, however, which is in some ways more attractive, is to replace the STRESS measure with what Carroll and Chang (see Carroll & Wish, 1974a) have, somewhat whimsically, called STRAIN, defined in this case as:

$$\text{STRAIN} = \left\{ \sum_i \left[\frac{\sum_j \sum_k (b_{jk}^{(i)} - \hat{b}_{jk}^{(i)})^2}{\sum_j \sum_k (b_{jk}^{(i)})^2} \right] \right\}^{1/2}, \tag{16.47}$$

where $b_{jk}^{(i)}$ is computed by (16.33) while the $\hat{b}_{jk}^{(i)}$'s are computed from $\hat{d}_{jk}^{(i)}$'s by the obvious analogue of (16.16) with $\hat{d}_{jk}^{(i)} = M_i(\delta_{jk}^{(i)})$. Then Phase 2 would entail finding the M_i optimizing STRAIN (with other parameters held constant); that is, Phase 2 would be made least squares in scalar products. Carroll and Chang implemented an (unpublished) quadratic programming procedure for optimizing the STRAIN criterion, but this has not yet been incorporated into the INDSCAL program to provide a fully nonmetric version of the INDSCAL procedure.

Takane, Young, and de Leeuw's (1977) ALSCAL (in its three-way implementation) provides a method for fitting a nonmetric version of the INDSCAL model, optimizing what they call SSTRESS, which is basically a least-squares criterion of fit of data to *squared* (weighted Euclidean) distances. ALSCAL also provides a metric option, and one for fitting the INDSCAL model to nominal scale data, but this will not be gone into further here as the ALSCAL procedure is dealt with extensively elsewhere in this book.

Ramsay's (1977) MULTISCALE procedure also provides alternative methods for fitting the INDSCAL model, utilizing a maximum likelihood criterion (under a number of different possible distributional assumptions). MULTISCALE is a metric technique, although it does allow an assumption of various monotonic nonlinear functions relating data to distances. Some of these (specifically integrated cubic B-splines) can be made sufficiently general to approximate as closely as desired a completely general monotonic function. This could be viewed as a quasi-nonmetric procedure in a somewhat different sense than in the earlier use of that term. MULTISCALE is also described extensively elsewhere in this book and so will not be discussed further here. For purposes of clarification, however, it should be pointed out that what Ramsay calls the *diagonal metric* corresponds to the INDSCAL model, while what he calls the *full metric* corresponds to what Carroll and Chang have called the IDIOSCAL model (see Carroll & Wish, [1974a,b] for further discussion of this model, methods of fitting it and its various special cases).

AN ILLUSTRATIVE APPLICATION OF INDSCAL TO
SOME COLOR DISSIMILARITIES

We now illustrate the INDSCAL model by an example which entails a reanalysis of some data on color perception collected by Helm (1964). Helm and Tucker (1962) had analyzed these data via a points of view analysis and found that about 10 points of view (that is, 10 different perceptual spaces) were required to account for the individual differences among their 14 subjects.

Our analysis in terms of the INDSCAL model has quite nicely accounted for these individual differences in terms of a single two-dimensional solution. Moreover, the unique dimensions from the INDSCAL analysis shown in Figure 16.5 were interpretable without rotation of axes. Dimension 1

corresponds essentially to a blue versus yellow (or, more accurately perhaps, a purple–blue to green–yellow) factor, and dimension 2 to a red
versus green (or purple–red to blue–green) factor. This accords very well
with physiological and psychophysical evidence strongly suggesting the
existence of blue–yellow and red–green receptors.

Included among Helm's subjects were four who were deficient, to various
degrees, in red–green color vision. In the INDSCAL analysis this deficiency
is reflected in the fact that these subjects all have lower weights for the
red–green factor (dimension 2) than do any of the normal subjects. The
effect of these differential weights can be seen in Figure 16.5 by comparing
the private perceptual spaces for the color-blind subjects with those for the
normals. The spaces for the color-deficient subjects are compressed in the
red–green direction, relative to the spaces for the normals, reflecting the
fact that red and green (for example) are much more similar to each other
for these subjects than they are for the normals.

Had we not known that these subjects were red–green color deficient,
we could have discovered this through inspection of the weights in the
subject space. In fact Subject N10 seems from this analysis to border on
a mild form of blue–yellow deficiency. This is based on the fact that his
or her weight for dimension 1 is about as small as some red–green deficient
subjects' weights for dimension 2. If such a deficiency exists for this subject,
this would seem to be a fact determined by the INDSCAL analysis but *not*
detected by other measures (in any case, such a deficiency was not reported
by Helm).

The inspection of the private spaces provides insight into the way in
which INDSCAL uses individual differences in perception to determine a
unique orientation of the coordinate axes. If the coordinate axes were
oriented in a different way (say, by a 45° rotation of the axes of the group
stimulus space), the private spaces for color deficient subjects could not
be compressed along a line from red to green, but would have to be compressed in some other direction. More generally, the *family* of transformations of the stimulus space generated by differential weights varies as
a function of the orientation of axes in the group stimulus space. Thus it
is that INDSCAL manages to seek out not only the optimal stimulus space,
but also an optimal and unique orientation of coordinate axes within that
space. It is a matter of empirical observation that this unique orientation
is also (in almost every case to date) a highly "interpretable" one. Thus,
INDSCAL avoids the problem of rotation of axes that so often complicates
two-way MDS and other multivariate behavioral studies. This is not at all
a coincidence, however, since INDSCAL is based on a psychological model
which postulates dimensions that are unique in the sense of being modifiable
(in salience, or perceptual importance) across, and perhaps even within,
individuals. If the INDSCAL model does accurately reflect the underlying

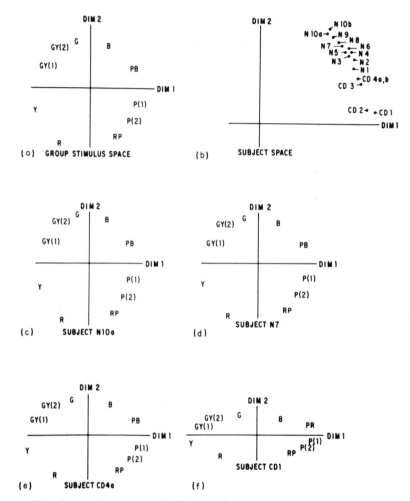

Figure 16.5. A two-dimensional INDSCAL analysis of Helm's (1964) data on color perception produced the group stimulus space shown in (a) and the subject space shown in (b). Private perceptual spaces for two color-deficient subjects (CD1 and CD4a) and for two subjects with normal color vision (N10a and N7) were derived from the group stimulus space by applying the subjects' respective weights (shown in the subject space) to the dimensions. The coding of colors (of constant saturation and brightness) is as follows: R = red; Y = yellow; GY(1) = green–yellow; GY(2) = green–yellow with more green than GY(1); G = green; B = blue, PB = purple–blue; P(1) = purple; P(2) = purple with more red than P(1); RP = red–purple.

psychological processes (at least to a good first approximation), then the coordinate axes from an INDSCAL analysis can be assumed to correspond to fundamental psychological dimensions.

16.6. MULTISCALE

JAMES O. RAMSAY

An important distinction in data analysis is between those analyses which are primarily exploratory and those which are mainly confirmatory. The former are designed to allow us to view the data in a variety of ways in order to uncover various interesting relationships. Exploratory tools should be as flexible as possible and tolerant of a wide range of types of data. The emphasis in such analyses is not so much on decisions about specific relationships or aspects of the data as on displaying what is there. ALSCAL, INDSCAL, and KYST were designed to be primarily exploratory instruments, although they are often employed for relatively confirmatory purposes.

Confirmatory analysis, on the other hand, is more sharply focused in specific aspects of the data and particular questions about them. It is assumed that the investigator has a fairly clear idea of the model to be employed, the behavior of the data, and the structure that he wishes to investigate. The goal is often to make a decision about some hypothesis. Perhaps the most familiar example in MDS of such a hypothesis is that a certain dimensionality is best for representing the data. Other questions might be whether the data from two or more groups can be represented by the same configuration, whether a weighted Euclidean model fits better than an unweighted one, or whether a configuration constrained in some way represents the data as well as an unconstrained configuration. Since questions are sharply focused and one needs as clear an answer as possible, there is considerable emphasis in confirmatory analyses on power or precision of estimation. One wants to use an estimation procedure which is optimal in some important sense, and this will imply that it is tuned to a fairly specific type of data.

MULTISCALE is a series of programs designed primarily for optimal analyses of certain kinds of data with a view to being useful for confirmatory analyses. Its rationale is primarily statistical and requires a number of assumptions about the random variation or noise in the data. While these assumptions limit the range of data which these programs can usefully analyze, they make possible a whole range of data analysis possibilities which would not be possible in more exploratory analyses. Thus MUL-

TISCALE is designed to complement programs like ALSCAL and KYST rather than replace them; and will often be used as the second stage in a serious multidimensional analysis. On the other hand, these programs also contain a variety of exploratory aspects which are made possible by the statistical assumptions that underly them.

The MULTISCALE programs are in development, and thus in the following discussion reference will be made to features which may not be available in earlier versions. At time of writing the only publicly available version is being distributed by International Educational Services, Chicago, Illinois, under the name MULTISCALE, and MULTISCALE results presented in this book were produced by that version. However, it is expected that a new version will shortly be available under the name MULTISCALE-II which will incorporate most of the features discussed. For a more detailed discussion of the statistical basis for MULTISCALE see Ramsay (1977, 1978a,b, 1980a,b) and Winsberg and Ramsay (1980).

Maximum Likelihood Estimation

Rather than defining a loss function which summarizes how bad the fit is and then minimizing it, MULTISCALE proceeds on a somewhat different basis. It computes the probability or likelihood of the sample for a given set of parameter values, and then tries to find those parameter values which will produce the largest possible probability. This principle is known as maximum likelihood estimation (MLE) and is the basis for a very large proportion of commonly used statistical analyses. In order to ascertain the probability of the entire set of observations, it is necessary to specify the probability of any specific datum given some particular set of parameter values. This means that the nature of the random variation or noise in the data must be completely specified. Thus, this specification, which is really a hypothesis about the data, is at the heart of MLE. If this assumption is seriously wrong, the desirable properties of MLE are not relevant, and the consequent analyses should be regarded as primarily exploratory.

However, if the statistical assumptions about the random variation in the data are correct, maximum likelihood estimates have a number of important advantages over many other estimates. These features as a rule pertain only to largish samples, but by and large also hold up reasonably well for modest sample sizes. First, it can be shown that no other estimates will have smaller estimation error (as defined by sampling variance). Thus, for large samples they are as precise as possible. Second, they behave in a very convenient way in that the estimates are normally distributed about the population values with a variance that is rather easy to compute. This allows us to construct regions for each parameter or set of parameters that have a certain predetermined probability of containing the population values. This is a very useful graphical aid in informing us as to the precision of estimates. Third, there is a rather simple rule whereby one model can be compared to another as to how well each fits the data. This permits us to test the significance of the improvement in fit as we move from a more specialized model to a more general one. The majority of hypotheses of practical interest in MDS can be expressed and tested in this way.

Since the statistical assumptions about noise or error are so central to MLE, it is a feature of MULTISCALE that the behavior of the data can be inspected graphically in order to allow the user to determine whether these assumptions hold satisfactorily. A variety of diagnostic statistics are made available to aid in inspecting various aspects of these assumptions. Moreover, MULTISCALE allows a number of alternatives for various aspects of these assumptions. However, even if one has serious doubts about the statistical basis for a particular MULTISCALE analysis, there are still a variety of program options which will make the results useful for more exploratory purposes.

The Statistical Assumptions

There are a number of aspects of the random variation in the data that have to be taken into account before a likelihood can be specified, computed, and maximized to obtain maximum likelihood estimates.

THE DISTRIBUTION OF ERROR

First of all, it is assumed that each datum arises from the imposition of noise on an errorless or population value. Let us refer to this ideal or errorless value as d^*, which will be the hypothetical perfect dissimilarity observation. We will need subscripts for this value later to indicate which stimuli and subject are involved in this datum, but this will suffice for now. Similarly, the actual observed value will be denoted simply by d. Datum d is assumed to arise from d^* by the influence of some random disturbance. It is the nature of this disturbance that must be specified.

One type of disturbance which is especially plausible in many applications is the lognormal distribution. Here it is assumed that d^* is multiplied by a random factor whose logarithm has a normal distribution with mean 0 and standard deviation σ. Another way to think of this is that the logarithm of d has a normal distribution with a mean equal to the logarithm of d^* and standard deviation σ. Figure 16.6 shows what the probability density function looks like, while the equation defining this function is as follows:

$$f(d) = \frac{1}{(2\pi)^{1/2}\sigma d}\, e^{-(\log d - \log d^*)^2/(2\sigma^2)}.$$

The lognormal distribution has a number of important features:

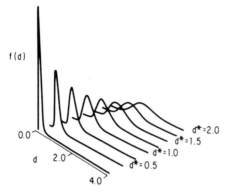

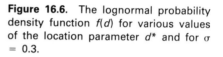

Figure 16.6. The lognormal probability density function $f(d)$ for various values of the location parameter d^* and for $\sigma = 0.3$.

1. It is defined only for positive values of d. This corresponds to the positive character of geometrical distance which is being used to represent d.

2. The actual variation of d about d^* or spread of the density function $f(d)$ increases roughly in proportion to d^*. Thus, the bigger the true value, the more noise there will be in the actual values arising from it. Again, physical distance measurements usually have this feature—our error in measuring a kilometer by any particular technique will usually be around a thousand times that in our measurement of a meter. Judgments of dissimilarity by a variety of techniques can also be seen to have this property; we are less sure of ourselves in absolute terms when we have to judge two very dissimilar stimuli than when we judge two highly similar stimuli.

3. The distribution is positively skewed, meaning that positive errors will tend to be larger on the whole than negative errors. This reflects that the fact that the positive character of d limits how big a negative error can be, while there is no upper limit on a positive error.

Of these features, the third seems to be the most troublesome in practice. It seems to be the case that the distribution of errors is often more symmetric than the lognormal distribution implies. This in general is not a very serious shortcoming from a practical point of view. However, MULTISCALE-II also permits one to assume that data are normally distributed (as opposed to their logarithms) with a mean of d^* and a standard deviation which is some power of d^*. This assumption captures the first two features of the lognormal distribution for positive powers but provides a symmetric error distribution.

THE INDEPENDENCE ASSUMPTION

MULTISCALE is based on the assumption that error or noise in any d is independent of that in any other datum. This implies that the probability of the entire sample can be computed by multiplying the probabilities of each datum. This assumption is difficult to verify in practice, but as a rule is not likely to be very critical for good estimation. It is known in other similar statistical procedures that estimates of σ can be somewhat distorted when there is a correlation between errors, but this parameter is not often of central importance. On the other hand, structural parameters like the coordinates of points in the configuration are usually estimated robustly even when errors are rather correlated. It is known that human judgments often display a mild serial correlation in psychophysical judgments. MULTISCALE-II permits the estimation of a serial correlation coefficient for a particular ordering of observations.

THE CONSTANT VARIANCE ASSUMPTION

In most analyses it will be satisfactory to assume that the standard deviation σ is the same for all observations. From time to time, however, there may be good reason to suspect that this is not so. One situation which can give rise to this suspicion is when the stimuli are of widely varying familiarity to the subject. One suspects that the variability of judgment when unfamiliar stimuli are involved will be greater than when both stimuli in the pair are well known. Thus, there will be reason to suppose that we should designate the standard deviation as σ_{ij} for stimuli i and j on the assumption that it will vary from pair to pair. It may be desirable to produce a separate estimate for each pair of stimuli, and MULTISCALE has an option which permits this when there are more than one subject involved in the rating. A more restricted alternative would be to suppose that σ_{ij} is specified as follows:

$$\sigma_{ij}^2 = \sigma \left(\frac{\alpha_i^2 + \alpha_j^2}{2} \right)^{1/2} .$$

In this instance, the variance is specified as an average of $\sigma^2 \alpha_i^2$ and $\sigma^2 \alpha_j^2$, and the coefficients or weights α_i and α_j determine the component of variance specific to each stimulus. MULTISCALE will also permit the use of this model for error variance, which has the advantage of involving fewer parameters to be estimated from the data than the model with σ_{ij} unrestricted. MULTISCALE-II will also estimate the standard deviation weights α_i after each analysis even when the standard deviation is held constant to permit an evaluation of the constant variance assumption.

It is likely in practice that the standard deviation will also vary from subject to subject. Different subjects are easily seen to differ in terms of the precision with which they make judgments due to a variety of factors such as motivation, educational level, skill at quantitative reasoning, and so forth. MULTISCALE-II permits the standard error to be estimated separately for each subject either along with the other aspects of the model or after the fact.

In summary, MULTISCALE permits the following types of variation in standard deviation σ_{ij}: none, stimulus-wise, subject-wise, and pairwise.

Transformations of the Data

A very important feature of programs like ALSCAL and KYST is the possibility of fitting a suitable order-preserving transformation to the raw data at the same time as the configuration and other aspects of the model are being estimated. In fact, it is seldom in the behavioral sciences that our data are in exactly the right form for fitting by strong models such as those used in MDS. We should as a rule be open to the possibility that the fit can be improved by some transformation of our original observations, and the capability of the nonmetric programs to do this is one of their most important features.

MULTISCALE also has various levels of data transformation capability. Because of the restrictions involved in MLE, it is necessary to restrict ourselves to only smooth continuous transformations, but this is hardly a serious constraint in practice. Of course, the more general the transformation, the more parameters will be consumed in its estimation. Therefore MULTISCALE allows the user to select one of three transformation families. These are as follows:

1. Scale: For each subject r a multiplier or regression coefficient v_r is estimated and the model fits $v_r d$ rather than d. It is $v_r d$ which is assumed to have the lognormal or normal distribution about d^*.

2. Power: For each subject r a power transformation $v_r d^{p_r}$ involving a regression coefficient v_r and an exponent p_r is estimated.

3. Monotone: For each subject r a continuous order-preserving transformation $f_r(d)$ is estimated using integrated B-splines. This family of functions is tremendously flexible and can accommodate any shape of transformation likely to be encountered in practice. The number of parameters estimated per subject depends on the flexibility desired and is under the control of the user.

These transformations might be called a posteriori since these are estimated in the maximum likelihood sense from the data. It is occasionally useful as well to have the data transformed prior to analysis. MULTISCALE-II permits transformations of the form

$$g(d) = \min\{ad^b - c, e\},$$

where constants a, b, c, and e are fixed by the user.

Distance Models

An important feature of MDS that has already been introduced is the nature of the distance function which is used to fit a particular datum or its transformation. This is the function which specifies the value of d^*.

INDSCAL and ALSCAL permit both an unweighted and a weighted Euclidean model, with the latter having the often useful feature that dimensions can be weighted or given psychological salience differently for different subjects. In geometrical terms, we say that the *metric* varies from subject to subject in the weighted case. MULTISCALE permits these options and extends them to include an even more general distance formula:

$$\text{Identity metric:} \quad d_{ijr}{}^* = \left[\sum_m^k (x_{im} - x_{jm})^2\right]^{1/2} ;$$

$$\text{Diagonal metric:} \quad d_{ijr}{}^* = \left[\sum_m^k w_{rm}(x_{im} - x_{jm})^2\right]^{1/2} ;$$

$$\text{Full metric:} \quad d_{ijr}{}^* = \left[\sum_m^k \sum_n^k (x_{im} - x_{jm})w_{rmn}(x_{in} - x_{jn})\right]^{1/2} .$$

In geometrical terms, we have the possibility not only that different dimensions will be given different weights, but also that the angle between axes will vary from subject to subject. One way to understand this is to see how three different subjects might visualize a pattern of nine dots that to you and me is square. Figure 16.7 shows three possibilities. If the unweighted Euclidean model is used, all three views will be represented as in View I. If the weighted Euclidean model in ALSCAL and INDSCAL is used, Views I and II will be correctly represented, but View III will be represented as a variation of View II. If the most general model is employed, all three views will be represented properly.

The full metric model has been discussed by Tucker (1973) and Bloxom (1978) as well as others. The square matrix of weights $\|w_{rmn}\|$ for subject r is required to be positive semidefinite by MULTISCALE.

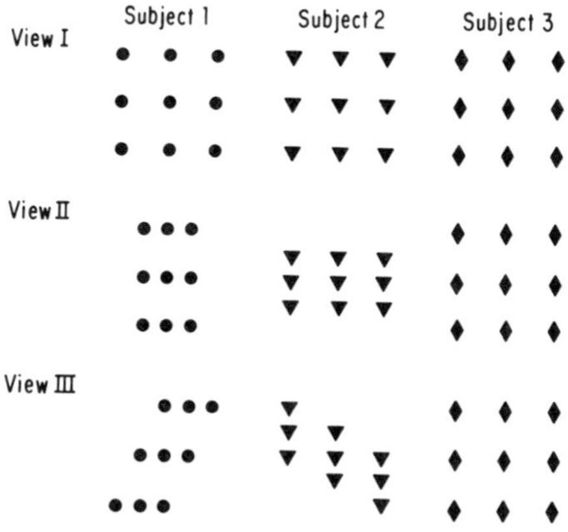

Figure 16.7. Three ways in which three subjects might see a pattern of points.

As has been pointed out elsewhere, there is an interesting variation among these distance models in terms of the degree of definition of the final configuration. For all three metrics the resulting configuration may be translated without altering the quality of the fit. For the identity metric, it may also be rigidly or orthogonally rotated. This does not change the angles between the axes, which are at 90°. For the diagonal metric, only translations are possible. But for the full metric, both translations and oblique rotations are permitted. This is rather handy when the configuration is determined a priori in some way (perhaps by physical measurements) and not estimated from the data. See Ramsay (1980b) for such an application.

Assessing a Single Fit

Once a particular set of data have been fit by some specified metric in a specified number of dimensions, the data analyst will naturally want some way to assess whether the fit was good or not, and will want to see ways in which the assumptions made prior to the analysis need modification. MULTISCALE has a range of such diagnostics, some of which have already been mentioned.

THE LOG LIKELIHOOD

MLE requires that the likelihood (or equivalently its logarithm) be maximized over the range of possible parameter values. Unlike STRESS or SSTRESS used in KYST and ALSCAL, however, the log likelihood is not normalized to lie within any particular limits. It may be negative or positive and has no upper limit. Its size will depend on the number of observations as well as the quality of the fit. Its usefulness is primarily in comparing two different fits, as we shall see in the next section.

THE STANDARD ERROR

We shall refer to the estimate of the standard deviation σ as the standard error since its interpretation is similar to that quantity in regression analysis. When the lognormal statistical assumption is employed, it is scale free; that is, its value does not depend on the units used to record the data, although it does depend to some extent on the data transformations. The standard error may be compared across two sets of data or between two analyses of the same set of data. In the lognormal case it will usually have a value between .0 and 1.0, with high-quality data yielding values around .3. Because of its usefulness, it is estimated in two ways. The value of the maximum likelihood estimate depends to some extent on the number of parameters being fit to the data, and a value corrected for these effects is also computed and termed the unbiased estimate. An unbiased estimate is also computed separately for each subject after all analyses to allow the user to spot those subjects whose data are especially noisy with respect to the model being employed. Of course, a relatively high standard error for a particular subject can mean many things: This subject is seeing the stimuli quite consistently but in a way different from what can be accommodated by the metric level and transformation type used, the subject is unable or unwilling to respond in a consistent and careful way, or the subject is using the response scale in some unexpected way. Each of these cases as well as others will require a particular action.

THE MULTIPLE CORRELATION

The maximum likelihood estimation process can also be viewed as a nonlinear regression problem if one ignores the fact that transformations of the data are also being estimated. A commonly used goodness-of-fit measure for regression problems is the multiple correlation coefficient, which is basically the correlation between the data (or transformed data) and the fitted values on the basis of the model. MULTISCALE displays the multiple correlation coefficient for the whole set of data and also for each subject separately.

THE STANDARD ERROR OF COORDINATE ESTIMATES

An important aspect of any analysis is how precisely parameters which are of particular interest are estimated. As mentioned, MLE makes possible the computation of approximate standard errors of estimates for coordinates. These standard errors will be especially useful for large sample sizes, but for even modest sample sizes can give the analyst a rough idea of how much noise is in the coordinate estimates. Approximately 95% confidence limits for a particular coordinate can be obtained by multiplying the standard error of estimate by 1.96 and both adding and subtracting this amount from the estimate.

CONFIDENCE REGIONS FOR POINTS

A simple extension of the idea of confidence limits for coordinates is the notion of confidence regions for each point in the configuration. These regions will be ellipsoidal in shape and require specialized plotting equipment to display. Figure 16.8 shows how a two-dimensional configuration might be plotted along with the 95% confidence regions for each point. As this figure illustrates, these regions can be extremely useful for showing which points or clusters of points can be regarded as truly distinct in the population, as well as for visually validating other types of structure in the data. MULTISCALE optionally plots the configuration in this way using Calcomp software. Interfaces between this software and other plotting equipment are widely available. The complete variance–covariance matrix of coordinate estimates is also displayed for users who wish to develop their own plotting system.

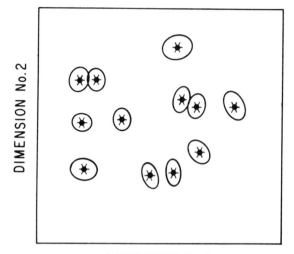

Figure 16.8. Elliptical 95% confidence regions for the locations of 12 points (data taken from 10 subjects).

DIAGNOSTIC PLOTS

It was emphasized at the outset that MLE requires rather strong assumptions about the data. It is seldom easy to determine whether a given set of data really satisfy these assumptions, so that it is important to be able to inspect various aspects of the data after the analysis is completed. MULTISCALE optionally produces a number of graphical displays to assist this process. For example, a plot of $f(d)$ against d^* for each subject can be useful for the detection of outliers, visual assessment of spread, and verification of aspects of the statistical assumptions. Of particular value is a diagnostic plot known in the statistical literature as a $q-q$ or quantile plot. For each subject, the standardized errors or discrepancies between $f(d)$ and d^* are computed. These are then ordered from largest to smallest. If the statistical assumptions are appropriate, these should have approximately a standard normal distribution. In order to verify this, these ordered standardized errors are plotted against the quantiles of the standard normal distribution. Figure 16.9 shows such a plot. In the event that the errors are distributed as assumed, the points will show little deviation from a diagonal straight line. Such plots are especially effective at detecting outliers or wild observations as well as systematic departures from the assumed distribution. Tables of $f(d)$, d^*, and standardized residuals are also displayed.

SERIAL CORRELATION

These techniques will be of little value in detecting a breakdown of the independence assumption, and in general this is an especially difficult assumption to verify. However, MULTISCALE-II can compute a measure of serial correlation for a particular ordering of the observations if desired.

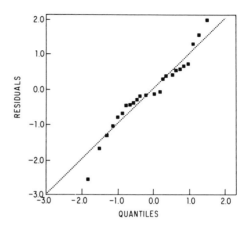

Figure 16.9. An example of a q-q plot for assessing the distributional assumptions in maximum likelihood multidimensional scaling.

CORRELATING THE ESTIMATED CONFIGURATION
WITH A TARGET

It is occasionally the case that one wishes to see how well the estimated configuration of points agrees with some configuration determined in some other way. MULTISCALE can compute a measure of the correlation between its estimated configuration and such a reference or target configuration.

Comparing Two Fits

A frequent goal in confirmatory analysis is the comparison of two different fits to the same data to determine which is to be preferred. Such comparisons fall naturally into two classes: first, those for which one model is a specialization of the other, and second, those for which this is not the case.

There are many examples of comparisons of the first kind, and the comparison of a fit in k dimensions with one in $k - 1$ dimensions has already been mentioned. Another good example would be comparing a fit using the diagonal metric model against one with the identity metric (weighted Euclidean against unweighted Euclidean in other words). In such cases, one arrives at the simpler model by fixing certain parameters in the more general model. For example, a $(k - 1)$-dimensional solution is equivalent to a k-dimensional solution in which all coordinates on the kth dimension are set to zero. An identity metric solution is equivalent to a diagonal metric solution in which all weights are set to one. In such comparisons, MLE makes possible a very simple statistical test based on the chi-square table which is appropriate for largish samples. One (a) doubles the respective log likelihoods, (b) computes the positive difference between these values, (c) also computes the positive difference between the number of parameters estimated in each model (which are printed out by MULTISCALE), and (*d*) looks quantity (*b*) up in a table of chi-square with the number of degrees of freedom computed in (*c*). This procedure can be used with a wide range of interesting hypotheses, including comparisons of two groups, comparison of a constrained configuration against an unconstrained configuration, and two different assumptions about the standard deviations σ_{ij}.

Comparisons of the second kind can also be carried out, although not on a statistical basis. MULTISCALE prints out a quantity called the AIC statistic which is basically the log likelihood corrected for the number of parameters being estimated. In other words, it is a measure of quality of fit per parameter used in fitting. Two AIC statistics are simply compared in terms of which is the smaller, with the fit producing the smaller AIC statistic being preferred.

Constrained Estimation

MULTISCALE can estimate the configuration subject to linear constraints on the coordinates. A large number of interesting hypotheses about the configuration can be expressed in these terms. For example, suppose we have three points whose coordinates are (x_{11},x_{12}), (x_{21},x_{22}), and (x_{31},x_{32}), respectively. If we have some reason to suppose point number 3 lies halfway between points 1 and 2, we can express this as the two equations

$$x_{11} + x_{31} - 2x_{21} = 0,$$

$$x_{12} + x_{32} - 2x_{32} = 0.$$

To test this hypothesis, we would estimate the configuration in two ways: first, with no constraints on the configuration, and second, with these two equations constraining the results. A comparison of log likelihoods in the manner described would then tell us whether the fit is improved significantly by relaxing these constraints, and hence whether the constraints should be thought of as holding in the population.

The Algorithms for Maximizing Log Likelihood

Techniques for maximizing or minimizing functions are the subject of a large and rather technical literature, and most users are content to leave this topic to specialists as long as the program works. Nevertheless, most algorithms used in practice either require or allow a certain amount of intervention by the user, and thus require a certain level of understanding. Moreover, these techniques are iterative in nature, improving estimates of the parameters in each iteration until further improvement is negligible, and thus require criteria for determining when iterations should be terminated.

MULTISCALE is designed rather like ALSCAL and KYST in that within each principal or main iteration each of a number of groups of parameter estimates is improved in turn. The modification of any group of parameters may involve multiple secondary iterations. Analogously with ALSCAL, this is an alternating maximum likelihood procedure (AMLESCAL if you insist on an acronym). Within any main iteration, the following four steps may be taken:

1. The configuration is updated. Early versions of MULTISCALE do this by an implicit equation process which is described in Ramsay (1977). Later versions incorporate a modified Gauss–Newton process primarily to incorporate fitting under constraints. There are two important practical differences between these two procedures: (a) The implicit equation approach produces relatively little improvement per iteration and therefore requires many more iterations; (b) on the other hand, it requires a small amount of computer memory and takes little time per iteration. Future versions of MULTISCALE will provide a choice between algorithms. For most unconstrained problems there is little difference between them in overall computation time.

2. The individual subject weights if any are updated. This is done by a modified Gauss–Newton process.

3. The parameters determining the transformation for each subject's data are updated. In the case of monotone transformations, a Gauss–Newton process is again employed.

4. The standard deviations σ_{ij} are computed. In the case of stimulus-wise variation in these, the standard error weights are updated.

The criteria determining when iterations should be terminated are generated internally by MULTISCALE for most applications using a rational procedure which depends on the amount of data being analyzed. The user can override these criteria when desired, however.

A considerable amount of work has gone into making MULTISCALE as user oriented as possible. Dissimilarity data can be entered in a variety of forms and all program and problem specification parameters are input in free format. The information input into the program such as dimensions of the problem, initial values of various parameters, dissimilarity data, and so on is organized into blocks, and these blocks can be entered in practically any order. The user can determine the file from which any particular block of input will be read, and also the files to which any of the output sections will be directed. All output can be in one of two modes: a narrow page mode designed for terminals, and a wide page mode for line printers. Computer memory is assigned dynamically meaning that only as much core is used as the problem requires.

Summary

The main objective motivating the development of MULTISCALE was to obtain the advantages of confirmatory analysis and efficient estimation in situations where the behavior of the data can be described explicitly. A wide range of statistical properties of the data can be accommodated within the programs so that most relatively continuous measures of dissimilarity or similarity can be fruitfully analyzed in a confirmatory sense. Nevertheless, it was not intended that exploratory capabilities be neglected, and a great deal of work has gone into producing secondary analyses and displays which might yield surprising and interesting insights. The programs have been designed to be as "friendly" as possible in the sense of requiring minimal effort in learning how to use them and in setting up a job. If MULTISCALE proves valuable in assisting researchers to gain important new understanding of human behavior, the labor involved in developing this tool will have been well worth while.

References

Bloxom, B. Constrained multidimensional scaling in N spaces. *Psychometrika,* 1978, *43,* 397–408.

Borg, I., & Lingoes, J. C. A model and algorithm for multidimensional scaling with external constraints on the distances. *Psychometrika,* 1980, *45,* 25–38.

Borg, I. (Ed.) *Multidimensional data representations: When and why?* Ann Arbor: Mathesis Press, 1981.

Carroll, J. D. Individual differences and multidimensional scaling. In R. N. Shepard, A. K. Romney, & S. Nerlove (Eds.), *Multidimensional scaling: Theory and applications in the behavioral sciences. Vol. I. Theory.* New York: Academic Press, 1972.

Carroll, J. D. & Arabie, P. Multidimensional scaling. In M. R. Rosenzweig & L. W. Porter (Eds.), *Annual Review of Psychology,* 1980, *31,* 607–649.

Carroll, J. D., & Chang, J. J. Analysis of individual differences in multidimensional scaling via an N-way generalization of Eckart–Young decomposition. *Psychometrika,* 1970, *35,* 283–319. (a)

Carroll, J. D., & Chang, J. J. A "quasi-nonmetric" version of INDSCAL, a procedure for individual differences multidimensional scaling. Paper presented at meetings of the Psychometric Society, Stanford, March 1970. (b)

Carroll, J. D., & Pruzansky, S. Use of LINCINDS as a rational starting configuration for INDSCAL. Submitted to *Psychometrika,* 1979.

Carroll, J. D., Pruzansky, S., & Green, P. E. Estimation of the parameters of Lazarsfeld's latent class model by application of canonical decomposition (CANDECOMP) to multiway contingency tables. Submitted to *Psychometrika,* 1979.

Carroll, J. D., Pruzansky, S., & Kruskal, J. B. CANDELINC: A general approach to multidimensional analysis with linear constraints on parameters. *Psychometrika,* 1979, *45,* 3–24.

Carroll, J. D. & Wish, M. Models and methods for three-way multidimensional scaling. In D. H. Krantz, R. C. Atkinson, R. D. Luce, & P. Suppes (eds.), *Contemporary devel-*

opments in mathematical psychology. Vol. 2. San Francisco: W. H. Freeman, 1974. Pp. 57–105. (a)

Carroll, J. D., & Wish, M. Multidimensional perceptual models and measurement methods. In E. C. Carterette & M. P. Friedman (Eds.), *Handbook of perception.* Vol. 2. New York: Academic Press, 1974. Pp. 391–447. (b)

Chang, J. J. Notes on NINDSCAL. Unpublished manuscript, Bell Laboratories, Murray Hill, N.J., 1972.

Chang, J. J., & Carroll, J. D. How to use INDSCAL, a computer program for canonical decomposition of *N*-way tables and individual differences in multidimensional scaling. Unpublished manuscript, Bell Laboratories, Murray Hill, N.J., 1972.

de Leeuw, J., & Heiser, W. Convergence of correction-matrix algorithms for multidimensional scaling. In J. C. Lingoes, E. E. Roskam, & I. Borg (Eds.), *Geometric representations of relational data.* Ann Arbor: Mathesis Press, 1979.

DeSarbo, W. S., & Carroll, J. D. Three-way metric unfolding. Unpublished manuscript, Bell Laboratories, Murray Hill, N.J., 1979.

Eckart, C. & Young, G. Approximation of one matrix by another of lower rank. *Psychometrika,* 1936, *1,* 211–218.

Green, P. E. (with Carroll, J. D.). *Mathematical tools for applied multivariate analysis.* New York: Academic Press, 1976.

Guttman, L. A general nonmetric technique for finding the smallest coordinate space for a configuration of points. *Psychometrika,* 1968, *33,* 469–506.

Harman, H. H. *Modern factor analysis.* Chicago: The University of Chicago Press, 1976.

Harshman, R. A. Foundations of the PARAFAC procedure: Models and conditions for an "explanatory" multimodal factor analysis. UCLA Working Papers in *Phonetics,* 1970, *16,* 86 pp. (Reprinted by University Microfilms International, Ann Arbor, Michigan, Order No. 10,085.)

Helm, C. E. Multidimensional ratio scaling analysis of perceived color relations. *Journal of the Optical Society of America,* 1964, *54,* 256–262.

Helm, C. E., & Tucker, L. R. Individual differences in the structure of color perception. *American Journal of Psychology,* 1962, *75,* 437–444.

Horan, C. B. Multidimensional scaling: Combining observations when individuals have different perceptual structures. *Psychometrika,* 1969, *34,* 139–165.

Kruskal, J. B. Nonmetric multidimensional scaling: A numerical method. *Psychometrika,* 1964, *29,* 1–27, 115–129.

Lingoes, J. C. New computer developments in pattern analysis and nonmetric techniques. In *Uses of computers in psychological research—The 1964 IBM Symposium of Statistics.* Paris: Gauthier-Villars, 1966.

Lingoes, J. C. Some boundary conditions for a monotone analysis of symmetric matrices. *Psychometrika,* 1971, *36,* 195–203.

Lingoes, J. C. *The Guttman–Lingoes nonmetric program series.* Ann Arbor: Mathesis Press, 1973.

Lingoes, J. C. A general survey of the Guttman–Lingoes nonmetric program series and additional programs in the Guttman–Lingoes Series. In J. C. Lingoes, E. E. Roskam, & I. Borg (Eds.), *Geometric representations of relational data.* Ann Arbor: Mathesis Press, 1979.

Lingoes, J. C. Some uses of statistical inference in multidimensional scaling. In I. Borg (Ed.), *Multidimensional data representations: When and why?* Ann Arbor: Mathesis Press, 1981. (a)

Lingoes, J. C. Testing regional hypotheses in multidimensional scaling. In I. Borg (Ed.), *Multidimensional data representations: When and why?* Ann Arbor: Mathesis, 1981. (b)

Lingoes, J. C., & Borg, I. CMDA-U: Confirmatory monotone distance analysis—unconditional. *Journal of Marketing Research,* 1978, *15,* 610–611.

Lingoes, J. C., & Borg, I. An exact significance test for dimensionality and for choosing between rival hypotheses in confirmatory multidimensional scaling. *U. M. Comp. Rpt.*, 1980, *1*, 1–22.

Lingoes, J. C., & Roskam, E. E. A mathematical and empirical study of two multidimensional scaling algorithms. *MMPP-71-1*. (Also in *Psychometrika Monograph Supplement*, 1973, *19*.)

Lingoes, J. C., Roskam, E. E., & Borg, I. *Geometric representations of relational data*. Ann Arbor: Mathesis Press, 1979.

Pruzansky, S. How to use SINDSCAL, A computer program for individual differences in multidimensional scaling. Unpublished manuscript, Bell Laboratories, Murray Hill, N.J., August 1969.

Ramsay, J. O. Maximum likelihood estimation in multidimensional scaling, *Psychometrika*, 1977, *42*, 241–266.

Ramsay, J. O. Confidence regions for multidimensional scaling analysis. *Psychometrika*, 1978, *43*, 241–266. (a)

Ramsay, J. O. *MULTISCALE: Four programs for multidimensional scaling by the method of maximum likelihood*. Chicago: National Educational Resources, Inc. 1978. (b)

Ramsay, J. O. Some small sample results for maximum likelihood estimation in multidimensional scaling. *Psychometrika*, in press. (a)

Ramsay, J. O. The joint analysis of direct ratings, pairwise preferences, and dissimilarities. *Psychometrika*, 1980, in press. (b)

Roskam, E. E. A comparison of principles for algorithm construction in nonmetric scaling. *MMPP-69-2*, Ann Arbor, Dept. of Mathematical Psychology, University of Michigan, 1969. (a)

Roskam, E. E. Data theory and algorithms for nonmetric scaling, I & II. *Technical Report*, Nijmegen, Holland, Dept. of Mathematical Psychology, University of Nijmegen, Holland, 1969. (b)

Roskam, E. E. A survey of the Michigan–Israel–Netherlands–Integrated Series. In J. C. Lingoes, E. E. Roskam, & I. Borg (Eds.), *Geometric representations of relational data*. Ann Arbor: Mathesis Press, 1979.

Roskam, E. E. A general system for nonmetric data analysis. In J. C. Lingoes, E. E. Roskam, & I. Borg (Eds.), *Geometric representations of relational data*. Ann Arbor: Mathesis Press, 1979.

Roskam, E. E., & Lingoes, J. C. MINISSA-I: A Fortran IV (G) program for the smallest space analysis of square symmetric matrices. *Behavioral Science*, 1970, *15*, 204–205.

Takane, Y., Young, F. W., & de Leeuw, J. Nonmetric individual differences multidimensional scaling: An alternating least squares method with optimal scaling features. *Psychometrika*, 1977, *42*, 7–67.

Torgerson, W. S. *Theory and methods of scaling*. New York: Wiley, 1958.

Tucker, L. T. Relations between multidimensional scaling and three-mode factor analysis. *Psychometrika*, 1972, *37*, 3–27.

Tucker, L. R., & Messick, S. J. Individual difference model for multidimensional scaling. *Psychometrika*, 1963, *28*, 333–367.

Winsberg, S., & Ramsay, J. O. Monotonic transformations to additivity using splines. *Biometrika*, 1980, in press.

Wish, M., & Carroll, J. D. Applications of individual differences scaling to studies of human perception and judgment. In E. C. Carterette & M. P. Friedman (Eds.), *Handbook of perception, Vol. 2*, New York: Academic Press, 1974.

Wold, H. Estimation of principal components and related models by iterative least squares. In P. R. Krishnaiah (Ed.), *Multivariate analysis*. New York: Academic Press, 1966.

Young, F. W. TORSCA-9: A FORTRAN IV program for nonmetric multidimensional scaling. *Behavioral Science*, 1968, *13*, 343–344.

Young, F. W. A model for polynomial conjoint analysis algorithms. In R. N. Shepard, A. K. Romney, & S. Nerlove (Eds.) *Multidimensional scaling: Theory and applications in the behavioral sciences*. Vol. I. New York: Academic Press, 1972.

Young, F. W. POLYCON: A program for multidimensionally scaling one-, two-, or three-way data in additive, difference, or multiplicative spaces. *Behavioral Science*, 1973, *18*, 152–155.

Young, F. W. Scaling conditional rank-order data. *Sociological Methodology*, 1975, 129–170. (a)

Young, F. W. An asymmetric Euclidian model for multi-process asymmetric data. *U.S.–Japan Seminar on Multidimensional Scaling*, 1975. (b)

Young, F. W., de Leeuw, J., & Takane, Y. *Multidimensional scaling: Theory and methods*. Hillsdale, N.J.: Erlbaum, in preparation.

Young, F. W., Null, C. H., & Sarle, W. Interactive similarity ordering. *Behavior Research Methods & Instrumentation*, 1978, *10*, 273–280.

Young, F. W., Sarle, W. S., & Hoffman, D. L. Interactively ordering the similarities among a large set of stimuli. In R. C. Golledge, & S. N. Rayner (Eds.), *Data analysis in multidimensional scaling*. Ohio State University Press, in press.

Young, F. W., Takane, Y., & Lewyckyj, R. Three notes on ALSCAL. *Psychometrika*, 1978, *43*, 433–435.

Appendix

MINISSA(M) is available in an MDS package containing numerous other useful programs from:

> James C. Lingoes
> Computing Center Station
> 1005 N. University Building
> University of Michigan
> Ann Arbor, Michigan 48109

Documentation for MINISSA(M) is available from:

> Mathesis Press
> 2664 Lowell Road
> Ann Arbor, Michigan 48103

POLYCON version 2.06 is distributed as POLYCON II along with test problems and their output by:

> Forrest W. Young
> L. L. Thurstone Psychometric Laboratory
> University of North Carolina
> Chapel Hill, North Carolina 27514

A more extensive description of POLYCON is also available: Young, F. W., Conjoint scaling. Publication number 118. L. L. Thurstone Psychometric Laboratory. April, 1973 (Revised March, 1977).

There are several versions of KYST that differ slightly in the manner in which they are programmed (e.g., the plot routine). However, all versions give comparable results. One version (KYST-1, 1973) can be obtained along with INDSCAL (Chapter 8), PREFMAP (Chapter 12), and MDPREF (Chapter 14) in an MDS package of 18 programs distributed by:

> Bell Laboratories Computing Information Library
> Irma Biren, Supervisor
> 600 Mountain Avenue
> Murray Hill, New Jersey 07974

The latest version (KYST-2A, August, 1977) is also available from Bell Laboratories as a separate program with extensive documentation: *How to Use KYST-2A, A Very Flexible Program to Do Multidimensional Scaling and Unfolding,* by J. B. Kruskal, F. W. Young, and J. B. Seery. SINDSCAL is available on a separate tape from the same source.

Documentation and a computer tape containing the source code, test data, and test data output for ALSCAL-4 is available from Forrest W. Young at the address given above. (The documentation for ALSCAL-4, *ALSCAL-4 User's Guide,* can be obtained separately without the tape.) PROC ALSCAL is distributed with SAS by:

> The SAS Institute
> P.O. Box 10066
> Raleigh, North Carolina 27605

MULTISCALE is available from:

> International Educational Services
> 1525 East 53rd Street
> Room 829
> Chicago, Illinois 60615

Documentation entitled: *MULTISCALE: Four Programs for Multidimensional Scaling by the Method of Maximum Likelihood,* by James O. Ramsay, is available as well.

Index